ADVANCES IN INTERDISCIPLINARY STUDIES OF WORK TEAMS

Volume 3 • 1996

TEAM LEADERSHIP

ADVANCES IN INTERDISCIPLINARY STUDIES OF WORK TEAMS

TEAM LEADERSHIP

Editors: MICHAEL M. BEYERLEIN
Center for the Study of Work Teams
Department of Psychology
University of North Texas

DOUGLAS A. JOHNSON
Center for the Study of Work Teams
Department of Psychology
University of North Texas

SUSAN T. BEYERLEIN
Center for Public Management
Department of Public Administration
University of North Texas

VOLUME 3 • 1996

 JAI PRESS INC.

Greenwich, Connecticut   *London, England*

CONTENTS

LIST OF CONTRIBUTORS

William P. Anthony

College of Business
Florida State University

Bruce J. Avolio

School of Management
Binghamton University

James R. Barker

Department of Communication
and Journalism
University of New Mexico

Alok Baveja

School of Business
Rutgers University

Janis A. Cannon-Bowers

Training Systems Division
Naval Air Warfare Center

Jonathan F. Cox

Center for the Study of Work Teams
University of North Texas

Don D. Daake

Business Department
Olivet Nazarene University
Bourbonnais, Illinois

Elaine M. Engle

Department of Psychology
University of Akron

Stanley M. Gully

Department of Psychology
Michigan State University

Dong I. Jung

School of Management
Binghamton University

Steve W.J. Kozlowski

Department of Psychology
Michigan State University

Ed L. Levine   Department of Psychology
                                          University of South Florida

Robert G. Lord   Department of Psychology
                                          University of Akron

Charles C. Manz   Department of Management
                                          Arizona State University

William D. Murry   School of Management
                                          Binghamton University

Christopher P. Neck   Department of Management
                                          Virginia Polytechnic Institute
                                              and State University

Ren Nygren   Florida Power Corporation
                                          St. Petersburg, Florida

Gayle Porter   School of Business
                                          Rutgers University

Eduardo Salas   Training Systems Division
                                          Naval Air Warfare Center

Anson Seers   Management and Marketing
                                              Department
                                          University of Alabama

Henry P. Sims, Jr.   College of Business and Management
                                          University of Maryland

Nagaraj Sivasubramaniam   School of Management
                                          Binghamton University

Greg L. Stewart   Owen Graduate School of Management
                                          Vanderbilt University

INTRODUCTION

This volume of the annual series on work teams focuses on leadership. A number of experts in academia and in business agree that leadership is the key to effective work teams. However, they do not necessarily agree on what is meant by "leadership," how leadership should be enacted, or what constitutes a "team." The papers in this volume were first presented at the third University of North Texas Symposium on Work Teams in May, 1995.

The presentations by the academic authors were accompanied by commentary from discussants chosen from business, by question and answer exchanges with an audience primarily consisting of business people, and by a panel discussion at the end of each day. Authors were thus able to test the expression of their theoretical work with people who were living it. Those exchanges and the opportunity for authors to hear each other present led to some revisions that appear in the papers in this volume. In that way, also, the themes of the chapters have become a little more integrated.

The topic of leadership has been one of the most thoroughly researched topics in organization science in the past 50 years. The number of articles, chapters, and books must number in the tens of thousands by now. So, why would there be anything new to add? The world of work is changing, and with it, the nature of leadership or our understanding of it is changing. The dominant paradigm in business has been that of command and control. There has been some evolution of leadership concepts and practices toward a more empowering approach focusing on the employees as human resources, but the research literature that helps us understand the direction and implications of that evolution and the practices that express the consequences of that evolution have only slowly replaced the command and control approach. The authors of the papers in this volume are at the cutting edge with their thinking, writing, and validation work on new approaches to understanding leadership.

Leadership is a term with many meanings. Many people seem to automatically hear the word "leader" when the term "leadership" is spoken. For those people, leadership represents a person, usually a few levels above the people who do the actual work in the organization's hierarchy. For others, leadership represents the top of the hierarchy—vice presidents and above— who set direction for the organization as a whole. With increasing empowerment and the continuing shift to work teams, leadership becomes shared with the workers—the people who provide the basic services to customers or assemble the products or invent ways to improve the products. Shared leadership involves listening to any employee who has expertise relevant to a problem or decision. Within a team, a leader may be permanent, like a supervisor, but do the same work as the other team members; a team leader may rotate, having been elected by team members who vote every six or 12 months; or be a team member who has emerged during the team meeting for half an hour to share his or her expertise. Consequently, leadership has become distributed throughout the organization: a matrix of influence sources.

Leadership also shows up in the work environment. Kerr and Jermier (1978) wrote about the idea of substitutes for leadership some time ago. They identified a number of sources of influence that guided the behavior of employees. For example, the reward system was so influential that rewarded behaviors emerged even when the supervisors and managers demanded other kinds of behaviors.

Culture in the organization has been identified as a leadership influence, too. Culture may be one of the most difficult concepts to work with in the whole organization science lexicon. After reviewing more than three dozen definitions, Ott (1989) suggested that culture can be viewed from three perspectives: basic cultural assumptions, beliefs and values, or patterns of behavior. Culture, as a work environment, is addressed in all three of those ways by the chapter authors in this volume. But like leadership, if we look at culture as the elephant that the blind men stumbled into in the jungles of India, each of the perspectives is equally legitimate, each has something valuable to contribute, and the real problem is that none of the perspectives is sufficient, by itself, to comprehend the whole. The different perspectives must be integrated to begin to get a sense of what the elephant, or leadership, or culture, really represents.

Organizations have become increasingly dynamic and complex in trying to cope with their increasingly turbulent environments. In other words, the elephant is changing and challenging our ability to understand even more now than in the past. Our understanding of leadership needs to be evolving in parallel to that change for the concept and its components to remain viable tools in making organizations effective. These papers should help bring readers up to date with the latest in understanding leadership.

Effective leadership of teams has become recognized as a key to industry competitiveness. Following Hackman's (1992) idea that critical leadership functions for teams are those "activities that contribute to the establishment and maintenance of favorable performance conditions" (p. 120), we view leadership as a matrix of influences with some embodied in the manager, some in team members, and some in the environment. We also agree with Hackman that leadership becomes more important, demanding, and complex as teams mature toward self-management.

An example of that complexity is captured by the stages of management role evolution. When an organization goes through transformation to new, more empowered designs, the role of the manager changes with it. Some writers (e.g., Wilson, George, Wellins, & Byham, 1994) describe the role change as five stages: (1) chain of command with authoritative style, (2) manager as central but slightly participative, (3) transition as members begin to link together in increasing participation, (4) some high involvement with partnership resulting in leader/ member status equality, and (5) high involvement with highly empowered members and the leader playing a support role. Toward the latter stages, leadership becomes a shared responsibility at all levels of the organization including team members. In addition, cues in the environment such as reward systems, function as substitutes for leadership by providing information that guides employee behavior. This volume addresses the relationship of those styles to team effectiveness, the fit of different forms of leadership with each other, and the role of leadership in generating high levels of team performance.

The papers in this volume are organized, so those with broader frameworks and more inclusive themes are at the beginning. Reading them first should allow the reader who is less familiar with the research literature on teams and leadership to develop a perspective that will aid in reading the later chapters. Papers in the second half of the book tend to address more specific themes and more generally integrate theory and practice.

The volume opens with a paper by Jonathan Cox and Hank Sims on leadership and team citizenship behavior. Sims and his colleagues, especially Chuck Manz, have published extensively on SuperLeadership for some years, including a paper in the first volume of this series. This year's paper provides an excellent overview of that work within the larger framework of a historical review of leadership literature. That sets the stage for a review of the work published on good citizenship behavior in organizations. Then the ideas of SuperLeadership as an approach to empowerment are presented as a means of obtaining good citizenship behavior with work teams. They also describe measurement instruments for assessing the leadership strategies that relate to the citizenship behaviors.

In the second paper, Chris Neck, Greg Stewart, and Chuck Manz present a model for balancing self-leadership for individual team members, self-leadership for the team as a whole, and team performance. They address the problem that arises when self-management by the individual suboptimizes self-management of the team, and present both behavioral and mental strategies to solve the problem. Balancing the two types of self-management depends on the individual, group dynamics, formal leadership, and substitutes for leadership. The balance leads to productive goal-oriented behavior and thereby is a key to performance.

Chapter 3 continues the theme of linking team leadership to team performance. Ren Nygren and Ed Levine offer an extensive coverage of the prior literature on leadership which they summarize by arguing that the leaders are responsible for identifying the key organizational success factors, taking steps to address those factors, and then enabling the teams and their members to perform at high levels. They summarize their ideas in a model that ties together factors in the team environment, team leader and member behaviors, and team outcomes. They remind us that measurement of team outcomes is not always straightforward, so assessing the links between the factors is a challenge in research and in practice.

In Chapter 4, Jim Barker focuses on the power and authority of the team. He addresses the issue of how empowerment for the team fits into the organization's basic system of control. His conclusion is that the organization needs a good fit between authority, control, and leadership, and that the sense of authority is more important than power. Of four types of control—simple, technological, bureaucratic, and concerted—the team depends on the last: day-to-day situations where groups of individuals act in concert with each other to control their own behavior. The team leader has a responsibility to help the team develop norms and rules based on appropriate values, so the concerted process works.

All of the papers in this volume directly or indirectly address leaders, team members, and the team environment and their interrelationships. However, some address the leader's role in creating the environment more explicitly than others. Chapter 5, by Alok Baveja and Gayle Porter, focuses on creating an environment that fosters the personal growth of the team members. Readers familiar with the work of Carl Rogers will recognize the philosophical framework for this chapter. Other readers will quickly perceive the convergence of Miles and Snow's (1994) work on the human investment model with this paper's argument that growing the employee to be fully functioning will provide the basis for outstanding performance. For Baveja and Porter, the key to an environment that makes that growth possible is the expression by the leader of genuineness, respectfulness, and empathy. Techniques of empowerment differ for leaders with different abilities to express those qualities in relationships.

Leadership comes in many forms, but for self-managed teams, shared leadership is probably the key to achieving effectiveness. In Chapter 6, Anson Seers focuses on leadership that emerges from the team members when the chemistry is right. Leadership depends on followership, so part of the right chemistry depends on communication; when the leader is not heard, there are no followers, so leadership does not exist. Like several other chapter authors, Seers recognizes that the authority to lead is granted by the followers. A true team exists when there are several kinds of interdependence: task, socio-emotional, outcome, and mutual expectations. Simply following is mere dependence which is not enough for optimal performance; interdependence is essential. The chemistry of balanced mutual influence among team members depends on a balance of directiveness, goal orientation, supportiveness, and participativeness expressed through the roles the team members adopt.

This volume began with one of the most intriguing new frameworks for understanding leadership: SuperLeadership and self-leadership. Another, equally inspiring framework is transformational leadership. Chapter 7 by Bruce Avolio, Dong Jung, Bill Murry, and Naga Sivasubramaniam flows out of the work Avolio has done with Bernie Bass (1988) on transformational leadership. Like Cox and Sims, Avolio and his colleagues have presented a continuum of leadership styles and related them to the level of team functioning. Highly developed teams depend on transformational leadership. Developing from a group to a highly developed team can be slow and difficult; the transformational leader guides that process by facilitating the development of a consensual value set that enables a shift from an "I" focus to a "we" focus: "unity in diversity." This framework is supported by a review of two studies using the Team Multifactor Leadership Questionnaire.

Chapter 8 by Bob Lord and Elaine Engle links together three levels of analysis to create some unique insights first addressed in Lord and Maher's recent book (1993). Organizational culture is described as the environment of the team, but culture is expressed in the behaviors of team members because of the shared values, beliefs, and assumptions that drive their behavior. Lord and Engle link culture, behavior, and leadership together by creating a model of information processing alternatives. In other words, people think about their experience differently, with different approaches, depending on the situation. For a leader to manage the culture or the behavior, those methods of information processing alternatives must be understood as avenues to change. Some of the options that are available to the leader will result in wasted effort, but some, when chosen to fit the situation, will provide competence enhancing change. For example, focusing on the method of cybernetic processing depends on active feedback loops in the group that reinforce old ways of doing things, so reliance on the expert and rational methods may be better ways to generate change.

In Chapter 9, William Anthony and Don Daake take on the toughest team of all: executives. The literature on top management teams suggests "top management" and "team" form an oxymoron; there are only top management *groups*. What can one do to move such a powerful and political group toward teaming? Anthony and Daake suggest an external facilitator will be essential. They provide a number of arguments to support this suggestion. Then they define the roles a facilitator should play to improve the strategic decision making performance of these groups.

Chapter 10 wraps up the volume with an emphasis on training leaders and teams. Steve Kozlowski, Stan Gully, Ed Salas, and Janis Cannon-Bowers present an excellent overview of training for teams that emphasizes integration of taskwork and teamwork skills. They add to the team leader's responsibilities that of trainer. That role has subcomponents depending on which leadership facet is relevant: mentor, instructor, coach, or facilitator. They then present a model that links the facets of the role to the developmental level of the team and the training responsibilities that are relevant. They also emphasize that the nature of the team's context and task influence the selection of the teamwork training; more focus on task relevant interaction must be added to training on social interaction as the task becomes more complex. One should not assume that skills for coordination and adaptability will naturally develop through experience; formal learning opportunities must be provided. A number of principles are presented to guide the decision making in providing those opportunities.

These papers each contribute valuable insights and perspectives to both the researcher planning further study of team leadership and the practitioner who must produce performance enhancing change with the work teams. Taken in combination, they provide a solid foundation with their summaries of the best existing thought and research and a launch platform for experimenting. Combining intriguing ideas, practices, and tools from various chapters should provide us all with opportunities to "push the envelope" on our understanding of team leadership.

Michael M. Beyerlein
Douglas A. Johnson
Susan T. Beyerlein
Editors

REFERENCES

Avolio, B.J., & Bass, B.M. (1988). Transformational leadership: Charisma and beyond. In J. G. Hunt, B. R. Baliga, H. P. Dachler, & C. Schriesheim, (Eds.), *Emerging leadership vistas* (pp. 29-50). Elsmford, NY: Pergamon Press.

Hackman, J.R. (1992). Group influences on individuals in organizations. In M.D. Dunnette & L.M. Hough (Eds.), *Handbook of industrial and organizational psychology*, Vol. 3, 2nd ed. (pp. 199-267). Palo Alto, CA: Consulting Psychology Press Inc.

Kerr, S., & Jermier, J.M. (1978). Substitutes for leadership: Their meaning and measurement. *Organizational Behavior and Human Performance, 22*, 375-403.

Lord, R.G., & Maher, K.J. (1993). *Leadership & information processing: Linking perceptions and performance*. London: Routledge.

Miles, R.E., & Snow, C.C. (1994). *Fit, failure & the hall of fame: How companies succeed or fail*. New York: The Free Press.

Ott, S.J. (1989). *The organizational culture perspective*. Pacific Grove, CA: BrooksCole.

Wilson, J.M., George, J., Wellins, R.S., & Byham, W.C. (1994). *Leadership trapeze: Strategies for leadership in team-based organizations*. San Francisco: Jossey-Bass.

FOREWORD

Leadership. Teams. It was but a short time ago when many practitioners believed teams and leadership were mutually exclusive. We believed somehow that teams which were empowered, autonomous, high performing, self-managing, or otherwise set apart from traditional supervisor/subordinate relationships, were also devoid of leadership, not unlike a ship without a rudder.

Just as the rudder provides the ship direction, so does leadership guide individuals and teams regardless of the organizational configuration. Work team leadership can come both from inside and outside the team. It can be highly formalized or quite informal, dogmatic or enlightened, and effective or ineffective. However, one thing is certain: like a ship without a rudder, if leadership is missing, the team's direction becomes unclear, and therefore its success is impossible to measure.

As a practitioner, I am convinced that leadership and self-managed teams are not antithetical. I learned this the old-fashioned way ... by trial and error. Through our own corporate journey to teams (teams with greater empowerment) we learned we could not ignore the need for leadership. Teams, although often skilled at self-management, still need strong, clear, and dedicated leadership from outside the team. As we have described the process at GTE Directories Corporation recently, "self-management means we're removing one layer of management; we're not throwing out the entire upper management structure."

In the past, we have watched several of our teams flounder without direction as we ignorantly believed they somehow would discern their own direction without outside help. We have more recently reassumed a more balanced leadership role and now provide direction and feedback regularly as we further empower our employees to manage themselves day by day. We provide a definition of the destination and a goodly supply of resources. The teams themselves determine to a greater (or sometimes lesser) extent the route to take and how the resources will be managed.

In the last few years, the output of research around teaming issues has risen dramatically, yielding an abundance of useful findings for both practitioners and academics. Those in search of new paradigms for teams are finally getting to the "heart of the matter" as the interplay of ideas and practical applications multiplies. In this latest compilation of symposium papers, one finds yet another tremendously relevant resource for those involved in both the study and application of teaming initiatives.

Each of the contributions in the present volume assists us from a particular vantage point in understanding the essence of leadership in team settings. For example, of particular help in comprehending how leaders can generate cultural change is Lord and Engle's exploration of culture and personality and their interrelationship. Also, as training is often regarded as one of the major considerations for any organization contemplating pursuit of "teaming," the paper by Kozlowski, Gully, Salas, and Cannon-Bowers provides a framework for understanding team leadership skills and the necessary approaches to skill development which can be taken. Review these and the other papers with a view toward finding "gems" here and there which, when added to the common body of practical wisdom about leadership and teams, provide clarity for our journey, making it perhaps a bit easier and certainly more interesting.

I encourage both practitioners and academic researchers to consider the kernels of truth contained herein as yet another step in launching further into the exploration of teams and that ever-so-elusive, ever-so-evolving, and ever-so-complex understanding of leadership. As we approach the new century, we can be fairly confident that the team "boat" will change its shape, its source(s) of energy, its crew, and its cargo. However, with a working rudder in the form of effective team leadership, it will be able to steer the course and negotiate the waters ahead.

David Rawles
GTE Directories Corporation
DFW Airport, Texas

ACKNOWLEDGMENTS

The editors wish to acknowledge the contributions of the authors who contributed outstanding papers and of the staff at the Interdisciplinary Center for the Study of Work Teams who organized the Third University of North Texas Symposium on Work Teams ... especially Liz Teal, Donna Metz, and the Symposium discussants. All of the papers in this book began as presentations at the Symposium. Representatives from 10 different public and private sector organizations served as discussants for the papers. Their reflections on the practical implications of the theories and the authors' opportunity to hear the presentations of the other academics led to improvements in all of the papers. Discussants (in alphabetical order) were:

Dave Bess, Electronic Data Systems (EDS)
Charles (Skip) L. Blechle, Shell Exploration & Production Company
Amy R. Brennan, Lockheed Martin
Stanley O. Horner, Advanced Micro Devices (AMD)
Mitchael (Mickey) Kaehr, Jostens
James (Sonny) N. McCutcheon, Convex Computer Corporation
Siobhan O'Brien, Microsoft
B.J. Parks, Alcatel Network Systems
Peter J. Sorenson, Boeing DS&G
J.N. (Jim) Underwood, AT&T Power Systems

Finally, our sincere thanks to Melanie Bullock for her careful work and attention to detail in working with the authors and editors, communicating with JAI Press, and organizing and typing the manuscript. Any errors that remain are the responsibility of the editors.

LEADERSHIP AND TEAM CITIZENSHIP BEHAVIOR:

A MODEL AND MEASURES

Jonathan F. Cox and Henry P. Sims, Jr.

ABSTRACT

This paper presents a conceptual model linking leadership to team citizenship behavior. We also describe the theoretical underpinnings and present questionnaire items for measures of leadership and citizenship constructs: the Leadership Strategies Questionnaire II and the Team Citizenship Questionnaire. Previous research on citizenship behavior (e.g., organizational citizenship behavior, Organ, 1988) has conceptualized citizenship behavior as a characteristic of individuals. The present model, however, treats citizenship as a group attribute critical to cohesion and effective teamwork. Discussion of leadership is organized around a typology of leader behavior developed by Manz and Sims (1991). Discussion will particularly emphasize how SuperLeadership (Manz & Sims, 1989)—an empowering approach to fostering responsible autonomy among followers—should promote positive citizenship among team members.

Advances in Interdisciplinary Studies
of Work Teams, Volume 3, pages 1-41.
ISBN: 0-7623-0006-X

INTRODUCTION

This paper proposes relationships between team leader behavior and citizenship among team members. Our discussion of leadership will particularly emphasize an empowering approach to leadership—*SuperLeadership*—previously defined by Manz and Sims (1989). Leadership will be conceptually related to a characteristic of team member behavior called *citizenship*, a behavioral construct relating to interpersonal support and helping behavior (e.g., Fisher & Locke, 1992; Organ, 1988). We propose that SuperLeadership can promote positive citizenship among team members and that citizenship, in turn, can enhance team effectiveness. This paper has both theoretical and pragmatic research implications for conceptualizing and measuring the behavior of team leaders and members.

The paper will begin discussing leadership by reviewing a typology of leader behavior (cf. Manz & Sims, 1991) that places SuperLeadership within a broader context of historical leadership research and theory. During our review, we will introduce several specific leader behavior dimensions from the typology that have been incorporated into a field-tested leader behavior description questionnaire, the Leadership Strategies Questionnaire II (LSQII) investigated by Cox (1994). Appendix A presents examples of items used on the LSQII to capture each leader behavior dimension in the typology.

Later sections of the paper will shift the emphasis to team citizenship behavior. This discussion will describe specific citizenship behavior dimensions that have been incorporated into a field-tested citizenship questionnaire, the Team Citizenship Questionnaire (TCQ). Appendix B presents examples of items used to capture each citizenship dimension described in the chapter. Further discussion will focus on the importance of citizenship behavior for team effectiveness and the relationship between leadership and team citizenship, with a particular emphasis on SuperLeadership. Finally, the paper will conclude with a set of research propositions suggesting a program of future research.

Leadership

The term *leadership* has long presented definitional problems for researchers and practitioners. Twenty years ago, for example, Stogdill (1974) observed that "there are almost as many definitions of leadership as there are persons who have attempted to define the concept" (p. 259). Unfortunately, the passage of time and the addition of hundreds of leadership studies has done little to clarify the precise meaning of the term.

In his review of leadership theory and research, Yukl (1989) offers a catchall definition of leadership as "influence processes involving determination of the group's or organization's objectives, motivating task behavior in pursuit of these objectives, and influencing group maintenance and culture" (p. 5). For our purposes, we define leadership mainly as a process of influence: if one influences another (typically a leader influencing a follower), then leadership takes place.

The New Reality of Leadership

Leadership has long been a lively topic of commentary and debate in academic circles and the popular press. Debate extends even to the fundamental importance of leadership (cf. Bass, 1990; Bennis, 1989; Bennis & Nanus, 1985; Pfeffer, 1977). What seems increasingly clear, however, is that the economic and social context of organizational leadership is changing rapidly and significantly. Intense global competition, for example, demands leaders who can choreograph large improvements in productivity, creativity, and quality.

At the same time, broad social changes in the post-war era are reflected in a labor force that brings higher expectations to the workplace (e.g., Carnevale, 1991). These social trends were evident more than 20 years ago to Walton (1972), who identified a mismatch between traditional, hierarchical, command-and-control leadership and employees' increasing demands for satisfying work, greater egalitarianism, and greater control over their work lives.

Many organizations have turned to team-based work design and other empowerment strategies in response to these economic and social pressures. However, these strategies fundamentally change the context of leadership and the roles, responsibilities, and behaviors required for leaders to be effective. Manz and Sims (1989, 1990, 1991) have recently proposed an approach to leadership, *SuperLeadership*, that addresses the new reality of leadership in empowered, team-based contexts.

SUPERLEADERSHIP: AN OVERVIEW

SuperLeadership is an approach that emphasizes empowerment of followers, that is, shifting employees "from dependence on external [top-down] management to independence" (Manz & Sims, 1990, p. 68). Manz and Sims present SuperLeadership as a plan of action for replacing conventional command-and-control with responsible employee self-direction and autonomy. They define a SuperLeader as "one who leads others to lead themselves" (p. 4). Central to SuperLeadership is employee self-management and initiative, or *self-leadership* in the parlance of Manz and Sims.

The first comprehensive exposition of SuperLeadership (Manz & Sims, 1989, 1990) was a prescription for practicing managers, rather than a tightly constructed psychological theory. More recently, Sims and Lorenzi (1992) have elaborated on the theoretical underpinnings of SuperLeadership, which include social learning theory and self-management theory. Still, SuperLeadership is as yet too new to have been explicated as a formal model of leadership. Sims and Lorenzi (1992) captured the present status of SuperLeadership by describing it as "a *perspective* rather than a theory" (p. 26).

Manz and Sims (1990) argue that substantial benefits accrue to leaders who replace external influence with employee self-leadership: costly oversight can be reduced, command bureaucracies can be trimmed to permit greater organizational flexibility and responsiveness, and management is freed from routine supervision to focus on longer-range planning issues. Furthermore, employee self-leadership may enable gains in quality and productivity that are impossible when leaders—formal "managers"—act alone. At Hewlett-Packard, for example, engineers in one plant were able to cut defects in half by modifying production processes. However, when "HP turned to its workers ... they practically rebuilt the operation—and slashed defects a thousandfold" (Port & Carey, 1991, p. 16). From a SuperLeadership perspective, this Hewlett-Packard plant is an example of self-leadership in action.

Competitive advantages offered by gains in productivity, flexibility, and quality need to be considered in light of one of the central challenges of SuperLeadership: employees may not react in a responsible way if given the opportunity. In their account of one organization's transition to more empowering leadership, Manz, Keating, and Donnellon (1990) illustrate how difficult it can be for managers to gain confidence in employees' capacity for responsible self-leadership. The challenge of transition can be compounded when employees "test" commitment to empowerment by contriving mistakes and gauging management's response, or when managers try to increase top-down control through manipulation and superficial empowerment (e.g., Manz & Angle, 1993).

Though not necessarily a formal theory per se, SuperLeadership is rooted in several theoretical perspectives in psychology and organizational behavior. The next section will place SuperLeadership in a broader historical context by providing a brief review of selected leadership theory. This review draws heavily on Yukl's (1989) integrative review of leadership as well as Bass's (1990) comprehensive reference work. A leadership typology developed by Manz and Sims (1991; Sims & Manz, 1996) provides an organizing framework for our research measure of leader behavior, the Leadership Strategies Questionnaire II (LSQII).

SUPERLEADERSHIP IN THE BROADER CONTEXT OF LEADERSHIP THEORY: THE MANZ/SIMS TYPOLOGY

Manz and Sims (1991; Sims & Manz, 1996) have recently proposed a leadership typology including four leadership archetypes, or strategies of leadership, that typify relatively "pure" patterns of connected leader behaviors: *Strongman, Transactor, Visionary Hero,* and *SuperLeader.* Table 1 provides

Table 1. Manz and Sims (1991) Leadership Typology

	Strongman	Transactor	Visionary Hero	SuperLeader
Leadership Focus	Commands	Rewards	Visions	Self-Leaders
Power Focus	Position/Authority	Reward/Exchange	Relational/Inspirational	Responsible Autonomy
Source of Wisdom and Direction	Leader	Leader	Leader	Followers with fall back to leader
Follower Response	Fear/conditional performance	Calculation/conditional performance	Emotional commitment to leader vision	Emotional Commitment based on self-led ownership
Major Leader Behaviors	• Directing • Commanding	• Interactive goal-setting • Contingent personal rewarding • Contingent material rewarding • Contingent reprimanding	• Communicating vision • Inspiration and persuasion • Idealism • Challenge to the status quo	• Becoming a self-leader • Modeling self-leadership • Encouraging self-set goals • Creating positive thought patterns • Developing self-leadership through reward and constructive reprimand • Promoting teamwork • Facilitating a self-leadership culture

Source: Manz and Sims (1991). Copyright 1991 by Charles C. Manz and Henry P. Sims, Jr. Adapted by permission.

Table 2.   Manz and Sims (1991) Leadership Typology
with Representative Theory and Research

Arechetype	Related Historical Theory/Research
Strongman	Theory X Leadership (e.g., McGregor, 1960)
	Initiating Structure—Ohio State Leadership Studies (e.g., Fleishman, 1973)
	Goal Setting Theory (e.g., Locke & Latham, 1990)
	Punishment Research (e.g., Arvey & Ivancevitch, 1980)
Transactor	Expectancy Theory (e.g., Vroom, 1964)
	Path-Goal Theory (e.g., House & Mitchell, 1974)
	Reinforcement Theory (e.g., Luthans & Kreitner, 1985)
	Punishment Research (e.g., Arvey & Ivancevitch, 1980)
Visionary Hero	Charismatic Leadership Theory (e.g., House, 1977)
	Transformational Leadership Theory (e.g., Burns, 1978)
SuperLeader	Behavioral Self-Management (e.g., Thoreson & Mahoney, 1974)
	Social Learning Theory (e.g., Bandura, 1977)
	Cognitive Behavior Modification (e.g., Meichenbaum, 1974)
	Goal Setting Theory (e.g., Locke & Latham, 1990)
	Participative Decision Making (Vroom & Yetton, 1973)

an overview of the Manz/Sims typology. This typology is an extension of the theoretical and empirical work of researchers like Burns (1978) and Bass and associates (e.g., Bass et al., 1987), who contrast transactional with transformational leadership. Fundamentally, Manz and Sims have extended the Burns' typology by adding the *Strongman* and *SuperLeader* archetypes. Theoretically, this typology is useful for contrasting SuperLeadership's emphasis on employee self-influence, or *self-leadership*, with alternative views of leader influence. Discussing the typology also allows description of the content of the Leadership Strategies Questionnaire II (LSQII; see Appendix A), which is structured around the typology.

The *Strongman, Transactor*, and *Visionary Hero* have been recognized in the traditional leadership literature, albeit by other names. In the following paragraphs, these three archetypes will be discussed and related to historical theory and variables. The theoretical underpinnings of SuperLeadership will then be introduced to illustrate how SuperLeadership differs from past conceptualizations of leadership. The four archetypes in the Manz/Sims (1991) typology and their related historical theories are summarized in Table 2. Where appropriate, the discussion that follows will include references to behavior dimensions that appear in the LSQII (see Appendix A).

Strongman

The first Manz/Sims archetype, *Strongman*, represents a prototypical "boss" who engages in highly directive and occasionally punitive and dictatorial leadership (cf. Schriesheim, House, & Kerr, 1976). Relying primarily on formal position power, Strongman leaders make key decisions without consultation. Based on their own judgment, they dictate a course of action to their subordinates and expect unquestioning compliance.

The Strongman archetype parallels the dominant view of leadership early in this century when "leadership was mainly a matter of how and when to give directions and orders to obedient subordinates. The strong directed the weak" (Bass, 1985, p. 5). The punitive aspects of the Strongman are similar to McGregor's (1960) conception of Theory X leadership, in which the leader assumes that passive, malingering followers require strong, directive leadership. Leadership research at Ohio State University (e.g., Fleishman, 1973) and research on punishment (e.g., Arvey & Ivancevich, 1980; Sims, 1980) also relate to Strongman leadership.

The Ohio State leadership studies. The punitive and directive aspects of the Strongman archetype can be seen in research on leadership conducted at Ohio State University in the 1950s (e.g., Fleishman, 1973). Analysis of questionnaire data from the Ohio State studies highlighted two broad behavioral factors related to leader effectiveness: *consideration* and *initiating structure* (Yukl, 1989). The *consideration* factor included behaviors reflecting interpersonal sensitivity and supportiveness, such as considering subordinates' feelings and consulting with subordinates before making decisions. However, more relevant to the Strongman, the *initiating structure* factor included leader behaviors related to defining the work roles and behavior of a leader's subordinates.

Schriesheim, House, and Kerr (1976) compared various operationalizations of *initiating structure* in behavior questionnaires derived from the Ohio State research. They found that different questionnaires operationalized this dimension in terms of (a) directive, structuring behavior, and (b) more explicitly autocratic and punitive oversight behavior. As presented by Manz and Sims (1991), the Strongman archetype is inspired by both of these interpretations.

For research purposes, the LSQII (Appendix A) captures the structuring aspects of Strongman leadership through questionnaire items covering two leader behavior dimensions: (a) *instruction and command*, commands and explicit directions about task performance from the leader; and (b) *assigned goals*, unilateral action by the leader to set explicit requirements for task performance. The punitive aspects of Strongman leadership are captured by two additional dimensions in the LSQII: (c) *intimidation*, implied or explicit threat from the leader; and (d) *non-contingent reprimand*, reprimand by the leader that is not clearly related to performance.

Goal setting theory.   A large body of past research on goal setting (e.g., Latham et al., 1988; Locke & Latham, 1990) has clearly demonstrated that goals can increase performance when combined with feedback on task performance. One particularly robust finding is that challenging, specific goals lead to higher performance than no goals, vague "do your best" goals, or unchallenging goals. Locke and Latham (1990) stress that commitment to goals is important for goal effectiveness; goal commitment is highest, they contend, "when people think they can attain the goal and when there are values associated with goal attainment" (p. 240). Past research on goal setting has found little difference in the effects of assigned goals versus participatively set goals. However, this distinction is important in the Manz/Sims typology and is preserved in the LSQII. The *assigned goals* dimension in the LSQII, discussed previously, captures the top-down quality of Strongman goal-setting for measurement purposes.

Punishment research.   Measurement of the punitive side of Strongman leadership—the *intimidation* and *non-contingent reprimand* dimensions of the LSQII—is inspired by research on punishment in organizations (e.g., Arvey & Ivancevich, 1980; Podsakoff et al., 1982; Sims, 1980). Two central findings have emerged from this research. First, non-contingent punishment has very strong, negative effects on subordinate satisfaction but little effect on performance. Second (and contrary to the predictions of reinforcement theory, discussed in the following text), contingent punishment has almost no effect on subordinate performance. More recently, Ball, Trevino, and Sims (1991) have documented relationships between incidents of leader reprimand and subsequent citizenship behavior by subordinates.

Transactor

The second Manz/Sims archetype, *Transactor*, leads by constructing and clarifying reward contingencies. Transactors engage in instrumental exchange relationships with subordinates by negotiating and strategically supplying rewards in return for achievement of goals. These rewards, in turn, evoke calculating compliance from subordinates. Four theoretical perspectives that are consistent with the Transactor archetype are path-goal theory (e.g., House, 1971; House & Mitchell, 1974), expectancy theory (e.g., Vroom, 1964), goal-setting theory (e.g., Locke & Latham, 1990), and reinforcement theory (e.g., Luthans & Kreitner, 1985).

These theoretical perspectives inspired three behavioral variables on the LSQII that capture the strategic give-and-take of Transactor leadership: (a) *contingent material reward,* (b) *contingent personal reward,* and (c) *contingent reprimand.* The *contingent material reward* scale measures the extent to which the leader supplies material rewards such as pay and bonuses in exchange for desired behavior. The *contingent personal reward* scale measures the leader's use of personal, non-material rewards such as praise and recognition contingent upon performance. The *contingent reprimand* scale captures the leader's use of verbal punishment (e.g., reprimand) when subordinate behavior or performance fails to meet goals or expectations.

These Transactor behavior variables reflect the theoretical perspectives mentioned previously by emphasizing contingent reinforcement by the leader. Goal-setting theory, discussed previously, touches on the standard-setting aspect of these leader behavior variables. Path-goal theory, expectancy theory, and reinforcement theory apply more directly to the Transactor archetype. These three perspectives will be briefly discussed following.

Expectancy theory and path-goal theory. According to expectancy theory, a cognitive theory of motivation, subordinates choose their level of effort based on: (a) their expectancy that effort will lead to performance, (b) the instrumentality of performance for achieving outcomes, and (c) the valence, or attractiveness, of the outcomes. Path-goal theory builds on the motivational framework of expectancy theory to suggest how leaders can influence subordinates. According to path-goal theory, one avenue to leader influence is strengthening the link between behavior and outcomes—the instrumentality of behavior. Leaders can strengthen instrumentality by providing structure, clarification, or coaching. Leaders may also influence subordinates by increasing the valence or desirability of outcomes for goal accomplishment.

House and Mitchell (1974) elaborated path-goal theory by arguing that the leader can shore up motivational deficiencies by compensating for limitations imposed by the work environment, the task, and the subordinate. Structuring, task-oriented leadership, for example, can clarify reward contingencies when work is complex or ambiguous. On the other hand, a relations-oriented approach might be more appropriate if the requirements for successful performance are well-known but the work itself is unsatisfying. Bass (1990) summarizes the research on path-goal theory by saying that "it suggests that to obtain the subordinate's effective performance and satisfaction, the leader must provide structure if it is missing and must supply rewards that are contingent on the adequate performance of the subordinate" (p. 633). Path-goal theory is positioned as a transactional leadership theory because of its emphasis on behavioral instrumentalities and clarification of reward structures.

Reinforcement theory. The reinforcement theory of motivation (e.g., Luthans & Kreitner, 1985; Scott & Podsakoff, 1982; Sims, 1977) is clearly related to Transactor leadership. In practice, reinforcement theory is compatible with path-goal theory except—in the behaviorist tradition—it lacks a cognitive component. Luthans and Kreitner (1985) focus specifically on organizational behavior modification—the application of reinforcement principles in organizational settings. One of their major conclusions is that a combination of positive reinforcement and extinction is more effective than contingent punishment in influencing behavior. They advocate that punishment, if administered at all, be strictly contingent on subordinate behavior. This recommendation is also consistent with past research on punishment, discussed above (e.g., Arvey & Ivancevich, 1980). Research supports the overall effectiveness of goal setting and leader contingent reward (Sims & Lorenzi, 1992).

Visionary Hero

The third Manz/Sims archetype, *Visionary Hero*, leads by inspiring followers and creating "highly absorbing and motivating visions" (Manz & Sims, 1991, p. 21). This leadership archetype captures the spirit of charismatic and transformational leadership theories (e.g., Bass et al., 1987; Burns, 1978; Conger, 1989). Yukl (1989) notes that these two perspectives overlap considerably but that transformational leadership tends to be defined more broadly than charismatic leadership. The LSQII includes four scales measuring aspects of Visionary Hero leadership. These scales will be described after charismatic and transformational leadership theory have been introduced.

Charismatic leadership theory. Charismatic leadership theory is closely associated with the work of House (1977) and Conger and Kanungo (1988). Like the definition of leadership generally, Yukl (1989) notes that the definition of charisma varies among different researchers. House (1977) described charismatic leaders as self-confident and convinced of their own beliefs and ideals. He viewed the identification of followers with the leader as a dynamic process of trust-building, where the leader's ability to inspire and to supply vision arouses commitment and dedication among followers.

Conger and Kanungo (1988; Conger, 1989) view charismatic leadership as an emergent, interactive process between leaders and followers. To Conger, charisma is *attributed* to leaders by followers. Identifying leader behaviors that evoke the attribution of charisma, then, is key to understanding the charismatic leadership process. Both House (1977) and Conger (1989) identified communication of vision as an important leader behavior. However, Conger also identified challenge to the status quo—a gadfly tendency to "buck the system"—as an important part of charismatic leadership.

Transformational leadership theory. Transformational leadership was originally proposed by Burns (1978) as an alternative to transactional leadership. According to Burns, the transformational leader inspires followers to look beyond their own immediate needs toward a longer-term view of the common good. An organizational study by Bass (1985) suggests that the inspiring aspects of transformational leadership can engender substantial commitment from followers. In this study, transformational leaders were "seen to lead the respondents to work 'ridiculous' hours and to do more than they ever expected to do" (Bass, 1985, p. 22).

Although Burns originally proposed that the effect of transformational leadership was positive, Bass (1985) later suggested that transformational leaders could have profoundly negative effects as well: both heroes and villains could qualify as transformational leaders. Also unlike Burns, who classified leaders as either transactional or transformational, Bass (1985, 1990) asserted that leaders use a mixture of both approaches. For Bass, then, transformational leadership is a supplement that augments, rather than replaces, transactional leadership. Although research on charismatic and transformational leadership is relatively new, research has associated transformational leader behavior with task commitment and with subordinate ratings of effectiveness (Bass, 1990).

Perhaps because this line of research is relatively new, the core characteristics of charismatic and transformational leaders have not yet shaken out. For measurement purposes, the LSQII includes four behavioral variables to represent the Visionary Hero archetype. The first two, *vision* and *idealism*, correspond to House's (1977) and Conger's (1989) conceptions of the charismatic leader. Items in the *vision* dimension pertain to the leader's communicating a guiding vision concerning organizational purpose, destiny, or overarching goals. The *idealism* dimension pertains to the leader's expressed dedication to fundamental personal beliefs, ideals, or overarching goals.

The third Visionary Hero scale, *stimulation and inspiration*, reflects House's (1977) and Bass's (1985) observations on the inspiring aspects of charismatic and transformational leadership. This dimension pertains to the leader's motivation of subordinates toward high(er) levels of performance and achievement. The fourth scale, *challenge to the status quo*—challenge to established ideas, routines, and conventions—corresponds to Conger's (1989) portrayal of the charismatic leader as one who advocates change.

SuperLeader

The archetypes discussed previously illustrate how three types of leaders position themselves as the primary agents of influence in their organizations. The Strongman influences followers through direction or threat; the Transactor acts on followers as a reinforcer or exchange agent; the Visionary Hero inspires or transforms followers. The role of the follower, except as target of influence, is largely absent in these approaches to leadership. In contrast, the SuperLeader emphasizes employee self-influence rather than external, top-down influence (Manz & Sims, 1990, 1991). Scully and coworkers (1994) describe SuperLeaders as "operat[ing] under the belief that followers are an influential source of wisdom and direction. These [Super]leaders create 'self-leaders' by evoking in them a sense of ownership" (p. 7). In essence, the SuperLeader is a leader who empowers followers.

The following paragraphs will discuss five theoretical perspectives that have inspired the conceptualization of SuperLeadership and the LSQII scales intended to measure SuperLeader behavior. These perspectives include: (a) behavioral self-management (e.g., Mahoney & Arnkoff, 1978; Thoreson & Mahoney, 1974), (b) social learning theory (e.g., Bandura, 1977a, 1977b), (c) cognitive behavior modification (e.g., Meichenbaum, 1977), (d) participative management, and, briefly, (e) goal-setting theory (e.g., Locke & Latham, 1990). Then, LSQII SuperLeader behavior scales will be introduced and defined along with related theory.

Behavioral self-management. Central to the SuperLeadership's emphasis on breaking traditional patterns of top-down influence is encouragement of behavioral self-control among subordinates. The self-management aspects of SuperLeadership are closely related to behavioral self-management theory. Four SuperLeader behavior variables in the LSQII especially pertain to leader encouragement of behavioral self-control: (a) *encourages self-goal setting*, (b) *encourages self-reward*, (c) *encourages finding natural rewards*, and (d) *encourages self-observation and evaluation*. Self-goal setting and self-reward are largely self-explanatory; they capture the extent to which the leader encourages subordinates to set their own performance goals and find ways to reward themselves for good performance (both without leader intervention). Items in the *natural rewards* scale refer to the leader's encouraging subordinates to find ways to get work done that are personally enjoyable. The *self-observation and evaluation* scale taps leader encouragement of subordinate self-observation of behavior at work and self-evaluation of performance (both without leader intervention).

Behavioral self-management (BSM) theory extends the principles of reinforcement theory to self-control of behavior: self-structuring one's own reinforcement environment is central to BSM. Mahoney and Arnkoff (1978) contend that before the emergence of BSM, behaviorism had assumed environmental determinism: the forces shaping behavior were seen to lie primarily in the environment rather than the individual. Research on self-control "ushered in the acceptance of a *reciprocal determinism* ... [where] the human organism was no longer viewed as a passive product of environmental influence, but as an active participant in his or her own complex development" (Mahoney & Arnkoff, 1978, p. 690).

BSM, closely associated with the work of Thoreson and Mahoney (e.g., 1974), has been used in clinical settings to modify behavior through self-influence strategies such as self-reinforcement, stimulus control, and rehearsal (Mahoney & Arnkoff, 1978; Thoreson & Mahoney, 1974). Luthans and Davis (1979) first suggested that BSM might also be applied by managers in organizational settings. They defined BSM as "the manager's deliberate regulation of stimulus cues, covert processes, and response consequences to achieve personally identified behavioral outcomes" (p. 43). At about the same time, Manz and Sims (1980) wrote an article on "Self-Management as a Substitute for Leadership" that drew upon the work of Thoreson and Mahoney. This article, which foreshadowed SuperLeadership, defined elements of self-management and introduced the question of how leaders can "lead others to lead themselves."

Luthans and Davis (1979) defined BSM as "the manager's deliberate regulation of stimulus cues, covert processes, and response consequences to achieve personally identified behavioral outcomes" (p. 43). Manz (1986) later offered a more generalized definition of BSM as "a set of strategies that aides employees in structuring their work environment" (p. 590). This definition was offered as part of a broader conceptualization of BSM in employment settings that more fully incorporated cognition into the process of employee self-influence (e.g., Bandura, 1977a, 1977b; Meichenbaum, 1977). Manz (1986) asserted that the behavioral outcomes of conventional BSM are often specified by upper-level management rather than by employees themselves. As such, he argued, conventional applications of BSM are more an internalized assertion of organizational control than true employee self-control.

In work that foreshadowed later developments in SuperLeadership, Manz (1986) argued that employee self-influence is fully expressed only when employees exercise self-management within a context of proactive self-determination and relative autonomy. He adopted the term *self-leadership* to capture this more comprehensive form of self-influence. Self-leadership, of course, subsumes effective behavioral self-management. However, Manz viewed self-led employees as setting their own agendas; they perceive and respond to—even anticipate—their own requirements and the requirements of the job itself rather than the demands of their supervisors. Recall that Luthans and Davis' (1979, p. 43) earlier definition of BSM incorporated "personally identified behavioral outcomes" that nod in the direction of Manz's self-leadership. However, Luthans and Davis were specifically addressing a managerial audience. Manz applied his idea of self-leadership to *all* employees. What he proposed was a community of self-leaders. SuperLeadership—leading others to lead themselves—later formalized much of this early thinking.

Social learning theory. Like behavioral self-management, encouragement of cognitive self-regulation is also central to the SuperLeadership perspective. According to Mahoney and Arnkoff (1978), reciprocal determinism was only half of the behavioristic revolution in the mid-1960s; the other half concerned "a reappraisal of the radical behavioristic neglect of 'private events'" (p. 690). One outcome of this reappraisal was the idea that thoughts, like behavior, could be modified using principles of behavior change. Social learning theory, which followed on the heels of this "covert conditioning revolution," provided a framework within which to view the effects of cognition on behavior (Mahoney & Arnkoff, 1978).

Closely associated with Bandura (e.g., Bandura, 1977a, 1977b, 1989), social learning theory rejects the environmental determinism of traditional behaviorism in favor of "triadic reciprocal causation" in which action, cognition, and the environment all affect behavior (Bandura, 1989, p. 1175). Social learning theory explains the acquisition and regulation of behavior in terms of "direct, vicarious, and symbolic sources of information" (Bandura, 1977a, p. 192). As such, it has both learning and motivational implications.

Bandura (1977b) posits two cognitive sources of behavioral control. The first involves interpretation, symbolic representation, and later symbolic construction of behavior consequences based on observation of models. The second source involves generating internal standards through self-goal setting, then comparing performance with these standards through self-observation. Contingent self-reward (positive appraisal) when performance is on-track with goals provides cues that guide and motivate continued improvement in performance. Discrepancies provide cues that stimulate reappraisal and perhaps cognitive or behavioral change to align goals and performance.

According to social learning theory, symbolic processes provide a link between goals and action (Bandura, 1989). One central mediator of these processes is self-efficacy or efficacy expectation, "the conviction that one can successfully execute the behavior required to produce the outcomes" (Bandura, 1977a, p. 193). Efficacy epitomizes the importance of internal representation to social cognitive theory, which links mind and behavior to an extent not admitted by conventional behaviorism. High self-efficacy results in higher self-set goals, firmer commitment to goals, and persistence in mastery attempts. Just as important, however, efficacy expectations affect anticipatory scenarios and affective reactions. Those with high self-efficacy "visualize success scenarios that provide positive guides for performance;" those with low efficacy are burdened by apprehensive cognitions and disruptive "failure scenarios that undermine performance" (Bandura, 1989, p. 1176).

Social learning theory emphasizes the importance of self as a cause of behavior. Analogously, SuperLeadership emphasizes the importance of the individual (i.e., subordinate) by stressing behavioral and cognitive self-regulation. One SuperLeader scale on the LSQII, *encourages efficacy expectations*—leader encouragement of the subordinate's confidence in her or his performance and ability—follows directly from social learning theory. Three additional LSQII scales measuring SuperLeader behavior, *encourages self-observation and evaluation, encourages self-reward*, and *encourages self-goal setting*, were mentioned previously in relation to BSM but are also consistent with social learning theory.

Cognitive behavior modification. Like social learning theory, cognitive behavior modification reflected the cognitive revolution of the 1960s and 1970s. Research by Meichenbaum (e.g., 1977) on self-instructional training is one prominent example of cognitive behavior modification. Meichenbaum's (1977) research was intended to "conceptualize cognitive events and to understand their role in behavior change" (p. 11). Central to self-instructional training is the "internal dialogue" of private consciousness, such as self-talk and its associated attributions, interpretations, self-reinforcements, and beliefs.

Self-instructional training promotes adaptive behavior by identifying and modifying self-statements and thought patterns. Two techniques that can be used to foster adaptive patterns of thought are cognitive modeling and rehearsal. Indicative of these techniques is "coping" imagery, where the person imagines a challenge and then imagines herself or himself successfully coping with the challenge. The goal of self-instructional training is to substitute adaptive thought patterns—patterns that aid coping—for maladaptive ones. Self-instructional training is an approach to cognitive restructuring that essentially promotes the adaptive "success scenarios" discussed by Bandura (1989). To capture the SuperLeader's emphasis on promoting adaptive thought patterns like those proposed by Meichenbaum (1977) and Bandura (1989), the LSQII includes a SuperLeader behavior scale called *encourages opportunity thought*. Items in this scale reflect leader encouragement of an opportunity-oriented rather than obstacle-oriented approach to adversity (Manz, 1992). This variable has been related to employee self-leadership by Manz and Sims (1990; Manz, 1992).

Goal setting theory. As previously discussed in the Strongman section, goal theory is linked to both the Strongman and SuperLeader archetypes. Clearly, the SuperLeader will want to move as far as possible toward self-goal setting by subordinates. The LSQII dimension *encourages self-goal setting* was mentioned previously in relation to BSM but is also clearly consistent with goal-setting theory.

Participative management. Theory on participative management does not directly relate to any of the behaviors articulated for the SuperLeadership archetype. However, it does bear on the status of SuperLeadership as a participative leadership perspective. Considered as a continuum, participation can range from autocratic decision making, where the supervisor acts alone, through joint consultation and decision making, to delegation, where the leader grants subordinates authority and responsibility for making decisions (Yukl, 1989).

Perhaps the most prominent theoretical statement on participative leadership has been offered by Vroom and Yetton (1973) and Vroom and Jago (1988). Vroom and Yetton (1973) outlined a normative theory concerning the appropriate degree of subordinate participation in decisions based on the importance of decision quality and decision acceptance by subordinates. Vroom and Jago (1988) revised this model to offer clearer guidance to the practicing manager and to incorporate concerns about time constraints and longer-term employee development. The Vroom and coworkers' models (e.g., Vroom & Jago, 1988; Vroom & Yetton, 1973) propose specific rules for decisions that require some degree of management involvement. For certain decisions, the prescriptions of these models apply to the SuperLeader as well. Furthermore, participation and joint decision making certainly are not inconsistent with SuperLeadership.

Fundamentally, according to the original Vroom and Yetton (1973) model, the default locus of decision making largely resides with the leader. In contrast to the contingencies covered by Vroom and coworkers (Vroom & Jago, 1988; Vroom & Yetton, 1973), however, SuperLeadership largely places the default decision making and control functions with the follower as long as the issues fall reasonably within her or his area of responsibility. Furthermore, the SuperLeadership perspective extends past work on participation by offering more specific behavioral prescriptions for increasing employee involvement. From a SuperLeadership perspective, these leader behaviors should produce a climate of extreme participation characterized by follower initiative, proaction, and responsible autonomy—that is, self-leadership. This is compatible with the earlier observations of Burns and Stalker (1961) on organic organization, which they claim is particularly well-suited to unstable environments. In the organic organization, directive leadership is supplanted by extensive employee involvement, shared authority, and lateral communication flows.

The LSQII includes two scales—*encourages self-problem solving* and *encourages initiative*—that broadly describe the extreme participation promoted by the SuperLeader and the follower independence that should result. Items in the *self-problem solving* scale describes the extent to which the leader encourages problem solving by the subordinate without direct supervisory input, approval, or assistance. The *initiative* scale describes the extent to which the leader encourages spontaneous innovation and assumption of responsibility by subordinates without input or approval from above.

Summary

The typology proposed by Manz and Sims (1991; Sims & Manz, 1996) was originally intended and written for a managerial audience. However, as shown by our review, the typology is deeply rooted in past leadership theory and research. For purposes of measuring leader behavior, the Leadership Strategies Questionnaire II (LSQII) was developed to include key behavioral dimensions representing each leadership strategy within the Manz/Sims typology.

Note that the four leadership archetypes identified by Manz and Sims (1991; Sims & Manz, 1996) have not been empirically proven to be necessarily clear-cut or exclusive. However, a recent second-order LISREL confirmatory analysis of these leader behavior dimensions has been conducted by Pearce, Cox, and Sims (1995). For the most part, their analysis generally supported the Manz and Sims typology. An exception was the aversive and directive aspects of Strongman leadership, which emerged as separate factors.

ESTABLISHING SELF-LEADERSHIP THROUGH TEAMWORK

In this section, we relate SuperLeadership to teamwork. Discussion will highlight the importance of leader encouragement of teamwork for establishing self-leadership—responsible autonomy and proactive independence—among followers.

The SuperLeader's mandate, "to lead others to lead themselves" (Manz & Sims, 1990, p. 5), follows directly from Manz's concept of self-leadership. Leaders become SuperLeaders, according to Manz and Sims (1991), by encouraging self-leadership among followers. In so doing, they claim, the SuperLeader harnesses "the strength and wisdom of many persons—by helping to unleash the abilities of the 'followers' (self-leaders) that surround them" (p. 22). Manz and Sims argue that the SuperLeader does this by using two points of leverage. First, the leader encourages employees to use several self-influence strategies, including those discussed in the last section. Second, the leader introduces supportive elements into the social context of work by promoting *teamwork* among subordinates. As will be clear later, we argue that the team-based context of SuperLeadership is conceptually linked to citizenship behavior among followers.

Manz and Sims (1990) treat the organizational context of self-leadership largely in terms of teamwork and cooperation; they consider teamwork an important part of the "self-leadership system" (p. 182). They argue that problems will arise at work that cannot be solved by individuals working alone; fresh perspectives or direct assistance will sometimes be necessary. Self-leadership under these conditions will sometimes require peer collaboration and cooperation. By encouraging this collaboration, SuperLeaders can foster a norm in which every employee is a potential resource for others. The team, then, becomes the unit of self-leadership.

Sims and Manz (1982; Manz & Sims, 1987, 1993) pursued their emphasis on teamwork and cooperation through a field study they conducted in a small, non-unionized, auto parts assembly plant in the southern United States. Operations in this plant were organized around small teams of employees for each segment of the production process. Sims and Manz discovered that these teams were springboards for self-leadership throughout the plant: teams collaborated within and between themselves to set their own production and quality targets, conduct and evaluate quality inspections, schedule production, and track inventory. They also selected their own members, assigned work, and handled internal discipline. Moreover, they performed all of these tasks without routine management intervention.

The daily examples of self-leadership exercised by these teams were punctuated by periodic meetings that amounted to group problem-solving sessions. Sims and Manz (1982) analyzed the content of discussion during these meetings. They found that the tone of these meetings was occasionally contentious, particularly when internal discipline was an issue, but also problem-focused, generally nondirective, involving, and centered on self-responsibility. Sims and Manz interpreted these meetings as pragmatic manifestations of self-leadership.

The plant observed by Sims and Manz (1982) is a textbook example of self-managing teamwork (e.g., Cummings, 1978; Hackman, 1987a, 1987b). Self-managing teams, carefully planned and implemented, can promote self-leadership where the unit of analysis is the group. The original conceptualization of self-management by Manz and Sims (1980) was oriented mainly to the individual follower. However, more recent statements (Manz & Sims, 1989, 1990, 1991) emphasize teamwork and cooperation among subordinates. A final SuperLeadership behavior scale in the LSQII— *encourages teamwork*—captures the team-based context of SuperLeadership. This scale includes items measuring the extent to which the leader encourages cooperation and coordinated action among subordinates.

CITIZENSHIP BEHAVIOR:
A LOGICAL TARGET OF SUPERLEADERSHIP BEHAVIOR

In this section, we shift attention to one aspect of the behavior of followers: citizenship behavior. We particularly emphasize citizenship behavior as a target of the SuperLeader. This section will begin by reviewing an established citizenship construct, *organizational citizenship behavior* (OCB, e.g., Organ, 1988), and discussing OCB as a behavioral outcome of SuperLeadership. We will then introduce the newer, related construct of anti-citizenship behavior (ACB, e.g., Fisher & Locke, 1992) and conceptually link leadership to citizenship behavior among followers. Then, we will extend the notion of *individual* citizenship to *team* citizenship. Throughout this section, discussion will describe several citizenship behavior dimensions that were incorporated into a questionnaire called the *Team Citizenship Questionnaire* (TCQ) investigated by Cox (1994). Appendix B presents examples of items on the TCQ broken out by dimension.

Organizational Citizenship Behavior

Organ (1988) defines *organizational citizenship behavior* (OCB) as "behavior [by the employee] that is discretionary, not directly or explicitly recognized by the formal reward system, and that in the aggregate promotes the effective functioning of the organization" (p. 4). Organ acknowledges that some OCBs— punctual attendance, for example—can have a beneficial cumulative effect for an individual and that the individual may consider these long-term benefits. Still, these behaviors qualify as OCB so long as they are unlikely to lead directly to formal rewards.

To Organ (1988), for example, a salesperson's extra (discretionary) effort to increase sales volume is *not* OCB if pay and promotional opportunities are tied to sales volume. In this case, the extra effort produces rewards for the individual directly as a matter of organizational policy. The key to OCBs, however, is that their returns are "not contractually guaranteed" and are "at most an inference on the part of the individual who contemplates such returns" (Organ, 1988, p. 5).

OCBs can benefit organizations either directly or indirectly. Moreover, they can focus personally on an individual coworker or more impersonally on the organization as an institution. Examples of OCB include volunteerism, assistance between coworkers, unusual attendance or punctuality, and active participation in organizational affairs (Farh et al., 1990).

OCB can be considered one of several classes of *prosocial organizational behavior* (POB) that have been identified by Brief and Motowidlo (1986). They defined the broader POB construct as:

> Behavior which is (a) performed by a member of an organization, (b) directed toward an individual, group, or organization with whom he or she interacts while carrying out his or her organizational role, and (c) [is] performed with the intention of promoting the welfare of the individual, group, or organization toward which it is directed (p. 711).

POB differs slightly from OCB in that it also encompasses prosocial gestures that do not promote effective *organizational* functioning per se. Organ (1988) illustrates this distinction through the example of an employee who helps a coworker cover up a potentially serious mistake. This act can be considered POB because it benefits the coworker. However, it does not qualify as OCB because it is ultimately dysfunctional for the organization as a whole.

Considered as individual events, OCBs are almost taken for granted—as when one employee helps another who is having difficulty with a task. Such acts are too small to be noticed by management or directly rewarded in a performance appraisal. Perhaps for this reason, OCBs seem to occur without a calculated expectation of tangible gain or compensation. Though individually inconsequential, however, Organ (1988) contends that OCBs have a beneficial cumulative effect for organizations that is reflected in a strong undercurrent of cooperation.

OCBs imply a selfless sensitivity to coworkers or the organization as a whole—a free willingness to cooperate as an organizational player—that is difficult or impossible to directly reward or specifically require in an employment contract. Smith, Organ, and Near (1983) stress the benefits of OCBs for "lubricat[ing] the social machinery of the organization" (p. 654). They liken OCB to spontaneous behavior that "goes beyond role prescriptions" (p. 653), noting that Katz (1964) considered such behavior essential for strong organizational social systems. The organization, then, gains a measure of systemic resiliency from these small, spontaneous acts of selfless sensitivity, cooperation, and uncompensated contribution.

Dimensions of Organizational Citizenship Behavior

Research specifically directed toward OCB is relatively recent, extending only from the early 1980s. Much of this early research has been directed toward defining and clarifying the OCB construct. Two OCB behavioral factors have been repeatedly identified in past research: *altruism* or *helping* behavior and *conscientiousness* or *generalized compliance* (e.g., Farh et al., 1990; Organ, 1988; Organ & Konovsky, 1989; Smith et al., 1983). These two dimensions are included in the Team Citizenship Questionnaire (TCQ), with sample items presented in Appendix B.

Altruism. The altruism dimension of OCB includes face-to-face behavior that directly aids others (Smith et al., 1983). Examples of altruistic behavior include volunteering for extra work or helping other employees who are new, who have been absent, or who have heavy work loads. Altruism increases the efficiency and flexibility of the work force; it reduces the need to devote organizational resources to "purely maintenance functions" and helps the social system accommodate environmental variance (Organ, 1988, p. 8).

Conscientiousness. The second dimension, conscientiousness, is more impersonal. It reflects behavior that is "indirectly helpful to others involved in the system" but is not targeted directly toward a specific coworker (Smith et al., 1983, p. 657). Examples of conscientiousness include above-average attendance and holding breaks to reasonable lengths. Conscientiousness signals an incremental investment in the productivity of the organization and lends a measure of orderly predictability to the social system.

Although the previously-mentioned two dimensions are well-documented, Organ (1988) notes that the dimensionality of OCB has not been definitively established. He suggested three additional OCB dimensions that had not been explored at the time of his review: *courtesy, civic virtue,* and *sportsmanship.*

The TCQ also includes items measuring courtesy and civic virtue among followers, with sample items presented in Appendix B.

Courtesy.   Whereas altruism involves helping others solve problems that have already arisen, *courtesy* reflects a degree of interpersonal sensitivity that helps avoid problems from the outset (Organ, 1988). An example of courtesy is being considerate of the impact of one's actions at work on others. The benefit of courtesy for the organization stems mainly from interpersonal conflict avoided.

Civic virtue.   Civic virtue suggests an incremental investment in the global welfare, not just the productivity, of the organization. It reflects citizenship, belonging, and constructive engagement. An example might be rank-and-file attendance at meetings that are not required. Organ (1988) contends that civic participation benefits the organization indirectly by "bringing more knowledge and points of view to bear upon the formulation of [organizational] policy" (p. 13). The short-term cost of civic virtue in terms of productivity, he contends, can be offset by the benefits of better long-term decisions for the organization. The benefits of civic participation to the organization—increased knowledge and expressed diversity of opinion—are indirect but, nevertheless, potentially substantial (Organ, 1988).

Sportsmanship.   Sportsmanship is defined primarily as the obverse of negative actions such as "complaining, petty grievances, railing against real or imagined slights, and making federal cases out of small potatoes"(Organ, 1988, p. 11). Sportsmanship spares the organization from the distracting dissipation of ceaseless grievances and infighting. This dimension has undergone some reconceptualization since its inception and now, on the basis of empirical analysis, is considered by Ball and coworkers (1991) to be a type of *anti-citizenship behavior*, which they relabeled *complaining*.

Teamwork.   Although teamwork has not traditionally been considered an OCB per se, the TCQ includes a teamwork dimension for exploratory purposes. Items in this dimension pertain to group coordination and cooperation. This dimension is unique to the TCQ; it is not included in previous citizenship measures.

A Related Construct: Anti-Citizenship

In their review of research on job satisfaction, Fisher and Locke (1992) reported research relating general job satisfaction to positive behaviors such as OCB. They also report research relating general job satisfaction to negative or "non-compliant" behaviors, defined by Puffer (1987) as "non-task behaviors that have negative organizational implications" (p. 615). Fisher and Locke focus particularly on behavioral responses to job *dissatisfaction*, which have not been explored as extensively as satisfaction-related behaviors. Conceptual typologies of likely responses to job dissatisfaction include physical and psychological withdrawal, perceptual adjustment, and protest actions (Fisher & Locke, 1992).

Based on preliminary research, Fisher and Locke (1992) developed an inductive taxonomy of negative behavioral responses to job dissatisfaction. In two early studies, a range of possible behaviors was identified by asking respondents about actions they took, considered taking, or had seen taken by others in response to job dissatisfaction. Subsequent research built on this initial item pool, categorized the items into dimensions, and developed ratings of the relative "badness" of the items. Dimensions from the Fisher and Locke taxonomy were later conceptualized as examples of *anti-citizenship behavior* (ACB) by Ball and coworkers (1991). Discussion of ACB is included to provide the reader with a better understanding of the contents of the TCQ investigated by Cox (1994). However, because the ACB construct is quite recent, ACB will not figure as prominently in the arguments to be developed later in this chapter.

Although it may at first seem that OCB and ACB are merely opposite ends of the same continuum, they may in fact be separate, coexisting dimensions (Schnake, 1991). Accordingly, reduced citizenship behavior need not necessitate a corresponding increase in anti-citizenship behavior. The absence of citizenship behavior, for example, might only signal passivity with respect to positive citizenship. Anti-citizenship behavior, however, involves active behavior that has specific negative implications for the organization. Ball and coworkers (1991) found a substantial negative (-0.74) correlation between organizational citizenship behavior and counterproductive behavior. However, their second-order factor analysis supported the conceptual distinctness of these two classes of behavior. This finding offers preliminary support for the separate dimensionality of OCB and ACB, although they appear to be negatively correlated.

Dimensions of Anti-citizenship Behavior

The dimensions identified by Ball and coworkers (1991) certainly do not exhaust the range of negative behaviors that might be exhibited by employees. Scales representing three ACB dimensions from Ball and coworkers, plus the *complaining* dimension described previously, are included in the TCQ investigated by Cox (1994). Recall that the *complaining* dimension was the reverse coding of the OCB *sportsmanship* as reconceptualized by Ball and coworkers.

In addition to *complaining*, ACB dimensions from Ball ad coworkers that are included in the TCQ are *physical avoidance or escape from the job as a whole, avoidance of the work itself*, and *defiance and resistance to authority*. The *physical avoidance* dimension reflects behaviors like chronically late arrival to work or falsely calling in sick. The *work avoidance* dimension reflects gold-bricking behavior like letting others do one's own work or looking busy while doing nothing. The *defiance and resistance* dimension reflects more overt negative behavior like deliberately ignoring rules and regulations or talking back to supervisors.

Summary

Although it continues to evolve as a construct, organizational citizenship behavior is rapidly emerging as an interpretable and practical indicator of employee behavior. OCB is also a coherent, theoretically-grounded, composite criterion of employee effectiveness; it includes a whole class of behaviors that are individually specified, yet conceptually unified (e.g., Fisher & Locke, 1992). Furthermore, OCB is under the volitional control of individual employees (e.g., Bateman & Organ, 1983; Organ, 1988).

Rapidly growing interest in the citizenship construct is reflected in the wide range of variables that have been related to OCB in recent research. Although a comprehensive review of these variables and their relationships to OCB is beyond the scope of this paper, past research has found relationships between various facets of OCB and employee demographic characteristics (Smith et al., 1983), perceived fairness (Farh et al., 1990; Moorman, 1991; Organ & Konovsky, 1989), job satisfaction (Bateman & Organ, 1983; Smith et al., 1983), supervisor punishment behavior (Ball et al., 1991), trust in management (Puffer, 1987), and task scope (Farh et al., 1990). The interested reader is referred to Organ (1988) for a thorough review of earlier OCB research.

SuperLeadership, Teamwork, and Citizenship Behavior

In this section, we argue that OCB is responsive to leadership, especially SuperLeadership. Further, because of the fundamental interactive nature of the concept, we argue the appropriateness of reconceptualizing the unit of analysis of citizenship to *team* citizenship.

According to Manz and Sims (1990, 1991), the SuperLeader directly encourages a norm of employee self-leadership. Ideally, this norm will become a mandate as the leader extricates herself or himself from the cycle of hierarchical command-and-control. Over time, lines of communication should become less vertical (hierarchical) and more horizontal as employees take on more responsibility for their own behavior. As the transition to self-leadership progresses, the SuperLeader serves less as a source of direction and command than "as a source of information and experience, as a sounding board, and as the transmitter of overall organizational goals" (Manz & Sims, 1991, p. 31). The role of consultant and facilitator, which typifies the SuperLeader's relationship with mature self-leaders, further reinforces the self-leadership norm. Ideally, the result is a cadre of nominal "followers" that have extensive, often decisive personal responsibility for their work and how they will carry it out. We contend that the personal responsibility mandated under SuperLeadership will foster employee behaviors that are consistent with Organ's (1988) conceptualization of OCB.

SuperLeadership and Direct Effects on Citizenship

References in the counseling psychology literature on therapy groups offer some suggestive parallels to a connection between OCB and mandated employee responsibility of the kind that should emerge under SuperLeadership. Antonuccio, Davis, Lewinsohn, and Breckenridge (1987), for example, found that group cohesiveness was positively related to nondirective leader behavior in eight psychoeducational therapy groups. These findings are consistent with earlier work by Angell and DeSau (1974), who experimentally explored the relationship between leadership and group process in leaderless, democratically-led, and directively-led therapy groups. Only the leaderless group showed increases in problem-solving behavior over time. The authors attributed this to the *absence* of direct leader support, which may have produced "discomfort, anxiety, and unusual behavior in the common social sense [that] are related to group growth and problem solving" (p. 55).

Seligman and Desmond (1975) offered a historical review of leaderless group therapy that supports the observations of Antonuccio and coworkers (1987) and Angell and DeSau (1974). According to Seligman and Desmond, proponents of leaderless group therapy observe that "patients are actually helped by their peers and are cast into a constructive role of 'helper'" (p. 281). Group cohesiveness and shared leadership result from leaderless therapy's "denial of leader role with resultant heightened 'group-centeredness' and individual sense of responsibility" (p. 282).

The generalizability of this research and commentary to non-therapeutic settings cannot be assumed. Still, this viewpoint is broadly consistent with the idea that an absence of hierarchical control can promote greater personal responsibility, mutual assistance, and collaborative problem-solving among self-led followers. It is also consistent with Manz and Sims's (1990, 1991) assertion that self-leadership, with its accompanying feelings of ownership, commitment, and personal responsibility, can fill the void created by dissolving hierarchical reporting structures.

Within the organizational psychology literature, Schnake, Dumler, and Cochran (1993) recently conducted an exploratory field study of the effects of SuperLeadership on OCB in a small manufacturing facility. These authors argued that SuperLeadership might promote OCB for two reasons. First, they proposed that SuperLeadership should enhance autonomy and control among followers, thus providing "greater opportunity to engage in discretionary behaviors such as OCB" (p. 355). Second, they proposed that SuperLeadership may increase intrinsic job satisfaction by enriching work and increasing feelings of competence among followers. Noting that intrinsic satisfaction has been found to be related to OCB in past research, they proposed that SuperLeadership might therefore have motivational effects that promote OCB.

Schnake and colleagues' (1993) study operationalized SuperLeadership in truncated form using eight items taken from an early version of Manz and Sims's (1987) Self-Management Leader Behavior Scale. These items covered three dimensions of self-management considered in Manz and Sims's early conceptualization of SuperLeadership, including *self-observation, self-expectation*, and *self-goal setting*. These early dimensions are roughly analogous to the *encourages self-observation and evaluation, encourages efficacy expectations*, and *encourages self-goal setting* dimensions on the present LSQII.

Schnake and coworkers (1993) were unable to confirm that these three dimensions explained additional variance in follower OCB beyond the well-established *consideration* and *initiating structure* leader behavior dimensions. One explanation they offered for these findings was that work at their field site may have been too structured for employee self-management, and hence for SuperLeadership, to have had strong effects. They urged continued exploration of SuperLeadership as a possible predictor of OCB in settings where broader task scope would more effectively capitalize on the potential of employee self-management.

These early results notwithstanding, we continue to expect that relationships between SuperLeadership and OCB will emerge through additional research in a range of work settings. We feel that relationships are particularly likely in research that measures additional relevant dimensions of SuperLeader behavior using instruments like the LSQII.

Summary

It seems reasonable that OCBs are likely to be promoted by the SuperLeader's emphasis on employee self-leadership rather than top-down direction. Mutual assistance and interpersonal cohesion imply altruism and courtesy, for example, setting aside for a moment the confrontational aspects of therapeutic introspection. Moreover, personal responsibility seems consistent with the OCB dimension of conscientiousness. On the other hand, several dimensions of ACB should be suppressed under SuperLeadership. Heightened sensitivity to personal responsibility vis-à-vis coworkers, for example, should reduce physical avoidance from the job, avoidance of the work itself, and retaliation. A SuperLeader orientation toward employee self-leadership, then, is expected to increase employee OCB and reduce ACB.

Indirect SuperLeadership Effects on Citizenship
Through Encouragement of Teamwork

The discussion to this point makes a case that OCB may be promoted directly through SuperLeadership's emphasis on self-leadership. The preceding findings are suggestive because they trace a possible connection between self-leadership and OCB-like behavior among self-led followers in interventions that are *not* explicitly team-oriented. Research and commentary discussed following will link OCB-like behavior specifically to *team* self-leadership. This discussion will be used as a foil to suggest that OCB should also result from the SuperLeader's encouragement of teamwork.

Citizenship and self-leadership in self-managed teams. The literature contains extensive discussions of self-managing teams. These organizational interventions are necessarily sweeping, systemic, and sometimes wrenching for the participants (cf. Rice, 1955; Trist et al., 1977; Walton, 1972). As a consequence, the generalizability of this research to work settings is to some extent offset by its complexity, which defies definite causal statements about leadership, self-management, and OCB. Nevertheless, self-managing work teams share important similarities to a SuperLeadership work context as portrayed by Manz and Sims (1990, 1991): they combine non-directive leadership with an emphasis on self-leadership and teamwork by team members.

Mature self-managed teams are also characterized by behavior strikingly akin to OCB. Consider, for example, some of the signal characteristics of self-managed workteams that have been observed by Hackman (1987a). These characteristics unite self-leadership, teamwork, and OCB:

1. Team members feel personally responsible and accountable for their work;
2. They self-lead by monitoring and directing their own performance and by taking corrective action on their own initiative (conscientiousness);
3. They actively help coworkers and constructively seek guidance, help, or resources from others (altruism).

In a similar vein, the Tavistock Institute characterized self-managing teams as facilitating social relationships and cooperation that seem reminiscent of OCB (Pearce & Ravlin, 1987).

Walton's (1972) description of a team-based food processing plant is a case-in-point of how work behaviors and relational patterns among self-managed team members seem to capture several aspects of OCB. For example, below-average absenteeism in the plant and broad employee involvement in developing and implementing new production techniques suggest a great deal of conscientiousness. Employee altruism was evident on-site in extensive mutual assistance and adjustment. Civic virtue, both within and outside the plant, was evident in extensive self-governance by shop-floor team members and unusual activity in public affairs in the surrounding community. This experiment, which also included extensive technical innovations not described here, reported impressive reductions in overhead and gains in quality.

Kolodny and Kiggundu (1980) illustrated the importance of OCB-like behavior to self-managing teams with their ethnographic account of woodlands harvesting teams. In attempting to explain large and consistent differences in productivity across different teams, the authors discovered that team productivity rested critically on behaviors that resemble altruism and courtesy as defined by Organ (1988). High-producing teams, for example, were characterized by extensive, informal altruism: experienced machine operators offered technical advice to each other on their radios and provided informal, after-hours training for less experienced operators. High-producing teams also reflected courtesy, as when operators saved support mechanics several trips to the field by making an extra effort to precisely explain the nature of a mechanical problem.

Consistent with Organ's (1988) description of OCB, Kolodny and Kiggundu (1980) observed spontaneous and informal support between members of high-producing teams. Moreover, when certain employees failed to exercise their option of OCB, group performance and interpersonal relations were disrupted. For example, Kolodny and Kiggundu observed that some machine operators generated substantial interpersonal friction and productivity losses by merely reporting mechanical problems but not making the extra effort to troubleshoot their cause in the field. In essence, they used mechanical problems as an opportunity to take a break while uninformed mechanics ran the gauntlet between the field and the machine shed.

Before turning away from this case, a final comment should be made regarding ACB. Earlier it was suggested that OCB and ACB may be only loosely coupled: they are not necessarily polar opposites of the same behavioral continuum. Kolodny and Kiggundu's (1980) study, however, illustrates how difficult it can be in practice to distinguish between passivity with respect to OCB and active ACB. The behavior of the non-communicative machine operators, for example, might plausibly be interpreted two ways. On one hand, it could be argued that their failure to troubleshoot problems before reporting them to mechanics represents passivity with respect to OCB dimensions such as courtesy and altruism. On the other hand, their conspicuous inactivity on the two-way radio might itself represent signal activity—avoidance of work or even attempted sabotage of the mechanics' efforts. The latter interpretation is supported by Kolodny and Kiggundu's description of how some operators resented the mechanics' overtime pay and working arrangements.

The mandate for positive citizenship in self-managed teams.   Factor analysis of the Ball and coworkers' (1991) citizenship instrument revealed the extent to which OCB and ACB can coexist independently. In their analysis of problem-solving conversations within self-managing teams, Sims and Manz (1982) reached a similar conclusion. They observed infrequent but memorable confrontations between group coworkers and individuals who were seen as lacking in some aspect of performance. For example, one confrontation involved direct feedback to a team member concerning her or his absenteeism (i.e., passivity with respect to OCB conscientiousness or active ACB job escape behavior) and the effect of this behavior on other team members.

Presumably, then, the glare of peer scrutiny in self-managed teams will tend to promote OCB and suppress ACB. Certainly, positive citizenship in various incarnations does seem to be important for effective team functioning (cf. Kolodny & Kiggundu, 1980). Perhaps this is because OCBs enhance resiliency by facilitating fluid mutual adjustment among employees (e.g., Organ, 1988; see also discussion of employee cooperation in self-managing teams by Rice, 1955).

SuperLeadership and self-managed teams.   Research on self-managed teams generally supports the idea that the SuperLeader will influence followers by promoting self-leadership and teamwork. Because employees work for themselves and each other, not for the boss, team members themselves are likely to encourage—if not demand—positive citizenship from their colleagues.

Hackman (1987a, 1987b) makes the connection between SuperLeadership and self-managed teams explicit. He observes that leaders of self-managing teams concern themselves mainly with broad planning and team facilitation rather than direct intervention with team members. Hackman likens this leadership approach to Manz and Sims's (1984) earlier (and abandoned) idea of "unleadership" in self-managed teams. (The term *SuperLeader* follows directly from and replaces this earlier definition of "unleader.")

Kolodny and Kiggundu (1980) paint a picture of SuperLeader-like leadership in their description of the harvesting teams. They found that effective team leaders largely acted as process consultants; they facilitated group work while deemphasizing micromanagement of employees. Similarly, in Manz and Sims' (1984) field study (see also Manz & Sims, 1987; Sims & Manz, 1982), leaders who were perceived as effective were those who encouraged employees to manage their own efforts.

Summary

Effective leaders of self-managed work teams seem primarily to facilitate teamwork and self-leadership. SuperLeaders create social systems that virtually mandate positive citizenship. In essence, we suggest the SuperLeader's encouragement of self-leadership and cooperative teamwork will enhance OCB and reduce ACB.

Research Propositions: The Model

In this section, we distill our discussion into a conceptual model and a summary of propositions suggesting logical relationships between various approaches to leadership from the Manz and Sims (1991) typology and citizenship constructs. The model entails OCB and ACB as *external criteria*, or targets of team leader behavior.

The predicted leader behavior/follower citizenship relationships are presented in Figure 1. In this figure, we use the generic clusters of leadership archetypes rather than specific leader behaviors, and show proposed relationships between leader archetypes and both team citizenship and team anti-citizenship. Note that the solid lines in this model, extending to OCB and ACB from the Strongman and SuperLeader archetypes, represent directional research propositions. Dotted lines, extending from the Transactor and Visionary Hero archetypes, represent exploratory, non-directional research questions. We see positive citizenship as the essence of teamwork and view the effective leader as one who has a capacity to generate teamwork among followers. Of course, the present model is merely a theoretical starting point for future empirical investigation of the relationships between leadership and team citizenship.

Strongman Leadership and Team Citizenship

We would expect Strongman leadership to be *negatively* related to OCB and *positively* related to ACB in teams. Recall that the Strongman archetype contains elements of highly directive and occasionally arbitrary and punitive leader behavior (cf. Manz & Sims, 1991; Schriesheim et al., 1976). The arbitrary and punitive aspects of this leadership profile are suggestive given past leadership research on the antecedents of OCB and on the effects of leader punishment.

Past research, for example, has found aspects of OCB to be positively related to perceived fairness in the workplace (Farh et al., 1990; Moorman, 1991; Organ & Konovsky, 1989). To the extent that capricious leader behavior is perceived as unfair, the arbitrariness implied by Strongman leadership is likely to reduce OCB among team followers.

Past research has also established positive relationships between job satisfaction and aspects of OCB (e.g., Bateman & Organ, 1983; Smith et al., 1983). Also, the punishment research previously cited has found leader punishment to reduce subordinate job satisfaction (Arvey & Ivancevich, 1980; Podsakoff et al., 1982; Sims, 1980). Together, these findings are also consistent with the proposition that the punitive side of Strongman leadership will negatively affect OCB in teams.

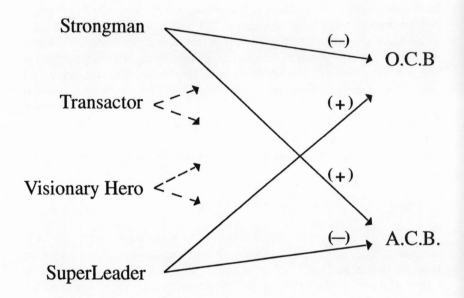

Note: Solid lines represent propositions
Dotted lines represent non-directional research questions

Figure 1. Diagram of Propositions and Research Questions Showing
Relationships Between Leadership Archetypes and Citizenship

Not only might Strongman leadership reduce OCB, but the Strongman's punitive approach may indeed generate active resistance akin to ACB. That is, Strongman behaviors such as threats and intimidation may produce negative responses such as complaining and withdrawal. Research suggests that close, punitive supervision can promote role ambiguity, resistant behavior, and conflict among coworkers (e.g., Day & Hamblin, 1964; Keller & Szilagyi, 1976;

Raven & French, 1958). In general, it seems plausible that leaders who behave in arbitrary and capricious methods are less likely to develop team commitment and the positive citizenship that would result.

SuperLeadership and Team Citizenship

In contrast to the Strongman, we would expect SuperLeadership to be *positively* related to OCB and *negatively* related to ACB in teams. To some extent, this contrasting expectation simply reflects the differing roles played by the Strongman and the SuperLeader in relation to followers. The Strongman's command-and-control approach sends a clear message that followers are primarily accountable to the leader. The SuperLeader, however, gradually removes herself or himself from the command-and-control cycle by emphasizing initiative, self-problem solving, and various self-leadership strategies (Manz & Sims, 1989, 1991). In addition, the SuperLeader actively encourages teamwork and reliance on peers for support and guidance (Manz & Sims, 1990). SuperLeadership, then, should encourage lateral accountability to peers among team members rather than vertical accountability to the leader.

The effects of lateral accountability in groups, such as corrective feedback and more active helping and support behavior, have been documented in research cited above (e.g., Angell & DeSau, 1974; Antonuccio et al., 1987; Sims & Manz, 1982). In a mature SuperLeadership system, increased peer accountability should focus the attention of team members on their coworkers rather than on the leader. This lateral focus should highlight the benefits of good citizenship (OCB) among mutually accountable and interdependent team members because of the greater likelihood and importance of reciprocation. On the other hand, resistant and counterproductive behavior (ACB) among team members should be relatively more costly. Under conditions of extensive lateral accountability, ACB would be ill-advised, both because it strains important lateral working relationships, and because it is less likely to be tolerated.

Transactor Leadership, Visionary Hero Leadership, and Team Citizenship

Relationships between citizenship and the Transactor and Visionary Hero archetypes seem less clear. In terms of Transactor leadership, a contingent reward pattern may create good will which, in turn, may promote OCB and/ or suppress ACB. On the other hand, reward policies can also promote an atmosphere of strategic give-and-take in which individuals do what they are paid to do, but do not go beyond role requirements in a way that suggests good citizenship.

With respect to Visionary Hero leadership, certainly the defining characteristic of the Visionary Hero is inspiration. Perhaps the enthusiasm resulting from inspiration can be translated into team commitment with positive citizenship effects. However, the commitment inspired by Visionary Hero behavior may also be primarily directed toward individual members rather than the team. If individualized inspiration occurs at the expense of team inspiration, citizenship effects may be negative.

The ambiguous effects of the Transactor and Visionary Hero archetypes on team citizenship stems from the ongoing, central involvement of these leaders in the work lives of followers. Like the Strongman, these leaders maintain a dependency relationship with followers. However, whereas the arbitrary and punitive aspects of Strongman leadership suggest clear citizenship effects, Transactor and Visionary Hero effects on citizenship seem more leader-specific. That is, citizenship effects are probably dependent on the behaviors that a specific Transactor rewards and the content of the inspiring messages that a specific Visionary Hero sends. Future research may provide a clearer picture of the circumstances under which these approaches to leadership have positive or negative effects on follower citizenship.

SUMMARY

Team applications are rapidly emerging as a new frontier in organizational design. The increasing popularity of teams, along with greater experience in application, highlights the interactive importance of leader and member behavior for effective team functioning.

The Manz and Sims (1991; Sims & Manz, 1996) typology was introduced to organize past research on leadership and to present a palette of leadership theories. This paper discussed a range of research from several sources to support our contention that SuperLeadership, with its emphasis on team member initiative, self-management, and lateral accountability, is a particularly effective approach to facilitative leadership in empowered team contexts. The constructs of organizational citizenship behavior (OCB) and anti-citizenship behavior (ACB) were introduced as potentially useful indicators of effective team member behavior and, by extension, effective teamwork. To aid future research, the paper has made periodic references to the Leadership Strategies Questionnaire II and the Team Citizenship Questionnaire. These instruments illustrate how leader behavior and team citizenship can be measured for research purposes. Sample questionnaire items, categorized by leadership and citizenship dimension, appear in the appendices to this paper. Complete copies of these formatted questionnaires are presented in Cox (1994), along with information on their developmental history and preliminary psychometric characteristics.

The preliminary conceptual model described at the end of the paper unites the Manz and Sims (1991) leadership typology with the OCB and ACB constructs. This model includes directional research propositions and non-directional research questions that present a challenge for future investigation of how the behavior of leaders and members contribute to effective teamwork.

APPENDIX A

Leadership Strategies Questionnaire II

Listed below are examples of items on the Leadership Strategies Questionnaire II (LSQII), categorized by dimension within the Manz and Sims (1991) leadership typology framework. Although dimension labels are presented for illustration, no labels appear in the actual LSQII.

The LSQII is designed to be administered to subordinates for purposes of describing the leadership behavior of their supervisor. Responses to each item are registered on a five-point, true/false scale as follows:

1 = if the statement is definitely not true of your supervisor;
2 = if the statement is not true;
3 = if the statement is neither true nor untrue;
4 = if the statement is true;
5 = if the statement is definitely true of your supervisor.

A complete copy the formatted LSQII is presented in Cox (1994), along with information on its developmental history and preliminary psychometric characteristics.

Strongman

Instruction and Command

He/she gives me instructions about how to do my job.
He/she provides commands in regard to my job.

Non-Contingent Reprimand

He/she is often critical of my work, even when I perform well.
I frequently am reprimanded by him/her without knowing why.

Intimidation

He/she behaves in a threatening manner.
He/she tries to influence me through threat and intimidation.

Assigned Goals

He/she establishes my performance goals.
He/she sets the goals for my performance.

Transactor

Contingent Material Reward

He/she will recommend that I am compensated well if I perform well.
He/she will recommend that I am compensated more if I perform well.

Contingent Personal Reward

When I do a job well, he/she tells me about it.
He/she gives me positive feedback when I perform well.

Contingent Reprimand

He/she lets me know about it when I perform poorly.
He/she reprimands me when my performance is not up to par.

Interactive Goals

He/she and I work together to decide what my performance goals should be.
He/she and I sit down together and reach agreement on my performance goals.

Visionary Hero

Vision

He/she provides a clear vision of who and what we are.
He/she provides a clear vision of where we are going.

Stimulation and Inspiration

He/she inspires me to get a lot more done than I could have if he/she were
    not around.
Because of him/her, I do more than I expected I could do.

Idealism

He/she is driven by higher purposes or ideals.
He/she has a strong personal dedication to higher purposes or ideals.

Challenge to the Status Quo

He/she isn't afraid to "buck the system" if he/she thinks it is necessary.
He/she is a non-traditional type who "shakes up the system" when necessary.

SuperLeader

Encourages Self-Goal Setting

He/she advises me to set goals for my own performance.
He/she actively encourages me to set goals for myself.

Encourages Self-Observation and Evaluation

He/she encourages me to judge how well I am performing.
He/she encourages me to keep track of my progress on tasks I'm working on.

Encourages Self-Reward

He/she encourages me to treat myself to something I enjoy when I do a task especially well.
He/she urges me to reward myself with something I like when I have successfully completed a major task.

Encourages Finding Natural Rewards

He/she encourages me to take time to do work tasks that I like to do.
He/she urges me to do tasks at work that make me feel good about myself.

Encourages Opportunity Thought

He/she advises me to look for the opportunities contained in problems I face.
He/she encourages me to view unsuccessful performance as a chance to learn.

Encourages Efficacy Expectations

He/she encourages me to have confidence in my ability to meet challenges at work.
He/she advises me to expect that I will perform well.

Encourages Self-Problem Solving

He/she encourages me to search for solutions to my problems on the job without his/her supervision.

He/she encourages me to find solutions to my problems at work without his/her direct input.

Encourages Initiative

He/she urges me to assume responsibilities on my own.

He/she advises me to make improvements in how I do my work on my own initiative without being told to do so.

Encourages Teamwork

He/she advises me to work together with other managers/supervisors who report to him/her as a team.

He/she encourages me to work together with other managers/supervisors who report to him/her.

APPENDIX B

Team Citizenship Questionnaire

Listed below are examples of items on the Team Citizenship Questionnaire (TCQ), categorized by dimension within the organizational citizenship behavior (OCB) and anti-citizenship behavior (ACB) categories. Although dimension labels are presented below for illustration, no labels appear in the actual TCQ.

The TCQ is designed to be administered to individuals for the purpose of describing the OCB and ACB of their colleagues in a supervisor-defined work group. Responses to each item are registered on a five-point, true/false scale as follows:

1 = if the statement is definitely not true of your colleagues who also report to your supervisor;

2 = if the statement is not true;

3 = if the statement is neither true nor untrue;

4 = if the statement is true;

5 = if the statement is definitely true of your colleagues who also report to your supervisor.

A complete copy of the formatted TCQ is presented in Cox (1994), along with information on its developmental history and preliminary psychometric characteristics. Note that the present TCQ was originally titled the Citizenship Behavior Questionnaire (CBQ) in Cox.

Organizational Citizenship Behavior

Conscientiousness

The attendance of my colleagues has been above the norm.
My colleagues obey company rules and regulations even when no one is watching.

Altruism

My colleagues help orient new people even though it is not required.
My colleagues willingly help others who have work-related problems.

Courtesy

My colleagues are mindful of how their behavior affects other people's jobs.
My colleagues consider the impact of their actions on co-workers.
My colleagues try to avoid creating problems for co-workers.

Civic Virtue

My colleagues have been reading and keeping up with organization announcements, memos, etc.
My colleagues attend meetings that are not mandatory, but are considered important.

Anti-Citizenship Behaviors

Avoidance or Escape from the Job as a Whole

My colleagues get away from the job by calling in sick when they are not really sick.
My colleagues avoid their jobs by coming in late or leaving early.

Avoidance of the Work Itself

My colleagues make frequent and/or long trips to the water fountain, vending machines, or restroom to avoid work.
My colleagues take frequent or extra long breaks to avoid doing work.

Defiance, Resistance to Authority

My colleagues talk back to their supervisor.
My colleagues resist the influence of their supervisor.

Complaining

My colleagues focus on what's wrong, rather than the positive side.
My colleagues tend to "make mountains out of molehills."

Teamwork

My colleagues work together as a team.
My colleagues work together.

ACKNOWLEDGMENT

We wish to thank the many colleagues who have provided encouragement and inspiriation. These include: G. Ball, B. Bass, M. Beyerlein, C. Fisher, E. Locke, C. Manz, D. Organ, P Podsakoff, J. Scully, L. Trevino, and many others. We are grateful for the support of the Maryland Business School, the Maryland Center for Quality and Productivity, the Maryland Dingman Center, and the Center for the Study of Work Teams at the Unviersity of North Texas.

REFERENCES

Angell, D.L., & DeSau, G.T. (1974). Rare discordant verbal roles and the development of group problem-solving conditions. *Small Group Behavior, 5*(1), 45-55.

Antonuccio, D.O., Davis, C., Lewinsohn, P.M., & Breckenridge, J.S. (1987). Therapist variables related to cohesiveness in a group treatment for depression. *Small Group Behavior, 18*(4), 557-564.

Arvey, R.D., & Ivancevich, J.M. (1980). Punishment in organizations: A review, propositions, and research suggestions. *Academy of Management Review, 5,* 123-132.

Ball, G.A., Trevino, L.K, & Sims, H.P., Jr. (1991). "Just" and "unjust" organizational punishment: Influences on subordinate performance and citizenship behavior. Unpublished manuscript, University of Nevada at Las Vegas.

Bandura, A. (1977a). Self-efficacy: Towards a unifying theory of behavioral change. *Psychological Review, 84,* 191-215.

Bandura, A. (1977b). *Social learning theory.* Englewood Cliffs, NJ: Prentice-Hall.

Bandura, A. (1989). Human agency in social cognitive theory. *American Psychologist, 44*(9), 1175-1184.

Bass, B.M. (1985). *Leadership and performance beyond expectations.* New York: Free Press.

Bass, B.M. (1990). *Bass and Stogdill's handbook of leadership: Theory, research, and managerial applications,* 3rd ed. New York: Free Press.

Bass, B.M., Waldman, D.A., Avolio, B.J., & Bebb, M. (1987). Transformational leadership and the falling dominoes effect. *Group and Organization Studies, 12,* 73-78.

Bateman, T.S., & Organ, D.W. (1983). Job satisfaction and the good soldier: The relationship between affect and employee "citizenship." *Academy of Management Journal, 26,* 587-595.

Bennis, W.G. (1989). *On becoming a leader.* Reading, MA: Addison-Wesley.

Bennis, W.G., & Nanus, B. (1985). *Leaders: The strategies for taking charge.* New York: Harper & Row.

Brief, A.P., & Motowidlo, S.J. (1986). Prosocial organizational behavior. *Academy of Management Review, 10,* 710-725.

Burns, J.M. (1978). *Leadership.* New York: Harper & Row.

Burns, T.R., & Stalker, G.M. (1961). *The management of innovation.* Chicago: Quadrangle Books.

Carnevale, A. (1991). *America and the new economy.* San Francisco: Jossey-Bass.

Conger, J.A. (1989). *The charismatic leader: Behind the mystique of exceptional leadership.* San Francisco: Jossey-Bass.

Conger, J.A., & Kanungo, R.M. (1988). Behavioral dimensions of charismatic leadership. In J.A. Conger & R.N. Kanungo (Eds.), *Charismatic leadership: The elusive factor in organizational effectiveness.* San Francisco: Jossey-Bass.

Cox, J.F. (1994). The effects of SuperLeadership training on leader behavior, subordinate self-leadership behavior, and subordinate citizenship. *Dissertation Abstracts International, 55,* 10B. (Publication No. 9507927)

Cummings, T.G. (1978). Self-regulating work groups: A socio-technical synthesis. *Academy of Management Review, 3,* 625-634.

Day, R.C., & Hamblin, R.L. (1964). Some effects of close and punitive styles of supervision. *American Journal of Sociology, 69,* 499-510.

Farh, J., Podsakoff, P.M., & Organ, D.W. (1990). Accounting for organizational citizenship behavior: Leader fairness and task scope versus satisfaction. *Journal of Management, 16*(4), 705-721.

Fisher, C.D., & Locke, E.A. (1992). A new look in job satisfaction research and theory. In C.J. Cranny, P.C. Smith, & E.F. Stone (Eds.), *Job satisfaction: How people feel about their jobs and how it affects their performance.* New York: Lexington Books.

Fleishman, E.A. (1973). Twenty years of consideration and structure. In E.A. Fleishman & J.G. Hunt (Eds.), *Current developments in the study of leadership.* Carbondale, IL: Southern Illinois University Press.

Hackman, J.R. (1987a). The psychology of self-management in organizations. In M.S. Pollock & R.O. Perloff (Eds.), *Psychology and work: Productivity change and employment* (pp. 85-136). Washington, DC: American Psychological Association.

Hackman, J.R. (1987b). The design of work teams. In J.W. Lorsch (Ed.), *Handbook of organizational behavior* (pp. 315-342). Englewood Cliffs, NJ: Prentice-Hall.

House, R.J. (1971). A path goal theory of leader effectiveness. *Administrative Science Quarterly, 16,* 321-338.

House, R.J. (1977). A 1976 theory of charismatic leadership. In J.G. Hunt & L.L. Larson (Eds.), *Leadership: The cutting edge.* Carbondale, IL: Southern Illinois University Press.

House, R.J., & Mitchell, T.R. (1974). Path-goal theory of leadership. *Journal of Contemporary Business, 3,* 81-97.

Katz, D. (1964). The motivational basis of organizational behavior. *Behavioral Science, 9,* 131-133.

Keller, R.T., & Szilagyi, A.D. (1976). Employee reactions to leader reward behavior. *Academy of Management Journal, 19,* 619-627.

Kolodny, H., & Kiggundu, M. (1980). Towards the development of a socio-technical systems model in woodland mechanical harvesting. *Human Relations, 33,* 623-645.

Latham, G.P., Erez, M., & Locke, E.A. (1988). Resolving scientific disputes by the joint design of crucial experiments by the antagonists: Application to the Erez-Latham dispute regarding participation in goal setting. *Journal of Applied Psychology, 75*(6), 753-772.

Locke, E.A., & Latham, G.P. (1990). Work motivation and satisfaction: Light at the end of the tunnel. *Psychological Science, 1*(4), 240-246.

Luthans, F., & Davis, T.R.V. (1979, summer). Behavioral self-management: The missing link in managerial effectiveness. *Organizational Dynamics*, 42-60.

Luthans, F., & Kreitner, R. (1985). *Organizational behavior modification and beyond.* Glenview, IL: Scott, Foresman.

Mahoney, M.J., & Arnkoff, D.B. (1978). Cognitive and self-control therapies. In S.L. Garfield & A.E. Borgin (Eds.), *Handbook of psychotherapy and therapy change* (pp. 689-722). New York: Wiley.

Manz, C.C. (1986). Self-leadership: Toward an expanded theory of self-influence processes in organizations. *Academy of Management Review, 11*, 585-600.

Manz, C.C. (1992). *Mastering self-leadership: Empowering yourself for personal excellence.* Englewood Cliffs, NJ: Prentice-Hall.

Manz, C.C., & Angle, H.L. (1993). The Illusion of self-management: Using teams to disempower. In C.C. Manz & H.P. Sims, Jr. (Eds.), *Business without bosses: How self-managing teams are building high performing companies* (pp. 115-130). New York: Wiley.

Manz, C.C., & Sims, H.P., Jr. (1980). Self-management as a substitute for leadership: A social learning theory perspective. *Academy of Management Review, 5*(3), 361-367.

Manz, C.C., & Sims, H.P., Jr. (1984). Searching for the "unleader": Organizational member views on leading self-managed groups. *Human Relations, 37*, 409-424.

Manz, C.C., & Sims, H.P., Jr. (1987). Leading workers to lead themselves: The external leadership of self-managing work teams. *Administrative Science Quarterly, 32*, 106-128.

Manz, C.C., & Sims, H.P., Jr. (1989). *SuperLeadership: Leading others to lead themselves.* New York: Prentice Hall.

Manz, C.C., & Sims, H.P., Jr. (1990). *SuperLeadership: Leading others to lead themselves.* New York: Berkeley Books.

Manz, C.C., & Sims, H.P., Jr. (1991, spring). SuperLeadership: Beyond the myth of heroic leadership. *Organizational Dynamics*, 18-35.

Manz, C.C., Keating, D.E., & Donnellon, A. (1990). Preparing for an organizational change to employee self-management: The management transition. *Organizational Dynamics, 19*(2), 15-26.

McGregor, D. (1960). *The human side of enterprise.* New-York: McGraw-Hill.

Meichenbaum, D. (1977). *Cognitive-behavior modification: An integrative approach.* New York: Plenum Press.

Moorman, R.H. (1991). Relationship between organizational justice and organizational citizenship behaviors: Do fairness perceptions influence employee citizenship? *Journal of Applied Psychology, 76*(6), 845-855.

Organ, D.W. (1988). *Organizational citizenship behavior: The good soldier syndrome.* Lexington, MA: Lexington Books.

Organ, D.W., & Konovsky, M. (1989). Cognitive versus affective determinants of organizational citizenship behavior. *Journal of Applied Psychology, 74*(1), 157-164.

Pearce, J.A., & Ravlin, E.C. (1987). The design and activation of self-regulating work groups. *Human Relations, 40*(11), 751-782.

Pearce, C., Cox, J.F., & Sims, H.P., Jr. (1995). A LISREL confirmation analysis of historical leadership archetypes. Unpublished manuscript, University of Maryland, College Park.

Pfeffer, J. (1977). The ambiguity of leadership. *Academy of Management Review, 2*, 104-112.

Podsakoff, P.M., Todor, W.D., & Skov, R. (1982). Effects of leader contingent and noncontingent reward and punishment behaviors on subordinate performance and satisfaction. *Academy of Management Journal, 25*, 810-821.

Port, O., & Carey, J. (1991, October 25). Questing for the best. *Business Week*, 8-16.

Puffer, S.M. (1987). Prosocial behavior, noncompliant behavior, and work performance among commission salespeople. *Journal of Applied Psychology, 72*(4), 615-621.

Raven, B.H., & French, J.R.P. (1958). Legitimate power, coercive power, and observability in social influence. *Sociometry, 21,* 83-97.

Rice, A.K. (1955). Productivity and social organisation in an Indian weaving mill, II. A follow-up study of the experimental reorganisation of automatic weaving. *Human Relations, 7*(3), 399-428.

Schnake, M. (1991). Organizational citizenship: A review, proposed model, and research agenda. *Human Relations, 44*(7), 735-759.

Schnake, M., Dumler, M.P., & Cochran, D.S. (1993). The relationship between "traditional" leadership, "super" leadership, and organizational citizenship behavior. *Group and Organization Management, 18*(3), 352-365.

Schriesheim, C.A., House, R.J., & Kerr, S. (1976). Leader initiating structure: A reconciliation of discrepant research results and some empirical tests. *Organizational Behavior and Human Performance, 15,* 197-321.

Scott, W.E., Jr., & Podsakoff, P.M. (1982). Leadership, supervision and behavioral control: Perspectives from an experimental analysis. In L. Frederickson (Ed.), *Handbook of organizational behavior management.* New York: Wiley.

Scully, J.S., Sims, H.P., Jr., Olian, J.D., Smith, K.G., Schnell, E.R., & Smith, K.A. (1994). Tough times make tough bosses: A meso-analysis of CEO leader behavior. *Leadership Quarterly, 5*(1), 59-83.

Seligman, M., & Desmond, R. (1975). The leaderless group phenomenon: A historical perspective. *International Journal of Group Psychotherapy,* 277-290.

Sims, H.P., Jr. (1977). The leader as a manager of reinforcement contingencies: An empirical example and a model. In J.G. Hunt & L.L. Larson (Eds.), *Leadership: The cutting edge* (pp. 121-137). Carbondale, IL: Southern Illinois University Press.

Sims, H.P., Jr. (1980). Further thoughts on punishment in organizations. *Academy of Management Review, 5,* 133-138.

Sims, H.P., Jr., & Lorenzi, P. (1992). *The new leadership paradigm: Social learning and cognition in organizations.* Newbury Park, CA: Sage.

Sims, H.P., Jr., & Manz, C.C. (1982, summer). Conversations within self-managed work groups. *National Productivity Review,* 261-269.

Sims, H.P., Jr., & Manz, C.C. (1996). *Company of heros: Unleashing the power of self-leadership.* New York: Wiley.

Smith, C.A., Organ, D.W., & Near, J.P. (1983). Organizational citizenship behavior: Its nature and antecedents. *Journal of Applied Psychology, 68*(4), 653-663.

Stogdill, R.M. (1974). *Handbook of leadership: A survey of the literature.* New York: Free Press.

Thoreson, E.E., & Mahoney, M.J. (1974). *Behavioral self-control.* Holt, Rinehart, & Winston.

Trist, E.L., Susman, G.L., & Brown, G. (1977). An experiment in autonomous working in an American underground coal mine. *Human Relations, 30*(3), 201-236.

Vroom, V.H. (1964). *Work and motivation.* New York: Wiley.

Vroom, V.H., & Jago, A.G. (1988). *The new leadership: Managing participation in organizations.* Englewood Cliffs, NJ: Prentice-Hall.

Vroom, V.H., & Yetton, P.W. (1973). *Leadership and decision making.* Pittsburgh: University of Pittsburgh Press.

Walton, R.E. (1972, November/December). How to counter alienation in the plant. *Harvard Business Review,* 70-81.

Yukl, G.A. (1989). *Leadership in organizations,* Rev. ed. Englewood Cliffs, NJ: Prentice-Hall.

SELF-LEADERS WITHIN
SELF-LEADING TEAMS:
TOWARD AN OPTIMAL EQUILIBRIUM

Christopher P. Neck, Greg L. Stewart,
and Charles C. Manz

ABSTRACT

An abundance of research has focused on self-management and self-leadership for *both* individuals and teams. However, very little work has been written about the integration of these two sets of literature. We attempt to integrate these individual and team self-regulation dimensions by developing a framework that examines the delicate balance between self-leadership for individual team members, self-leadership for the team as a collective whole, and team performance.

INTRODUCTION

Recently, a plethora of material has been written about self-managing and self-leading teams in the workplace (e.g., Cohen & Ledford, 1994; Hackman, 1986;

Advances in Interdisciplinary Studies
of Work Teams, Volume 3, pages 43-65.
Copyright © 1996 by JAI Press Inc.
All rights of reproduction in any form reserved.
ISBN: 0-7623-0006-X

Lawler, 1986; Lawler et al., 1992; Manz & Sims, 1986, 1987, 1993; Orsburn et al., 1990; Stewart & Manz, 1995). Additionally, a large amount of attention has focused on self-management and self-leadership for individuals (e.g., Hackman, 1986; Luthans & Davis, 1979; Manz, 1983, 1986; Manz & Neck, 1991; Neck & Manz, 1992). Relatively little work, however, has been written about the integration of these two sets of literature (Manz, 1990).

Possibly, one explanation for this lack of integration involves a quandary related to combining these two streams of research. Specifically, the paradox revolves around the issue of simultaneously increasing both self-leadership for individuals and group-level self-leadership (Markham & Markham, 1995). In other words, does maximizing self-leadership for individuals result in optimal performance for the team as a whole? This question highlights a critical but overlooked dual aspect of self-managing/self-leading teams—that is, the self-regulation of the team as a collective *and* the self-regulation of individual team members. We provide insight into this dual team focus and begin to fill the void in the literature (discussed previously) by integrating these individual and team self-regulation dimensions. This blending is further achieved through the development of a framework that explains how specific external and internal team forces interact to influence the relationships among individual self-regulation (self-leadership for individual team members), team self-regulation (self-leadership for the team as a collective whole), and team performance.

In order to develop this comprehensive framework, we first briefly review the teams and self-management literature and then clarify and describe the term team self-leadership. Next, we use social learning theory to integrate specific external and internal factors as a mechanism for creating an optimal balance between individual and team self-leadership.

AN OVERVIEW OF THE TEAMS AND SELF-MANAGEMENT LITERATURES

As mentioned previously, a vast amount of attention has been focused on self-management and self-leadership at both the individual and teams level of analysis. We will briefly examine the literature streams within this area.

Self-managing Teams

The topic of self-managing work teams (SMWTs) is receiving increased emphasis in both academic and practitioner literature (e.g., Cohen & Ledford, 1994; Hackman, 1986; Katzenbach & Smith, 1993; Lawler, 1986, 1992; Manz & Sims, 1987, 1993; Orsburn et al., 1990; Walton, 1985). The theoretical basis for SMWTs derives primarily from socio-technical systems (STS) theory. STS theory prescribes joint optimization of the social and technical aspects of work (Cummings, 1978; Emery & Trist, 1969; Susman, 1976). This optimization frequently results in the adoption of self-managing teams, because "a group can more effectively allocate its resources when and where required to deal with its total variance in work conditions than can an aggregate of individuals each of whom is assigned a portion of the variance" (Susman, 1976, p. 183).

SMWTs are provided with relatively whole work tasks, and are allowed increased autonomy and control over their work (Hackman, 1986; Manz, 1992a). Moreover, teams are responsible for many traditional management functions such as assigning members to various tasks, solving within-team quality and interpersonal problems, and conducting team meetings (Lawler, 1986; Manz & Sims, 1993). Applications of teams have spanned both the manufacturing and the service sector. Many specific case studies of teams mainly involving manufacturing and clerical work have been reported, including a dog food plant (Walton, 1977), coal mines (Trist et al., 1977), a financial investment firm (Sims, Manz, & Bateman, 1993), a paint manufacturing plant (Poza & Markus, 1980), small parts manufacturing (Manz & Sims, 1987), an airline (Cohen & Denison, 1990), an independent insurance firm (Manz & Angle, 1986), a mental health hospital (Shaw, 1990), a warehouse (Manz et al., 1990), a paper mill (Manz & Newstrom, 1990), and a telecommunications company (Cohen & Ledford, 1994).

Benefits that have been attributed to the implementation of self-managing teams include increased productivity, quality, and improved quality of work life for employees, as well as decreases in absenteeism and turnover (Cohen & Ledford, 1994; Gustavsen & Héthy, 1989; Herbst, 1962; Lawler, 1986; Manz & Sims, 1987; Saporito, 1986; Verespej, 1990). SMWTs and a socio-technical perspective have also been advocated as a means for improving organizational flexibility and thereby promoting adaptation to a rapidly changing business environment (Manz & Stewart, forthcoming; Trist, 1977). While there is definitely a need for additional research that further clarifies the benefits of adopting a team-based organizational structure, the general conclusion is that empowered teams improve organizational effectiveness (U.S. Department of Labor, 1993).

Self-management and Self-leadership

Kerr and Jermier (1978) developed the concept of substitutes for leadership by suggesting that characteristics of employees, of work tasks, or of organizations can serve as substitutes for managerial action. Manz and Sims (1980) introduced the self-management construct as a specific substitute for leadership by drawing upon psychological research (e.g., Thoresen & Mahoney, 1974) to identify specific methods for personal self-control. These methods include self-observation, self-goal setting, incentive modification, and rehearsal. In short, self-managing employees take personal responsibility for their work behavior.

Manz (1986) later argued that a more comprehensive and higher level of self-influence exists than the concept of self-management as it had been written about in the literature. This higher level of self-regulation is referred to as self-leadership, and addresses governing standards that guide both behavior focused self-management processes and individual cognitions.

From a control theory perspective (Carver & Scheier, 1982), self-management primarily concerns regulating one's behavior to reduce discrepancies from externally set standards (Manz, 1986). Self-leadership goes beyond reduction of discrepancies from standards in one's immediate behavior and addresses the utility and rationale for the standards, themselves. The individual self-leader is viewed as the ultimate source of standards that govern his or her behavior (Manz, 1986). Individuals are seen as not only capable of monitoring their own actions but also determining which actions are most desirable. Primary components of self-leadership include setting personal standards for performance, building natural rewards into work, and thought self-leadership. In particular, the concept of thought self-leadership has recently been explicated in detail to explain how employees can create constructive thought patterns to lead themselves cognitively (Manz & Neck, 1991; Neck & Manz, 1992; Neck & Milliman, 1994; Neck et al., 1995).

DEFINING TEAM LEVEL SELF-LEADERSHIP

As we have stated, a fairly extensive literature has been developed for both self-managing/self-leading teams and self-management/self-leadership. However, virtually no consideration has been given to the integration of these two areas. To move toward an integration of team and self-leadership concepts, we begin by describing team level self-leadership. Once this construct has been developed, we shall move to a discussion of specific factors that influence the extent to which teams actually lead themselves.

Team Level Self-leadership

Before we proceed, however, it is important to highlight that our main focus here is on team self-leadership as opposed to team self-management. Similar to the individual level self-leadership/self-management distinction, with self-leading teams, workers are involved more with strategic issues concerning *what* they do and why in addition to the issue of *how* they do it (the *how* tends to be the more dominant focus with SMWTs in the workplace; Manz, 1990, 1992a). Consequently, self-leading teams (as opposed to self-managing teams) encompass a broader form of group self-regulation as the team itself is more directly involved in establishing the direction for its work efforts (again, not just how to carry out the directions; Manz, 1990).

The group-as-a-whole perspective (Wells, 1985) provides a basis for understanding self-leadership as a team level construct. This view sees team behavior as something more than a mere summation of individual inputs. The team is the unit of analysis, and the behaviors of the group as a whole (rather than a simple aggregation of individual behaviors) are the key focus. Team level self-leadership is thus defined in terms of behaviors of the group as a collective, rather than in terms of individual member or leader activity.

Team self-leadership can be described as active control exercised by work group members over themselves and their immediate environment that results in productive goal-oriented behavior (Manz, 1992a; Manz & Sims, 1986). Similar to individual self-leadership strategies, team self-leadership actions can be separated into behavioral and cognitive components. The behavioral component consists of team actions that are observable, while the cognitive component represents thought patterns for the team as a whole.

Behavioral Aspects of Team Self-leadership

Specific practices in the behavioral realm include self-observation, self-goal setting, antecedent modification, consequent modification, and rehearsal. While each of these constructs has been developed at the individual level, they have not been described at the group level of analysis. We thus review these practices with an emphasis on how they can be applied at the team level.

Team Self-observation

Self-observation is the process of gathering information about one's behavior (Andrasik & Heimberg, 1982; Manz & Sims, 1980). At the team level, self-observation represents the team's collective effort to purposefully observe (and record) behavior and performance, as well as to attempt to understand the antecedents and consequences that are associated with those actions. Self-observation is a self-initiated process, suggesting that this behavior must be done by the team. This means that independent self-observation by either individuals or a leader is insufficient to explain the team level construct. Rather, team self-observation encompasses the group working as a collective to measure and understand its behavior. An example is the group seeking information needed to compare its performance with its production goals.

Team Goal-setting

Self-goal setting involves teams developing their own goals. A goal is defined as "what the [team] is trying to accomplish; it is the object or aim of an action"

(Locke et al., 1981, p. 126). Individuals can have personal goals that are coordinated with and necessary for achieving team goals, but the focus for teams is the shared goals of the team as a whole. The self-influence component also requires the group as a collective (rather than an individual leader) to establish the goals. Goal setting by the group thus represents an element of self-leadership for the team that will encompass, but is not defined by, individual goals of team members or leaders.

Team Antecedent Modification

Antecedent modification is accomplished when the team behaves proactively to alter its environment. Much of human behavior follows specific cues or stimuli (Luthans & Kreitner, 1975; Skinner, 1969). Teams can remove stimuli that cue undesirable behavior and increase exposure to stimuli that cue desirable behavior (Andrasik & Heimberg, 1982; Mahoney & Arnkoff, 1979). By changing environmental conditions that affect behavior, team self-leadership occurs. These attempts to change the environment are collectively performed by the team, and are not synonymous with individual attempts to modify antecedents that cue behavior. An example is the team deciding to alter the configuration of its work space.

Team Consequent Modification

Consequent modification generally accompanies antecedent modification. Consequences come in two forms: reinforcement and punishment. Teams can reinforce their own behaviors by providing rewards to one another and to the group as a whole that strengthen or increase those behaviors. These rewards can be either tangible or intangible (Bandura, 1986). Tangible rewards might include monetary bonuses, time off, or purchasing new equipment. Intangible rewards might include increased satisfaction, joy from working as a team, or a feeling of respect for the work accomplished by the team. Punishment involves applying negative consequences in order to reduce undesirable behaviors. An example of punishment is a team deciding that everyone must work late in order to make up for excessive socialization. In order to be considered team self-influence, the group must collectively administer and receive rewards and sanctions.

Team Rehearsal

Rehearsal is another step associated with the self-leadership process. Rehearsal is a form of practice, and can be conducted either overtly or covertly (Manz & Sims, 1980). Rehearsal builds efficacy by allowing teams to visualize themselves completing tasks (Bandura, 1986; Manz & Sims, 1981). An example of rehearsal might be several team members practicing a presentation they must make to the rest of the organization. Consistent with the team-level of analysis, this practice must once again be initiated and directed by the team as a whole rather than by a leader.

Advanced Behavioral Techniques

Advanced forms of team self-leadership go beyond these basic self-regulation techniques and encompass efforts to formulate long-term goals and strategy (Manz, 1992a). The circle of influence expands from determining *how* things are to be done, and encompasses *what* will be done, as well as *why* it should be done. Advanced behavioral self-leadership for teams thus implies processes similar to and/or including strategic planning. Teams engaging in these advanced behaviors plan new methods of work production, as well as examine the standards that guide their behavior. This allows teams to actually lead themselves, instead of just managing behavior to achieve external objectives (Manz, 1986).

Cognitive Aspects of Team Self-leadership

Having discussed how individual-level techniques of behavioral self-leadership apply to teams, we now focus on cognitions. Constructive cognitions concern thought patterns of the team as a collective, and have been labeled "teamthink" (Neck & Manz, 1994). An underlying assumption of the teamthink framework is the emergence of a group pattern of thinking that is more than the existence of a simple collection of separate individual minds (Neck & Manz, 1994). This notion of a "group mind" has been further asserted by various researchers including LeBon (1985), Bion (1961), Freud (1960), and McDougall (1921). For example, Freud (1960) observed "that individuals in groups tend to subjugate their individuality and act as though they were of one mind." Similarly, Bion (1961) asserted that a group's mentality exists beyond that of the individual group members in that the group's mentality connects group members by an unconsciously implied agreement.

Accordingly, the basic premise of teamthink is that, similar to self-leading individuals, self-leading work teams can enhance their performance through the collective application of specific cognitive strategies that result in constructive synergistic team thinking (Neck & Manz, 1994; Manz & Neck, 1995). These collective cognitive strategies include beliefs and assumptions, self-talk, and mental imagery.

Team Beliefs and Assumptions

Theorists have suggested that many problems individuals encounter result from dysfunctional thinking (Ellis, 1975; Burns, 1980). These theorists argue that cognitive distortions establish the foundation for ineffective thinking that hinders personal effectiveness, and even leads to some forms of depression. These distorted thoughts are based on some common dysfunctional beliefs and assumptions that are activated by potentially troubling situations. Most of the types of individual-level beliefs involved have corresponding analogs at the group level.

An example of an individual level dysfunctional assumption is called "all or nothing" thinking. This refers to the tendency to evaluate things in extreme, black or white categories (Burns, 1980). Similarly, a group can adopt "all or nothing" beliefs. This can be especially problematic for cohesive decision-making groups that are vulnerable to dysfunctional within-group processes. If a risk does not seem overwhelmingly dangerous, the team as a whole is frequently inclined to minimize its importance and proceed without further preparation instead of developing contingency plans in case the risk materializes (Janis, 1983).

Another example of a distinctive team belief is an illusion of group morality. Janis (1983) argues that groups that succumb to groupthink believe unquestioningly in the inherent morality of their in-group. This belief inclines the members to ignore the ethical or moral consequences of their decisions.

Team Self-talk

Self-talk or self-verbalization at the individual level is defined as what we covertly tell ourselves (Ellis, 1962). Self-talk can serve as a tool for self-influence directed at improving the personal effectiveness of employees and managers (Manz, 1986, 1992b; Manz & Sims, 1990). Weick (1979) recognized this cognitive strategy in group-level phenomenon when he argued that "[o]rganizations are presumed to talk to themselves" (p. 133). Group verbalizations (the self-talk of the group) might significantly influence group performance (Janis, 1983; Neck & Manz, 1994). More specifically, it is proposed that within a cohesive self-managing team, there is a tendency for members to put social pressure on any member who expresses verbalizations that deviate from the group's dominant form of dialogue (which is derived from dominant group beliefs). This pressure is exerted by other group members to assure that the deviant member does not disrupt the consensus of the group as a whole. This tendency toward group enforced, conformity dialogue may lead to defective decision making on the part of the group (Janis, 1983).

Team Mental Imagery

A variety of definitions exist for the term mental imagery. In sports psychology, mental imagery describes methods involving individual rehearsal of a physical task in the absence of observable movement (Corbin, 1972;

Richardson, 1967). In clinical psychiatry, mental imagery is defined as "the mental invention or recreation of an experience that in at least some respects resembles the experience of actually perceiving an object or an event, either in conjunction with, or in the absence of, direct sensory stimulation," (Finke, 1989, p. 2). In the management literature, mental imagery has been described as a process in which: "we can create and, in essence, symbolically experience imagined results of our behavior before we actually perform" (Manz, 1992b, p. 75). These views suggest that, in general, mental imagery refers to imagining performance of a task prior to its physical completion. For example, an individual can potentially enhance a presentation performance by visualizing the details and successful completion of a presentation in his or her mind before it is actually delivered. Similarly, a decision-making group or work team could potentially enhance its performance through the utilization of group mental imagery to establish a common vision. Because members of successful groups tend to share a common vision (Napier & Gershenfeld, 1987), self-managing teams faced with strategic decisions should benefit from interactively creating a common image regarding what they want to accomplish, as well as visualizing effective means for doing so.

Thought Patterns

Thought patterns can be described as integrated patterns of thinking that tend to be repeated when triggered by situational events, or as, "habitual ways of thinking" (Manz, 1992b). Individuals may engage in both negative and positive chains of thought (habitual ways of thinking) that affect emotional and behavioral reactions (Manz & Neck, 1991; Neck & Manz, 1992). An example of the types of thought patterns a person could adopt are called opportunity thinking and obstacle thinking (Manz, 1992b).

Opportunity thinking involves a pattern of thought that focuses on opportunities, worthwhile challenges, and constructive ways of dealing with challenging situations. More specifically, opportunity thinking involves a realistic appraisal of difficult situations that leads to the necessary preparation and application of skills to overcome existing challenges. Opportunity thinkers view challenging or difficult situations as temporary occurrences that will be overcome.

Obstacle thinking, on the other hand, involves a focus on the negative aspects (the obstacles) involved in challenging situations—such as reasons to give up and retreat from problems. Obstacle thinkers view troubling occurrences as permanent events that happen repeatedly and that can rarely be conquered.

The nature of one's thought pattern is directly related to his or her performance (Manz & Neck, 1991; Neck & Manz, 1992). In other words, if thought patterns are constructive (i.e., focus on opportunities and potential ways of overcoming challenges, rather than obstacles), the potential for enhancing subsequent performance is established. If, on the other hand, a person engages in "obstacle thinking," subsequent performance is more likely to be hindered. An example of team opportunity/obstacle thinking can involve the group's perception of its ability to overcome a particular challenge. If a self-leading work team is faced with a technical problem that affects the quality of its product, it can view this occurrence as an "opportunity" to focus the groups energies and to utilize the decision-making and technical skills of the team, or as an "obstacle" that will prevent the team from producing a product of high quality. If the work team believes that this technical problem is an insurmountable obstacle, then it is practically assured that the product's quality will suffer. On the other hand, if the team feels that this technical problem is an opportunity to further improve the product, the probability of producing a high quality product is enhanced. This conclusion is based on the logic that team members are more likely to exert more effort and persist longer in addressing the challenge when they believe they are capable of overcoming it (e.g., Bandura, 1986 on self-efficacy). Thus, if the team believes problems are "opportunities" to overcome challenges, rather than "obstacles" that will lead to failure, its performance should be enhanced.

Seligman (1991) described a related thought pattern that individuals can adopt. He argued that individuals tend to evoke one of two habits of thinking, optimism or pessimism. When confronted by a bad situation, optimists "perceive it as a challenge and try harder," whereas pessimists believe "bad events will last a long time, and will undermine everything they do," (pp. 4-5). A similarly unrealistic dysfunctional thought pattern related to optimism can be enacted by self-managing teams (Neck & Manz, 1994).

Teams may adopt an overly optimistic pattern of thought as a result of a shared illusion of invulnerability. Subsequently, the group may be willing to take extraordinary, unnecessary risks (Janis, 1983). Thus, opportunity thinking and optimism will likely need to be tempered with realism (or probabilistic thinking) to produce positive outcomes. Viewing problems as challenging opportunities can be beneficial unless unrealisticly extreme thinking leads teams down destructive paths. Indeed, being alert for positive opportunities while at the same time watching out for and constructively planning and preparing to overcome problems might be the ideal cognitive mix. This logic is supported by the writings on relapse prevention for individuals (cf. Marx, 1982).

Summary

In general, the concept of teamthink suggests that similar relationships found between individual cognitions and performance can hold for team cognitions and performance. In sum, self-leading work teams can enhance their performance through the collective application of specific cognitive strategies that result in constructive synergistic team thinking. This collective team cognition might manifest itself in thought patterns such as opportunity/ obstacle thinking and/or optimism/pessimism.

FACTORS INFLUENCING SELF-LEADERSHIP AT THE TEAM LEVEL

Having described the concept of team level self-leadership, we now move to a discussion of factors that can influence a team's efforts to lead itself. Our basic premise is that effective team level self-leadership is achieved through a balance of individual member self-leadership and self-leadership for the team as a collective whole.

This view proposes that while a self-leading team needs effective self-leading individuals, it is more than a group of independent self-leaders. Individual efforts must be coordinated in order to attain a high level of self-leadership for the group as a whole. This suggests a trade-off, or balance, between the self-leadership of individual team members and the self-leadership of the team as a collective.

A balance between individual and group collectivity is especially critical because of the vulnerability of self-leading teams to "pressures toward conformity" among their members (Manz & Sims, 1982; Manz & Neck, 1995; Neck & Manz, 1994). We propose that optimal self-leading team effectiveness occurs when a collection of self-leaders (a self-leading work group) work as a coordinated group, while at the same time maintaining their uniqueness of creativity, contributions, and beliefs (Neck & Manz, 1994; Manz & Neck, 1995). As Neck and Manz (1994) argue:

> ... By maintaining their separate belief systems, members are able to critically examine the decision-making process without being influenced to conform to a group view that overwhelms individual viewpoints ... the group reaches a decision of the quality that could not have been reached by adding the efforts of each separate member (p. 941).

We predict that if the members of a self-leading team lose the unique value of their own separate identity and viewpoint, suboptimal performance will result (Neck & Manz, 1994; Manz & Neck, 1995). Consequently, this suggests that self-leading teams should strive diligently to achieve an optimal balance between team coordination and individual self-leadership. Social learning theory provides a framework for describing the factors that affect this balance.

Social Learning Theory as a Foundation

Social learning theory (SLT; Bandura, 1968, 1976, 1977a, 1977b, 1986) posits that the best explanation of human behavior is a set of continuous, reciprocal

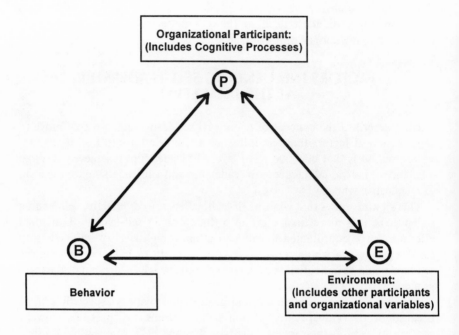

Figure 1. Social Learning Theory Model of Behavior

interactions among three primary sets of variables stemming from the person, the behavior, and the environment. Figure 1 (adapted from Bandura, 1977b) attempts to clarify this relationship. In short, SLT posits that the environment, E, the behavior itself, B, and the person, P (including internal cognitions) reciprocally interact to explain individual actions. Because SLT encompasses the elements that we see as critical to self-regulation for teams, we utilize this framework to discuss how external and internal group forces influence collective self-leadership for a team.

Bandura (1986) suggests that all relationships in the SLT triad cannot be simultaneously researched. He, therefore, advocates focusing on the explicit relationships that are most pertinent to a specific research question. In the present case, we seek to describe the development and practice of team self-leadership behavior, which most closely correspond with the behavioral, B, element of Bandura's model. We accomplish this by examining the impact of external and internal forces, which respectively correspond with environmental forces, E, and person factors, P. In brief, our theory of team leadership focusing on self-leadership illustrates how team behavior, B, is influenced by both external, E, and internal, P factors. While other approaches are certainly possible, this focus best captures the process through which internal and

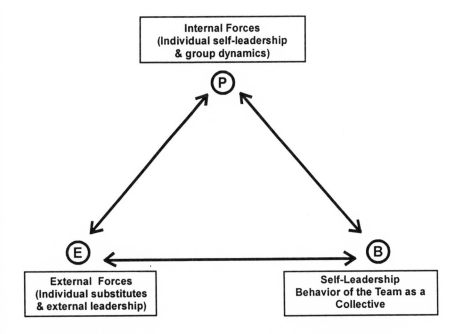

Figure 2.   Social Learning Theory Application to Self-leading Teams

external group forces work together to achieve an optimal balance between individual self-leadership and collective self-leadership. Figure 2 provides an overview of this process.

With social learning as our theoretical context, we will next elaborate on these external and internal team self-leadership forces. A graphical depiction of these elements is portrayed in Figure 3.

Internal Influences

Internal leadership forces that affect the team self-leadership balance can be classified broadly as either (a) individual inputs of group members, or (b) group dynamics representing interactions among individuals. The effect of individual self-leadership is discussed first and then group dynamics.

Individual Self-leadership

In general, each person contributes to the team by providing both technical and social inputs (Emery & Trist, 1969). An exhaustive review of all potential inputs is beyond the scope of our present discussion. We thus focus specifically

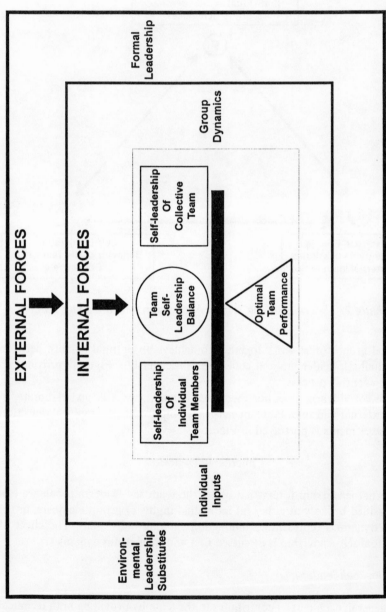

Figure 3. Depiction of Elements Impacting the Synergistic Relation Between Individual Self-leadership and Team Self-leadership

56

on the leadership inputs that team members contribute. Outside the role of a designated leader (which will be discussed later), these inputs can be described within the context of self-leadership. In essence, self-leading individuals are the basic building blocks of a self-leading team.

Self-leading individuals take responsibility for controlling their own behavior. Although influenced by external forces (Mills, 1983), the ultimate source of behavioral control is internal (Manz et al., 1987). Self-leaders thus make sure that work is accomplished. Effective self-leaders also examine the standards that regulate their behavior, and make changes needed to align their behavior with internal standards (Manz, 1986).

While the purpose of this paper is not description of self-leadership at the individual level, the effect of individual self-leadership on teams is substantial. The impact of self-leading individuals on teams can be demonstrated through a few practical illustrations.

The first illustration concerns team goal setting and achievement. Team goals are generally achieved as individuals attain personal goals, as long as individual and team goals are consistent with one another. The absence of hierarchical control necessitates that self-leadership of individual contributions occur in a timely, efficient manner. Team goal setting can thus result from individual self-leadership—team goals will be accomplished as individual goals (consistent with the goals of the team) are achieved.

Another illustration concerns the combined effect of individual attempts to engage in self-leadership by altering work processes and strategic focuses. Individuals who establish new directions for their personal behavior will likely feel constrained by current team activities, and therefore feel a need for the team to alter some of its strategic focuses. As individual members discuss and integrate their various personal desires for change, pressure is placed on the team as a whole to rethink its strategic direction. Ultimately, this interaction can result in redefinition of team goals.

The combination of self-leading individuals can also influence the team's decision-making process. As we have already discussed, there is a natural tendency for cohesive groups to fall victim to "groupthink." Competent self-leading team members, on the other hand, will tend to more openly voice their individual viewpoints and concerns and thereby help the team avoid this dysfunctional tendency. Again, constructive, opportunity-oriented, yet realistic team thinking is promoted by combining the inputs of competent self-leaders.

Group Dynamics

In addition to maintaining individual self-leadership, team members must somehow coordinate their efforts. The process through which a collective of individuals achieves coordination has been labeled group dynamics (Forsyth, 1990; Lewin, 1948). Included in the conceptualization of group dynamics are factors such as team structure, team communication, and team decision making. Although this list is not exhaustive, these factors can be used to illustrate how group dynamics link self-leading individuals to one another. These dynamics are ultimately seen as the driving force that translates individual behaviors into a coordinated whole that constitutes team self-leadership.

Group structure provides team members with roles. Although these roles are often dynamic, they help define an area of contribution for each individual. Team member roles can generally be classified as either task or socio-emotional (Benne & Sheets, 1948). Task roles influence team self-leadership via their impact on work completion and planning. Definition of work roles assures that important tasks are completed. Roles such as strategic planner and quality controller also influence the group to examine its practices and look for ways to improve future performance. Socio-emotional roles are different in that they contribute mostly to social dimensions of team activity. These roles link task roles together, and provide a mechanism for coping with intragroup conflict. Walton (1977) suggests that positive social relations are essential for cooperative groups, implying that team self-leadership is impossible without a proper mix of socio-emotional roles.

Group communication facilitates both behavioral and cognitive facets of self-leadership. Team level self-performed observation, goal setting, antecedent modification, and rehearsal require shared perceptions, and shared perceptions result from communication. Teamthink is also largely an outcome of group communication, as attitudes and beliefs are strongly influenced by words and actions of referent others. Without effective communication, the team will not coordinate itself and collective direction is impossible.

Decision making is another area where group dynamics influence team behavior. The team's ongoing communication will influence its collective beliefs and, consequently, its view of potential problems or opportunities. The team's internal dynamics can determine whether a pattern of "groupthink" or "teamthink" develops.

Overall, the internal influences of individual self-leadership and group dynamics can work together to achieve a balance of effort that is both unique and coordinated. This balance is critical. Teams without individualism are susceptible to groupthink, while teams that lack group integration are unable to develop synergy.

External Influences

The primary external influences that affect the team self-leadership balance can be grouped into the following categories: substitutes for leadership and formal leader behaviors. This section explores the impact of both on team level self-leadership.

Environmental Substitutes for Leadership

The type of work performed by the team represents one factor that has been advanced as a substitute for leadership. Work activities with clear boundaries can be more suitable for teams than ambiguous work activities without definable task boundaries (Cummings, 1978). Kerr and Jermier (1978) also assert that clearly defined tasks are more supportive of self-management than are non-routine tasks. Routine tasks with clear boundaries allow the team to exercise self-leadership without being dependent on outside sources of control. Behavioral forms of self-management like self-observation and goal setting are obviously dependent on the ability to clearly define tasks. This suggests that behavioral focused self-management strategies may yield the greatest benefit within teams that are working in settings that involve routine tasks with clearly defined boundaries (e.g., manufacturing and clerical settings). Indeed, a behavioral emphasis on task completion appears to be less optimal for teams that are working on non-routine tasks that have undefined boundaries.

However, teamthink and team-level strategic planning appear to be more congruent with ambiguous tasks. Ambiguous tasks require the team to constantly adjust to change. Only advanced forms of self-leadership appear capable of altering team activity to meet changing environmental needs in a timely manner. Positive thought patterns can also help the team define ambiguity as an opportunity rather than as an obstacle. The impact of the nature of the task on team self-leadership thus appears to depend on the form of self-leadership employed. Clearly defined tasks are beneficial for more behaviorally focused self-management practices, while ambiguous tasks may stimulate and necessitate more advanced forms of team self-leadership.

Human resource management practices represent another cluster of substitutes for leadership that influence team self-leadership. These human resource practices include staffing processes, motivation and compensation policies, and training programs. Kerr and Jermier (1978) point out that self-leadership is most appropriate for high-ability individuals. In the same way, teams with the combination of requisite technical abilities are more capable of leading themselves than teams lacking these abilities that must look to outside sources for critical inputs, thereby reducing their ability to control their own behavior. A selection process that provides teams with members that together possess all the skills needed to complete tasks (or the ability and motivation to obtain needed skills) can thus facilitate the creation of truly self-leading teams.

Compensation policies that assess and reward team development also facilitate team self-leadership. A focus on team-level regulation can serve as a stimulus that encourages teams to accept responsibility for their own actions. In contrast, reward systems that motivate employees to focus on maximization of individual contributions at the expense of team performance can actually harm team coordination and cooperation (Lawler, 1986). This implies that team self-leadership can be facilitated by providing teams with rewards for overall team development and productivity. Moreover, team control over at least some rewards can contribute to team-level consequent modification.

The final method by which human resource management contributes to self-leadership is training. Self-leading teams need to have the capacity to regulate their own behavior, and case studies suggest that many teams initially lack self-regulation skills (Stewart & Manz, 1995). Teams must also learn both social and technical skills. Organizations that provide formal means for learning these skills will advance team self-leadership at a faster rate than will teams not providing such training.

The Role of the Formal Leader

While both the nature of work tasks and general human resource practices represent possible substitutes for formal leadership, the actions of a team leader constitute a more direct influence. Strong leadership (whether from an internal or external team leader) can overwhelm much of the group interaction and can thereby become a force that is essentially external to other self-leading team processes. This reasoning is why formal leadership is classified as an external team influence. In short, a dominant leader can halt team efforts to engage in self-leadership because the leader (rather than the team) assumes responsibility for behavioral control. Stewart and Manz (1995), for example, address a variety of potential effects by providing a typology of team leader behaviors, along with an analysis of their expected impact on team self-leadership.

The typology classifies leader actions along two dimensions. The first dimension is autocratic-democratic, and the second is active-passive. Autocratic leadership tends to inhibit team self-leadership, whether it is active or passive. This is because autocratic leadership externally structures work activity, and seeks to retain ultimate control over team behavior. These practices reduce the likelihood that teams will engage in either behavioral or cognitive forms of collective self-leadership.

On the other hand, democratic leader actions can facilitate team self-leadership. Active, democratic leadership teaches self-leadership skills and helps the group learn how to coordinate itself. Active leadership is thus beneficial for teams in the early stages of self-leadership development. Passive forms of democratic leadership are, however, better suited for advanced teams that have the capacity to lead themselves. Passive leader behaviors provide assistance, but allow the team to set its own course and lead itself.

Combining Internal and External Leadership Forces

While both internal and external forces impact team self-leadership, the harmony between these influences is perhaps the most critical determinant of effective leadership for teams. Teams with strong, autocratic leadership are unable to develop the ability to effectively regulate their own behavior. Paradoxically, teams that lack initial external direction are often unable to learn the skills necessary to behaviorally and cognitively lead themselves.

In a similar way, teams need environmental support to help them acquire the resources needed for self-leadership. Leadership substitutes take the place of hierarchical control, and help the team manage its boundaries so that it can lead itself. However, substitute factors can also inhibit teams if they create a setting that overwhelms team level initiative. An example of such an inhibiting factor is the rigid structure of some organizations. The rigid structure and requirements of precise coordination can create a situation where teams must simply comply with external demands, thereby minimizing the opportunity for team self-leadership (Manz & Stewart, forthcoming).

SUMMARY

This paper has focused on the often overlooked issue of simultaneous self-leadership for individuals and team self-leadership. In summary, we examined the question, "Does maximizing self-leadership for individuals result in optimal performance for the team as a whole?" The answer to this question involves striking a balance between individual team member self-leadership and team self-leadership as a collective whole. This suggests that while a self-leading team needs effective self-leading individuals, it is more than a group of independent self-leaders. Individual efforts must be coordinated in order to attain a high level of self-leadership for the group as a whole. We posit that various factors, internal and external to the team, impact this balance. These elements include individual inputs, group dynamics, formal leadership, and environmental leadership substitutes.

There are several significant implications suggested by the ideas presented in this paper. The combined effects of these implications will determine whether or not teams achieve optimal performance. First, there is an important distinction between a self-managing team and a self-leading team. A movement toward self-leading teams implies a tremendous step towards greater employee empowerment. Our position is that the range of influence for workers should be expanded to include a greater role in setting the direction of their own team and organization. A movement in the direction of self-leading teams also requires that increased attention be given to the critical balance between individual members and the group as a whole. Employees who work cooperatively as a coordinated self-leading group, while at the same time maintaining their individual uniquenesses, will experience optimal team outcomes.

Overall, a challenge exists for both academics and practitioners to further examine the elements that impact the effectiveness of self-directed teams. We suggest that special attention should be placed on the factors that affect the "self-leadership balance" described here. In the years to come, the highest performing organizations are likely to be the ones that can foster a self-leadership balance that simultaneously optimizes both individual and team level contributions.

REFERENCES

Andrasik, F., & Heimberg, J.S. (1982). Self-management procedures. In L.W. Frederikson (Ed.), *Handbook of organizational behavior management* (pp. 219-247). New York: Wiley.

Bandura, A. (1968). A social learning interpretation of psychological dysfunctions. In P. London & D. Rosenhan (Eds.), *Foundations of abnormal psychology* (pp. 293-344). New York: Holt, Rinehart & Winston.

Bandura, A. (1976). Social learning theory. In J.T. Spence, R.C. Carson, & J.W. Thibaut (Eds.), *Behavioral approaches to therapy* (pp. 1-46). Morristown, NJ: General Learning Press.

Bandura, A. (1977a). Self-efficacy: Toward a unifying theory of behavior change. *Psychological Review, 84,* 191-215.

Bandura, A. (1977b). *Social learning theory.* Englewood Cliffs, NJ: Prentice-Hall.

Bandura, A. (1986). *Social foundations of thought and action: A social cognitive theory.* Englewood Cliffs, NJ: Prentice-Hall.

Benne, K.D., & Sheats, P. (1948). Functional roles of group members. *Journal of Social Issues, 4*(2), 41-49.

Bion, W.R. (1961). *Experience in groups.* New York: Basic Books.

Burns, D.D. (1980). *Feeling good: The new mood therapy.* New York: William Morrow.

Carver, C.S., & Scheier, M.F. (1982). Control theory: A useful conceptual framework for personality—social, clinical, and health psychology. *Psychological Bulletin, 92,* 111-135.

Cohen, S.G., & Denison, D.R. (1990). Flight attendant teams. In J.R. Hackman (Ed.), *Groups that work and those that don't* (pp. 382-397). San Francisco: Jossey-Bass.

Cohen, S.G., & Ledford, G.E., Jr. (1994). The effectiveness of self-managing teams: A quasi-experiment. *Human Relations, 47,* 13-43.

Corbin, C.B. (1972). Mental practice. In W.P. Morgan (Ed.), *Ergogenic aids and muscular performance.* New York: Academic Press.

Cummings, T. (1978). Self-regulated work groups: A socio-technical synthesis. *Academy of Management Review, 3,* 625-634.

Ellis, A. (1962). *Reason and emotion in psychotherapy.* New York: Lyle Stuart.

Ellis, A. (1975). *A new guide to rational living.* Englewood Cliffs, NJ: Prentice-Hall.

Emery, F.E., & Trist, E.L. (1969). Socio-technical systems. In F.E. Emery (Ed.), *Systems thinking* (pp. 281-296). London: Penguin Books.

Finke, R.A. (1989). *Principles of mental imagery.* Cambridge, MA: MIT Press.

Forsyth, D.R. (1990). *Group dynamics,* 2nd ed. Pacific Grove, CA: Brooks/Cole.

Freud, S. (1960). *Group psychology and the awareness of ego.* New York: Bantam.

Gustavsen, B., & Héthy, L. (1989). New forms of work organization: An overview. In P. Grootings, B. Gustavsen, & L. Héthy (Eds.), *New forms of work organization in europe.* Oxford, UK: Transaction Publishers.

Hackman, J.R. (1986). The psychology of self-management in organizations. In M.S. Pollack & R.O. Perlogg (Eds.), *Psychology and work: Productivity change and employment* (pp. 85-136). Washington, DC: American Psychological Association.

Herbst, P.G. (1962). *Autonomous group functioning and exploration in behavior theory and measurement.* London: Tavistock.

Janis, I.L. (1983). *Groupthink*. Boston: Houghton Mifflin.

Katzenbach, J.R., & Smith, D.K. (1993). *The wisdom of teams: Creating the high performance organization*. Boston: Harvard School Press.

Kerr, S., & Jermier, J. (1978). Substitutes for leadership: Their meaning and measurement. *Organizational Behavior and Human Performance, 22,* 375-403.

Lawler, E.E., III. (1986). *High involvement management*. San Francisco: Jossey-Bass.

Lawler, E.E., III. (1992). *The ultimate advantage: Creating the high involvement organization*. San Francisco: Jossey-Bass.

Lawler, E.E., III, Mohrman, S.A., & Ledford, G.E., Jr. (1992). *Employee involvement and total quality management: Practices and results in Fortune 1000 companies*. San Francisco: Jossey-Bass.

LeBon, G. (1985). *The crowd: A study of the popular mind*. London: Ernest Ben.

Lewin, K. (1948). *Resolving social conflicts: Selected papers on group dynamics*. New York: Harper.

Locke, E.A., Shaw, K.N., Saari, L.M., & Latham, G.P. (1981). Goal setting and task performance. *Psychological Bulletin, 90,* 125-152.

Luthans, F., & Davis, T. (1979). Behavioral self-management (BSM): The missing link in managerial effectiveness. *Organizational Dynamics, 8,* 42-60.

Luthans, F., & Kreitner, R. (1975). *Organizational behavior modification*. Glenview, IL: Scott Foresman.

Mahoney, M.J., & Arnkoff, D.B. (1979). Self-management: Theory, research and application. In J.P. Brady & D. Pomerleau (Eds.), *Behavioral medicine: Theory and practice* (pp. 75-96). Baltimore: Williams and Williams.

Manz, C.C. (1983). *The art of self-leadership: Strategies for personal effectiveness in your life and work*. Englewood Cliffs, NJ: Prentice-Hall, Inc.

Manz, C.C. (1986). Self-leadership: Toward an expanded theory of self-influence processes in organizations. *Academy of Management Review, 11,* 585-600.

Manz, C.C. (1990). Beyond self-managing work teams: Toward self-leading teams in the workplace. In R. Woodman and W. Pasmore (Eds.), *Research in organizational change and development* (pp. 273-299). Greenwich, CT: JAI Press.

Manz, C.C. (1992a). Self-leading work teams: Moving beyond self-management myths. *Human Relations, 45,* 1119-1140.

Manz, C.C. (1992b). *Mastering self-leadership: Empowering yourself for personal excellence*. Englewood Cliffs, NJ: Prentice-Hall.

Manz, C.C., & Angle, H. (1986). Can group self-management mean a loss of personal control: Triangulating on a paradox. *Group and Organization Studies, 11,* 309-334.

Manz, C.C., & Neck, C.P. (1991). Inner leadership: Creating productive thought patterns. *The Academy of Management Executive, 5,* 87-95.

Manz, C.C., & Neck, C.P. (1995). Teamthink: Beyond the groupthink syndrome in self-managing teams. *Journal of Managerial Psychology, 10,* 7-15.

Manz, C.C., & Newstrom, J. (1990). Self-managing teams in a paper mill: Success factors, problems and lessons learned. *International Human Resource Management Review, 1,* 43-60.

Manz, C.C., & Sims, H.P., Jr. (1980). Self-management as a substitute for leadership: A social learning theory perspective. *Academy of Management Review, 5,* 361-367.

Manz, C.C., & Sims, H.P., Jr. (1981). Vicarious learning: The influence of modeling on organizational behavior. *Academy of Management Review, 6,* 105-113.

Manz, C.C., & Sims, H.P., Jr. (1982). The potential for groupthink in autonomous work groups. *Human Relations, 35,* 773-784.

Manz, C.C., & Sims, H.P., Jr. (1986). Leading self-managed groups: A conceptual analysis of a paradox. *Economic and Industrial Democracy, 7,* 141-165.

Manz, C.C., & Sims, H.P., Jr. (1987). Leading workers to lead themselves: The external leadership of self-managing work teams. *Administrative Science Quarterly, 32,* 106-128.

Manz, C.C., & Sims, H.P., Jr. (1990). *Superleadership: Leading others to lead themselves.* New York: Berkeley.

Manz, C.C., & Sims, H.P., Jr. (1993). *Business without bosses: How self-managing teams are building high performance companies.* New York: Wiley.

Manz, C.C., & Stewart, G.L. (Forthcoming). Attaining flexible stability by integrating total quality management and socio-technical systems theory. *Organizational Science.* Providence, RI: INFORMS.

Manz, C.C., Mossholder, K.W., & Luthans, F. (1987). An integrated perspective of self-control in organizations. *Administration and Society, 19,* 3-24.

Manz, C.C., Keating, D., & Donnellon, A. (1990). Preparing for an organizational change to employee self-management: The managerial transition. *Organizational Dynamics, 19,* 15-26.

Markham, S.E., & Markham, I.S. (1995). Self-management and self-leadership re-examined: A levels of analysis perspective. *Leadership Quarterly, 6,* 343-359.

Marx, R.D. (1982). Relapse prevention of managerial training: A model for maintenance of behavior change. *Academy of Management Review, 7,* 433-441.

McDougall, W. (1921). *The group mind.* Cambridge: Cambridge University Press.

Mills, P.K. (1983). Self-management: Its control and relationship to other organizational properties. *Academy of Management Review, 8,* 445-453.

Napier, R.W., & Gershenfeld, M.K. (1987). *Groups: Theory and experience.* Boston: Houghton Mifflin.

Neck, C.P., & Manz, C.C. (1992). Thought self-leadership: The influence of self-talk and mental imagery on performance. *Journal of Organizational Behavior, 13,* 681-699.

Neck, C.P., & Manz, C.C. (1994). From groupthink to teamthink: Toward the creation of constructive thought patterns in self-managing work teams. *Human Relations, 47,* 929-952.

Neck, C.P., & Milliman, J.F. (1994). Thought self-leadership: Finding spiritual fulfillment in organizational life. *Journal of Managerial Psychology, 9,* 9-16.

Neck, C.P., Stewart, G.L., & Manz, C.C. (1995). Thought self-leadership as a framework for enhancing the performance of performance appraisers. *Journal of Applied Behavioral Science, 31,* 278-302.

Orsburn, J.D., Moran, L., Musselwhite, E., & Zenger, J.H. (1990). *Self-directed work teams.* Homewood, IL: Business One Irwin.

Poza, E.J., & Markus, L. (1980, winter). Success story: The team approach to work restructuring. *Organizational Dynamics,* 3-25.

Richardson, A. (1967). Mental practice: A review and discussion, Part I. *Research Quarterly, 38,* 95-107.

Saporito, B. (1986). The revolt against "working smarter." *Fortune, 114*(2), 58-65.

Seligman, M.E.P. (1991). *Learned optimism.* New York: Alfred Knopf.

Shaw, R.B. (1990). Mental health treatment teams. In J.R. Hackman (Ed.), *Groups that work [and those that don't]* (pp. 330-348). San Francisco: Jossey-Bass.

Sims, H.P., Jr., Manz, C.C., & Bateman, B. (1993). The early implementation phase: Getting teams started in the office. In C.C. Manz & H.P. Sims, Jr., *Business without bosses: How self-managing teams are building high performance companies.* New York: Wiley.

Skinner, B.F. (1969). *Contingencies of reinforcement.* New York: Appleton-Century-Crofts.

Stewart, G.L., & Manz, C.C. (1995). Leadership for self-managing work teams: A typology and integrative model. *Human Relations, 48,* 347-770.

Susman, G.I. (1976). *Autonomy at work: A socio-technical analysis of participative management.* New York: Praeger.

Thoresen, C.E., & Mahoney, M.J. (1974). *Behavior self-control.* New York: Holt, Rinehart and Winston.

Trist, E. (1977). Collaboration in work settings: A personal perspective. *The Journal of Applied Behavioral Science, 13,* 268-278.

Trist, E., Susman, G.I., & Brown, G.R. (1977). An experiment in autonomous working in an American underground coal mine. *Human Relations, 30,* 201-236.

Verespej, M.A. (1990). Self-directed work teams yield long-term benefits. *Journal of Business Strategy, 11*(6), 9-12.

U.S. Department of Labor. (1993). *High performance work practices and firm performance.* Washington, DC: Office of the American Workplace.

Walton, R.E. (1977). Work innovations at Topeka: After six years. *Journal of Applied Behavioral Science, 13,* 422-433.

Walton, R.E. (1985). From control to commitment in the workplace. *Harvard Business Review, 63,* 77-84.

Weick, K.E. (1979). *The social psychology of organizing.* Reading, MA: Addison-Wesley.

Wells, L., Jr. (1985). The group-as-a-whole perspective and its theoretical roots. In A.D. Coleman & M.H. Geller (Eds.), *Group Relations Reader 2.* Washington, DC: A.K. Rice Institute.

LEADERSHIP OF WORK TEAMS:
FACTORS INFLUENCING TEAM OUTCOMES

Ren Nygren and Edward L. Levine

ABSTRACT

Self-Directed Work Teams (SDWTs) represent an increasingly popular approach to work restructuring which has affected thousands of organizations and millions of workers since the mid-1980s. This SDWT popularity explosion has created several critically important research issues. First, it is thought that effective SDWT leadership involves the transfer of control of day-to-day job activities from managers to employees, however, few investigations have focused on how this transition of control affects leaders and team members. Second, many investigators have examined the relationship between SDWT outcomes and a single set of variables such as leader behavior, organizational factors, or team member behavior; yet, few authors have elaborated a systemic view encompassing the variety of intra-organizational factors thought to influence SDWT outcomes. This paper (a) highlights the dynamics of managers' transition from traditional supervision to SDWT leadership, (b) sets forth a systemic model encompassing factors thought to influence SDWT outcomes, and (c) identifies important SDWT research issues.

Advances in Interdisciplinary Studies
of Work Teams, Volume 3, pages 67-104.
Copyright © 1996 by JAI Press Inc.
All rights of reproduction in any form reserved.
ISBN: 0-7623-0006-X

INTRODUCTION

Organizations throughout the United States and in many other countries have made or are considering fundamental changes in the way organizational members do their jobs. The traditional approach to organizing the work of employees involved supervisors controlling when and how employees performed their jobs. This system emerged during the Industrial Revolution, largely in response to the need to control the activities of a large number of uneducated workers performing menial or repetitive tasks on assembly lines (Taylor, 1911). In the decades following the Industrial Revolution, this system of supervisors controlling employees' work remained intact, even though the educational requirements, job responsibilities, and the complexity of tasks facing workers steadily increased. At the time of this writing, organizations throughout the world are facing increased competition, decreasing internal resources, and internal and external pressure for increased efficiency (Applebaum & Batt, 1994; Cascio, 1993; Cummings & Malloy, 1977; Fisher, 1993; Manz, 1992; Trist, 1977).

This combination of factors is forcing organizational leaders to rethink fundamentally how their managers and employees accomplish work (Fisher, 1993). This situation often involves traditionally hierarchical organizations making the transition from supervisory control of employees' activities to a variety of schemes aimed at increasing employees' control of their own activities including: participative management (Lawler, 1986; Tannenbaum & Schmidt, 1958), voluntary and obligatory employee participation (Kanter, 1982), representative industrial democracy (Stymne, 1986), employee self-management (Bass, 1990), employee empowerment (Cameron & Ulrich, 1986), and self-directed work teams (SDWTs; Cohen & Ledford, 1994; Fisher, 1993; Manz & Sims, 1987).

Of these approaches, SDWTs have attracted considerable attention and interest in recent years. In fact, the application of SDWTs in organizations has risen dramatically in the last three to five years as evidenced by (a) articles written in the popular press (e.g., Brown, 1994; Dumaine, 1994; Fisher, 1993; Funk, 1992; Gilbert, 1985; Hirschhorn, 1991; Katzenbach & Smith, 1993; Kayser, 1994; Kolb, 1992; Larson & LaFasto, 1989; Luthans & Davis, 1979; Mackay, 1993; Manz, Keating, & Donnellon, 1990; Orsburn et al., 1990; Sweeny & Allen, 1988; Varney, 1989;), (b) the proliferation of training and implementation programs offered by a wide variety of consultants (Fisher, 1993), and (c) the creation of university-based centers devoted to their study (M.M. Beyerlein, personal communication, November 11, 1994).

Despite this groundswell of popular and practical interest in the topic of SDWTs, surprisingly few qualitative or quantitative investigations of SDWTs have been reported. When one considers the changes SDWTs are bringing to the roles of employees and managers in organizations, several fundamentally important research issues become apparent.

First, it is thought that individuals charged with leading or managing employees organized into SDWTs must develop a leadership skill set fundamentally different from that used by traditional supervisors and managers (Fisher, 1993; Kolb, 1992; Manz & Sims, 1987). While many researchers report that managers and supervisors experience difficulty in transitioning from traditional leadership behaviors to this new set of SDWT leadership behaviors (Fisher, 1993; Gilbert, 1985; Manz & Sims, 1987; Wall, Kemp, Jackson, & Clegg, 1986), few systematic, empirical studies have investigated the behavioral requirements for this new leadership role.

Second, several theorists have suggested that the presence or absence of certain organizational or contextual factors can impact the behavior of team leaders (Fisher, 1993; Hackman, 1990; Larson & LaFasto, 1989) and the behavior of team members (Druskat, 1994; Hackman, 1990; Marchington et al., 1994; Varney, 1989). Yet, little is known about how such organizational factors interact with leader behavior to influence team members' behaviors and team outcomes.

Third, the SDWT concept and the fundamental change it brings to the supervision of employees' activities is thought to impact profoundly employees' behavior within organizations (Cummings & Malloy, 1977; Fisher, 1993; Manz & Sims, 1987; Marchington et al., 1994; Poza & Markus, 1980; Trist & Bamforth, 1951; Trist et al., 1977; Wall et al., 1986; Walton, 1977); yet, relatively few studies have examined how leader behavior, organizational factors, and team outcomes impact team members' behavior.

And finally, few studies have examined how leader behavior, organizational factors, and resulting team member behaviors are related to objectively measured team outcomes (Beekun, 1989; Cohen & Ledford, 1994). Given the current widespread interest in and application of SDWT concepts in organizations throughout the world, determining the answers to these fundamentally important research issues is imperative.

Despite the fact that little is known about the relationship between leader behavior, organizational factors, team member behavior, and team outcomes, traditional managers and employees are being reengineered into SDWTs at an ever increasing rate (Fisher, 1993). In fact, it would seem that up to this point, many organizations implementing SDWTs have largely assumed that (a) the act of implementing SDWTs somehow brings with it managers' transition from "control retaining" behaviors to "control releasing" behaviors, (b) the organizational context in which SDWTs operate will shift to support them, (c) team members will begin to engage in functional team oriented behaviors, and (d) the SDWTs will achieve the desired team outcomes. The search for and presentation of supporting, contradicting, or yet-to-be-discovered evidence related to these beliefs represents the objective of this paper.

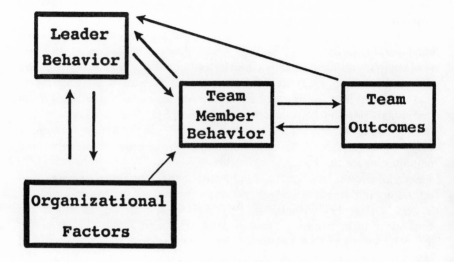

Figure 1. Self-directed Work Team Leadership Model

Though little empirically derived information is available regarding the collective or systemic interaction between leader behavior, organizational factors, team member behavior, and team outcomes within a SDWT environment, it may be helpful to begin thinking about a model which, given future research on this issue, could serve to organize our understanding of the dynamic relationships among these variables. To help develop a theory of performance called for by Campbell (1990), such a working model is presented in Figure 1.

The model depicted in Figure 1 delineates the theorized relationships between organizational factors, leader behavior, team member behavior, and team outcomes. First, organizational factors (e.g., physical surroundings) are thought to influence both leader behavior and team member behavior. In certain situations, organizational factors (e.g., resources made available to the team) could be influenced by leader behavior. Second, leader behavior is thought to influence organizational factors and team member behavior. Also, leader behavior is thought to be influenced by team member behavior and team outcomes. Third, team member behavior is thought to influence team outcomes. Also, team member behavior is thought to be influenced by team outcomes.

After a definition of a SDWT is offered and selected background issues are attended to, including what type of organizational role might be reserved for a SDWT leader, the remaining sections of this paper elaborate upon each of the elements depicted in Figure 1. Pertinent research is used to (a) lay a groundwork of foundational information about SDWTs, (b) further develop and explain the proposed model, and (c) highlight important SDWT research issues which remain largely uninvestigated. We conclude the paper by (a) highlighting the proposed model's heuristic value, (b) acknowledging the proposed model's shortcomings, and (c) specifying research directions that merit further study.

SELF-DIRECTED WORK TEAMS

Definition

A review of published literature regarding SDWTs shows that they are known by a variety of names including teams with responsible autonomy (Trist & Bamforth, 1951), self-managing teams (Walton, 1977), self-managed work teams (Manz & Sims, 1987), self-directed work teams (Fisher, 1993), self-designing teams and shared leadership teams (Cohen & Ledford, 1994) and autonomous work groups (Wall et al., 1986). The teams cited in these investigations share a common theme of employee self-management, and their differences in name can be attributed to the differences between their tasks and their organizations' culture and climate. To minimize confusion, the label self-directed work team (SDWT) will be used in this paper from this point forward.

With regard to SDWTs, several authors have suggested important characteristics of these teams. For instance, Orsburn and coworkers (1990) emphasize that since SDWTs plan, set priorities, organize, coordinate with others, measure, and take corrective action, they represent the conceptual opposite of the assembly line and traditional supervision. Hackman (1986, 1987) has pointed out that SDWTs often have discretion over decisions, methods of work, assignment of team members to jobs, feedback about performance, and certain elements of compensation decisions. Manz and Sims (1987) emphasize that these teams are characterized by a high degree of decision making autonomy and behavioral control at the work-group level. Fisher (1993) offers a concise yet comprehensive SDWT definition which will facilitate a review of the relevant literature and to provide the reader with a simple and specific SDWT schema:

> Self-directed Work Team: A group of employees who have day-to-day responsibility for managing themselves and the work they do with a minimum of direct supervision. Members of SDWTs typically handle job assignments, plan and schedule work, make production and/or service related decisions, and take action on problems (p. 15).

Having established a working definition of what a SDWT is, it seems important to discuss the characteristics of the more widely studied work groups so that distinctions between the two can be made. This is important because a substantial body of literature exists regarding work group processes and productivity (Hackman, 1990; Levine, 1973; Steiner, 1972), and a full accounting of this literature is beyond the scope of this paper.

The label work group is used to refer to an enormous number of social and organizational forms, and this situation has created some confusion in work group research (Hackman, 1990). As suggested by Hackman (1990), work groups have three attributes: (a) they are intact social systems with clear boundaries and member roles, (b) they have one or more tasks to perform, and (c) they operate as a collective within a larger organizational context.

Considering the characteristics of a SDWT and work group cited previously, key similarities and differences become apparent. Work groups and SDWTs are similar in that (a) members work jointly to produce some product, (b) members develop specialized roles, (c) clear boundaries of group/team responsibilities are apparent, (d) members and non-members are readily identifiable, and (e) members interact in real time. In terms of differences, SDWTs appear to have a more clearly specified charter with regard to self-management, decision making, and day-to-day control of activities. More specifically, many SDWTs engage in decisions regarding peer selection, appraisal, and compensation. Finally, the leadership role in work groups is not always clearly specified, whereas the SDWT definition specifies that the team is in charge of its own activities (within certain organizational constraints). Because SDWTs seem to represent a special form of the more widely studied work group, the literature reviewed from this point forward is primarily limited to studies investigating teams which conform to the aforementioned SDWT characteristics and definition.

Assumptions Underlying SDWTs

While industrial/organizational psychologists have long been interested in how individuals and groups accomplish work, relatively little research has been conducted about how SDWTs accomplish work and what benefits or improvements they provide organizations above and beyond the more traditional approaches used to organize work. Considering the apparent paucity of high quality studies about the benefits SDWTs provide to organizations (Cohen & Ledford, 1994), one might wonder why they have become so popular and so widely embraced. There appear to be at least four key assumptions which account for their conceptual appeal and current popularity.

The first assumption involves the belief that a direct result of implementing SDWTs is increased employee involvement in their work. Following this line of reasoning, when employees are given responsibility for making day-to-day decisions regarding their work, it is assumed that their level of commitment to their decisions, plans, and ultimately their jobs also increases. This increased employee involvement then translates into improved product quality, better service, and process improvements. The SDWTs are then assumed to provide tangible, improved operating results above and beyond what the organization could achieve using more traditional approaches to employee supervision. While a handful of quantitative studies suggest that SDWTs give organizations improved productivity (Beekun, 1989; Cohen & Ledford, 1994; Goodman, 1979), this belief seems more commonly rooted in the voluminous popular business literature which documents examples of SDWT success stories (Brown, 1994; Fisher, 1993; Funk, 1992; Gilbert, 1985; Hirschhorn, 1991; Katzenbach & Smith, 1993; Kayser, 1994; Kolb, 1992; Mackay, 1993; Sweeny & Allen, 1988). Unfortunately, the writers and readers of many of these articles often fail to realize or acknowledge that the cases selected consist of an extremely small and probably unrepresentative sample from the much larger population of organizations experimenting with SDWT concepts.

Second, organizational leaders often perceive that their organizations are locked in competition against others for profits, market share, and customers. Considering this competitive outlook, these leaders view the notion of a team and its popular definition of a group of people working together to achieve a goal as an intuitively appealing strategy for winning in the competitive business environment. Additionally, many of these leaders draw upon their own past experiences with sporting, project, or community teams as evidence of team effectiveness and value. These beliefs combine to fuel the assumption that team synergy surpasses the sum of each individual's contribution and that teams are the way to win in the modern, competitive business environment.

Third, the implementation of SDWTs often involves reducing or eliminating entire layers of highly paid supervisors and managers. These reductions of salaried employees cut expenses and improve organizational profitability in the short term. These short-term gains in profitability support the assumption that teams help the organization become more cost effective, however, this belief may or may not be true, since studies investigating the utility of SDWTs are not readily available (W.F. Cascio, personal communication, August 18, 1994).

Fourth, the current popularity of SDWTs may represent a manifestation of the declining motivation to manage seen in individuals studied in at least two separate investigations (Howard & Bray, 1988; Miner & Smith, 1982). More specifically, Miner and Smith (1982) suggested that the decline in college students' motivation to manage, as measured between 1960 and 1980, presents organizations with a population of young managers who have less motivation to manage others. Similarly, the Management Continuity Study of Howard and Bray (1988) produced data suggesting that individuals now possess considerably less need for advancement than did the individuals studied in the original Management Progress Study (Bray et al., 1974). If one assumes that shifting the responsibility for day-to-day control of activities from managers to workers through SDWTs may be linked to the declining motivation to manage apparently held by modern supervisors and managers, the findings of Miner and Smith (1982) and of Howard and Bray (1988) suggest a rather subtle explanation for the popular appeal of SDWTs.

While these four assumptions clarify and most likely support the underlying popularity of SDWTs, they also tend to crystallize scientific skepticism regarding the utility of SDWTs. These issues represent fertile avenues of research for social scientists because large numbers of organizations are transitioning to SDWTs and their managers and supervisors are being required to adjust to this new way of leading employees.

Social Scientists Discover SDWTs

Formal research regarding SDWTs first appeared in 1951 when Trist and Bamforth documented several problems, including absenteeism, stress, worker dissatisfaction, and decreased productivity, resulting from changes in coal mining technology and work organization in a British coal mine. Their investigation and conclusions, based on a qualitative methodology involving repeated discussions and long interviews with key informants, revealed fascinating insights as to how miners' perceptions regarding their involvement in work decisions affected their job performance.

Briefly, Trist and Bamforth (1951) concluded that the introduction of large-scale long-wall mining techniques had stripped the miners of their accustomed decision making and work allocation responsibilities inherent in the traditional hand-got methods of coal mining. As a remedy for the decreases in productivity and job satisfaction, and increases in employee absenteeism and stress, Trist and Bamforth recommended that these problems could be solved by "... restoring responsible autonomy to primary groups throughout the system and ensuring that each of these groups has a satisfying sub-whole as its work task, and some scope of flexibility in work-pace" (p. 38).

While the Trist and Bamforth investigation has been credited as the first investigation of SDWTs (Fisher, 1993), it seems ironic that this seminal investigation was prompted by the elimination of the SDWT concept in the coal mine. Further, the period between 1951 and 1995 is marked with ever increasing popular interest in employee empowerment and the SDWT concept (e.g., Brown, 1994; Dumaine, 1994; Fisher, 1993; Funk, 1992; Gilbert, 1985; Hirschhorn, 1991; Kayser, 1994; Katzenbach & Smith, 1993; Kolb, 1992; Larson & LaFasto, 1989; Luthans & Davis, 1979; Mackay, 1993; Manz et al., 1990; Orsburn et al., 1990; Sweeny & Allen, 1988; Varney, 1989), but few quantitative investigations (e.g., Beekun, 1989; Cohen & Ledford, 1994; Manz & Sims, 1987; Walton, 1977) regarding their usage in modern organizations have been published. What is perhaps even more striking than the scarcity of quantitative research about SDWTs themselves is the paucity of research about leadership of SDWTs.

The Seeming Paradox of SDWT Leadership

Prior to developing and outlining the leader behavior component of the Self-Directed Work Team Leadership Model, one might wonder why leadership and self-direction are not mutually exclusive. In fact, confusion regarding the seeming paradox surrounding leadership of a team of employees who are supposed to be self-directed is a common point of misunderstanding (Fisher, 1993; Lawler, 1986; Manz & Sims, 1986, 1987). Based on these accounts, it seems that even the most autonomous, independent, or otherwise self-reliant work teams need some amount of direction, support, and/or linkage to their organization's larger supra-system. For example, while a SDWT installing roofs on pre-fabricated trailer homes might have the responsibility for the daily assignment of individual team members to specific tasks, the team would typically rely on their coordinator (e.g., team leader) to give them guidance on clarifying customer requirements, facilitating communication with internal suppliers, and communicating information about production forecasts.

Manz and Sims (1987) have suggested that this set of leader behaviors involves encouraging team members to engage in self-reinforcement, self-criticism, self-goal setting, self-observation/evaluation, self-expectation, and rehearsal; yet, it seems that additional leader behaviors may be required for effectiveness in the SDWT environment (Hackman, 1990; Larson & LaFasto, 1989; Levine, 1973; Tjosvold, 1984). The set of leader behaviors independently suggested by these researchers seems substantially different from the traditional management control paradigm behaviors (Fisher, 1993); and, this insight leads to the question: "What leader behaviors are required for leader effectiveness in the SDWT environment?" This important research question remains open to further investigation.

SDWT Leadership in Organizations

With regard to the actual organizational positions involving SDWT leadership, researchers generally report two to three layers of leadership supporting the activities of these teams. For instance, Manz and Sims (1987) investigated a SDWT system in place at a medium-sized auto parts manufacturer and discovered three layers of leaders including upper plant management, work team coordinators, and an elected team leader within each team. Similarly, Fisher (1993) reports that SDWTs are generally supported by three layers of leaders which include operations team leaders (e.g., those responsible for leading teams), management team leaders (e.g., those responsible for leading operations team leaders), and culture team leaders (e.g., those responsible for organization-wide empowerment and cultural change). The immediate leaders of SDWTs, as evidenced in the previous descriptions, typically operate in an overseer or coordinator role at the organizational level immediately above the team itself. These leaders, most probably known as foreman or first line supervisors in a traditional management schema, represent the individuals called team leaders from this point forward.

Self-directed Work Teams Summary

SDWTs represent an increasingly popular approach to organizing the work of employees in organizations. Although SDWTs have been in existence for several decades, relatively little research has been conducted about why and how they work. Considering the growing interest in and application of SDWTs in organizations, at least two important research issues have been raised and remain as yet uninvestigated.

First, the Trist and Bamforth (1951) investigation sparked extensive interest in socio-technical considerations in aligning the demands of jobs and technology with the social and human needs individuals bring to work. Unfortunately, many of the suggestions made by Trist and Bamforth (1951), Tannenbaum (1968), Sundstrom and coworkers (1990), and others regarding the need for careful matching of SDWT concepts with jobs and people are apparently going unheeded in the modern business world. While some companies are evaluating jobs and people carefully to determine if SDWTs make sense in a given setting, it would seem that many companies are engaging in an SDWT frenzy, converting thousands of employees into teams on an almost overnight basis. Little is known about the organizational and human costs of improperly creating and implementing SDWTs in organizations, however, one can imagine that such costs would be staggering.

Second, managers and supervisors are being asked to exchange their long-held control of employees' activities for a new set of coaching and facilitating behaviors. This change is striking, but what is even more amazing is the fact that the precise form of these new leadership behaviors and their concomitant utility remains largely uninvestigated. Many theorists, including Fisher (1993), Hackman (1990), and Manz and Sims (1987) believe that how the leader of a team behaves will affect team members' behaviors and team outcomes, yet few empirically-based studies have been conducted to verify this assumption (Cohen & Ledford, 1994). If these new behaviors are important for effective leadership in the SDWT environment, then organizations need to re-train their managers with skills appropriate for leadership in this new environment. If, on the other hand, the new behaviors are no better than traditional leadership behaviors or if intra-organizational factors other than leader behavior are relatively more important in determining team outcomes, organizations and managers can spend their time, effort, and money on activities other than leader re-training.

LEADER BEHAVIOR

First, as we have stated relatively little research has been conducted and/or published regarding leader effectiveness and/or ineffectiveness in the SDWT environment. In fact, the careful review of SDWT literature conducted in the preparation of this paper yielded some qualitative coverage of this issue in the popular business literature (e.g., Brown, 1994; Larson & LaFasto, 1989; Mackay, 1993; Manz et al., 1990) and substantially fewer quantitative investigations (Beekun, 1989; Cohen & Ledford, 1994; Manz & Sims, 1987). However, based on the results of the vast quantity of leadership research conducted during this century, the assumption that SDWT leader behaviors influence (a) team members' behavior, and (b) certain organizational factors, justifies at least a brief review of key behavioral theories of leadership effectiveness. Prior to exploring this assumption, research relevant to our understanding of how leader behavior influences employee and group performance is presented.

Early Studies of Leader Behavior

One of the first formal and empirical investigations regarding leadership behavior was initiated by Shartle (1950) and continued by Hemphill and Coons (1957). These Ohio State University Leadership Studies sought to improve psychologists' understanding of leadership effectiveness by studying the behavior of leaders. Adopting a factor analytic approach, these researchers identified two broad factors of leadership behavior and named them *consideration* and *initiating structure* (Hemphill & Coons, 1957). Consideration was defined as the degree to which a leader acts in a friendly and supportive manner, displays concern for subordinates, and shows concern for their welfare. Initiating structure was defined as the degree to which the leader structures and organizes his or her role and subordinates' roles toward achieving the group's goal(s). From this initial study, several survey instruments designed to measure leaders' standing on these factors were developed including (a) the Leader Behavior Description Questionnaire (LBDQ) (Hemphill & Coons, 1957), (b) the Supervisory Behavior Description Questionnaire (SBDQ) (Fleishman, 1972), (c) the LBDQ—Form XII (Stogdill, Goode, & Day, 1962), and (d) the Leadership Opinion Questionnaire (LOQ) (Fleishman, 1989). The constructs of consideration and initiating structure, as well as the instruments used to measure them, have received widespread acceptance and application in hundreds of investigations of leadership over the past 35 years (Yukl, 1989).

At roughly the same time as researchers at Ohio State were investigating leaders' behaviors, a similar research effort began at the University of Michigan. Leader behaviors and their influence on group outcomes were investigated in a number of businesses including insurance (Katz et al., 1950), transportation (Katz et al., 1951), and manufacturing (Katz & Kahn, 1952). Likert (1961, 1967) presented and summarized the three behavioral clusters discovered in the University of Michigan research as (a) task-oriented behavior (helping subordinates establish goals, coordinate/plan work, providing resources), (b) relationship oriented behavior (concern for relationships with subordinates), and (c) participative leadership (facilitating subordinate participation in decision making, conflict resolution, and group discussion).

Leader Behavior, Employee Performance, and Employee Satisfaction

The Ohio State and University of Michigan studies improved our understanding of the clusters of behaviors which comprised effective leadership. These research efforts also highlighted the many ways that leader behavior influences a host of employee and organizational outcomes, including productivity, ratings of group or unit effectiveness, and job satisfaction. With regard to productivity, Katz and coworkers (1951) found that groups of railroad-section workers were less productive when supervised by individuals who performed employees' tasks, failed to delegate, and did not otherwise exercise their leadership role. Similarly, Tannenbaum (1968) concluded that the control patterns of leadership behavior have important and predictable effects on the reactions, satisfaction, feelings of tension, and well-being of employees. Expanding on this line of research, Levine (1973) demonstrated that groups with higher and equally distributed amounts of control, where control was based on behaviors of the type engaged in by effective group leaders, had better problem-solving performance, higher member satisfaction, and more positive socio-emotional interactions.

In terms of perceived effectiveness, several researchers have established a relationship between leader behavior and employee ratings of their group's effectiveness (Christner & Hemphill, 1955; Seltzer & Numeroff, 1988; Stogdill, 1965). Similarly, numerous investigations have confirmed a strong relationship between leader behavior and job satisfaction in educational settings (Petty & Lee, 1975), hospitals (Oaklander & Fleishman, 1964; Szabo, 1981), industrial settings (Badin, 1974; Fleishman & Simmons, 1970; Skinner, 1969), and government organizations (Miles & Petty, 1977).

Investigators of leader behavior in the area of participative leadership also discovered important relationships between leader behavior and employee performance. Researchers discovered that the leader behaviors and employee responses in systems using participative leadership led to (a) improved decision quality, (b) greater acceptance of decisions, (c) better understanding of decisions by people who must implement them, (d) development of decision-making skills among subordinates, (e) enrichment of subordinate jobs by making them more interesting, and (f) facilitation of conflict resolution and team building (Yukl, 1989). These findings, based on a wide variety of empirically-based investigations, sound strikingly similar to the assumed beliefs and benefits thought to underlie the current popularity of SDWTs.

SDWT Leadership Behavior

In the SDWT arena, managers trained and experienced in traditional supervision are faced with the most challenging and striking paradox in modern leadership, leading employees to lead themselves (Manz & Sims, 1987). This transition presumably requires leaders to adopt a significantly different repertoire of leadership behaviors than those required for successful leadership in the structure of a traditional organization. More specifically, the centralized and hierarchical patterns of communication, decision making, and controlling behaviors characterizing traditional supervision apparently need to be replaced with behaviors aimed at helping team members (employees) learn to lead themselves. Table 1, adapted from Levine, (1973), Schriesheim, House, and Kerr (1976), Lord, Foti, and DeVader (1984), and Manz and Sims (1987) outlines a sampling of the fundamental behavioral changes thought to be associated with effective performance in this new role.

It is widely acknowledged that this leadership transition represents a significant behavioral change for individuals occupying supervisory and managerial roles in organizations which implement SDWTs (Fisher, 1993; Manz & Sims, 1987, 1991; Manz et al., 1990; Wall et al., 1986), however, empirically-based studies investigating these new leadership behaviors and their relation to team member behavior and subsequent team outcomes have rarely been published. Despite this lack of specific research, some investigations have touched on the issue of leadership behavior in the SDWT environment.

In an interesting investigation of SDWTs, Poza and Markus (1980) reported the results of a field study involving the design and start-up of a Sherwin-Williams automotive paint factory in Richmond, Kentucky. Although this study employed the weakest possible quasi-experimental design of no control group and post measurement only (Cook et al., 1990), these investigators reported successful and contagious innovations within this plant and the Sherwin-Williams organization as a whole.

More specifically, Poza and Markus (1980) observed (a) reduced staff needed to operate the plant, (b) an absenteeism rate 63 percent below the Sherwin-Williams' plant average, (c) 30 percent higher productivity, (d) 94 percent of production rated as excellent by Sherwin-Williams technical department, (e) no lost time accidents in 1,108 days of operation, and (f) positive quality of work life indicators including high employee satisfaction with the design and

Table 1.   Behavioral Transition from Traditional to SDWT Leadership

Traditional Leaders	SDWT Leaders
Establish employee's performance goals.	Help team members learn how to set their own goals.
Organize employees' activities.	Encourage employees to organize tehir work.
Emphasize production.	Ask team members to make "emphasis decisions."
Control/filter the flow of information (communicate only what they want employees to know).	Communite "need to know" information quickly.
Gather, interpret, and tell employees about organizational information.	Set-up systems to funnel organizational information directly to team members.
Initiate/direct employees' actions.	Teach team members to initiate their own activities.
Monitor employees' performance.	Encourage team members to monitor (gather) performance data.
Evaluate employees' performance.	Help team members learn to evaluate performance data.
Reward employees' performance.	Facilitate system (s) for team members to reward their performance.
Establish work norms for employees.	Encourage team members' to establish team norms.
Resolve employees' conflicts.	Coach team members on skills to process and manage conflicts.
Determine and provide employee training.	Encourage team members to identify and address training opportunities.

content of jobs, the quality of teamwork, and the overall organizational climate. The researchers attributed these results to the successful design and implementation of a SDWT system of work structuring and overall plant management.

While citing a host of socio-technical considerations important to an SDWT start-up, Poza and Markus included a brief mention of the key transition required of team leaders from "... supervisory roles that emphasized expediting and checking-the-checkers activity ..." (p. 19) to a role as " ... team facilitators and consultants ... to the point where they could move away from their previous roles in more traditional plants and take up a helping, coordinating, and consulting role" (p. 21). The development of and initial transition to this new team leader skill set occurred through a two-and-one-half-day team building session designed by an unnamed organization development consultant, the plant manager, and his direct subordinates, however, details regarding the specific learning objectives, content, or training methodology of this team-building session were not reported. Finally, Poza and Markus concluded that "[it] is not easy for supervisors to adjust to their new role as team leaders in this kind of plant. Some make it, others don't" (p. 23).

Given the positive organizational results documented in this investigation, it seems that benefits are potentially available to organizations which commit to SDWTs. What remains unclear, however, is the exact relationship between leader behavior, organizational factors, team member behavior, and subsequent team outcomes. Prior to focusing attention on effective leadership of SDWTs, a brief review of what is known about ineffective team leadership behaviors follows.

Ineffective Team Leader Behavior

Illustrating a potential dark side of SDWTs, Manz and Angle (1987) presented an interesting case study regarding a small insurance company's transition from the industry's traditional individual agent form of work organization to a system involving self-managed work teams. While the conclusions drawn by Manz and Angle appear to rely almost solely on qualitative evidence, some interesting insights were developed regarding the leadership of these self-managed work teams comprised of insurance agents. Of particular interest are the largely ineffective team leader behaviors documented by Manz and Angle which included (a) putting pressure on teams to be productive, (b) attending meetings and prodding members to participate, and (c) offering to direct employees to participate in the study.

In this particular organization, it seems that the introduction of self-managed work teams actually came to represent a loss of individual control and personal discretion as perceived by the normally free roaming insurance agents. To make matters worse, the newly formed teams of salespeople were challenged by an "autocratic" team leader apparently bent on controlling team members' activities. As mentioned previously, these observations of apparently ineffective team leader behavior led Manz and Angle to call for additional research. They asked: "What behaviors are appropriate for self-managed group leaders, and how should their behavior vary in different kinds of work settings?" (p. 331).

Effective Team Leader Behavior

In an attempt to discover information regarding the behavioral requirements of the SDWT leader, Manz and Sims (1987) identified 21 "salient leader behaviors" exhibited by the external leaders of self-managed work teams in a medium-sized manufacturing setting. Using the behaviors identified, these investigators developed the Self-Management Leadership Questionnaire, a paper and pencil measure of leadership behaviors for coordinators of SDWTs. This measure was then administered to 276 hourly employees. These ratings were then factor analyzed using a principal components approach, and a varimax rotation yielded a six factor solution. Manz and Sims labeled these six leader behavior clusters as "... coordinator encourages [the team to engage in] (a) self-reinforcement, (b) self-criticism, (c) self-goal setting, (d) self-observation/self-evaluation, (e) self-expectation, and (f) rehearsal" (p. 116). Factor scores on these clusters were then correlated with subjective ratings (e.g., "His/her overall effectiveness is very high") of team coordinator effectiveness made by team members and the internal leaders of the teams. Nine of 12 resulting correlation coefficients exceeded 0.50, and all 12 coefficients were significant at the $p < 0.01$ level. These findings led Manz and Sims to conclude that SDWT leaders must release control of certain leadership functions to team members so that they may take responsibility for and direct their own activities.

While the Manz and Sims (1987) study represents one of the first empirical investigations of the leadership role in the SDWT environment, several important questions remain unanswered. First, the behavioral taxonomy suggested by Manz and Sims (1987), while largely acceptable as an initial effort to understand the behavioral requirements of the SDWT leader role, appears to lack team leader behaviors suggested by other researchers as important including (a) the dynamics of how control is exercised within the team (Levine, 1973), (b) the fostering of team spirit, solidarity, and commitment (Larson & LaFasto, 1989), and (c) the handling of conflicts and disagreements (Hackman, 1990; Levine, 1973).

Second, while there appears to be a strong correlation between certain SDWT leader behaviors and subjective ratings of leader effectiveness, the linkage between leader behavior and perceived leader effectiveness is probably mediated by other important variables. For instance, some might question whether the leadership behaviors elicit certain team member behaviors which positively influence team outcomes and result in team members' perception that their leader is effective.

Third, some might wonder about the impact of organizational factors on the perceived effectiveness of the SDWT leader and the behavior of team members. And fourth, many theorists assume that these new leadership behaviors positively impact team processes and team outcomes, however, empirical evidence supporting this relationship is not readily available.

Because it was not practical for Manz and Sims (1987) to include objective measures of team outcomes in their analyses (H.P. Sims, Jr., personal communication, June 2, 1995), one wonders whether subjectively measured leadership effectiveness is a correlate of objectively measured team outcomes. More specifically, subjectively measured leadership effectiveness is, at best, a correlate of team outcomes and, at worst, might only represent an indication of the leader's likability. Hence, the inclusion of objectively measured team outcomes in an investigation of leader behavior, perceived leader effectiveness, and objectively measured team outcomes would lend support for the construct validity of the Manz and Sims (1987) SMLQ in specific, and the notion that leader behavior impacts team outcomes, in general.

Leader Behavior Summary

Based on the leader behavior research conducted regarding traditional leader and employee interactions, it seems clear that how a leader behaves affects employee behavior, satisfaction, and performance. This conclusion supports the assumed leader behavior, organizational factor, team member behavior, and team outcomes relationships set forth in the Self-Directed Work Team Leadership Model. However, the leader behavior research reviewed thus far also leads to several important questions.

As stated earlier, it seems that the leader behavior taxonomy proposed by Manz and Sims (1987) is reasonable and largely acceptable, however, the taxonomy does not include certain leader behaviors identified as important by other researchers such as Levine (1973), Larson and LaFasto (1989), and Hackman (1990). For example, Levine (1973) demonstrated the importance of amount and distribution of control within groups (teams) and their impact on team outcomes and member satisfaction. Based on these findings, one might presume that SDWT leaders ought to engage in behaviors aimed at making sure that the relative amount of control allotted to teams is high and equally distributed among members. Leader behaviors involved with distribution of control would, for example, include encouraging increased interaction between team members when control seems unequally distributed. Larson and LaFasto (1989) point out that team leaders need to foster team spirit, solidarity, and commitment. Such leader behaviors would include encouraging team members to "... include membership in the team as an important aspect of self" (p. 77). Finally, Levine (1973), Tjosvold (1984), and Hackman (1990) have emphasized the importance and value of handling disagreement in effectively functioning groups. Leader behaviors in this area include encouraging team members to discuss disagreements and providing team members with appropriate mechanisms (e.g., team meetings, exercises, training, outings) for handling conflict and releasing tension. The addition of certain key leader behaviors to the six cluster taxonomy set forth by Manz and Sims (1987) would seem both important and appropriate. A full accounting of the original taxonomy and proposed additions are presented in Table 2 as "Amended Self-Directed Work Team Leader Behaviors" (adapted from Hackman, 1990; Larson & LaFasto, 1989; Levine, 1973; Manz & Sims, 1987).

Second, since it seems that leaders of SDWTs are pressed to engage in behaviors which are somewhat different from the traditional leadership behaviors discovered and studied over the past 50 years, one wonders about

Table 2.   Amended Self-directed Work Team Leader Behaviors

---

1. **Foster team spirit:**
   He/she encourages us to discuss our team's purpose.
   He/she encourages us to learn about one another's strengths and abilities.
   He/she encourages us to learn about one another's developmental needs.
   He/she encourages us to talk about significant team accomplishments.
   He/she provides us with opportunities to build our team.
   He/she encourages us to include membership in the team as an important aspect of self.
2. **Encourage interaction:**
   He/she encourages us to offer our ideas when solving problems.
   He/she encourages us to ask one another about ideas and opinions.
   He/she encourages us to consider one another as equals.
3. **Process conflict:**
   He/she provides us with methods to work through disagreements.
   He/she encourages us to discuss disagreements.
   He/she encourages us to release tension when we experience conflict.
4. **Encourage self-goal setting:**
   He/she prompts us to define the goals for our own team.
   He/she encourages us to establish our own task goals.
5. **Encourage self-expectation:**
   He/she encourages our group to think we can do very well in our work.
   He/she encourages us to expect high performance from our group.
6. **Encourage rehearsal:**
   He/she encourages us to go over an activity before we attempt it.
   He/she helps us to go over a new task before we actually begin the task.
7. **Encourage self-observation/evaluation:**
   He/she encourages us to be aware of our level of performance.
   He/she encourages us to know how our performance stands.
   He/she encourages us to judge how well we are performing.
   He/she encourages us to think about how we are going to do a job before we begin the job.
8. **Encourage self-reinforcement:**
   He/she encourages us to praise each other if we have done a job well.
   If we do an assignment especially well, then he/she encourages us to feel positive about ourselves.
   He/she encourages us to feel good about ourselves if we do a job well.
9. **Encourage self-criticism:**
   He/she expects us to be tough on ourselves when our performance is not up to standard.

---

the impact of these new leader behaviors on team member behavior in the SDWT environment. Also, little is known about the relationship between leader behavior and objectively measured team outcomes. As mentioned previously, this leads to the question, *do* team leaders who behave as suggested by Levine (1973), Manz and Sims (1987), Larson and LaFasto (1989), and Hackman (1990), actually elicit certain team member behaviors and higher team outcomes than do team leaders engaging in a more traditional set of leadership behaviors?

ORGANIZATIONAL FACTORS

Several theorists suggest that organizational factors play a critical role in the implementation, leadership, and functioning of SDWTs (Druskat, 1994; Fisher, 1993; Katzenbach & Smith,1993; Larson & LaFasto, 1989; Marchington et al., 1994; Mowday & Sutton, 1993; Orsburn et al., 1990). For this reason, it seems important to view SDWTs not in isolation but instead within the larger context of the organizational system in which they function. Accordingly, the term "organizational factors" has been included in the Self-Directed Work Team Leadership Model.

Prior to specifying the nature of the organizational factors which are thought to be involved with the model, it should be noted that a comprehensive investigation of the melange of organizational factors potentially impacting the leadership and performance of SDWTs is beyond the intended scope of this paper. Accordingly, a summary of key organizational factors has been prepared based on the writings and thoughts of several subject matter experts. In the following sections, the positions of these theorists and research efforts highlighting the impact of these factors on SDWTs are reviewed and discussed.

Specific Organizational Factors

Many theorists including Druskat (1994), Orsburn and coworkers (1990), Marchington and coworkers (1994), Varney (1989), and Pearce and Ravlin (1987) have suggested that organizational factors can influence team processes and thereby influence team outcomes. Although these researchers suggest that the organizational factors influence team members and team outcomes alone, it seems reasonable to assume that they would also influence the behavior of the SDWT leader. This assumption is consistent with the model's proposed relationship between organizational factors and leader behavior, team member behavior, and team outcomes.

To highlight specific organizational factors thought to influence the leadership and performance of SDWTs, an integrative summary, adapted from M.M. Beyerlein (personal communication, April 11, 1995), Druskat (1994), Sundstrom and coworkers (1990), Orsburn and coworkers (1990), Larson and LaFasto (1989), Varney (1989), Pearce and Ravlin, (1987), and Hackman (1986, 1987) detailing each of the nine key organizational factors and their potential influence(s) on SDWTs and their leaders is presented in the following list:

1. Resources available, including information, materials resources, training, and coaching;
2. Team size which impacts intermember communication, team decision making, diversity of human resources, and so forth;

3. Physical surroundings such as co-location, physical barriers to contact, availability of a meeting area, work layout, and sources of stress;
4. Clearly defined team goals which define the team's purpose and outputs can provide a common objective and minimize ambiguity and anxiety;
5. Organizational norms that provide a shared agreement among members about behavior and a shared understanding about such things as quality, cost, and delivery standards;
6. The reward system which can unite or divide members in their work efforts;
7. Trust between the levels of the organization which determines how committed team members will become to the organization's goals;
8. Meaningful feedback about the team's contribution to the overall organizational system, including hard data on performance;
9. The amount of cooperation and support the team receives from other teams and/or support functions within the organization.

Based on these organizational factors thought to influence the leadership and performance of SDWTs, it seems clear that the inclusion of the organizational factors term in the Self-Directed Work Team Leadership Model is both necessary and appropriate. Research regarding the influence of organizational factors on SDWT leadership and performance can be divided into qualitative/anecdotal and quantitative investigations.

Qualitative/Anecdotal Research Regarding Organizational Factors

Abundant qualitative/anecdotal accounts of organizational factors and their influence on SDWTs are found in the popular business literature (e.g., Dumaine, 1994). These accounts offer qualitative support for the conclusion that organizational factors can and do influence the implementation, leadership, and maintenance of SDWTs.

More specifically, Larson and LaFasto (1989) conducted extensive interviews with the leaders and members of a wide variety of teams, including, for example, surgical and sports teams. During these interviews, they asked individuals about the characteristics, features, and attributes of effectively functioning teams. While these questions serve to elicit information about a wide variety of variables impacting team functioning, the list of characteristics set forth by Larson and LaFasto (1989) includes several organizational factors thought to be important to SDWT implementation, leadership, and functioning. The Larson and LaFasto characteristics of effectively functioning work teams are presented in Table 3.

It is interesting to note that the characteristics set forth by Larson and LaFasto (1989) are quite similar to the organizational factors identified by Druskat (1994), Sundstrom and coworkers (1990), Orsburn and coworkers

Table 3. Characteristics of Effectively
Functioning Work Teams

Effectively Functioning Teams Have:

1. A clear, elevating goal.
2. A results-driven structure.
3. Competent members.
4. Unified commitment.
5. A collaborative climate.
6. Standards of excellence.
7. External support/recognition.
8. Principled leadership.

Note: Adapted fromm Larson and LaFasto (1989).

(1990), Varney (1989), Pearce and Ravlin (1987), and Hackman (1986). Considering this insight, it would seem that the available qualitative research lends support to the notion that organizational factors do impact the implementation, leadership, and performance of SDWTs.

Quantitative Research Regarding Organizational Factors

Quantitative research regarding the influence of organizational factors on SDWT leadership and performance is difficult to find. In fact, the literature review conducted in preparation of this paper yielded only one published study which indirectly sheds light on the impact of organizational factors on team leader behavior, team member behavior, and team outcomes.

Trist, Susman, and Brown (1977) reported an investigation involving autonomous work group principles in a central Pennsylvania underground coal mine. The management of the mine "believed that increased involvement of workers in decision making and an overall improvement in work quality through the use of autonomous work groups might be a means to improve safety, as well as increase productivity ..." (p. 204). Trist and coworkers (1977) were able to set-up a quasi-experimental design involving an autonomous mining group (treatment) and two traditional mining groups (control) within the same mining company. While the authors readily acknowledged several threats to their experiment's internal validity including (a) diffusion of the experimental (autonomous) treatment and (b) control versus autonomous group rivalry, they reported positive gains for the autonomous mining group including fewer mining violations, fewer accidents, decreased absenteeism, decreased costs per ton of coal mined, increased productivity, decreased disruption due to changing conditions and technology, and generally improved employee attitudes.

Although positive results were achieved, an attempt to convert the entire mine to autonomous work teams failed due to at least two organizational factors stemming from management and union difficulties at the research site. These factors, although not explicitly stated as such by Trist and coworkers (1977), included low trust and unclear project goals.

Notwithstanding this disappointment, Trist and coworkers (1977) offered timely insight regarding benefits to organizations which encourage front line supervisors to transition their control of employees' activities to the employees themselves. While crew members assumed responsibility for day-to-day operations, foreman were freed to plan, study mining laws, identify potential breakdowns, contribute to the overall mine development plan, and act as a resource person for crew members. While these benefits certainly sound appealing, Trist and coworkers (1977) offered little information as to how individual foremen should go about making the transition from their traditional control paradigm to the approach prescribed by the authors. Additionally, no attempt to establish a relationship between leader behavior, team member behavior, and/or team outcomes was reported.

Summary of Organizational Factors Research

Based on the qualitative research and limited quantitative research regarding the influence of organizational factors on SDWT leadership and performance, such factors do appear to influence leader behavior, team member behavior, and team outcomes. These tentative conclusions support the proposed relationships between organizational factors, leader behavior, team member behavior, and team outcomes set forth in the Self-Directed Work Team Leadership Model. A key question that remains unanswered, however, is how such organizational factors might interact with leader behavior and team member behavior to impact team outcomes. For example, one wonders to what extent leader behavior matters given the presence of relatively favorable or unfavorable organizational factors (Howell et al., 1990). Gathering such information is critically important for understanding the dynamic and complicated issue of leadership effectiveness and ineffectiveness in the SDWT environment.

TEAM MEMBER BEHAVIOR

According to the Self-Directed Work Team Leadership Model, team member behavior is thought to be impacted by leader behavior, by the favorability of a host of organizational factors, and by the outcomes that the team achieves. Also, how team members behave is thought to impact leader behavior and the team outcomes. Prior to reviewing what is known about team member behavior in a SDWT environment, an attempt is made to elaborate the difference between team member behavior (team processes) and team outcomes.

Differentiating Team Member Behavior and Team Outcomes

Discussions regarding measurement of team member behavior and team outcomes reveal that the constructs are often inextricably combined in many situations. This blurring of behavior and outcomes may be due to the apparent temporal overlap between team member behavior and team outcomes. Stated more simply, one wonders whether effective or ineffective team outcomes are brought about by functional or dysfunctional team member behaviors, or do effective or ineffective team outcomes cause team members to engage in functional or dysfunctional behaviors. This distinction between behavior and outcomes is depicted in the model by the dual arrows between team member behavior and team outcomes. In other words, it is suggested that, at least initially, behavior leads to outcomes, but, as members gain experience in their team environment, behavior both precedes and results from team outcomes. While these distinctions may seem overly academic, it is important to realize that practical discussions of team member behavior and of team outcomes are in many cases identical. In this section of the review, then, the discussion focuses on team member behavior with the understanding that team outcomes shall be addressed shortly.

Qualitative and Quantitative Research Regarding Team Member Behavior

As in previous sections of this review, qualitative and quantitative investigations regarding the behavior of team members within the SDWT environment are not abundant. However, available and relevant information from published accounts is presented following.

With regard to qualitative research on team member behavior within the SDWT environment, a number of perspectives on effective and/or productive team work are available in the popular business literature (e.g., Funk, 1992; Kayser, 1994; Larson & LaFasto, 1989). These accounts offer qualitative support for the conclusion that team members' behavior impacts team outcomes, however, few authors do more than imply the relationships suggested in the Self-Directed Work Team Leadership Model. Despite this lack of qualitative support for the overall relationships specified in the model, these writings do contain a wealth of information about functional and dysfunctional team member behaviors and how they are thought to impact team outcomes.

More specifically, several authors including Orsburn and coworkers (1990), Hackman (1990), Varney (1989), and Larson and LaFasto (1989) have suggested positive and negative team member behaviors. An integrative

Table 4. Functional and Dysfunctional Team Member Behaviors

Activity	Functional Behaviors	Dysfunctional Behaviors
	Communicating:	
Information sharing.	Share information.	Hoard information.
Communicating.	Open communication.	Guarded communication.
Disagreeing.	Share true feelings.	Withhold feelings.
Giving feedback.	Give constructive FB.	Give person centered FB.
Listening.	Individuals listen.	Individuals interrupt.
Seeking and using feedback.	Seek constructive FB.	Ignore feedback.
	Working with Other Team Members:	
Working together.	Cooperating to attain goals, support others.	Competing (self-advancement).
Initiating change.	Change/Improve processes.	Resist changes/improvements.
Interpersonal relations.	Support others.	Create tension, hostility.
Conflict management.	Resolve conflicts.	Highlight/ignore conflicts.
Role clarity.	Ask/negotiate about others' roles.	Don't ask/assume.
Individual development.	Seek knowledge/training.	Resist knowledge/training.
Meetings.	Accomplish goals.	Waste time, stray off agenda.
Team involvement.	All participate, involved.	Few involved.
Team support.	Members give/get help.	Members do not help others or seek help when they need it.
	Making Decisions and Taking Action:	
Decision making.	Cooperative, informed decisions.	Arbitrary, selfish decisions.
Problem solving.	Use PS techniques.	Resist PS techniques.
Planning.	Individuials involved/contribute.	Individuals check-out.
Implementing plans.	Individuals take responsibility.	Individuals ignore and blame.

summary of these functional and dysfunctional intra-team behaviors, organized according to team activities, is presented in Table 4.

In terms of quantitative research on team member behaviors in the SDWT environment, few studies have been conducted. In fact, the issue of employee behavior in the SDWT environment, while seeming to be a key element underlying the "increased productivity assumption" of teams, has been largely ignored in the SDWT investigations conducted to date. It seems that many researchers have assumed a behavioral linkage between increased motivation/ satisfaction and improved performance (cf. Wall et al., 1986). As mentioned previously, some investigations shed light on the relationship between team members' behaviors and team outcomes.

Researchers investigating team processes have generally focused on one or more of three team processes including (a) communication (Glickman et al.,

1987; O'Reilly & Roberts, 1977; Siegel & Federman, 1973), (b) cohesion (Dailey, 1980; Gladstein, 1984), and (c) coordination (Dailey, 1980; Glickman et al., 1987). Following the line of research established by these authors, Brannick, Roach, and Salas (1993) conducted an investigation of the convergent and discriminant validity of measures of critical aspects of team processes that contribute to team outcomes. Although the primary focus of this investigation involved issues of process measurement and construct validity, information was presented regarding the relationships between team processes (scored as frequency of behaviors) and team outcomes.

More specifically, the interactions between 52 two-person teams flying simulated F-16 aircraft missions were analyzed for five team processes including giving suggestions, accepting suggestions, cooperation, coordination, and team spirit. As mentioned previously, these processes were constituted by the frequency of team members' behaviors in these areas. Significant correlations were found between the behaviors involving giving suggestions, accepting suggestions, cooperation, and coordination and two team outcomes including (a) time required to shoot down enemy MIG fighter planes, and (b) the number of radar locks by the MIG on the F-16. The results of this investigation support the notion that team members' behaviors do influence objectively measured team outcomes.

Based on the previously cited qualitative and quantitative studies, it seems that team members' behaviors do impact team outcomes. Also, it seems reasonable that the system of SDWTs would affect the behavior of employees placed in them. Again, these assertions are consistent with the relationships specified in the Self-Directed Work Team Leadership Model. A study of SDWTs in a European manufacturing setting further investigated these proposed relationships.

Wall and coworkers (1986) examined the effects of autonomous work groups on employees' attitudes and behaviors. Employing a quasi-experimental approach involving four conditions and three measurement occasions, Wall and coworkers conducted their investigation within two locations of a large, non-unionized, British manufacturer of confectionery. The primary aim of their study was to examine the effects of SDWTs on employees' attitudes, behaviors, work motivation, job satisfaction, group performance, organizational commitment, mental health, and turnover rates. In terms of findings, they reported positive autonomous work group effects on perceived group autonomy and job satisfaction but no clear effect on internal work motivation, organizational commitment, mental health, and extrinsic job satisfaction.

With regard to group performance, the SDWTs produced at levels below target for almost two years, however, they eventually stabilized at a level equal to the control factories. Because the SDWTs managed themselves, the organization achieved reduced supervisory expenses. However, turnover rates were found to be higher for the SDWTs. This surprising and somewhat contradictory finding was attributed to lower unemployment in the region with SDWTs (e.g., it was easy to leave and find another job), and increased disciplinary action by supervisors. Interestingly, this latter reason was explained as occurring due to a host of organizational factor variations including (a) increased time demands on fewer supervisors, (b) organizational pressure to get the Greenfield site up and running, (c) an over-reliance by supervisors on the company's disciplinary procedures, and (d) team members' reluctance to sanction other team members who broke team norms.

Wall and coworkers (1986) also discovered that SDWTs directly and indirectly affected team leaders through team members' behavior. More specifically, they concluded that Greenfield site managers experienced (a) high levels of stress, (b) interpersonal and interfunctional conflict, (c) pressure for production output, (d) difficulties involved in communicating, intervening, disciplining, and providing the resources and conditions necessary for team members to work effectively and efficiently. In fact, one of the conclusions reached by Wall and coworkers was that "... clearly there were costs in terms of personal stress arising from the difficulties involved in managing and maintaining the system" (p. 298). In this sense, then, team member behavior can be viewed as influencing leader behavior.

Summary of Research on Team Member Behavior

Based on the qualitative and quantitative research available regarding employee behavior in the SDWT environment, several conclusions can be drawn. First, it seems that SDWT systems require certain cooperative/ collaborative "teaming" behaviors which may or may not be required as frequently in non-SDWT environments. Comparisons of the behavioral requirements of the same job performed in team and non-team environments would highlight different behavioral requirements, if such differences exist. This question represents a potentially important avenue for future research.

Second, qualitative and quantitative evidence regarding team member behavior in the SDWT environment seems to suggest that certain functional behaviors lead to improved team outcomes and that certain dysfunctional behaviors lead to poorer team outcomes. Similarly, researchers including Brannick and coworkers (1993) have demonstrated the relationships between team member behavior and team performance, however, empirical studies replicating these findings in an SDWT setting have not been published. The results of such studies would either confirm or refute the findings of the qualitative investigations. Certainly, the team process (behavior) clusters of giving suggestions, accepting suggestions, cooperating, coordinating, and fostering team spirit (Brannick et al., 1993; Dailey, 1980; Gladstein, 1984; Glickman et al., 1987; O'Reilly & Roberts, 1977; Siegel & Federman, 1973) represent useful constructs for measurement of team processes.

Third, little quantitatively-derived information is available regarding the influence of organizational factors on team member behaviors. While many theorists including Fisher (1993), Funk (1992), Marchington and coworkers (1994), Varney (1989), Larson and LaFasto (1989), and Sweeny and Allen (1988) have suggested that a host of organizational factors impact employee behavior in the SDWT environment, no quantitative investigation of this linkage has been published. Given the impact that organizational factors are thought to have on team member behaviors, such research would reveal the extent to which these factors determine team members' behaviors in the SDWT environment.

Finally, the relationship between leader behavior and team member behavior in the context of an SDWT has not been fully investigated. While several theorists (Fisher, 1993; Hackman, 1990; Larson & LaFasto, 1989) have stated that leader behavior has a significant impact on employee behavior in the SDWT environment, little research confirming or refuting these assertions has been conducted. Such research is critically important to understanding exactly which leader behaviors elicit team member behaviors leading to increased or decreased team outcomes. Also, little is known about how team member behaviors influence leader behavior, however, this relationship seems important (cf. Wall et al., 1986). Clearly, many questions remain about the overall relationships between team member behavior, leader behavior, organizational factors, and team outcomes.

TEAM OUTCOMES

Team outcomes may be conceptualized as the results of a team's effort toward achieving some goal or set of goals. For example, the goal (i.e., desired outcome) of NASA's Apollo Moon Project was to place a man on the moon by the end of the 1960s (Larson & LaFasto, 1989), and the team accomplished that goal. The members of this NASA team (i.e., the scientists, engineers, astronauts, and others) presumably behaved in certain ways to accomplish such team processes as giving suggestions, accepting suggestions, cooperating, coordinating, and fostering team spirit in order to attain their desired outcome/goal. It is at this point of the review, then, that attention is turned to the construct of Team Outcomes.

In addition to or instead of goal accomplishment, other measures can reveal the "effectiveness" of teams. Indeed, indices of effectiveness of a team's processes may sometimes be used for goal achievement. We elaborate on this point in the next section. Accordingly, this portion of the paper is divided into (a) a section containing information about such indicators of team processes, and (b) a section presenting investigations of SDWTs which involved actual measurement of team outcomes in field settings.

Indicators of Team Processes

A common point of confusion among lay people discussing SDWTs is the interchangeability of the terms team process and team outcomes, however, they, in fact, represent related yet substantially different constructs and should not be used interchangeably. For example, a commonly used survey of team effectiveness contains questions regarding team activities such as "mission, planning, and goal setting," "roles," "operating processes," "interpersonal relationships," and "intergroup relations" (Organization Design and Development, Inc., 1992). These effectiveness scales, in fact, seem to be more reflective of organizational factors and team processes (i.e., the context in which a team operates and what a team does in pursuit of its goal) than team outcomes (i.e., whether or not the goal is attained).

Varney (1989) has suggested that team functioning in such areas as planning and organizing, problem definition and solution, control systems, and follow-up activities can help diagnose causes of team outcome problems. Within this section, then, it seems important to clearly delineate the difference between team processes and team outcomes. Team processes (e.g., planning and organizing, follow-up) represent tactical, behavioral steps underlying a strategy for attaining desired team outcomes (i.e., goal achievement).

Also, it is important to note that these tactical team processes are in many cases constituted by team members' behavior. As such, the indicators of team processes covered ought to be thought of as aggregates of members' behavior and as reflections of the team's functioning. More specifically, team members' behaviors also constitute such process dimensions as giving suggestions, accepting suggestions, cooperating, coordinating, and fostering team spirit (Brannick et al., 1993).

As stated earlier, indicators of team outcomes rely heavily on team processes. Varney (1989) suggests that four team processes are key indicators of how effective a team will be in attaining its goal. These key indicators and their theorized relationship to team outcomes appear in Table 5.

As mentioned previously, a variety of survey instruments designed to assess the effectiveness of team processes such as those suggested by Varney (1989) are available through the popular teams literature and a variety of consulting firms. Information regarding the reliability and validity of such instruments is generally not available, however, their usefulness in stimulating discussion among team members and leaders about team functioning seems clear (R. Melecci, personal communication, February 17, 1995).

Measuring SDWT Outcomes

It should first be noted that measuring team outcomes and attributing these team achievements solely to the processes and efforts of the team presents a

Table 5.   Key Indicators of Team Effectiveness

1. Planning and organizing: How well does the planning and organizing of the team prepare it to accomplish its tasks and goal(s).
2. Problem definition and solution: How well does the team define and solve the problems that it faces.
3. Control: How effective are the control systems the team establishes to ensure that results are achieved as planned.
4. Follow-up: How well does the team follow-up and/or take corrective action when needed.

Note: Adapted from Varney (1989).

very difficult measurement challenge. In fact, almost every field investigator of SDWTs who attempts to measure team outcomes readily acknowledges the host of alternative explanations for observed team outcomes. For example, Trist and coworkers (1977) carefully collected team outcome data including absenteeism, productivity, and supply costs; yet, these investigators at times questioned the true influence of the SDWT concept on team outcomes based on a host of threats to their experiment's internal validity (Cook et al., 1990; Crano & Brewer, 1986). Such problems are generally inherent in field research methodologies and the published investigations of SDWT outcomes should be viewed with such limitations in mind.

Quantitative studies reporting measures of SDWT outcomes have included decreased absenteeism and turnover rates (Beekun, 1989; Poza & Markus, 1980; Trist et al., 1977; Walton, 1977), fewer accidents and increased productivity (Beekun, 1989; Cohen & Ledford, 1994; Goodman, 1979; Poza & Markus, 1980; Trist et al., 1977), positive ratings of team and/or leader effectiveness (Applebaum & Batt, 1994; Manz & Sims, 1987; Poza & Markus, 1980; Wall et al., 1986), and decreased production costs (Wall et al., 1986; Poza & Markus, 1980). While generally not stated in these studies, one might reason that the teams investigated engaged in behaviors and processes identified in the previous discussions as important to effective team functioning. A final study involving the use of SDWTs to accomplish organizational objectives highlights the measurement of team outcomes.

Walton (1977), using a naturalistic observation strategy (Crano & Brewer, 1986), documented the start-up and stabilization of General Foods Gaines dry dog food plant in Topeka, Kansas, which was staffed by SDWTs from its inception. With regard to the teams' performance and overall plant performance, several measures of team outcomes (operating goals) were gathered. For example, while standard industrial engineering principles suggested a work force of 110 employees to staff the plant, by adopting the SDWT approach, General Foods was able to successfully start and run the plant with six teams comprised of six team leaders (one "external" leader per team) and 63 team members. Also, Walton reported that the plant operated for 44 months, from start-up, without a lost time accident, registered absenteeism rates from 0.8% to 1.4% between 1971 and 1974, and recorded a relatively low turnover rate of 10% per year. Walton attributed these outcomes to the work restructuring approaches, however, he did not offer more specific explanation(s) such as team leader behavior, organizational factors, team member behavior, or the potentially reinforcing effects of positive performance feedback for the results attained by this plant.

It is also interesting to note that Walton reported that after three years, "... a number of indices of the positive work culture had declined ... not a steep decline—rather a moderate erosion" (p. 429). Walton concluded that the slippage in indices such as openness, candor, identification with plant management, and helping among team members was attributable to (a) the departure of three of the original six team leaders and their subsequent replacement by team leaders whose personal styles varied widely, (b) the start-up of a neighboring canned dog food plant using traditional work structures (i.e., not teams), and (c) a lack of significant new challenges for the dry dog food plant to handle. Based on these findings, it would seem that the SDWT approach needs ongoing maintenance and management continuity in order to remain both viable and productive. Also, these conclusions lend additional support for the assertion that leader behavior and organizational factors can and often do impact SDWT processes and outcomes.

Summary of Team Outcomes Research

Based on the qualitative and quantitative research discussed in the previous sections, several conclusions regarding the issue of team outcomes seem apparent. First, there is substantial qualitative and somewhat more tentative quantitative evidence that SDWTs yield positive outcomes including improved productivity, increased team member satisfaction, decreased accidents, and so forth. Second, the exact reason(s) why SDWTs yield such benefits remains unclear. Third, the benefits associated with the use of SDWTs may erode over time. These and other apparent research issues are addressed in the final section.

EVALUATION OF OUR MODEL
AND DIRECTIONS FOR FUTURE RESEARCH

The research presented throughout this paper clearly demonstrates that SDWTs represent a cogent and increasingly popular form of organizing employees to accomplish work. It also seems clear that leader behavior, organizational factors, and team member behavior each play a role in determining the outcomes a SDWT achieves. To this end, the model proposed in this paper offers heuristic value. Certain shortcomings, however, are evident as well.

In terms of heuristic value, the proposed model offers managers and organizations a systemic view of the dynamic mix of intra-organizational factors which seem to influence SDWT outcomes. While the individual relationships between the variables included in the model have been qualitatively and quantitatively investigated by several authors, the value of integrating these findings in a holistic view of SDWT functioning seems apparent. It is in this sense, then, that the authors of this paper acknowledge that the individual relationships specified in the proposed model are not new, however, their representation as a system of factors responsible for team outcomes may represent a step toward clearer organization of our understanding of SDWT functioning.

When one considers this systemic view in relation to studies conducted to date, a number of shortcomings in our model become apparent. First, it remains unclear exactly what roles leader behavior, organizational factors, and team member behavior play in an SDWT's outcomes. More specifically, quantitative evidence supporting and specifying the exact nature of the causal relationships suggested in the model is not available as yet in the published literature. Second, while the model seeks to establish a systemic view of the intra-organizational factors influencing team outcomes, factors external to organizations also clearly influence team outcomes. For example, external competition, national and global events, and shifting consumer demands can impact organizational factors, leader behavior, team member behavior, and team outcomes. It is readily acknowledged that such extra-organizational factors can impact SDWT outcomes, however, their inclusion in the model proposed in this paper has been withheld until our understanding of the intra-organizational determinants of SDWT outcomes is more fully developed. When one considers the influence and likely relationships that exist between these intra-organizational variables and SDWT outcomes, several important research questions become apparent.

Leader Behavior

First, based on the leader behavior research reviewed in this paper, it seems reasonable to assume that leader behavior affects organizational factors and team member behavior, however, the precise nature of these relationships remains largely unknown. It seems reasonable to assume, for instance, that leaders who (a) work to influence organizational factors to facilitate team processes (e.g., they acquire the resources the team needs to do their job), and (b) behave in ways that encourage team members to exercise control over their own activities create situations in which SDWTs succeed. Similarly, it seems reasonable to assume that leaders who (a) do not work to influence organizational factors to facilitate team processes (e.g., they ignore team requests for resources the team needs to do their job), and (b) behave in ways that are inconsistent with team members exercising control over their own activities create situations in which SDWTs have difficulty achieving desired outcomes. With regard to leader behavior, future SDWT research ought to (a) refine and/or confirm the precise form of SDWT leader behaviors suggested in the available literature, and (b) establish quantitatively the relationship between leader behavior, team member behavior, and team outcomes.

Organizational Factors

The influence of organizational factors on SDWT systems is not well understood. Available research suggests that organizational factors including team resources, team size, physical surroundings, team goals, organizational norms, organizational reward systems, intra-organizational trust, performance feedback, and cooperation and support from other groups and teams affect leader behavior, team member behavior, and ultimately team outcomes. It seems reasonable to assume, for instance, that team leaders and SDWT members functioning in an organization characterized by sufficient resources, clear team goals, appropriate reward systems, and high levels of intra-organizational trust would stand a greater chance of displaying positive and functional behaviors and ultimately achieving desired team outcomes. Similarly, it seems reasonable to assume that team leaders and SDWT members functioning in an organization characterized by insufficient resources, unclear or non-existent team goals, inappropriate reward systems, and low levels of intra-organizational trust would stand a lesser chance of displaying positive and functional behaviors and ultimately fall short of achieving desired team outcomes. With regard to organizational factors, future SDWT research ought to (a) establish a comprehensive listing of organizational factors which influence leader behavior and team member behavior, (b) determine if such factors are specific to or are generalizable across SDWT applications within and between industries and cultures, (c) determine the weight or relative impact each factor has on leader behavior and/or team member behavior, and (d) examine how organizational factors might interact with certain combinations of leader behavior and team member behavior to influence team outcomes.

Team Member Behavior

Our understanding of team members' behavior in the SDWT environment is improving, however, few studies have sought to verify the assumed relationships between team member behavior, leader behavior, and team outcomes. It seems reasonable to assume, for instance, that functional team member behaviors lead to better team outcomes and also reinforce leader behaviors aimed at encouraging team members to manage their own activities. Similarly, it seems reasonable to assume that dysfunctional team member behaviors are likely to lead to poorer team outcomes and fail to reinforce leader behaviors aimed at encouraging team members to manage their own activities. In fact, it seems likely that such dysfunctional team member behaviors might tempt or cause team leaders to retain control of team members activities, thus establishing a pattern inconsistent with the principles underlying both self-management and SDWTs. With regard to team member behavior, future SDWT research ought to (a) establish the precise form of functional and dysfunctional team member behaviors, (b) examine the relationship between such team members behaviors and objectively measured team outcomes, and (c) evaluate the utility of training programs and developmental activities aimed at improving team members' teamwork skills.

Team Outcomes

The overall utility of SDWTs remains uncertain. While some researchers have established a relationship between SDWTs and increased productivity (Beekun, 1989; Cohen & Ledford, 1994; Poza & Markus, 1980; Walton, 1977), the generalizability of these findings over an extended time period across industries, organizational cultures, and international borders remains uncertain. Unfortunately, we simply do not know if SDWTs consistently yield organizational benefits which outweigh the time and resources required for their implementation and maintenance. With regard to team outcomes, future SDWT research ought to (a) examine the effect of goal (e.g., desired outcome) difficulty and value on team member motivation and behavior, (b) establish the relationship between subjective measures of perceived team effectiveness and objective measures of team outcomes, (c) examine the effect of immediate and delayed feedback (e.g., the number of parts successfully installed by a manufacturing team vs. the long-term outcomes of a strategic planning team) on team member behavior and leader behavior, and (d) evaluate the utility of SDWT systems compared to traditional work organization approaches.

CONCLUSIONS

This paper has highlighted available and needed research regarding factors thought to influence team outcomes. Given the current SDWT popularity explosion in the United States and elsewhere, determining the answers to the questions outlined in this paper is critically important for at least three reasons.

First, an improved understanding of the factors influencing team outcomes will more clearly identify situations in which establishing SDWTs does and does not make sense. Certainly, SDWTs make a great deal of sense within appropriate socio-technical specifications, however, one wonders how much consideration is given to such specifications by the literally thousands of organizations which are converting their entire work forces to SDWTs. As stated earlier, the costs associated with improperly implementing SDWTs are unknown, however, such costs are probably staggering considering the individual and organizational resources required for such substantial work system changes.

Second, an improved understanding of the factors influencing team outcomes will lend support to the commonly held assumptions thought to underlie the current popularity of SDWTs. Also, additional quantitative investigations will help establish the precise nature of the causative relationships thought to exist between factors contributing to positive and negative team outcomes. Such evidence will be helpful in justifying the appropriateness and value of SDWTs.

Third, an improved understanding of the factors influencing team outcomes will help organizations and practitioners who design and implement SDWT systems do their jobs more successfully. Each inappropriate application of an SDWT system contributes to the concern that SDWTs are a fad destined to follow in the ranks of other widely misapplied organizational interventions. This possible outcome is almost sure to happen if social scientists fail to pursue the answers to these critically important and timely research challenges.

ACKNOWLEDGMENTS

This paper represents a portion of Dr. Nygren's doctoral dissertation. Special thanks are offered to Mike Brannick, Melanie Bullock, Jan Cannon-Bowers, Vanessa Druskat, and Tammy Nygren for their assistance in the review and preparation of this manuscript.

Correspondence concerning this chapter should be addressed to Dr. Ren Nygren, Florida Power Corporation, 3201 34th Street South, D2V, St. Petersburg, FL 33711.

REFERENCES

Applebaum, E., & Batt, R. (1994). *The new American workplace*. Ithaca, NY: ILR Press.
Badin, I.J. (1974). Some moderator influences on relationships between consideration, initiating structure, and organizational criteria. *Journal of Applied Psychology, 59*, 380-382.
Bass, B.M. (1990). *Bass & Stogdill's handbook of leadership*. New York: The Free Press.
Beekun, R.I. (1989). Assessing the effectiveness of sociotechnical interventions: Antidote or fad? *Human Relations, 47*(10), 877-897.
Brannick, M.T., Roach, R.M., & Salas, E. (1993). Understanding team performance: A multimethod study. *Human Performance, 6*, 287-308.
Bray, D.W., Campbell, R.J., & Grant, D.L. (1974). *Formative years in business: A long-term AT&T study of managerial lives*. New York: Wiley-Interscience.
Brown, T. (1994, September 5). Greatness that endures. *Industry Week,* 12-22.
Cameron, K.S., & Ulrich, D.O. (1986). Transformational leadership in colleges and universities. In J.C. Smart (Ed.), *Higher education*, Vol. 2., *Handbook of theory and research* (pp. 1-42). New York: Agathon Press.

Campbell, J.P. (1990). Modeling the performance prediction problem in industrial and organizational psychology. In M. Dunnette (Ed.), *Handbook of industrial & organizational psychology*, Vol. 1., 2nd ed. (pp. 687-726). Palo Alto, CA: Consulting Psychologists Press, Inc.

Cascio, W.F. (1993). Downsizing: What do we know? What have we learned? *Academy of Management Executive, 7*, 95-104.

Christner, C.A., & Hemphill, J.K. (1955). Leader behavior of B-29 commanders and changes in crew members' attitudes toward crew. *Sociometry, 18*, 82-87.

Cohen, S.G., & Ledford, G.E. (1994). The effectiveness of self-managing teams: A quasi-experiment. *Human Relations, 47*(1), 13-43.

Crano, W.D., & Brewer, M.B. (1986). *Principles and methods of social research.* Newton, MA: Allyn and Bacon.

Cook, T.D., Campbell, D.T., & Peracchio, L. (1990). Quasi-experimentation. In M. Dunnette (Ed.), *Handbook of industrial & organizational psychology*, Vol. 1, 2nd ed. (pp. 491-576). Palo Alto, CA: Consulting Psychologists Press, Inc.

Cummings, T., & Malloy, E. (1977). *Improving productivity and the quality of work life.* New York: Praeger.

Dailey, R.C. (1980) A path analysis of R & D team coordination and performance. *Decision Sciences, 11*, 357-369.

Druskat, V.U. (1994). Effectiveness in self-managed work teams: A literature review and competency analysis. Unpublished manuscript, Boston University.

Dumaine, B. (1994, September 5). The trouble with teams. *Fortune*, 86-92.

Fisher, K. (1993). *Leading self-directed work teams.* New York: McGraw Hill, Inc.

Fleishman, E.I. (1972). *Examiner's manual for the supervisory behavior description questionnaire.* Washington, DC: Management Research Institute.

Fleishman, E.I. (1989). *Examiner's manual for the leadership opinion questionnaire (LOQ)*, Rev. ed. Chicago: Science Research Associates.

Fleishman, E.I., & Simmons, J. (1970). Relationship between leadership patterns and effectiveness ratings among Israeli foreman. *Personnel Psychology, 23*, 169-172.

Funk, J.L. (1992). *The teamwork advantage.* Cambridge, MA: Productivity Press.

Gilbert, G.R. (1985). Building highly productive work teams through positive leadership. *Public Personnel Management, 14*, 449-454.

Gladstein, D.L. (1984). Groups in context: A model of task group effectiveness. *Administrative Science Quarterly, 29*, 499-517.

Glickman, A.S., Zimmer, S., Montero, R.C., Guerette, P.J., Campbell, W.J., Morgan, B.B., & Salas, E. (1987). *The evolution of teamwork skills: An empirical assessment with implications for training* (Tech. Rep. No. 87-016). Orlando, FL: Naval Training Systems Center.

Goodman, P.S. (1979). *Assessing organizational change: The Rushton quality of work life experiment.* New York: Wiley-Interscience.

Hackman, J.R. (1986). The psychology of self-management in organizations. In M.S. Pollack & R.O. Perloff (Eds.), *Psychology and work: Productivity, change, and employment* (pp. 89-136). Washington, DC: American Psychological Association.

Hackman, J.R. (1987). The design of work teams. In J.W. Lorsch (Ed.), *Handbook of organizational behavior.* Englewood Cliffs, NJ: Prentice-Hall.

Hackman, J.R. (1990). *Groups that work [and those that don't].* San Francisco, CA: Jossey-Bass.

Hemphill, J.K., & Coons, A.E. (1957). Development of the leader behavior description questionnaire. In R.M. Stogdill and A.E. Coons (Eds.), *Leader behavior: Its description and measurement.* Columbus, OH: Bureau of Business Research, Ohio State University.

Hirschhorn, L. (1991). *Managing in the new team environment.* New York: Addison-Wesley Publishing Company, Inc.

Howard, A., & Bray, D.W. (1988). *Managerial lives in transition: Advancing age and changing times.* New York: Guilford Press.

Howell, J.P., Bowen, D.E., Dorfurun, P.W., & Kerr, S. (1990). Substitutes for leadership: Effective alternatives to ineffective leadership. *Organizational Dynamics, 19*(1), 21-38.

Kanter, R.M. (1982). Dilemmas of managing participation. *Organizational Dynamics, 11,* 5-27.

Katz, D., & Kahn, R.L. (1952). Some recent findings in human relations research. In E. Swanson, T. Newcomb, & E. Hartley (Eds.), *Readings in social psychology.* New York: Holt, Rinehart, & Winston.

Katz, D., Maccoby, N., & Morse, N. (1950). *Productivity, supervision, and morale in an office situation.* Ann Arbor, MI: Institute for Social Research.

Katz, D., Maccoby, N., Gurin, G., & Floor, L. (1951). *Productivity, supervision, and morale among railroad workers.* Ann Arbor, MI: University of Michigan, Institute for Social Research.

Katzenbach, J.R., & Smith, D.K. (1993, March-April). The discipline of teams. *Harvard Business Review,* 111-120.

Kayser, T.A. (1994). *Building team power.* New York: Irwin.

Kolb, J.A. (1992). Leadership of creative teams. *The Journal of Creative Behavior, 26,* 1-9.

Larson, C.E., & Lafasto, F.M. (1989). *Teamwork: What must go right, what can go wrong.* Newbury Park, CA: Sage.

Lawler, E.E. (1986). *High involvement management: Participative strategies for improving organizational performance.* San Francisco: Jossey-Bass.

Levine, E.L. (1973). Problems of organizational control in microcosm: Group performance and group member satisfaction as a function of differences in control structure. *Journal of Applied Psychology, 58,* 186-196.

Likert, R. (1961). *New patterns of management.* New York: McGraw-Hill.

Likert, R. (1967). *The human organization: Its management and value.* New York: McGraw-Hill.

Lord, R.G., Foti, R.J., & DeVader, C.L. (1984). A test of leadership categorization theory: Internal structure, information processing, and leadership perceptions. *Organizational Behavior and Human Performance, 34,* 343-378.

Luthans, F., & Davis, T. (1979, summer). Behavioral self-management: The missing link in managerial effectiveness. *Organizational Dynamics,* 42-60.

Mackay, A. (1993). *Team up for excellence.* New York: Oxford University Press.

Manz, C.C. (1992). Self-leading teams: Moving beyond self-management myths. *Human Relations, 45*(11), 1119-1140.

Manz, C., & Angle, H. (1987). Can group self-management mean a loss of personal control: Triangulating a paradox. *Group & Organization Studies, 11,* 309-334.

Manz, C.C., & Sims, H.P., Jr. (1987). Leading workers to lead themselves: The external leadership of self-managing work teams. *Administrative Science Quarterly, 32,* 106-128.

Manz, C.C., & Sims, H.P., Jr. (1986). Beyond imitation: Complex behavioral and affective linkages resulting from exposure to leadership training models. *Journal of Applied Psychology, 71,* 571-578.

Manz, C.C., & Sims, H.P., Jr. (1989). *Superleadership: Leading others to lead themselves.* New York: Prentice Hall Press.

Manz, C.C., & Sims, H.P., Jr. (1991). Superleadership: Beyond the myth of heroic leadership. *Organizational Dynamics, 19,* 18-35.

Manz, C.C., Keating, D.E., & Donnellon, A. (1990, autumn,). Preparing for an organizational change to employee self-management: The managerial transition. *Organizational Dynamics,* 15-26.

Marchington, M., Wilkinson, A., Ackers, P., & Goodman, J. (1994). Understanding the meaning of participation: Views from the workplace. *Human Relations, 47*(8), 867-877.

Miles, R.H., & Petty, M.M. (1977). Leader effectiveness in small bureaucracies. *Academy of Management Journal, 20,* 238-250.

Miner, J.B., & Smith, N.R. (1982). Decline and stabilization of managerial motivation over a 20 year period. *Journal of Applied Psychology, 67*, 297-305.

Mowday, R.T., & Sutton, R.I. (1993). Organizational behavior: Linking individuals and groups to organizational contexts. *Annual Review of Psychology, 44*, 195-229.

Oaklander, H., & Fleishman, E.A. (1964). Patterns of leadership related to organizational stress in hospital settings. *Administrative Science Quarterly, 8*, 520-531.

Organization Design and Development, Inc. (1992). *Team effectiveness profile: How is your team working?* Organization Design and Development, Inc.

Orsburn, J., Moran, L., Musselwhite, E., Zenger, J., & Perrin, C. (1990). *Self-directed work teams: The new American challenge.* Homewood, IL: Business One Irwin.

O'Reilly, C.A., & Roberts, K.H. (1977). Task group structure, communication, and effectiveness in three organizations. *Journal of Applied Psychology, 62*, 674-681.

Pearce, J.A., & Ravlin, E.C. (1987). The design and activation of self-regulating work groups. *Human Relations, 40*, 751-782.

Petty, M.M., & Lee, G.K. (1975). Moderating effects of sex of supervisor and subordinate on relationships between supervisory behavior and subordinate satisfaction. *Journal of Applied Psychology, 60*, 624-628.

Poza, E., & Markus, M. (1980, winter). Success story: The team approach to work restructuring. *Organizational Dynamics*, 3-25.

Schriesheim, C.A., House, R.J., & Kerr, S. (1976). Leader initiating structure: A reconciliation of discrepant research results and some empirical tests. *Organizational Behavior and Human Performance, 15*, 297-321.

Seltzer, J., & Numerof, R.E. (1988). Supervisory leadership and subordinate burnout. *Academy of Management Journal, 31*, 439-446.

Shartle, C.A. (1950). Studies of leadership by interdisciplinary methods. In A.G. Grace (Ed.), *Leadership in American education.* Chicago: University of Chicago Press.

Siegel, A.I., & Federman, P.J. (1973). Communications content training as an ingredient in effective team performance. *Ergonomics, 16*, 403-416.

Skinner, E.W. (1969). Relationships between leadership behavior patterns and organizational-situational variables. *Personnel Psychology, 22*, 489-494.

Steiner, I.D. (1972). *Group process and productivity.* New York: Academic Press.

Stogdill, R.M. (1948). Personal factors associated with leadership: A survey of the literature. *Journal of Psychology, 25*, 35-71.

Stogdill, R.M. (1965). *Managers, employees, and organizations.* Columbus, OH: Ohio State University, Bureau of Business Research.

Stogdill, R.M., Goode, O.S., & Day, D.R. (1962). New leader behavior description subscales. *Journal of Psychology, 64*, 259-269.

Stymne, B. (1986). Industrial democracy and the worker. *International Review of Applied Psychology, 35*, 101-120.

Sundstrom, E., De Meuse, K.P., & Futrell, D. (1990). Work teams: Applications and effectiveness. *American Psychologist, 45*, 120-133.

Sweeny, P.J., & Allen, D.M. (1988). Teams which excel. In R. Katz (Ed.), *Managing professionals in innovative organizations: A collection of readings* (pp. 262-266). Cambridge, MA: Ballinger Publishing Co.

Szabo, D.M. (1981). *A relationship between job satisfaction of staff nurses with perceptions they hold of their head nurse's leadership behavior.* Unpublished masters thesis, Villanova University, Philadelphia.

Taylor, F.W. (1911). *Principles of scientific management.* New York: Harper & Brothers.

Tannenbaum, A.S. (1968). *Control in organizations.* New York: McGraw Hill.

Tannenbaum, R., & Schmidt, W. (1958). How to choose a leadership pattern. *Harvard Business Review, 36*, 95-101.

Tjosvold, D. (1984). Cooperation theory and organizations. *Human Relations, 13*(9), 743-767.
Trist, E. (1977). Collaboration in work settings: A personal perspective. *Journal of Applied Behavioral Science, 13*, 268-278.
Trist, E.L., & Bamforth, K.W. (1951). Some social and psychological consequences of the longwall method of coal-getting. *Human Relations, 4*, 3-38.
Trist, E., Susman, G., & Brown, G. (1977). An experiment in autonomous working in an American underground coal mine. *Human Relations, 30*, 201-236.
Varney, G.H. (1989). *Building productive teams*. San Francisco: Jossey-Bass Publishers.
Wall, T.D., Kemp, N.J., Jackson, P.R., & Clegg, C.W. (1986). Outcomes of autonomous work groups: A long-term field experiment. *Academy of Management Journal, 29*, 280-304.
Walton, R.E. (1977). Work innovations at Topeka: After six years. *The Journal of Applied Behavioral Science, 13*, 423-433.
Yukl, G.A. (1989). *Leadership in organizations*. Englewood Cliffs, NJ: Prentice Hall.

COMMUNAL-RATIONAL AUTHORITY AS THE BASIS FOR LEADERSHIP ON SELF-MANAGING TEAMS

James R. Barker

ABSTRACT

This paper argues that our considerations of leadership in self-managing teams must fit with the form of authority and type of control that characterizes self-managing environments. It describes the emergence of *communal-rational authority* in the team-based organization and the system of *concertive control* that this authority legitimizes. Effective team leaders in a concertive system must become skilled in facilitating three critical control functions: (a) *directing* their fellow team members' activity, (b) *monitoring* their peers for compliance with the team's directions, and (c) *eliminating* any behavioral *deviation* from the team's directions. By framing team leadership in terms that are consistent with concertive control and communal-rational authority, we can more effectively teach leaders and organize our existing knowledge about leadership on teams.

Advances in Interdisciplinary Studies
of Work Teams, Volume 3, pages 105-126.
Copyright © 1996 by JAI Press Inc.
All rights of reproduction in any form reserved.
ISBN: 0-7623-0006-X

INTRODUCTION

The last few years have witnessed a dramatic increase in the number of practitioners and scholars studying and implementing self-managing teams in a variety of different organizations. Naturally, our knowledge, both theoretical and applied, is dramatically proliferating along with this exploding interest in teamwork. A key area of interest in our study of self-management has been the character and the practice of leadership both within and outside the team.

In my study of teams, I have been fortunate to draw on the years personally spent as the "leader" of a self-managing team working for a large trucking company. The lessons learned from this experience coupled with my ongoing research into self-management and control have led to my concern with how we think about leadership in teams today. Briefly stated, I am concerned that we need to articulate our thinking about teamwork in terms of the type of authority that characterizes a self-managing environment and the control system that effectively "fits" such an environment. That is, I am concerned that we refrain from viewing "leadership" in isolation. Leadership in self-managing teams does not happen in an organizational vacuum. This leadership occurs within a particular system of control based on authority that the team members see as legitimate. And this system of control and authority indelibly shapes the character and practice of team leadership.

To be effective, leadership in a team-based environment must fit the needs of that system. That is, the leadership that occurs on teams must fit, systemically, with the *type* of control and *form* of authority that occurs in this environment. In a team-based environment, two things must occur for leadership to be effective. First, the leadership must be seen by the team members as being legitimate. Second, the leadership must be functional in that it must help the team accomplish its goals. In short, the leadership that occurs must facilitate the team's ability to make its system of control work.

My purpose, then, is to articulate how this fit works. I will describe the fundamental characteristics of control and authority in a team environment and how leadership responds to these characteristics. When we discuss control and authority in organizations, we are attempting to understand the highly complex processes of meaning creation that mark collective human interaction. If we can understand these complex processes, the processes of how we make day-to-day organizational life meaningful for ourselves, we can gain a much richer understanding of leadership and how it must occur in daily practice. Instead of bemoaning how the forces of control and authority always seem to work against us in teams, we can begin learning how to make these forces work to our advantage.

Elsewhere (Barker, 1993; Barker & Tompkins, 1994) I have argued that the term "concertive control" best characterizes the system of control that emerges in a team environment. The term "concertive" refers to the team members acting *in concert* with each other to develop a means for their own control. In this paper, I will argue that a particular form of authority, *communal-rational authority* (a term first coined in Barker & Tompkins, 1993), exists in a self-managing team environment. Communal-rational authority legitimizes the concertive control system that develops as teams mature. And team leaders have an important role to play in the development of an effective concertive control system.

For team leaders to function effectively in a concertive system that is legitimized by communal-rational authority, they must become skilled in facilitating three critical control functions: (a) directing their fellow team members' activity, (b) monitoring their peers for compliance with the team's directions, and (c) eliminating any behavioral deviance from the team's directions. These are three skills that the traditional supervisor could do relatively easily. However, because of the form of authority that legitimizes control on self-managing teams, the team leader cannot "manage" in a traditional sense. The team leader must lead a group of peers, and this leadership must be consistent with the system of control and the form of authority that develops in a self-managing environment. By framing team leadership in terms that are consistent with concertive control and communal-rational authority, we can more effectively teach leaders, facilitate the process of leadership, and organize our existing knowledge about leadership on teams.

To make these arguments, I will first explain the relationship between concertive control and communal-rational authority. I will detail how communal-rational authority draws from and builds on more familiar types of organizational authority. Next I will describe how this type of authority necessitates a special view of the three leadership skill areas previously listed. Last, I will discuss the implications that this perspective on authority and control has for assimilating our current knowledge about team leadership.

CONTROL AND AUTHORITY
IN THE TEAM-BASED ORGANIZATION

The emergence of the self-managing design has radically reshaped our thinking about the possibilities of action in the modern organization. Today we practically assume as a matter of course that the team-based organization heralds a new work design that will transcend the stultifying effects of bureaucratic authority, the core base of the modern organization, and replace it with a dynamic new design based upon an open, flexible authority structure that extends from a consensual, normative ideology, not a system of formal rules (Alvesson, 1987; Lawler, 1989; Parker, 1992).

Several organizational theorists have touched on the role of authority in the team-based organization. Normally, these theorists "touch on" authority by describing elements of how the team-based organization controls member behavior. For example, Mintzberg (1980, 1989) described the appearance of organizations designed around ideological structures, interpersonally enacted systems of norms and beliefs rather than the traditional, hierarchically-mandated systems of standards and procedures. Ideology, in this sense, refers to the interactive (an inherently persuasive) process of exerting influence by promoting or assimilating particular attitudes, values, and behavioral norms. Ideology, then, provides a means for both worker motivation and control (Morgan, 1986).

Ouchi (1980) saw the rise of "clan-like" organizations that socialized their members according to implicit ideological traditions which produce for the workers a culturally coherent "point of view." This "point of view" functions as a theory for the workers that defines what is and is not appropriate behavior at work: "A member who grasps such an essential theory can deduce from it an appropriate rule to govern any possible decision, thus producing a very elegant and complete form of control" (p. 139).

Tompkins and Cheney (1985) described "concertive" organizations in ways similar to that of Mintzberg and Ouchi. They characterized some contemporary organizations, such as the self-managing team environment, as fostering collaborative behavior by framing organizational roles and expected behaviors around traditional common value systems. Employees work in "concert" with each other as guided by the value system, which evokes powerful premises that shape day-to-day collective interaction (such as decision making on a team). The strength of these traditional value systems constrains worker behaviors in ways functional for the organization.

Concertive Control in Self-managing Teams

Control in any organization is systemic in nature. That is, an organization cannot exist without some system of controlling the behaviors of the individual members so that they act in ways functional for the organization. The classical organizational theorist, Chester Barnard, defined an organization as "a system of consciously-coordinated activities or forces of two or more people" (1968, p. 73). The preeminence Barnard gave to "consciously-coordinated activities or forces" indicates that control is the primary communication system in any organization. An organization will not exist for long unless its members are working well together to help the organization achieve its goals. If a team becomes consumed by internal conflicts and begins to miss its production goals, then the organization's system of control has been affected in a negative way, and this problem will have to be corrected.

All organizations, then, have a system of control, but not all organizations have the same type of control system. In today's organizations, we see control systems as generally falling into four broad types. Edwards (1981) originally identified the first three types of control, which I summarized in a recent study of teams:

> First is "simple control," the direct, authoritarian, and personal control of work and workers by the company's owner or hired bosses, best seen in nineteenth-century factories and in small family-owned companies today. Second is "technological control," in which control emerges from the physical technology of an organization, such as in the assembly line found in traditional manufacturing. And third and most familiar is bureaucratic control, in which control derives from the hierarchically based social relations of the organization and its concomitant sets of systemic rational-legal rules that reward compliance and punish noncompliance (Barker, 1993, p. 409).

As discussed previously, Tompkins and Cheney (1985) identified a fourth type of control, *concertive control*, which they used to describe control in today's team-based organizations. The term "concertive" best describes control in the self-managing environment, because team members must work closely in "concert" with each other to accomplish the organization's goals. In the course of doing this, the team members create a unique system of self-control that revolves around the team's own values, norms, and rules (Barker, 1993).

To create a functional (i.e., effective) system of concertive control, a self-managing team must reach consensus on a set of common values, which refers to a shared, collective sense of what is important for the team to be able to work together effectively. The team members must then shape their work behavior around these values. The term for value-based behavior such as this is norms. For example, when a self-managing team first forms, the team members will have to decide for themselves what exactly it means to be a good teammate on this team. The team members will have to negotiate among themselves a set of values for doing good work on the team: coming to work on time, learning all the job skills required on the team, participating in team decision making, and so forth.

Out of this value consensus, the team members will start to place expectations on each other to behave in ways consistent with these values. The teammates will expect each other to come to work on time, and they will take notice and probably confront their comrades who show up late. They will begin to put pressure on each other to learn all the job skills needed on the team. The team now has created a set of norms.

Norms are the behavioral component of values. When we act in a way consistent with a value, we are acting out a norm. Thus, a self-managing team has to reach consensus on a set of *values* (a shared sense of what is important for the team's success) and a set of norms (behavioral expectations drawn from the values) that *control* the behavior of the team members so that they act in accordance with the values.

To survive and thrive over time, teams have to turn these value-based norms into rules. Norms are something we "know." That is, we carry our understanding of norms in our head. We know what our values for being good team members are, and we know what we need to do to behave in accordance with those values. Let's assume that a new worker comes into an already established team. This new worker was not present when the original team members created their value consensus and norms. Plus, the team cannot afford to spend a lot of time letting this new team member gradually come to understand the complex meanings behind the team's values and norms. How will this person quickly learn how to behave on this team?

To meet this need, the team will have to tell the new team member how to behave. They will have to tell this person the "rules" for how to be a good team member. This may take the form of the team giving the new member a copy of the team's "code of conduct." Or the team leader may sit down with the new member and say, "Let me tell you how we work together on this team." Values and norms take much time and experience to learn, but a new worker can grasp the team's rules very quickly.

If norms are the behavioral component of values, then rules are the rational component. Rules are rational; they are intellectually analyzable. Whenever someone presents us with a rule, we can easily understand it and quickly shape our behavior to fit the rule. Continuing the previous example, let's continue to assume that the new worker is coming onto a team that has the value-based norm, "To be a good team member, you must come to work on time, every day." The team leader then orients the new teammate by saying, "Our work day here starts at 7:00 a.m. The team expects you to be on time everyday." The team leader has just given the new worker a rule. By understanding rules such as these, the new employee can then easily understand how to act in accordance with the team's values.

Rules are essential because of a self-managing team's need to exist over time by readily adapting to change and, especially, to turnover. Team values and norms take a long time for new members to learn. But if the team socializes new members into a set of rules, the new workers can quickly infer what the underlying values and norms are and shape their behavior accordingly.

In teams and groups we use values, norms, and rules to create a sense of shared meaning that is functional for us; it enables us to accomplish our goals on the team or group. In fact, most of the decision making and group development models presented to teams in training sessions seek to get the group members to reach value consensus, form norms, and set rules. For example, many team members have been exposed to development models such as Tuckman's (1965) famous "forming, storming, norming, and performing" sequence. When teams or groups are "forming" and "storming," they are trying to reach value consensus. When they are norming, they are creating norms. When the team reaches the performing stage, they are setting rules for themselves.

A self-managing team creates its necessary system of control through the team members acting *in concert* with each other to form value consensus, norms, and rules. This concertive system is the way that the team makes its work behavior functional, or controlled. Teams are successful to the extent that they have an effective system of concertive control. Leaders in the team environment must work to facilitate the useful development of the team's concertive system. They must ensure that concertive control works for them, not against them. But that leadership will not work unless it also fits with the form of authority that occurs in the team-based organization.

Authority in Self-managing Teams

Because of the character of a concertive control environment, workers in a team-based system will experience work and enact their job-related behaviors in terms of their own value-based norms and rules rather than from the traditional, hierarchical-based, system-of-job standards and procedures so often associated with work organizations. This means that the concertive design initiates a substantive change in the adoptive organization's formal authority structure.

Authority, in the traditional sense, refers to that which legitimately influences, governs, or determines an actor's behavior in an organization (Barnard, 1968; Simon, 1976). Most often and very familiar to us, our conceptualizations of authority in work organizations stem from Weber's (1978) model of rational-legal (or bureaucratic) rules and hierarchial directives. Workers shape their job behaviors around the rational set of procedures and standards (the bureaucracy's "rules") for productive performance as mandated by the organization's hierarchy.

The concertive, team-based organization asserts a more egalitarian form of authority. Here authority stems from the team's values and the socially constructed behavioral norms and rules it produces rather than from the most rationally efficient method of doing work or from an unquestioned managerial directive. Socializing and assimilating new members to these values, norms, and rules is more important for the team than learning the "rational" procedures and standards. Thus, the emerging concertive design changes organizational authority from the classical (and traditionally observed) rational and hierarchial (bureaucratic) model common to work organizations to a more negotiated authority model centered on values and enacted norms and rules.

Weber's Classical Forms of Authority

To gain a clearer understanding of the character of authority in the concertive, self-managing, system, I will contrast this form with Weber's (1978) classical forms of organizational authority, which constitute the foundation for how we think about authority and control today. Authority, to review, refers to what organization actors accept as a legitimate agency for governing their behaviors. Any form of authority has certain claims to legitimacy, which justifies why actors should accept the authority or see it as having the power to influence their behaviors. Leaders take on particular leadership roles based on the form of authority operating in the organization. Weber identified three forms of legitimate authority that occur in the modern organization: charismatic, traditional, and rational-legal (or bureaucratic).

Weber (1978) defined charismatic authority as the ability to influence others through exemplary or extraordinary character attributes. Weber associated charismatic authority with change, because charismatic leaders often challenge accepted "rational" rule systems and seek to establish new, radically different systems. While not all concertive organizations begin with a charismatic founder articulating a company mission, many organizations changing to self-managing teams draw on charismatic authority to justify both the change itself and the transition process to the new design.

For Weber, traditional authority rested on the "established belief in the sanctity of immemorial traditions and the legitimacy of those exercising authority under them" (1978, p. 215). Weber primarily associated this type of authority with the personal loyalty demanded of a patriarch: "Obedience is owed not to enacted rules [the rational-legal model] but to the person who occupies a position of authority by tradition ..." (1978, p. 227). In the modern organization, we would normally see elements of traditional authority in the small, family-owned business. For example, the owner's daughter or son might come to lead the business through tradition (passing the company on the next generation) rather than through that person's own leadership abilities.

Weber (1978) defined rational-legal (or bureaucratic) authority as "resting on a belief in the legality of enacted rules and the right of those elevated to authority under such rules to issue commands" (p. 215). As discussed previously, rationality means that the rules are, as Weber wrote, "intellectually analyzable" (1978, p. 244). That is, in a rational rules system, organizational actors will understand the intent and purpose of the rules, use them to make sense of their daily work experience, and develop mechanical patterns of behavior in accordance with the rules.

Thus, teams and bureaucracies have in common the need for rational rules to facilitate their existence over time. And, as I will describe at the end of this paper, this commonality is both good and bad for the concertive organization. But, bureaucracies and concertive organizations do have many key differences. For example, leaders in a bureaucracy "manage" in the conventional sense. They ensure that the workers follow the rules of the bureaucracy. Team leadership works somewhat differently from traditional management, which I will discuss following.

For Weber, rational-legal authority was the most powerful form. He argued that charismatic or traditional organizations would eventually take on bureaucratic attributes. And, because of its system of highly rational rules, the bureaucracy was best situated to survive over time. For better or for worse, the bureaucracy would become the dominant organization, a point that we are very aware of today.

The concertive organization, with its focus on self-managing teams, represents something of a hybrid form of authority. That is, authority in the concertive organization reflects elements of the classical types that Weber originally described, particularly elements of traditional and rational-legal authority. But, this form of authority is still different.

Charismatic authority does have a role to play in the concertive organization, however, this role is mainly to serve as a legitimating agent for change or dramatic action. For example, a senior level manager, or even an owner, often emerges as the charismatic champion of the change within organizations that are revitalizing themselves by implementing self-managing teams. This person, or perhaps a small group, becomes convinced that the company must make the change to teams and works almost unceasingly, relying on individual personal charisma and position, to advocate and to help bring about the change (Sheridan, 1991). Of particular importance, the charismatic champion for the change to self-managing teams probably was very involved in developing the company's mission statement, which sets in motion an essential framework of values for the team.

The championing of the new design by a senior executive and subsequent development of the company's mission statement also influences workers to accept the change and adopt its concepts. Company executives see the many popular advocates of self-managing teams as legitimate information sources and consider their claims about teams as legitimate reasons for making the change in design. Company employees then grant legitimacy to the change to teams because of the corporate champion's position and advocacy of this "new, important, and productivity enhancing" organizational design.

The model of charismatic authority that the team concept presents here is in line with Weber's classical view. Charismatic authority influences and helps bring about the design change in an organization converting to self-management. Thus, charismatic authority may serve as both a catalyst for change and a legitimizing agent for the transition to teams. Once the change to teams, or the dramatic action, is set in motion by the charismatic leader, the importance of charismatic authority diminishes. Other legitimizing agents then begin to play a more important role. In fact, Weber asserted that once charismatic authority had influenced changes in an organization and had, essentially, "run its course," the organization would tend back toward a bureaucratic rational, rule-based system of authority. I will return to this point later, but first I will examine the influence that traditional authority has on the concertive organization.

Communal Authority in the Concertive Organization

Weber's view of traditional authority as based on the power of a patriarchal figure does not readily apply to the established organization that changes to a concertive design. The connection is found, however, in the value-intensive nature of team member activity and the "traditions" set in motion by the corporate mission statement so critical to concertive designs.

Advocates of self-management strongly advise executives in organizations converting to teams to draft and articulate mission statements based on traditional values (e.g., Peters & Waterman, 1982). These mission statements present the company's values in an abstract manner (e.g., "We are a principled organization," "We are an ethical organization," etc.) so organizational members can perceive them in different ways to meet different conditions. The value statements in the mission form premises for what is and is not acceptable behavior in the organization. Organizational members will identify with these value statements and develop patterns of behavior congruent with these values (Barker, 1993). And this process will have a powerful effect on the behavior of team workers. According to Mintzberg, a strong, behavior-governing, ideology begins to emerge from this process:

> Behaviors reinforce themselves over time, and actions become infused with value [from the mission]. When those forces are strong, ideology begins to emerge in its own right (1989, p. 226).

Thus, in the concertive design, a system of values set in motion by the mission statement, rather than the patriarch, becomes the legitimate source of influence. The mission's abstract values have strong, positive connotations and call out behavioral parameters general enough to guide behavior in a number of different situations (i.e., "what *should* we do" as opposed to the rational-legal "this is *how* we should do this"). The mission statement, normally formed and presented by senior executives, focuses on values "traditionally" seen as good and positive. No one wants to be thought of as being unethical, unprincipled, or unconcerned with meeting customer needs. As Mintzberg suggested, when employees enact these values they will identify with the values and thus incorporate them into their identity. Bullis and Tompkins (1989) explained and provided empirical support for this process:

> As members identify more strongly with the organization and its values, the organization becomes as much a part of the member as the member is a part of the organization. Members then allow organizational decision premises [which come from the shared value systems presented by the mission statement] to be inculcated into them (p. 289).

The mission statement, then, essentially serves the same function as Weber's patriarch. Because of its set of traditional values, employees give the mission statement legitimacy and feel obligated and expected to act according to its tenants. Through their actions, they internalize the "traditional" authority of the mission statement. They take ownership of these corporate values and begin to develop their own sets of values to guide their collective actions on the team. The leader's role now becomes one of cultivating the teams' obligations to their values and developing their expectations of each other's behavior.

The company mission statement mobilizes a complex set of value-based worker activities. A new team, faced with learning self-management, will have to learn how to work together as a team, a process that the team leader must facilitate. They do this by reaching consensus on a set of important, *team-defined*, values. For example, assume that this new team has a company vision statement that says: "We are a self-managing organization that prizes the effective contributions of every member." The team members will have to reach consensus on what exactly constitutes "effective member contributions." They will have to decide for themselves what constitutes good teamwork on the team. They will have to reach consensus as to proper support of each other on the team, such as coming to work on time or learning all the different job skills required by the team. Thus, the team is creating a system of value-based authority that members see as a legitimate source of control.

As the team members negotiate consensus on a set of workable values, they also create a set of normative parameters that will help them put those values into action. If the team reaches consensus on the value that "for our team to be effective, we all have to come to work on time," then behavioral norms will soon follow. Team members will note whether or not their teammates are arriving at work on time and confront those workers who are violating the norm.

For example, a self-managing team has reached consensus on the value that "meeting customer needs is our top priority." On a Friday, the team discovers that an unforeseen parts shortage means that they cannot finish an important customer shipment until the next day when new parts arrive. The team leader calls everyone together for a brief meeting to determine how to deal with this problem. The team wants to meet the customer's needs and get the shipment to the customer as soon as possible. The team decides to work on Saturday to finish the shipment. The team selects one team member to coordinate with the stockroom so they can get the parts as soon as they arrive. Another team member volunteers to coordinate shipping the order on Saturday. Another team member arranges to have the production building open and the heat turned on while they are working overtime. The team draws from the influence of their value consensus to help them decide how to behave in ways functional for the organization.

In my study of teams at "ISE Communications" (Barker, 1993), I described the importance of the team members' ability to control their own behavior through agreeing on values and establishing behavioral norms:

The teams will develop behavioral norms that put their values into action in consistent patterns applicable to a variety of situations, just as team members applied their norm of working overtime to meet customer demands to a variety of situations requiring extra work. Thus the teams could turn their value consensus into social norms or rules. The teams had manifested the essential element of concertive control; their value-based interactions became a social force that controlled their actions, as seen in Larry's willingness to forego his plans in order to work overtime for the team. Authority had transferred from ISE's old supervisory system to the team's value consensus (pp. 423-424).

The power of this value-based form of authority as a legitimizing agent for normative control is so strong that workers in the self-managing environment sometimes become "possessed" by the process. They begin to view the workplace as if it were a traditional home and the team members were family members. As Soeters (1986) wrote:

The employees develop a family feeling. The integration processes eventually result in a situation where everybody speaks alike concerning the same things. This happens regardless of their region of origin or position in the organization (p. 305).

The concertive design offers a different source of traditional authority than seen in Weber's classical view. Instead of a patriarch, employees identify and grant authority to a system of values that they created and to which they hold allegiance. Their consensus on these strong and compelling values creates a feeling of family, or more aptly, *community*. Team members want to act in ways functional for their team, their organizational community. They enjoy the sense of community they feel in working together effectively as a team. This is the *communal* base for authority in the concertive system. And team leaders must cultivate this communal attribute and keep the team continually focused on their values.

The value intensive influence of communal authority allows the self-managing team to function without the direct supervision that marks bureaucratic and hierarchical organizations. The value-based communication found in a concertive system provides team members with the parameters they need to manage themselves. This is what allows the organization to accrue the benefits of self-management such as streamlining costs by eliminating supervisory positions, by increasing productivity and quality through increased employee involvement and commitment, and by eliminating bureaucratic procedures, thus speeding decision making and employee action. The team members identify strongly with their values, and this communally-based authority becomes a legitimate force for controlling their actions.

Rational Authority in the Concertive Organization

In my study of ISE (Barker, 1993), I argued that self-managing teams will develop value-based norms and then, over time, standardized rules for team behavior, such as decision making. Teams will socialize and assimilate their members into these norms and rules. Thus, the value-based norms become "rationalized"; that is, easily understandable for new members coming onto the team. These rules then function to legitimize a powerful system of control over both new and old team members alike. In the concertive organization, team members normally create this set of rational rules themselves instead of having it thrust upon them by a traditional supervisor. The team leader must assist the team with creating functional rules which work for them. On the other hand, the team leader must help the team to avoid creating unnecessary rules that will ultimately keep the team from acting quickly and effectively.

In the team design, this normative process of creating new forms of rational authority stems from the interactions of the team members over time. Team members make their own decisions, gather their own information, and take collective responsibility for their team's performance. For team members to accomplish this, they must form patterns of behaviors that they can all understand and use to help them make sense of the work environment. This is an example of the process Weick (1979) called "organizing":

> Organizing is like a grammar [controlling rules] in the sense that it is a systematic account of some rules and conventions by which sets of interlocked behaviors are assembled to form social processes that are intelligible to actors. It is also a grammar in the sense that it consists of rules for forming variables and causal linkages into meaningful structures ... that summarize the recent experience of the people who are organized (pp. 3-4).

This process means that the team will invent their own set of rational rules, based on their original value consensus and norms, for how to act in ways functional for the organization.

The example I used previously to demonstrate the influence of communal authority on the teams also shows the rational authority of these normative behaviors. When a problem arose, the team had a normative system for dealing with it; the team leader called a brief meeting, and the team decided to work overtime to meet the customer's needs. They also had behavioral patterns for ensuring that their decision worked. A team member coordinated for late shipping. Another member arranged for the building to be opened. In this situation, the team members would experience interpersonal pressure to work overtime to help ensure that the team met its collective commitment to its customer. This system of functional behaviors extends from a negotiated ideology based on the team's values and not from a set of objective bureaucratic rules.

This rational system of rules exerts influence on (or is granted authority by) team members for several reasons. First, the team members have enacted these rules from their original value consensus, as based upon the company's mission statement. The communal authority of their value consensus legitimizes how the team makes their rational rules. Second, as I have discussed, the normative rules that the teams develop are rational. They are enactable behaviors that allow the team to work on its own and still be productive. The team members see these behavioral rules as the legitimate ways of working together as a team. Third, because the team's behaviors have elements of communal and rational authority, the team can legitimately demand willful obedience to these negotiated rules as a condition of team membership. A member who does not follow these rules, such as a person who refuses to work overtime (with no acceptable excuse) in the previous example, will face increasing pressure from the team members either to behave by their rules or leave the team. For example, as one work team member at ISE told me, "Poor performers don't last." Another team worker, described to me how the team members take on leadership roles to sanction their own behavior:

> We've had occasions where we've had a person say, "I refuse to sit on the [assembly] line." And we had to remind him, "Hey, you are a part of the team and you go where you're needed and you do it" (Barker, 1993, p. 425).

Essentially, these normative behaviors create a discipline for the team members to follow. Discipline, in this sense, refers to organizing collective behavior to make it purposeful, functional, and controlled (Barker & Cheney, 1994). The patterns of normative behavior enacted by the team "disciplines" their actions so that the team functions effectively (makes its own decisions, solves its own problems, supervises its own behaviors, etc.). Again, the leader's role here is to ensure that this discipline is working for the team, not against it. To work, the team-based, concertive system needs legitimacy from both communal values and disciplined, rational behaviors. The team's rational behavior enacted from their value consensus provides the concertive control system, its essential source of *rational authority*.

As with communal values, rational rules and the authority they entail play an important role in the concertive design. Here the rules are normative behaviors negotiated by the team members within the context of the organization's ideology as opposed to bureaucratic standards mandated by the hierarchy. The team's value-based, rational rules, which the team members themselves have negotiated, create a new rationality that allows the concertive organization to function without the constraints common to more bureaucratic designs. These negotiated behavioral rules allow the team to make quick decisions, adapt to changing conditions and crises, and increase productivity. The organization streamlines its structure while workers increase their commitment to the company and its product. While the rules have changed on the surface, from bureaucratic to negotiated, the underlying authority of the rules, rationality, has not changed.

The concertive, team-based organization draws its legitimizing authority from a blend of communal values and rational rules. That is, team members develop a legitimate system of control by negotiating consensus on particular communal values and by developing a system of normative rules from these values. Team leaders must lead within the constraints of this form of legitimized authority. While this form of authority blends and builds on Weber's original forms of organizational authority, *communal-rational authority* is still different in its own right. And it brings with it a particular set of leadership requirements.

COMMUNAL-RATIONAL AUTHORITY AND THE PROBLEM OF LEADERSHIP

To briefly review, communal-rational authority is a form of authority that legitimizes the system of control common to the team-based environment. This system, concertive control, functions, as does any system, to regulate activity in the organization so that the firm can achieve its goals. Concertive control regulates team activity, and the team members accept this control because of its foundation in communal-rational authority.

Three functions characterize any system of control. These three functions allow the system to be self-regulating, to stay focused on achieving the organization's goals. Additionally, our experience with traditional forms of management make these functions very familiar to us. The clearest articulation of these characteristics of a control system comes from the work of Tompkins (1990; also Tompkins & Cheney, 1985).

The first function is *directing*. This function consists of "categories of messages such as informing, advising, suggesting, even outright ordering, or issuing a statement of purpose, objectives, or core value premises" (Tompkins, 1990, p. 228). Through direction, workers can understand what they have to do to be effective, to meet the goals of the company. In the traditional organization, managers were very adept at providing direction, but the communal-rational authority of the team requires that direction occur in a complementary manner. The team has to direct itself based on its own values and normative rules. The team leader has to facilitate this process.

The second function is *monitoring*. In systems theory, this function is the feedback or deviation-counteracting loop in any process of control (Tompkins, 1990, p. 228-229). In the traditional organization, the supervisor monitored by checking the worker to *confirm* that the worker understood the directions and to *evaluate* how well the worker had complied with the directions. If a supervisor had directed a worker to ship 10 boxes of computer parts by noon, that supervisor would confirm that the worker understood the order and then check the worker's progress at about 10:00 a.m. or so to see how well the worker was complying with the directive. But in a concertive environment, the team members themselves must monitor their own compliance with their directives. Again, the team leader must facilitate this process.

The final function is *deviation elimination*, the familiar dispensing of rewards and punishments (Tompkins, 1990, p. 229). This is the function that ensures that the control process works. In the traditional organization, the supervisor punished workers for not meeting the directions and rewarded workers for achieving work goals (remember deviation elimination does include both punishments and rewards). In the concertive system, the team members themselves must identify and eliminate their own deviations. They must discipline their own behaviors. As with the other functions, the team leader must facilitate this process.

At first look, these three necessary components of a control system seem rather harsh and more characteristic of bureaucratic management rather than team leadership. However, we should remember that these three elements are essential components of any control system. All organizations, team-based or otherwise, must have a control system that directs and monitors member behavior and that eliminates any behavioral deviance. The key difference is that the system of control does not have to become manifest in the same way in all organizations. Because of the communal-rational authority that characterizes concertive organizations, teams will direct, monitor, and eliminate deviance among their members in ways much different than those methods found in the familiar bureaucracy.

In a concertive control system, with its communal-rational authority, the team leader faces a unique challenge. The leader cannot manage the team members in the traditional sense. That style of management does not fit the form of authority that exists in the team environment. Team members who have taken ownership of strong communal values and who have created powerful normative rules will resist a leader who tries to direct, monitor, and eliminate deviation in the same way as would a traditional supervisor.

The team leader must lead. The team leader must influence, persuade, inspire, and coach other team members. The team leader must practice what Drucker (1994) called the "liberal art" of management. The team leader must cultivate a creative process on the team, rather than a stultifying system of control. Team leaders cannot accomplish these three essential functions by themselves. But these functions must still be accomplished for the team's system of concertive control to work. The team leader must find a way to ensure that the team accomplishes these functions in a manner that is *consistent* with communal-rational authority. That is one of the many responsibilities that a team leader assumes, and that responsibility holds true whether the team leader was appointed by senior management, elected by the team, or emerged through the course of team interaction.

How can a team leader persuade the team to accomplish these three functions themselves? Leaders can learn how to do this if we rethink the function of leadership in terms of the requirements of communal-rational authority. What I will offer next are some initial suggestions as to how leaders can accomplish these essential functions in a concertive control system. I will also assert that by thinking of leadership and control functions in terms of communal-rational authority, we can reorganize our current knowledge of leadership into a more useful framework.

Team Leadership and Directing

When viewed from the framework of communal-rational authority, the leader's responsibility for directing differs from the traditional managerial function of giving orders. The team can and should give itself orders based on its negotiated values and normative rules. The team leader's responsibility now becomes one of focusing and persuading. In the early stages of team development, the leader has to understand that the team needs to reach consensus on key values, and the leader should focus the team toward identifying what the team members believe to be the elements of "doing good work on the teams." In later stages, the team leader must persuade the team to adopt norms and rules for dealing with recurring decisions or persistent problems, such as how to choose between competing customer demands and to hold themselves accountable to these rules.

The essential requirement here is that the leader facilitates the team toward establishing parameters for its actions. In organizations of diverse members, we learn how to work together by creating an acceptable sense of order out of the chaos of competing goals and desires. This sense of order is a set of behavioral parameters, such as value-based norms and rules. Examples of these parameters include the norm that all team members should be at work on time, the norm that the team will always build the "Acme" order first because Acme is the company's best customer, or the norm that the team will hold a 15 minute meeting each morning.

What the leader does here is not to give orders, but to *direct* the team toward discussing and setting these parameters. When the team is discussing and setting parameters, it is, at the same time, reaching consensus on values and establishing normative rules. If the team has value consensus and a set of normative rules, they can give *themselves* good orders.

But the team leader must also face a very serious problem for the team—time management. For those of us who have worked in teams, time often becomes the biggest enemy of self-management. The hectic pace of today's work environment means that a team will always be pressed for time. Unfortunately, "doing" teamwork demands much time and energy from the team members. And today's competitive business environment does not give time freely. The leader will be pressured to assume the role of traditional manager and give orders to the team.

The team will also find it easy to get carried away with making rules rather than taking the time to think through the necessity and usefulness of the rules. For example, a team that has a rule that everyone must come to work on time may tire of dealing with a few workers who are consistently tardy and, out of frustration, develop a very rigid, Draconian rule governing tardiness, such as docking workers a day's pay for being a few minutes late. Taking this path of least resistance will only increase the number of complaints to the human resources department and ultimately degrade the team's performance.

In this situation, a team leader could help the team to see the problems associated with creating a powerfully constraining rule as a way out of a difficult situation. The leader also might facilitate the team in drawing up a corrective "contract" between the tardy workers and the team that provides a clear set of performance objectives and with an equally clear set of consequences for noncompliance. A contract such as this would address the specific situation and not force the team into creating an unnecessary and unwieldy general rule for tardiness.

When time pressures the team, the leader's skill is all the more important. The leader must keep the team focused on its values and its *useful* rules. The leader must help the team to find the time that it needs to work effectively. That is all part of the leader's responsibility to direct the team toward its goals.

Team Leadership and Monitoring

The monitoring function requires that the leader facilitate the team's ability to supervise itself. The team has to establish its own system of checks and balances as a means of monitoring its own work activity. As a start, the leader should ensure that the team members reach consensus on their values for self-monitoring and that they establish a set of norms that pertain to the evaluation of their own effectiveness.

The team leader may help establish a formula for the team to *confirm* that all the members understand the goals and directions of the team, such as having a few team members brief back the decisions made at a team meeting to the rest of the group. The team leader may facilitate a regular feedback session with senior management and the team to *evaluate* the team's performance.

When the pressures of daily business life swell, senior management will apply their own path of least resistance that short-circuits concertive control. They may direct their communication, especially in terms of monitoring, to the team leader. A senior manager may use the excuse, "I've got 10 teams to worry about. I don't have time to talk to the whole team, so I want to talk to the team leader." When this happens, the team leader tends to take on more and more responsibility, such as filling out a weekly report on customer orders shipped. Gradually, the team leader will assume more and more of the traditional supervisory role, which means that the team's leadership will not be in synch with its base of communal-rational authority.

The team leader has to resist this pressure to assume the traditional first-line supervisor role, and senior management has to be supportive. The team leader must keep the team focused on creating and implementing their own systems of monitoring (including confirming and evaluating activities). Keeping the team focused on its need to self-monitor and self-evaluate is the key to achieving this control function.

Team Leadership and Eliminating Deviation

Self-discipline is the hardest function for the team to perform. The traditional supervisor can discipline errant behavior much more easily than can a group of peers. Here, the team leader's key task is to get the team to confront the issue directly. That is, the leader has to persuade the team that they must acknowledge their need to discipline each other from time to time, and that they should reach consensus on a set of appropriate values and behavioral norms for disciplinary situations.

Again, the path of least resistance is for the team to turn over disciplinary cases to the leader or to adopt a set of Draconian rules, neither of which work over the long term. The leader's first line of action is to prepare the team to deal with disciplinary situations. The leader's second line of action is to have had some training in mediation (*not* conflict management) skills. A team leader can be very effective in playing the role of the "cooler head that prevails" in difficult disciplinary situations.

The team leader also must remember that control in a self-managing environment revolves around the team's values, norms, and rules. As discussed previously, teams can easily get carried away with creating rational rules. Diverse teams, especially, face a natural tendency to create strong systems of rational rules (Barker, 1993), and these rules can be very useful for the team. However, these rational rules make the team vulnerable to the pitfalls of any bureaucracy. The team can get bogged down by its own rules and find itself unable to easily change and adapt to new business situations.

More importantly, concertive control, with communal-rational authority as its legitimizing agency, creates a very powerful system of control. In the bureaucracy, authority rested with the organization's structure and hierarchy. Traditional authority rested with the patriarch. Charismatic authority rested with a particular person. *Communal-rational authority rests with the peer pressure of the team* (Barker, 1993). The team controls itself. The team directs, monitors, and rewards or punishes itself. The team becomes very powerful, and the leader must ensure that the team exercises this power carefully. If not, the team environment can become a very oppressive place to work. When this happens a potentially fatal deviation has occurred that must be eliminated.

The leader must be able to recognize when the team is becoming bogged down by its rules and when the team environment is becoming oppressive. The team leader must be able to take some type of corrective action. As Hackman and Walton (1986) have suggested, the team periodically needs to review its norms and rules and evaluate how well they are working for the team. Leaders must facilitate this process, even at the expense of short-term productivity. Also, the leader must be able to turn to senior management for help if the team's system of control appears to be getting out of hand.

The team leader should not forget that eliminating deviation also means dispensing rewards. The leader should focus the team toward establishing its own system of recognizing outstanding behavior, even if senior management does not follow suit. The team needs a systemic mechanism for patting itself on the back.

CONCLUSIONS

In this paper, I have argued that we must consider the leadership of self-managing teams in terms of the form of authority and system of control that "fits" a team-based environment. Authority in the team-based organization rests with the values and rational rules of the team members themselves. Control in the team environment is concertive in nature. That is, a system of control develops from the team members working in concert to control themselves in terms of communal-rational authority. This is a different form of authority and a different system of control than exists in other types of organizations. And this form of authority and system of control have their own requirements for leadership.

What I have done here is to illustrate communal-rational authority and to demonstrate its importance in determining appropriate leader actions. I have also described how control works as a system with its functions of directing, monitoring, and eliminating deviation and how this system of control also requires appropriate leader actions in a team environment. Finally, I have identified some of the problems that leaders on teams face and offered some initial suggestions for how leaders can act in ways consistent with communal-rational authority and concertive control.

I also offer this depiction of concertive control requirements as a useful framework for organizing our current knowledge about team leadership. For example, Hackman's (1986) concepts of "clear, engaging direction" (p. 101) and monitoring and action-taking (pp. 120-123) as essential elements of team leadership readily complement the framework I have discussed here. Much of our other practical and theory-based knowledge about leading teams also complements this description of concertive control and communal-rational authority in team-based organizations (e.g., Larson & LaFasto, 1989; Manz & Sims, 1987, etc.).

As another example, many of the authors in this volume presented behavioral strategies or principles for leading self-managing teams. These strategies, such as Nygren and Levine's model of key leadership variables, Cox and Sims' model of team citizenship, and Baveja and Porter's depiction of the Growth-oriented Workplace, are readily compatible with the three components of a concertive control system that I explained previously. Seers argues in this volume that effective leadership results from good team chemistry. I have maintained here that a good chemistry for control in teams requires directing, monitoring, and deviation elimination behaviors that fit the needs of communal-rational authority.

In this paper, then, I have offered a new perspective on control and authority in team-based organizations that the reader can use to categorize and integrate many of the strategies for effective leadership discussed by the other authors in this volume. I encourage other writers studying teams to consider this model as an anchor for their suggestions about leadership in the self-managing organization.

Last, we should always be cautious in our thinking about the mixture of authority, control, and leadership in the team-based organization. The concertive organization still draws much of its authority from the rational rules, and as such, will always be closely related to the familiar bureaucracy in terms of control and authority. And, the concertive organization will always be pressured by time to become more and more bureaucratic, a point Mintzberg (1989) also described: "In effect, time blunts ideology, converting enthusiasm into obligation, traditions into dogmas, norms into rules. Administration thereby replaces ideology at the center of power" (pp. 287-288).

The concertive organization faces a constant tension that pulls it toward a purer type of bureaucratic control, a system of control that the self-managing organization was designed to transcend. But, dealing with that tension is part of the "art" of leadership in the team-based firm.

ACKNOWLEDGMENT

I wish to thank Linda R. Macdonald her assistance in developing this paper.

REFERENCES

Alvesson, M. (1987). Organizations, culture, and ideology. *International Studies of Management and Organization, 17*, 4-18.
Barker, J.R. (1993). Tightening the iron cage: Concertive control in self-managing teams. *Administrative Science Quarterly, 38*, 408-437.
Barker, J.R., & Cheney, G. (1994). The concept and the practices of discipline in contemporary organizational life. *Communication Monographs, 61*, 19-43.

Barker, J.R., & Tompkins, P.K. (1993, November). Organizations, Teams, Control, and Identification. Paper presented at the annual meeting of the Speech Communication Association, Miami.

Barker, J.R., & Tompkins, P.K. (1994). Identification in the self-managing organization: Characteristics of target and tenure. *Human Communication Research, 21*, 247-264.

Barnard, C.I. (1968). *The functions of the executive*. Cambridge, MA: Harvard University Press.

Bullis, C.A., & Tompkins, P.K. (1989). The forest ranger revisited: A study of control practices and identification. *Communication Monographs, 56*, 287-306.

Drucker, P.F. (1994, November). The age of social transformation. *Atlantic Monthly, 247*(5), 53-80.

Edwards, R. (1981). The social relations of production at the point of production. In M. Seyferrell & M. Aiken (Eds.), *Complex organizations: Critical perspectives*. Glenview, IL: Scott Foresman.

Hackman, R.J. (1986). The psychology of self-management in organizations. In M.S. Pallak & R.O. Perloff (Eds.), *Psychology and work: Productivity, change, and employment* (pp. 89-136). Washington, DC: American Psychological Association.

Hackman, R.J., & Walton, R.E. (1986). Leading groups in organizations. In P.S. Goodman and Associates (Eds.), *Designing effective work groups* (pp. 72-119). San Francisco: Jossey-Bass.

Larson, C.E., & LaFasto, F.M.J. (1989). *Teamwork: What must go right/what can go wrong*. Newbury Park: Sage.

Lawler, E.E. (1989, March). Substitutes for hierarchy. *Incentive*, 39-45.

Manz, C.C., & Sims, H.P., Jr. (1987). Leading workers to lead themselves: The external leadership of self-managing work teams. *Administrative Science Quarterly, 32*, 106-128.

Mintzberg, H. (1980). Structure in 5's: A synthesis of the research on organizational design. *Management Science, 26*, 322-341.

Mintzberg, H. (1989). *Mintzberg on management: Inside our strange world of organizations*. New York: The Free Press.

Morgan, G. (1987). *Images of organization*. Newbury Park, CA: Sage.

Ouchi, W.G. (1980). Markets, bureaucracies, and clans. *Administrative Science Quarterly, 25*, 129-141.

Parker, M. (1992). Post-modern organizations or postmodern organization theory? *Organization Studies, 13*, 1-17.

Peters, T.J., & Waterman, R.H., Jr. (1982). *In search of excellence: Lessons from America's best-run companies*. New York: Harper & Row.

Sheridan, J.H. (1991, February). A philosophy for commitment. *Industry Week*, 11-13.

Simon, H.A. (1976). *Administrative behavior: A study of decision-making processes in administrative organizations*, 3rd ed. New York: The Free Press.

Soeters, J.L. (1986). Excellent companies as social movements. *Journal of Management Studies, 23*, 299-312.

Tompkins, P.K. (1990). On risk communication as interorganizational control: The case of the Aviation Safety Reporting System. In A. Kirby (Ed.), *Nothing to fear: Risks and hazards in American Society* (pp. 203-239). Tucson, AZ: University of Arizona Press.

Tompkins, P.K., and Cheney, G. (1985). Communication and unobtrusive control in contemporary organizations. In R.D. McPhee & P.K. Tompkins (Eds.), *Organizational communication: Traditional themes and new directions* (pp. 179-210). Newbury Park, CA: Sage.

Tuckman, B.W. (1965). Developmental sequences in small groups. *Psychological Bulletin, 63*, 384-399.

Weber, M. (1978). *Economy and society*, G. Roth & C. Wittich (Trans. and Eds.). Los Angeles: University of California.

Weick, K. (1979). *The social psychology of organizing*. Reading, MA: Addison-Wesley.

CREATING AN ENVIRONMENT FOR PERSONAL GROWTH:
THE CHALLENGE OF LEADING TEAMS

Alok Baveja and Gayle Porter

ABSTRACT

Along with basic teaming skills, personal development is an important factor in creating a high functioning work force. More than 30 years ago, Carl Rogers offered guidelines for relationships, leading to an environment in which individual growth will occur. Applying this to team-structured organizations, we refer to such an environment as a *GRowth-Oriented Workplace* ("GROW"). To examine this framework we specify necessary leader characteristics, how this environment leads to more focused employee energies, evidence of employee growth suggested by Total Quality Management (TQM) principles, and general strategies for developing leaders who will create this environment.

Advances in Interdisciplinary Studies
of Work Teams, Volume 3, pages 127-143.
Copyright © 1996 by JAI Press Inc.
All rights of reproduction in any form reserved.
ISBN: 0-7623-0006-X

Corporations underestimate the shift in mindset and behavioral skills that team leaders need.
—David Nadler as quoted by Caminiti, 1995, p. 93

The skills you'll need—the patience to share information, the trust to let others make decisions, and the ability to let go of power—do not develop overnight.
—Caminiti, 1995, p. 94

... in my early professional years I was asking the question, How can I ... change this person? Now I would phrase the question in this way: How can I provide a relationship which this person may use for his own personal growth?
—Rogers, 1961, p. 32

Work teams are producing a revolution in many organizations across the country by increasing productivity. Phrases such as "let go of power and control" and "employee empowerment" have become a reality. Learning and growth, for individuals and the organization, have become a primary focus, instead of the supplemental, benevolent efforts of the past. Supervisors are now evolving into team leaders and coaches—shepherds rather than sheepherders (Fisher, 1993). The traditional system, "if you coerce people long enough they will yield," is being replaced with, "if you nurture people long enough, they will reveal."

Increasingly, to be competitive, organizations must reduce costs while achieving greater quality in their products and services. Quality output requires a quality work force, which requires quality leadership. To achieve more with less, we often refer to the synergy that occurs with good team processes, when the "whole" becomes greater than the sum of the parts. When there is need for improved outcomes, further improving the team process, for greater synergy, is one potential. Increasing the value of each of the parts, the individual team members, will also add to the total. Perhaps, in all the attention to teaming, we have somewhat lost sight of the fact that there is still a place for individual development.

"Teams are not antithetical to individual performance" (Katzenback & Smith, 1993, p. 14). As Smith and Berg (1987) point out, the group is enhanced, not weakened, as individuality is legitimated. If the leaders and team members become the best they can be—quality individuals—the initiatives targeting better output through use of teams will benefit from this resource. We must develop leaders who will provide the conditions for personal growth among team members.

The opening quotations pose a problem and one solution. The irony is seen in the date sequence. The problem is expressed in the 1990s; the solution dates back to the 1960s. Carl Rogers' 1961 book, *On Becoming a Person*,[1] is now considered a classic work on the human potential for growth and creativity.

In this book, Rogers described how certain characteristics in an organization will result in members who are more self-responsible, more creative, more cooperative, and better able to adapt to new problem situations. We propose that the current leadership challenge is to provide the proper environment for such personal development to occur among all workers. We refer to this environment as a *G*Rowth-*O*riented *W*orkplace ("GROW").

What we offer here is an application of Rogers' work to the topic of team leadership. In this paper we will (1) identify the traits which are essential corner stones for "GROW," (2) explain the impact of an environment for growth through examples from physical systems, (3) relate effects of "GROW" to popular TQM principles, and (4) offer development alternatives to foster the necessary leader characteristics.

A FORMULA FOR GROWTH-ORIENTED LEADER/MEMBER RELATIONSHIPS

Rogers summarized the desired leadership characteristics and resulting team member growth in the following manner:

"If I can create a relationship characterized on my part:

- by a genuineness and transparency, in which I am my real feelings;
- by a warm acceptance of and prizing of the other person as a separate individual;
- by a sensitive ability to see his world and himself as he sees them;

Then the other individual in the relationship:

- will experience and understand aspects of himself which previously he has repressed;
- will find himself becoming better integrated, more able to function effectively;
- will become more similar to the person he would like to be;
- will be more self-directing and self-confident;
- will become more of a person, more unique and more self-expressive;
- will be more understanding, more accepting of others;
- will be able to cope with the problems of life more adequately and more comfortably" (Rogers, 1961, pp. 37-38).

There is little need to adapt or translate Rogers' growth outcomes, to see their value in today's organizations and, particularly, in team-based structures. Work designs for employee involvement are closely linked to employee self-

G	R	U		E_g
0	0	1		0
0	1	0		0
0	1	1		0
1	0	0		0
1	0	1		0
1	1	0		0
0	0	0		0
1	1	1		1

Figure 1. Truth Table—Environment for Growth (E_g) is a Function of Genuineness (G), Positive Regard (R), and Empathic Understanding (U)

management and the elimination of expensive control process (e.g., Lawler, 1992). In current competitive business conditions, organizations need employees who are secure in themselves to cope with rapidly changing conditions. They require employees who are open and accepting of others in order to work cooperatively in problem solving and decision making.

We refer to the three described leader characteristics as genuineness, positive regard, and empathic understanding. Genuineness implies an awareness of one's own feelings, and a willingness to *be* and to express, via words and behavior, the various emotions and attitudes that exist in oneself. Rogers argues that this genuineness provides a reality to any relationship. It is extremely important to be *real*, even in the case when the feelings are not seemingly conducive to a good relationship.

Positive regard refers to an acceptance based on a consideration for the other person as someone of unconditional self-worth. This acceptance implies a respect and liking for the other individual as a separate person, who is free to feel (whether positive or negative) in his or her own way. Such a positive regard enables the other person to feel a safety in the relationship, thereby stimulating growth.

Finally, any form of acceptance, to be meaningful, has to be accompanied by a continuing desire to empathize with another individual's feelings and worldviews. It is only when an untiring effort is made to see another's actions and thoughts from his or her point of view that the individual then starts to explore his or her *own* feelings. In this freedom of exploration lies the basis of growth for the individual.

Each of these elements in a leader contributes to providing an environment for growth. Further, we believe that all three must be present at some identifiable level. That is, evidence of all three traits creates a sufficient condition for an environment for growth, but none can be missing entirely. If a leader is genuine but does not have positive regard for another individual, that leader may communicate feelings in a way that will make others feel less safe and secure. This will be counter-productive to the process of the individual's growth. On the other hand, with a leader who is accepting of others' feelings but not genuine, the individual is likely to remain cautious and not comprehend the empathy that exists.

This idea can be summarized using the concept of a truth table where the environment for growth (E_g) is a function of genuineness (G), positive regard (R), and empathic understanding (U). In the truth table, shown as Figure 1, a zero represents the absence of the trait and a one represents its presence. The figure displays, in a mathematical manner, the mental model we have discussed. For example, the second row demonstrates the condition in which the leader has positive regard but no genuineness and no empathic understanding. This leader will not be able to provide the non-zero condition, identified as an environment for growth. For the leader to create an environment for growth, he or she must possess each of these traits, as shown in the final row of the truth table.

In other words, it is a multiplicative formula in which any element with a zero value causes the result to also be zero. This mathematical representation is expressed as:

$$E_g = f(G \times R \times U).$$

To achieve an environment for growth, the leader must be genuine, have a positive regard for each team member, and understand others through true awareness of their perspective. By presenting these components in a mathematical formula, we offer a framework for future research. Potential issues to explore might include: the relative contribution of each component corresponding to various outcomes, the most desirable balance among factors, or the importance of moderating influences. As organizations expand outside the United States, the combination of these leader traits, and transferability of an environment for growth, may become an aspect of competitive strategy.

We consider each of the three leader characteristics to have discrete non-zero levels, such as low/medium/high. The number of incremental states, and the value at which differences are noted, is not addressed at this time. It is mentioned here only to depict that leader characteristics will be perceived in general levels or categories, and behaviors must accumulate to some threshold before this perception shifts to a higher state. Token gestures will not suffice. The degree to which members believe the leader is genuine, has positive regard, and has empathic understanding, is an ongoing judgment, and consistency is critical.

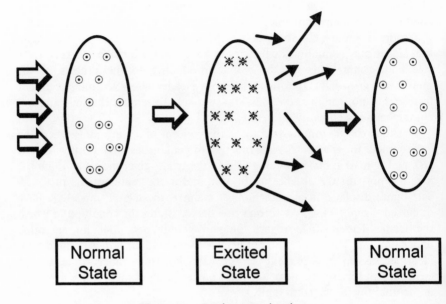

Figure 2.   Pre-laser Technology

WHY "GROW" MAKES A DIFFERENCE

Daniels (1994) remarks that difficulties arise when all employees are thrust into empowerment instantaneously. A preferable situation is to increase discretionary action more gradually, rewarding success in new activities by granting further empowerment as it is sought. We take that example a step farther and propose that any empowerment is risky if there is not an adequate environment for growth already in place. Unless people have developed an understanding of themselves, learned to be unique and self-expressive, and have come to accept others, even the initial introduction of discretionary power may cause confusion or be approached with suspicion.

Team and leader training often takes the form of process techniques, such as conflict resolution, problem solving, and group decision making. Such training is sometimes painful to participants and meets with varying responses. This may be due to neglecting the deeper issues of personal philosophy about relationships for individual growth. We propose that employees who have experienced an environment for growth will be able to learn these skills more quickly and less painfully.

An environment for growth is a means to focus employee energy. A good analogy can be drawn from physics and the principles used to generate laser beams.[2] When incident photons (packets of energy) are applied to atoms which are in a normal state, the atoms change to an excited state. In a short time

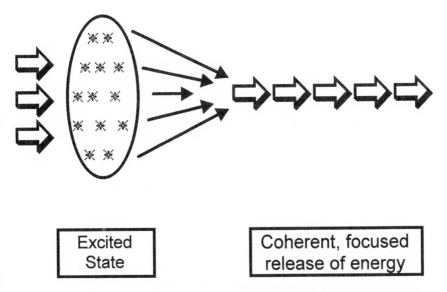

| Excited State | Coherent, focused release of energy |

Figure 3. Laser Technology

these excited atoms return to their normal state by emitting a photon (energy) of the same frequency as was absorbed. This photon release, however, is random in direction and phase, as shown in Figure 2. There is no coherence to the release.

Laser technology, shown in Figure 3, is an alteration to this process. When the atoms are already in an excited state, application of photons still creates a release of energy, but the released photons are of the same frequency, phase, and polarization. This focused energy is a coherent source of light. The phenomenon is most effective when the number of excited atoms is greater than the number of normal-state atoms. With this critical mass of excited atoms, the rate of energy radiated will actually exceed the rate that was absorbed. Providing a spark creates the population inversion (critical mass of exited atoms).

In human terms, the normal state of employees is, too often, either stagnant or frustrated. We apply energy to this normal state in the form of empowerment, or initiatives in various other forms. This does, typically, generate new energy from the employees, but it may be random, unfocused, and not coherent. As a result, the burst of energy subsides and conditions tend to revert to the normal state. The human factor may complicate this by making it increasingly difficult to generate the energy response. After becoming excited over past programs, which subsequently deteriorated, the employee's response becomes more cautious and somewhat cynical.

We believe an environment for growth establishes a preexisting excited state among individual employees. Already in a pattern of personal growth, the energy provided through an intervention such as empowerment will create a focused release of employee energy. Efforts then move in a common direction; there is coherence. Having a growth-oriented workplace can provide an ongoing spark among the employees, population inversion occurs (a critical mass of excited employees), and the energy released exceeds that applied. .

The intent of this analogy is not to reduce human beings to atoms to be manipulated, but only to demonstrate that the underlying principles of behavior bear similarity to those of physical systems. Our society has made tremendous advances by applying laser technology to fields as diverse as medicine, construction, and entertainment. We believe the application of this principle to organizational functioning is equally beneficial to a wide variety of users. Rather than create random energy, we need to generate coherent effort.

The environment for growth must be in place and receive constant attention to maintain a critical mass of workers in an excited state. An empowerment program, or' an intervention of some other type, then becomes a focusing mechanism. This approach is in line with research on organization climate and culture (e.g., Pfeffer, 1981; Schneider, 1987; Smircich, 1983) in recognizing the importance of the organization's internal environment. However, it is much more specific in calling for a particular influence in that environment and describing the employee reactions which are expected to follow. Each organization remains unique; the similarity is in the process, which allows that uniqueness to unfold through personal growth of team members.

"GROW"—THE NEXT FAD?

The cynicism mentioned previously is often a strong force against implementing change in organizations. A new buzzword, a book with a catchy title, or a flashy consultant's program meets with resistance. Such things have come and gone in the past. Each time, there are companies that report outstanding results, while others fail to thrive using that same prescription. Perhaps we are too anxious to find a complete "package of goods" to solve our problems. By looking for the deeper essence in management trends, we might be able to identify some constants that do not fade with time. Certain applications may enjoy cycles of more and less popularity, but the core value should not be allowed to wash away with alterations in method.

Many of the quality initiatives in recent years fall within the broad category of Total Quality Management (TQM). Those who have experienced improvement through TQM may believe its customer focus and participation emphases represent enduring wisdom. But others have become disillusioned and state openly that TQM is indeed a fad and its time may already have passed. Daniels (1994) reviews a study by Ernst & Young covering 584 companies. Their results revealed a wide range of failings in quality improvement activities across industries as varied as auto, computer, banking, and health care. We do not want to promote "GROW" as the trend to replace TQM. Instead, we suggest that the effects of a growth-oriented workplace help explain *why* TQM works so well for those who have succeeded—what the core value is that we need to retain.

Based on a consolidation of resources (e.g., Anderson, Rungtusanatham, & Schroeder, 1994; Dean & Bowen, 1994; Dean & Evans, 1994; Pierce, 1991), we summarize the quality focus into four general principles of TQM. The first is to satisfy the requirements of internal and external customers. Second, is the empowerment of employees to satisfy those requirements and solve problems. This is achieved through involvement and accountability at all levels and reduced hierarchy throughout the organization. The third principle is continuous process improvement—the incremental, ongoing enhancement of product quality and the productivity of the organization. Finally, management excellence is achieved by creating a vision and implementing this vision through employee involvement at all levels. These four summary principles are not replaced by an environment for growth. The employees' response to "GROW" is the essence of how these principles can succeed.

When the leader is genuine, has positive regard, and practices empathic understanding, the team members are in an environment where personal growth can occur. Rogers (1961) elaborates on this process of growth as the progression of certain tendencies. The first tendency is moving away from facades. This represents getting past a fear of exposing the true self. Rather than indulging in constant impression management (cf. Gardner, 1992; Morrison & Bies, 1991), the team members begin to display genuineness, similar to the leader. Along with the willingness to be oneself is an accompanying tendency to be less inclined to conform to expectations imposed by others when they do not coincide with self.

There is also movement *toward* a number of things. One of these is self-direction. Increased autonomy involves some fear and feelings of vulnerability, but the individual will be increasingly willing to make choices and learn through the consequences of those choices. Closely related is the move toward openness to experience. With the freedom to *be* one's feelings, comes a growing trust and authority in one's own experiences. Actions are then self-propelled—guided more by the person's own judgment and less by the evaluation of others. The tendency toward experiencing and discovering truth for oneself leads to perceiving experience as a friendly resource, not a frightening enemy.

An important tendency is the move toward "being process." As opposed to being some*thing*, being process refers to viewing the self as an ever-changing composite of feelings, ideas, and experiences. There is no closed system of

Table 1. The Effects of "GROW" as a Foundation for
Successful Implementation of TQM Principles

	TQM Principles			
Effects of "GROW"	Satisfy Customer	Continuous Improvement	Employee Involvement	Employees Empowered
Away from Facades	√			
Toward Trust of Self	√			
Toward Acceptance of Others	√			
Toward Being Process		√		
Toward Being Complexity		√		
Toward Openness to Experience		√	√	
Away from Meeting Expectations			√	√
Toward Self-direction				√

beliefs, no unchanging set of principles. The person is not a fixed entity, but a process of becoming. From this perspective, each person can begin to appreciate the fluid process of change. It becomes less disturbing that feelings are not the same from day to day, because factors change. There is less striving for conclusions and end states.

Along with being process, people also move toward "being complexity." Awareness of all the complex, changing, and sometimes contradictory feelings in relationships will become a positive, when there is nothing hidden from self— nothing feared in self. As fear diminishes, trust and acceptance are possible. The two final tendencies are movement toward trust in self and toward acceptance of others. Trusting self means daring to live by the values found within and to express one's own unique perceptions and ways of doing things. From this foundation it also easier to accept the uniqueness of others.

These trends correspond to each of the principles of TQM as shown in Table 1. Moving away from facades, toward trust of self, and toward acceptance of others is crucial to establishing successful working partnerships. Satisfying customer requirements is based on partnering with those people for problem solving and identification of new potentials. Moving toward being process and being complexity are key to the philosophy of continuous improvement, in which we recognize that one does not have to be wrong to get better. As a personal growth process this can only occur through openness to experience.

Becoming involved in implementation of a shared vision (rather than following instructions and keeping suggestions to oneself) is a new role for many team members. It is important they be open to this experience, not coerced into taking it on as added responsibility. When employees truly participate, they are no longer simply meeting others' expectations. The most distinct move away from others' expectations is the move toward self-direction that occurs through empowerment to solve problems.

In several cases, current research supports this intersection of Rogers' growth trends with TQM principles, and the view that leaders must create a conducive environment for the desired outcome. For example, employee self-direction can be linked to leaders' encouragement that team members set their own goals, monitor and evaluate their behavior, and self-reinforce (Manz et al., 1990; Manz & Sims, 1987).

DEVELOPING LEADERS WHO PROVIDE "GROW"

Attention thus far has been focused on characteristics that are needed in a leader to create an environment for growth and the positive effects of this environment for developing team members. The remaining question is how to develop the leaders who will initiate the process. When we speak of genuineness, positive regard, and empathic understanding, these are things that come about as a combination of personal beliefs and the effective implementation or display of those beliefs. Therefore, development activities can first be separated by whether the leaders have the beliefs and want to learn the behavior, or are not yet convinced they can believe in these factors.

The non-believers can be further described according to their readiness to accept a change to the assumptions under which they have operated successfully in the past. The believers will also vary on their readiness to perform, on the job, the behaviors that communicate these beliefs to team members. Figure 4 uses these distinctions to suggest four development strategies: structural interventions, awareness programs, self-efficacy combined with techniques, and technique training only.

1. Leaders With Opposing Beliefs That Seem Not Readily Changeable

It is an unproductive trap to focus energies on forcing people to change their ideas to conform with a particular set of beliefs. Heilman (1983) researched a similar issue in attitudes about women in the work force and the faulty assumption that to eliminate the consequences of gender stereotypes we must do away with the stereotypes themselves. The option Heilman describes is to change environmental structures of organizational procedures and practices, to hinder the occurrence of stereotyping consequences, whether or not the individuals' ideas have changed.

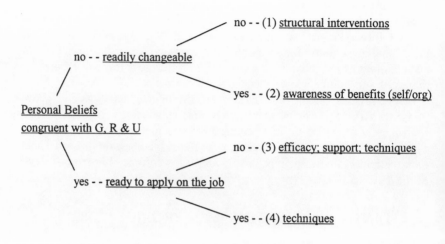

Figure 4.   Strategies for Developing Leaders Who Will Create
an Environment for Growth

Similarly, an organization can be structured so that the most advantageous path for a manager is to encourage growth in employees. For our concerns, the relevant structures would include reward systems, as well as job descriptions and career paths. The job of the leadership is to adhere to and support those structures to the best of their ability. The development program, therefore, focuses on making clear what those structures are and that they are important to the performance ratings and rewards of the leader.

The outcome of structurally influencing leaders' behavior in some cases will exceed mere compliance, because attitudes sometimes follow behavior (cf. Festinger, 1957). This may happen gradually over an extended period of time, but the principle of self-fulfilling prophecy (Eden, 1990; Rosenthal, 1994) indicates people often become what we communicate as our expectations. The structures communicate certain expectations. People may need to resolve the dissonance created between their behavior to adhere to these conditions and their opposing personal beliefs, so beliefs may change over time.

This is in line with the idea of incremental change. Do not push too hard to sell new ideas in one move when those ideas are radically different from established beliefs. Make the first change in surrounding issues that influence behavior and reinforce the desired behaviors (organizational rewards are important here). If attitudes show no change over time, the manager will become conspicuously *un*-genuine in relations with team members. Thus, the worst case outcome is clear identification of a leader who is, in fact, unable to contribute toward organizational goals.

2. Leaders Who are Receptive to Changing Their Assumptions

Although the proposed beliefs are different from assumptions utilized in the past, some people will be receptive to considering their merit. In this case the development program consists of helping the leaders see such a change as a net gain. The content should create an awareness of benefits to both self and the organization. Some people may welcome the idea that they can be more of themselves on the job when they are convinced that the organizational systems truly support this. Again, rewards must be linked to accomplishments such as team trust, flexibility, and incremental improvement. Organizational messages supporting "GROW" must be consistent.

Part of such an awareness program could be incremental goals toward testing out these new attitudes. For example, the leader might keep a journal of critical incidents with team members, including how situations evolved based on displaying either genuineness or impression management. Activities wherein leaders discuss sample incidents may be helpful for seeing the implications of their assumptions.

3. Leaders Who Believe But Lack Confidence in Behaviors

Some leaders may believe the characteristics are desirable, and welcome the opportunity to work under these assumptions, but still be skeptical that they can effectively execute the change in related behavior. These are not skills taught in typical courses on management or supervision. Self-efficacy refers to the belief in one's ability to perform (Bandura, 1986). A development program based on building self-efficacy perceptions provides substantiation that people *can* perform behaviors previously unfamiliar.

Included in this strategy are actual techniques of how to behave in support of creating an environment for growth. Added to that is practice in the new behaviors and follow-up to increase transfer of learning (Decker & Nathan, 1985; Gist et al., 1991). People also need to believe that the organization is supporting this activity. Again, it is important that rewards are designed to reinforce creating an environment for growth, not just talk about it. By simply taking part in the development program, each leader has access to support by knowing other leaders who also are experimenting with new behaviors. This support, in itself, is a valuable asset for the leader's personal growth and development.

4. Leaders Who Feel Ready But Could Use Additional Techniques

Some will believe in both the value of these new assumptions and their ability to utilize them in the workplace. At the same time, they recognize there may be nuances to these new behaviors that they do not, as yet, appreciate. They may come into the development program asking questions like, "how do I communicate both positive regard and genuineness, while delivering bad news or discussing poor performance?" They want to learn how to optimally combine these ideas with the full range of their leadership responsibilities. Techniques, such as suggested phrases, timing, and the settings for these interactions, are most appropriate. Along with these techniques, there again must be the opportunity to practice new behaviors and receive feedback on their effectiveness.

Common Themes Through the Four Development Strategies

One common theme throughout the four strategies is the need for firm and apparent organizational supports. In option 1, the substance of the program is communicating structural supports. In options 2 and 3, organizational support is critical to success. Option 4 seems to have the least reliance on the organization's structure, but there is still a need for that element to be clearly defined. Even with the most willing and able leaders, it is important not to dampen enthusiasm or create cynicism with contradictory messages from the organization. "Regardless of the strength of a belief an individual might hold, the degree to which that belief will influence behavior is dependent upon situational factors" (Heilman, 1983, p. 270, with additional reference to the work of Ajzen & Fishbein, 1973). This need for organizational support is related to the vision of top management being communicated through concrete actions. The structure of reward systems is extremely important (for related discussion see Daniels, 1994; Lawler, 1992).

A second theme across the development strategies is the potential for incremental advancement or continuous improvement. The entire list of strategies could be a progression that some individuals may experience over time (initial resistance, gradual acceptance of changing beliefs, questioning whether new beliefs will translate effectively to behaviors on the job, and, finally, enhancing these behaviors). Consultant David Nadler estimates that 15 percent of managers are natural team leaders; another 15 percent could never lead a team because it runs counter to their personality; and the group in between can learn the skills, but they do not come naturally (Caminiti, 1995). That majority in the middle would probably benefit from one of the two middle strategies for development. Options 1 and 4 address the issues specific to Nadler's "non-team-leader" personalities (option 1) and offer a means for continual improvement to even those who seem to take to it naturally (option 4).

These strategy descriptions are less than complete, in that they cover only the type of development program and not precise content. For example, we make reference to techniques, but the exact techniques are not provided. A great deal of future work is needed to determine how various leader behaviors are perceived by team members in relation to the characteristics targeted. Our intent here is to provide a framework for such additional research. As the knowledge evolves we can also further define leader development.

Each of the four referenced conditions (believers/non-believers; willing/willing & able) can be translated into a measurable attitude, behavior, or perception, so it is possible to assess a current state and monitor changes. This measurement potential is important both for advancing research on team leadership and for practitioners seeking a means of assessment. By recognizing that different strategies are available for differing degrees of leader readiness, an organization may establish a plan for continuous improvement—for developing leaders who will build an environment for growth.

CONCLUSIONS

Applying Rogers' work to the challenge of team leadership is not a cry for "back to basics" leadership, just as it is not proposed as a replacement for current trends. It is recognition that we need to stop and examine what is good in the solutions that are working and whether those components are missing in cases where the same proposed solution has failed. When Rogers wrote about the type of relationships that foster personal growth and development, he began by examining therapist/client relations, and found his conclusions applicable to other relationships, including those in business organizations. The reasoning was sound at that time and translates well to problems we are facing more than 30 years later.

The relationships that establish an environment for growth certainly can benefit many organizations, regardless of the way in which they structure their work force. However, in companies utilizing work teams, participatory decision making, and a quality emphasis, it seems even more critical. The described leader characteristics and resulting "GROW" appear as a continuing thread of potential that has resurfaced with team initiatives. As an essence underlying successful programs with a variety of names, we should endeavor to develop and retain this foundation, regardless of what the next management trend is called.

Human beings are a resource that add value to operations, but they may seldom achieve their full potential to contribute. Our "GROW" model suggests that leaders operating within this paradigm can create fertile ground for employees' personal development. In all probability individuals will be unable to achieve similar development without an appropriate leader/member relationship. The organization relinquishes achievement opportunities when team members cannot develop their potential—when there is not an environment for growth.

ACKNOWLEDGMENT

The authors wish to express their appreciation to Dr. N.P. Sastry for the suggestions which initiated this collaboration.

NOTES

1. Throughout this paper, we refer to Rogers' primarily in terms of passages from this text as a summary of his work and philosophy. Additional readings are included in the references under Hall and Lindsay (1965) and Rogers (1977).
2. This general explanation is available in most physics texts. As a basic source we have drawn from Sears, Zemansky, and Young (1986).

REFERENCES

Ajzen, K., & Fishbein, H. (1973). Attitudinal and normative variables as predictors of specific behaviors. *Journal of Personality and Social Psychology, 27*, 41-57.

Anderson, J.C., Rungtusanatham, M., & Schroeder, R.G. (1994). A theory of quality management underlying the Deming management method. *Academy of Management Review, 19*(3), 472-509.

Bandura, A. (1986). *Social foundations of thought and action.* Englewood Cliffs, NJ: Prentice-Hall.

Caminiti, S. (1995, February 20). What team leaders need to know. *Fortune*, 93-100.

Daniels, A.C. (1994). *Bringing out the best in people.* New York: McGraw-Hill.

Dean, J.W., & Bowen, D.E. (1994). Management theory and total quality: Improving research and practice through theory development. *Academy of Management Review, 19*(3), 392-418.

Dean, J.W., Jr., & Evans, J.R. (1994). *Total quality management, organization, and strategy.* Minneapolis, MN: West.

Decker, P.J., & Nathan, B.R. (1985). *Behavior modeling training.* New York: Prager.

Eden, D. (1990). *Pygmalion in management.* Lexington, MA: Lexington Books.

Festinger, L. (1957). *A theory of cognitive dissonance.* Palo Alto, CA: Stanford University Press.

Fisher, K. (1993). *Leading self-directed work teams: A guide to developing new team leadership skills.* New York: McGraw-Hill.

Gardner, W.L. (1992, summer). Lessons in organizational dramaturgy: The art of impression management. *Organizational Dynamics*, 51-63.

Gist, M.E., Stevens, C.K., & Bavetta, A.G. (1991). Effects of self-efficacy and post-training intervention on the acquisition and maintenance of complex interpersonal skills. *Personnel Psychology, 44*(4), 837-861.

Hall, C.S., & Lindsay, G. (1965). *Theories of personality.* New York: Wiley.

Heilman, M.E. (1983). Sex bias in work settings: The lack of fit model. In B.M. Staw & L.L. Cummings (Eds.), *Research in organization behavior*, Vol. 5 (pp. 269-298). Greenwich, CT: JAI Press

Katzenback, J.R., & Smith, D.K. (1993). *The wisdom of teams.* Boston: Harvard Business School Press.

Lawler, E.D., III. (1992). *The ultimate advantage: Creating the high-involvement organization.* San Francisco: Jossey-Bass.

Manz, C.C., & Sims, H.P. (1987). Leading workers to lead themselves: The external leadership of self-managing work teams. *Administrative Science Quarterly, 32*, 106-128.

Manz, C.C., Keating, D.E., & Donnellon, A. (1990). Preparing for an organizational change to employee self-management: The managerial transition. *Organizational Dynamics, 19*(2), 15-26.

Morrison, E.W., & Bies, R.J. (1991). Impression management in the feedback seeking process. *Academy of Management Review, 16*(3).

Pfeffer, J. (1981). Management as symbolic action: The creation and maintenance of organizational paradigms. *Research in organizational behavior*, Vol. 3, (pp. 1-52). Greenwich, CT: JAI Press.

Pierce, R.J. (1991). *Leadership, perspective, and restructuring for total quality*. Milwaukee, WI: ASQC Quality Press.

Rogers, C.R. (1961). *On becoming a person*. Boston: Houghton Mifflin.

Rogers, C.R. (1977). *Carl Rogers on personal power*. New York: Delacorte Press.

Rosenthal, R. (1994). Interpersonal expectancy effects: A 30-year perspective. *Current Directions in Psychological Science, 3*(6), 176-179.

Schneider, B. (1987). The people make the place. *Personnel Psychology, 40*, 437-453.

Sears, F.W., Zemansky, M.W., & Young, H.D. (1986). *University Physics*, 7th ed. Reading, MA: Addison-Wesley.

Smith, K.K., & Berg, D.N. (1987). *Paradoxes of group life: Understanding conflict, paralysis and momentum in group dynamics*. San Francisco: Jossey-Bass.

Smircich, L. (1983). Concepts of culture and analysis. *Administrative Science Quarterly, 28*, 339-358.

BETTER LEADERSHIP THROUGH CHEMISTRY:
TOWARD A MODEL OF EMERGENT SHARED TEAM LEADERSHIP

Anson Seers

ABSTRACT

This paper analyzes the concept of shared, internal team leadership for self-directed work teams. It draws on literature from several traditional areas of research, including role theory, leader behavior, group effectiveness, studies of organizational coordination, and social psychological studies of leader emergence. The analysis suggests that the role-making process within self-directed work teams can produce a set of interdependent roles in which team members share leadership by influencing other members with respect to certain group functions while following the lead of other group members on different group functions.

Advances in Interdisciplinary Studies
of Work Teams, Volume 3, pages 145-172.
Copyright © 1996 by JAI Press Inc.
All rights of reproduction in any form reserved.
ISBN: 0-7623-0006-X

INTRODUCTION

In recent years, both interest in and use of self-directed work teams (SDWTs) has grown exponentially. In large part, the popularity of teams may be attributable to the emergence of global business competition, which has left companies scrambling for more effective strategies. This has led to a major restructuring of the American workplace. Organizations have "downsized" by finding substitutes for human effort not only by replacing production employees with advanced technology, but more significantly by replacing great numbers of administrative and managerial employees with the adoption of less labor-intensive methods of coordinating work activities. Delegating a greater degree of responsibility for the coordination of work to the very people doing that work is a key strategic advantage of adopting SDWTs. Yet one can often hear cynicism expressed about SDWTs in that the presumed motivation, and apparent effect, of these programs is mainly to substitute informal, internal team leaders who are relatively modestly compensated for formal, external leaders who are relatively well compensated.

Some, but not all, applications of SDWTs manage to avoid "dumping" responsibilities that formerly justified healthy managerial salaries onto a regularly compensated team member. Some organizations allow for an internal team leader who gets a slight compensation premium to split leadership responsibilities with an external facilitator. Many organizations, though, strive toward an egalitarian model where all members are cross-trained and equally compensated on a pay-for-knowledge system. In this paper, we ask how leadership might be effectively shared among team members. We analyze how a particular social structure may develop so as to provide a mechanism through which the members of these teams effectively receive direction for their work efforts in exchange for contributing to the team's ability to generate internal leadership. Thus, it may be possible that the team as a functional unit substitutes for the external leadership formerly provided by administrative and managerial employees, as opposed to a single emergent leader arising from the ranks.

For our analysis, we will define leadership as the direction and coordination of employee efforts via interpersonal influence. This definition accords, except for one key element, with many that have been applied in leadership theory and research (e.g., Fiedler, 1967). That exception is that we eschew the assumption made either implicitly or explicitly in much of the leadership literature of the past 40 years that the necessary agent of such directional influence is an organizational superordinate (e.g., Fiedler, 1967; Graen & Cashman, 1975; House & Dessler, 1974).

A great deal of the leadership research and theory generated over the last 40 years builds on the leader behavior approach. Two ubiquitous dimensions have emerged from decades of study of effective leadership behavior. It is mainly the labels for the two most fundamental aspects of leadership behavior that differentiated much of the theory and research on leadership from the 1950s through the 1970s. Simultaneous research programs conducted through the 1950s and 1960s at the University of Michigan and at Ohio State University were the most influential in this period. The Michigan studies (Kahn, 1956) labeled these two general dimensions of leader behavior as "production-centered leadership" and "person-centered leadership." The Ohio State studies (Stogdill & Coons, 1957) labeled task leadership as "initiating structure" and relationship leadership as "consideration." In the 1970s, attention turned to how leadership interacted with situational factors, but much of the work on contingency models of leadership was still built on the premise that task and relational behavior defined leadership.

Leadership research plateaued in the 1980s, as interest shifted to self-directed work teams, which are less reliant on external leadership. Exemplary of research in the 1980s is the work on self-management (Manz, 1986; Manz & Sims, 1987). This approach has addressed how organizational employees could be less reliant on external supervision, and in turn, how managers should shift from actually directing, coordinating, and controlling the work activities of employees to encouraging employees to assume these responsibilities for themselves.

However, in their 1987 study of the leadership of self-managed teams, Manz and Sims concluded by suggesting that "... self-management principles ultimately operate at the individual level" (p. 128). Thus, these principles do not focus on the social and structural mechanisms of teams as functional units of employees. All, most, a few, or none of the members of any supposedly self-directed team might actually enthusiastically and effectively take on the self-management behaviors described by Manz and Sims (1987). If most or all of the employees change their individual behavior patterns to be self-managing, reductions in the ranks of lower and middle management may become feasible. But if few or none of the employees successfully adopt the self-management behaviors described by Manz and Sims (1987), eliminating lower and middle management jobs may lead to the inefficiencies and ineffectiveness of inadequate direction, coordination, and control. This suggests that a pertinent question is: by what behavioral mechanisms can a team direct, coordinate, and control member work activities so as to be less reliant on external supervision?

One possibility is that most or all of the employees successfully adopt self-managing behaviors. In this case they may proceed from thinking independently about how to direct and control their own activities to learning, perhaps by trial and error, how to informally coordinate their work activities with those of other employees by mutual adjustments (Van de Ven et al., 1976). In this state of affairs, those lower and middle managers whose jobs get eliminated should not be sorely missed.

Yet another possibility is that a single dominant individual may emerge from the peer group as an informal leader. In this case, most employees need not substantially change the patterns of behavior that they have learned for the operation of traditional workgroups. Except for the single emergent leader, group members can continue to play a subordinate role. They can carry out required task activities under the direction, coordination, and control of another individual, who plays a leadership role modeled after that of an external leader. In this case, self-directed work teams may simply substitute an internal, informal, and modestly compensated individual leader for an external, formal, more highly compensated supervisor. Some organizations have accepted this scenario quite readily, as it still allows for the cost savings occasioned by reducing the ranks of middle management.

However, neither of these scenarios allows organizations to fully tap the potential of self-directed work teams. When most employees continue to rely on other individuals to address the direction, coordination, and control of their efforts, the full abilities of employees are not being used. Yet even when self-managing employees individually accept responsibility to direct and control their own efforts, they may not be fully able to efficiently and effectively coordinate their efforts as a team. Coordination is inherently an attribute involving combinations of individuals. If we concentrate on turning individual employees into self-managers, we may end up with the analogue of an all-star team in which each individual competes for the limelight even though teamwork suffers. An effective team approach should provide a social structure that facilitates coordinated teamwork and provides for each team to exercise self-direction and control, not just the employees within the teams.

The importance of this distinction can better be seen if one appreciates role theory and research. As noted previously, individual role behavior is largely determined by expectations. The expectations are often more implicit than explicit. Nonetheless, research over several decades confirms that people will generally conform to what is expected of them. High expectations breed success, while low expectations invite mediocrity. More importantly, the kind of group roles described in the preceding paragraph evolve as individuals are relied upon to play a particular part in the task and interpersonal activities of a group. Research has shown that training employees as individuals is generally not an effective way to change the role structure of a group. Far more effective is a process called role negotiation, in which members explicitly discuss their expectations and how they will change the ways in which they rely on each other (Harrison, 1973). Groups generally affect members more than individual members affect groups, despite the paradoxical fact that the only actions that define the group are those performed by its members.

These considerations from role theory and research predate the popularity of self-directed work teams. Nonetheless, they suggest the possibility that members of a team could implicitly or explicitly negotiate a set of roles that effectively divide leadership of the team among several or even all of the members. A similar notion, albeit one that has emanated from the technical and practical reactions of managers within organizations rather than from academic research and theory, underlies the concept of starpoint leadership. Starpoints refer to specific functions for which an external supervisor traditionally maintained responsibility, but which must be assumed by the members of a self-directed work team. Examples include quality, cost control, safety, and housekeeping. Under any form of management system, such objectives may often be described as everybody's responsibility, yet the practical realization is that these unfortunately deteriorate into becoming nobody's responsibility.

Sports analogies also offer insight on the notion of shared team leadership. One can hear attributions, often from team coaches, of the relative success or failure of a team to the chemistry of that team. The importance of chemistry for a set of people expected to mesh their personal efforts in a particularly effective way seems intuitively obvious. Chemistry identifies that state of affairs such that team members seem to naturally react to each other in optimal ways. They tap their compatibilities so as to synergistically combine their individual human efforts into an integrated, whole team effort that is greater than the sum of its parts. Chemistry seems to be of greatest importance in highly interdependent team sports where the coach, as an external leader, has relatively little ability to lead the actual flow of task activity, such as basketball. The parallel to self-directed work teams should be obvious: when teams develop their ability to optimally mesh individual member efforts, external supervision is least necessary. The direct substitution is of mutual influence between members rather than external leadership influence. The problem is that chemistry amounts to a label for our ignorance. If knowledge of how to achieve positive chemistry was readily obtainable, one could read about it in management textbooks. Unfortunately, it is not there yet.

However, thinking about the idea has merit. In a chemical reaction, one substance combines with another substance, yielding a third substance different from the first two. In general, the key to such a reaction is that the first two substances differ from each other in complementary ways. If we have a substance A, no matter how many additional units of substance A that we add, we still have substance A. Team chemistry must obviously develop between the members rather than being an attribute embodied within team members. Thus, the most fundamental implication of the notion of team chemistry is that diversity among members is necessary. If the idea of team chemistry is ever to transcend a label for our ignorance, we need to identify complementary attributes that prospective team members may bring to their interaction.

Thus far we have yet to address how we might identify an appropriate set of complementary attributes of team members. Two general considerations seem warranted. First, such attributes would need to be related to task performance. Unless these attributes predict greater performance, they amount to a distraction from the productivity goals of an organization. Second, an appropriate set of attributes should also apply to performance in groups or teams in general. Not only will different teams have different tasks, but each team may have more or less variety in its tasks, and its list of task responsibilities may change over time.

We can find research evidence pertaining to performance of groups in general in the social-psychological literature on group dynamics and performance. Over several decades, researchers have investigated factors such as the emergence of leaders, cohesiveness, and group development. For our analysis, we will define as a workgroup any set of employees who are assigned to the same work unit and who interact on a regular basis. We will define as a work team only those workgroups whose members actually perceive their interdependencies as critical to their task effectiveness. Thus, whether an outside observer would determine that a group's assignments require the members to work in an interdependent fashion is not deemed to be a critical distinction. This usage is consistent with sports definitions of teams. Even four bowlers who simply pool their individual scores thus constitute a team *because they identify themselves as an interdependent team*. The extent to which a team can function independently of external supervision defines the extent to which it can be regarded as self-directing. Teams are thus defined as a special kind of group. Much research and theory developed for either teams or groups will also apply to the other, but some theory and research applicable to one will not apply to the other. Thus, we will not simply use groups and teams interchangeably. We will, however, carefully review the large body of research on groups for important implications for work teams.

CONCEPTUAL FOUNDATIONS

The underpinnings of a model of shared, internal team leadership can be drawn from the literature of group dynamics, leadership, and organizational coordination mechanisms. Models of workgroup effectiveness (Campion et al., 1993; Gladstein, 1984; Hackman, 1987; Kolodny & Kiggundu, 1980; Shea & Guzzo, 1987) provide a conceptual starting point. However, such models have been of limited use in providing knowledge that could be applied in practice by leaders, for several reasons. First, we have little empirical evidence bearing on the models. Among the models previously referenced, empirical studies that addressed the Hackman (1987) or Shea and Guzzo (1987) models seem to be nonexistent. The only evidence on the Gladstein (1984) and Campion and coworkers (1993) models was that reported in their own studies. The major exception is the empirical literature on socio-technical systems (Cummings,

1977). But here we have the opposite problem. Even though several empirical studies have employed a socio-technical approach, no clearly articulated model has been advanced for this approach that achieves the specificity presented by the other models. The core proposition of the socio-technical approach remains the rather abstract premise that effectiveness results from the joint optimization of social and technical subsystems.

Another problem is the overly coarse nature of group effectiveness models (Goodman et al., 1987). These models have been designed to address overall effectiveness, so it is not surprising that they are so broad in scope that their identification of variables tends toward generality. Such group effectiveness models imply an assumption that all factors that might be related to group functioning should be enumerated. Goodman and his associates suggested that we need to develop more fine-grained models. They argued that "Current models of group effectiveness are specified in too general a fashion. Lists of loosely connected variables will not generate new insights into group functions" (Goodman et al., 1987, p. 133). By moving toward more fine-grained models, construct specification and subsequent measurement should be improved, which, in turn, should stimulate more empirical studies of ongoing workgroups and teams in organizations.

A related problem concerns the lack of clarity in the definition of workgroup effectiveness. As effectiveness per se is not a very clear construct, workgroup effectiveness often gets defined in a general fashion rather than in a specific way (Goodman et al., 1986). Among the models referenced above, Hackman's (1987) model did identify specific dimensions of effectiveness. The Campion and coworkers' (1993) study took a fairly comprehensive approach to operationalize effectiveness. In this study, managerial assessments, employee satisfaction, and a composite index of six production statistics were used. The different outcome measures were predicted by different combinations of 19 characteristics, covering job design, interdependence, group composition, context, and process. While this model was specified in somewhat more detail than earlier models, what it seems to yield over earlier models is a longer list of loosely connected variables.

Furthermore, these general models of workgroup effectiveness may lead us to highlight aspects bearing on work in groups that have more to do with the context than the substance of teamwork. For example, Kolodny and Kiggundu (1980) emphasized that much of the productivity of wood harvesting crews was a function of the growth density of the trees in the area to be cut. Models that direct our attention to factors over which group members have little or no control may actually distract us from focusing on how group members can change to more effective ways of working together.

For our analysis, we will use knowledge developed by group researchers and theorists, but we wish to restrict our focus to leading teamwork, defined as the effective integration of group member efforts. We can keep the general frameworks of workgroup effectiveness models in mind for a context in which to consider team leadership, but we must regard much of what those models address as beyond the scope of leading teams to better integrate member efforts.

Coordination

Studies of workgroup coordination have focused on the integration of group member efforts. Organizational theorists have long regarded coordination as a necessary condition for effective organizational performance (Hage, 1980). Despite its importance, coordination is one of the least developed and most rarely investigated constructs in organization theory (Cheng, 1984).

Cheng (1984) indicated that conceptual confusion is a main reason for this dormancy. By distinguishing coordination from related concepts such as cooperation, coordinating process, and effectiveness, he defined coordination as "the extent to which the work activities of organizational parts/members are logically consistent and coherent" (Cheng, 1984, p. 833). According to this definition, coordination within a system concerns the quality of the functional articulation that exists among the components of the system in the process of achieving unity of efforts. A high level of coordination can be achieved when the work activities performed by various components are integrated in such ways that they supplement and complement one another. By contrast, fragmented activities within an organization result in misuse of members' efforts.

Coordination within a system can be achieved by various means. Litterer (1973) suggested three general types: directive, facilitated, and voluntary. Directive coordinating is achieved through hierarchical and/or administrative systems. Various work activities are linked together by placing them under a central authority or by developing formal procedures to carry out routine coordinating automatically. Facilitated coordinating is concerned with integrating work activities of subsystems in an organization by creating new departments or positions responsible for coordinating. Both directive and facilitated coordinating are based upon the development of formal devices and structural mechanisms.

Even where quite elaborate structural mechanisms are used, there will still be some areas where various work activities need to be integrated for better performance. Much of this integration may depend on voluntary means of coordination. Thus, voluntary coordination depends on individuals within organizations to identify problems and negotiate mutually acceptable solutions to those problems.

Studies of Workgroup Coordination

Paradoxically, studies of coordination, for example, Argote (1982), Cheng (1983), and Van de Ven, Delbecq, and Koenig (1976) have investigated it more as a technological rather than a behavioral phenomenon. Nonetheless, this research bears examination for its implications for leading teamwork. Van de Ven, Delbecq, and Koenig (1976) performed a study on the relationship between characteristics of work-unit technology and mechanisms for coordinating work activities within a workgroup. Van de Ven and coworkers (1976) found that an impersonal mode of coordination, that is, the programing of pre-established plans and formalized rules, was heavily used when the degree of workflow interdependence and technological uncertainty for a work unit was low. In the impersonal mode of coordination, relatively little human discretion was exercised in the decisions about important matters of group activities such as setting goals and the division of labor, because most activities are standardized and formalized.

Personal and group modes of coordination were found to be employed more frequently than impersonal modes when the work-unit task was technologically uncertain and required a high level of interdependence among group members. In the personal mode, mutual adjustments were made by individual role occupants to feedback from other individuals conveyed by either vertical or horizontal communication. In the group mode, scheduled or unscheduled group meetings served as a mechanism for mutual task adjustments among group members.

Argote (1982), in a study of 30 hospital emergency units, investigated the effect of input uncertainty on the relationship between various means of coordination and workgroup effectiveness measured in terms of the promptness of care, the quality of nursing, and the quality of medical care. She found that the appropriateness of various means of coordination depended on the level of uncertainty characterizing workgroup inputs. The use of programmed means of coordination made a greater contribution to the effectiveness of emergency units under the conditions of low-input uncertainty than under high-input uncertainty. By contrast, the use of non-programmed means of coordination was more appropriate than programmed means when the work units had inputs with high levels of uncertainty.

Cheng (1983) performed a study of the relationship between technological interdependence, coordination, and workgroup performance. He examined the influence of technological interdependence on the level of coordination within a workgroup and on the relationship between coordination and performance of the workgroup. From a sample of 127 research units, he observed that technological interdependence was positively related to the level of coordination. Both quantity and quality of output were explained by the level of coordination within a workgroup. Moreover, the relationship between coordination and performance was moderated by the level of technological interdependence. Accordingly, Cheng (1983) argued that technological interdependence is a contingency variable in the coordination-organizational performance relationship.

Cheng (1984) also investigated the influence of uncertainty on coordination as well as the effect of coordination on output performance from 111 research units. He found significant positive relationships between coordination and output quantity and quality. Although uncertainty had a significant moderating effect on both the coordination-output quantity and the coordination-output quality relationships, the directions of its effects were opposite. The relationship between coordination and output quality became more positive as level of uncertainty increased. A less positive relationship, however, was found between coordination and output quantity as level of uncertainty became higher.

Leadership Implications of Coordination Studies

Unlike the models of group-task effectiveness, studies of workgroup coordination have maintained a fairly specific focus. The practical implications of this work are thus more clear. When leading a group, it becomes increasingly important to facilitate the coordination of member efforts as tasks become increasingly interdependent. When there is workflow uncertainty, coordination is also particularly important. The mode of coordination is also important. As long as technological uncertainty and interdependence are relatively low, impersonal programmed coordination mechanisms such as rules and procedures are sufficient. But under conditions of uncertainty and task interdependence, employees must make adjustments to accommodate each other as they interact in their work. This mutual adjustment requires increased communication among the parties to these working relationships. Thus, the leadership functions of facilitating working relationships characterized by open communications take on increased importance.

Working Relationships in a Workgroup

The development of working relationships has been understood as "a progress from role-specified surface encounters to a greater degree of mutual exchange and task-related efficacy" (Gabarro, 1987, p. 184). A similar argument was made by Seers (1989) in proposing that the reciprocal working relationship between a member and the peer group, which he assessed by the newly introduced construct of team member exchange quality (TMX), is the prime mechanism through which workgroup members negotiate coordinated roles. The synergistic gain of workgroups can be achieved when the members develop high levels of exchange qualities in the role making process. The results of well-developed roles among the members of a workgroup are manifested in working relationships that are characterized by trusting, supportive attitudes and by cooperative interdependence beyond a "minimal task relationship."

Over the years, team building has been the most widely recognized strategy for improving team working relationships. A variety of reviews of the team building literature is available: Beer (1976), Dyer (1987), Liebowitz and DeMeuse (1982), and Woodman and Sherwood (1980). Team building interventions usually attempt to improve problem solving and interpersonal relations. The central premise is that joint problem solving enhances members' ability to work together effectively. Woodman and Sherwood (1980) noted that team building interventions focus mainly on general feelings and attitudes. These interventions may foster openness in communication, but team members are then left to their own devices if they wish to translate this openness into improved cooperation. Proponents of team building have not established and validated constructs for empirically testing models of an underlying process by which it would necessarily produce greater coordination or cooperation. Thus, as noted by Buller and Bell (1986), because of the "failure to specify and test relationships between independent variables, causal mechanisms, and criteria of performance. ... It is simply not clear why team building affects performance, if it does at all" (p. 306).

By way of contrast, the literature of social psychology offers a relatively solid foundation for examining the ongoing interaction process among group members while they are working together on group tasks (Hackman & Morris, 1975). A particularly useful conceptual tool from this literature is Homans' (1950) idea of the emergent system within a workgroup. An emergent system elaborates the rudimentary required system of task requirements into an integrated social system. Several scholars have suggested that a workgroup might perform better if it has a well-developed emergent system. Among the components of a workgroup's emergent system, the socio-emotional features have received the most emphasis. Although the social interaction among group members may have implications for group effectiveness, emergent task-related interaction may be more fundamental to the development of working relationships and to the effects of working relationships on workgroup effectiveness. Recently, students of working relationships (Gabarro, 1987; Janz & Tjosvold, 1985; Seers, 1989) have reached back to social exchange theory (Homans, 1950, 1961; Thibaut & Kelley, 1959) for a conceptual foundation.

Gabarro (1987) proposed that working relationships are different from social relationships. Although working relationships can be treated as a substantial form of social interactions, they have a distinctive nature in that their primary purpose is task achievement and that an organizational or task-related context is the interaction setting. He enumerated several factors that are more prominent in working relationships than in social ones.

The exchange relationships among workgroup members are based on rewards and costs relevant to task attainment. Consequently, development of working relationships is more influenced by the task-specific attributes of each party than by the conventional source of development of socio-emotional relationships. Furthermore, "disclosure about self is less important than openness concerning task on organizational issues" (Gabarro, 1987, p. 182), because working relationships require only partial inclusion of a person's life.

In this analysis, roles and role-related behaviors distinguish working relationships among the broader category of social relationships. Gabarro (1987) argued that most working relationships develop by virtue of roles and that members of organizations begin their interaction with an "institutionalized role relationship." Roles and role definitions also influence working relationships through their impact on the distribution of power, especially in the hierarchical working relationships. In addition, role expectations affect the interaction among role occupants and resulting working relationships.

Seers (1989) investigated the reciprocal role relationship between an individual work team member and the peer group as a whole. This exchange relationship was defined in the context of an ongoing workgroup as the member interacts with interdependent members of the role set (Katz & Kahn, 1978). The roles of team members are defined and modified over time through the reinforcement of reciprocal actions. Any member of the role set can send expectations for the behavior of an individual in a focal role and can respond to subsequent behaviors. An implicit process of negotiation occurs as various role senders interact with a focal role occupant. Some of the sent role expectations may be inherently contradictory, some may be too vague, and some may call for a behavior that a focal member is unwilling or unable to display. When a focal member does exhibit behavior consistent with role sender expectations, those expectations and behaviors are reinforced. Further, each focal member is actually a member of a role set in relation to other individual members.

A complete mapping of all these interpersonal interactions and reinforcements clearly exceeds human cognitive capacities. Yet an abstracted summary map representing a general pattern of expectations, behaviors, and reinforcements emerges such that members can identify behavior that is part of their role and distinguish it from behavior that is not part of their role. This resulting role must represent some manner of compromise between the idealized expectations of various role senders, as well as of a focal role occupant. Thus, member roles become defined in relation to the group and its other members through the reinforcement of reciprocal actions (Jacobs, 1970). The pattern of reciprocation that evolves for different members of a group will vary along with the abilities and interests of the individual, as well as with the needs of the other members and the variation in demands placed upon the group as a whole.

Exchange Quality In Team-Member Relationships

Seers (1989) proposed the construct of team member exchange quality (TMX) as a tool for assessing the reciprocity between a member and the peer group. Team member exchange quality assesses this reciprocity with respect to the member's contribution of ideas, feedback, and assistance to other members and, in turn, the member's receipt of information, help, and recognition from other team members. Thus, the quality of the team member exchange relationship indicates the effectiveness of the member's working relationship to the peer group.

Team member exchange quality would therefore be related to, but distinct from, other peer-related variables such as perceptions of cohesiveness and satisfaction with coworkers. Cohesiveness involves the perception of the group as a whole, while team member exchange quality involves the perception of one's role within the group. We might surmise that if perceptions of team member exchange within a group were uniformly high, the group would approximate the ideals sought in team building (Dyer, 1987) where members perceive the group to be both well coordinated and cohesive. Coworker satisfaction involves one's affective reaction to peers in the workplace rather than the perception of a reciprocal behavior pattern in relation to the peer group. Here we may surmise that the quality of the exchange relationship with the peer group would be a major influence on the affective reaction to those peers.

Team member exchange would also be related to, but distinct from, the leader-member exchange (LMX) construct developed by Graen and his associates (Graen, 1976; Graen & Cashman, 1975). The two constructs are similar in that both constructs focus on the nature and degree of reciprocity between parties to an exchange relationship rather than attributes or behavioral styles of either party to the relationship. Both constructs are based on the logic that relationships rather than jobholder positions are the building blocks of organizational structure. In both cases, the reciprocity must be analyzed in terms of the resources each party may bring to bear on the exchange process. The leader-member exchange construct is designed to jointly address employee role making and supervisory leadership, while the team member exchange construct was conceptualized to jointly address employee role making and work team dynamics.

Seers (1989) found that TMX added to the prediction of job attitudes by LMX. Further, TMX varied systematically between teams in relation to the autonomy given to the teams by higher managers and it varied systematically within teams in relation to job attitudes. Perhaps of greatest interest was the relationship between TMX and job performance, as moderated by the instrumentality of peer reactions for one's job motivation. For those high on team member exchange quality, rated performance was relatively high and not significantly related to peer motivation. Peer motivation was significantly related to rated performance for those low on team member exchange quality such that only respondents reporting high peer motivation were rated as equivalent in performance to members of the high exchange quality group.

Thus, while effective job performance was found consistently for members high on TMX, not all those who were low on TMX were mediocre performers. Apparently those who sought greater peer reward and recognition were attempting to earn it through stronger job performance.

Certainly, the peer group should be of particular importance in team-oriented management systems. With increasing interest in the development of self-managed teams, management of the reciprocal exchange between individual members and the team itself may be a key device for establishing the role of individual employees as team players. Individuals experiencing high quality team member exchanges may be able to contribute their efforts in a cooperative and collaborative fashion and receive social rewards in the bargain. Groups in which most members experience high quality team member exchange relationships should be effective teams as well as provide satisfying experiences to members. Thus, we should also consider the average level of team member exchange across a group as a meaningful variable at the aggregate level. If a group's average score on team member exchange reflects the level of member teamwork, then members of work teams expected to be self-managing should report a higher level of team member exchange quality than traditional group members, and team effectiveness ought to be positively related to team member exchange at the group level of analysis.

In a follow-up to the Seers (1989) study, Seers, Petty, and Cashman (1995) investigated the differentiation, with respect to TMX and other group dynamics variables, of teams expected to operate as self-managed teams from groups expected to operate as traditional workgroups. In the same plant where the original study was conducted, teams were separated into team and traditional categories when plant managers decided to revitalize their team approach, concentrating on those areas where they saw the greatest opportunity for success with a team approach. Except for supervisory satisfaction, none of the variables included in this study differed between the resulting team and traditional groups before they were separated. After the separation, measures reflecting the way in which team members worked together did differ significantly, although other important variables such as task autonomy and intrinsic work satisfaction were not sensitive to the changes. Furthermore, team member exchange explained differences between the two groups beyond any attributable to all of the other group dynamics variables. Also, team member exchange emerged from the group level analysis as the variable most closely associated with gains in group production efficiency, with cohesiveness having a marginally significant relationship. From these findings, we suggest that group dynamics bear further scrutiny in self-directed work teams, and that workgroup autonomy involves an additional set of forces beyond those brought into play by task autonomy and the enrichment of individual tasks.

A dissertation by Lee (1989) further investigated group level correlates of effectiveness, indicating that reciprocal behavior within teams appears to facilitate the coordination of member efforts toward the attainment of greater group effectiveness. Lee (1989) assessed 35 work units within a 600 bed hospital. The majority of these units contained between 10 and 17 employees. Through interviews with the unit heads, Lee (1989) assessed the degree of coordination achieved in each work unit, as well as the degree of task differentiation and the extent to which the work of the unit involved pooled, sequential, and reciprocal interdependencies. The level of team member exchange characterizing the unit was assessed by averaging the responses of the members within each unit. Task differentiation, interdependence, group size, and TMX were found to predict coordination at the work unit level of analysis.

While we have some evidence that reciprocal team member exchange can provide us with some insight into how team members can work together, teamwork remains a sports metaphor that is occasionally and casually applied in the management literature. Prior to the work of Kozlowski and coworkers (1996) teamwork had not been articulated as a management construct. Little published research directly addresses either teamwork or the psychology of workgroup autonomy, despite the introduction of terms such as autonomous workgroups and socio-technical systems four decades ago (Trist & Bamforth, 1951). This literature has not benefitted from the concentration of efforts to develop specific measures and models comparable to those that have guided research and theory building in other areas such as work design and leadership. We need to learn a great deal more about principles that may bridge the personal, interpersonal, and group levels of analysis.

ROLE-MAKING REVISITED

Ironically, the construct of organizational role has long been positioned (Katz & Kahn, 1966, 1978) as a conceptual mechanism for bridging across levels of organizational analysis. Katz and Kahn pointed out that the construct of organizational role had failed to deliver on its potential in this respect. Yet, progress has been made over the years in extending our knowledge of the psychological, social psychological, and social dynamics of organizational behavior. With the contributions that have been made in this literature since Katz and Kahn (1966) leveled their criticism, we may now be approaching the actual application of the role construct in the fashion envisioned decades ago. Much greater theoretical development is needed to establish whether teamwork can become a generally useful construct, and in particular, how useful role making concepts such as team member exchange can be in bridging the individual and team levels of analysis. Yet, little of this theoretical development may necessarily be original. Decades of work from social psychology may be highly relevant, even though little contemporary work on SDWTs has explicitly addressed much of this literature.

Extensive reviews of this literature have been published over the years, (e.g., Homans, 1950; Jacobs, 1970; Levine & Moreland, 1990) which facilitates our ability to draw on literature accumulated over several decades. That literature has established that roles are socially constructed frameworks for the patterns of behavior exhibited in a particular context. Much of this literature applied a symbolic interaction perspective to the analysis of group roles (see Zurcher, 1983). In these analyses, the process through which individuals construct, maintain, and modify their sense of personal identity is examined. Goffman (1959) contributed a particularly insightful analysis of how the role enactment process allowed individuals, by interacting with the other individuals populating the context of interest, to define their own self-identities in ways that compromised between the sometimes contrasting perspectives of the self and the other relevant actors of that social context. The reactions of other group members provide systematic data with which the individual must square his or her self-concept (Bem, 1967). While much of the literature on symbolic interaction is quite dated, its basic paradigm still informs contemporary research on human social identity (Deaux, 1993; Ethier & Deaux, 1994).

Analyses of work roles focus on interaction in context, such that identities become defined in terms of the behaviors occurring in that context, for example, identification as a reliable member of a workgroup or team. Of special interest is the process through which people acting individually to establish their identity in relation to all the other people in a particular context simultaneously provide identity and meaning to their collective structure. Roles may be described as the basic building blocks of organizations. A set of interdependent roles constitutes a social structure, in the sense that Allport (1962) described event patterns as social structure. As described by Katz and Kahn (1978), roles constitute patterns of behavior established by the interaction of members of a social unit. These roles allow individuals to know both what others expect of them and what to expect from others. Roles constitute the central medium of social exchange between groups and their individual members. Certainly members contribute behaviors to the group, and the pattern of rewards returned to the individual by group members reinforces certain behaviors and discourages others.

Exchange Between Individual and Group

Analyses of the role making process generally look at the interaction between the occupant of a focal role and those interdependent others that constitute the role set. When the set of interdependent actors comprise a work team, the identity of the team as a functional unit may closely approximate that of the role set (Seers, 1989). Focal members may generalize across the perceived expectations of the other team members into a summary notion of what their team expects of them. They learn the role over time through a process of socialization (Moreland & Levine, 1982), but it is important to keep in mind that much of the reality they are learning is simultaneously being socially invented by the very group interaction in which they are participating. When the role making process takes place in a newly formed team, it simultaneously constitutes the process of group development (Moreland & Levine, 1984).

While individuals gain favorable self-validation from effective exchange with the group, the group as a social entity also profits from the social exchange processes of its members. The systemic character of groups evolves through attributes established across the roles developed by members. As members come to conform to their role expectations, those expectations shared in common across the members become the norms of the group. Just as importantly, as members enact their individual identities as group members, they enact the very identity of the group. Acting in concert, they consensually validate (Festinger, 1950; Weick, 1979) their social reality. A group that is generally successful in gaining productive contributions from its members through effective roles and positive norms will best be able to achieve organizational goals. From this perspective, the group owes not only its identity to how it is perceived by its members, but also the entirety of its performance.

Thus, in the present analysis we disagree with those who take their premise from Durkheim's assertion that "If, then, we begin with the individual, we shall be able to understand nothing of what takes place in the group" (1898, p. 104). We also disagree with the early counterpoint offered by Allport (1924) that since groups had no tangible existence they were undeserving of study. Only by conceptualizing both the individual member and the group as initial elements for our analysis, and then examining how social exchange across these two levels of analysis reciprocally reshapes both the member and the group can we advance theoretical models that can accommodate what has been learned in nearly a century of study.

Role theory offers a particularly useful framework because it can address the task functions of groups and their members simultaneously with the psychological and social facets of group behavior. A very important implication of roles for the members of a work team, as noted by Sarbin and Allen (1968), is that when the members of a workgroup know what they will need to do and how interdependent others will react, less communication is needed for the coordination of their activities. Thus, misunderstandings, wasted efforts, and their associated psychological tensions are minimized, and time is used more efficiently. Empirical evidence exists that role differentiation benefits group performance (see Roger & Reid, 1982).

THE EMERGENCE OF LEADERS

As member roles also become differentiated, varying levels of status become attached to those roles. Thus, a status hierarchy becomes characteristic of the group. As particular group members grow into high status roles, they gain interpersonal power. As they then exercise that power, they become the emergent leaders of the group. Decades of research studies have documented these processes. Barnard's (1938) analysis noted that two individual group members often emerged into complementary leadership roles. One of these leaders was generally the member most respected for his contributions to the accomplishment of tasks within the group. The other was generally the best-liked member, who was most respected for his contribution and support of friendly interaction among members. Further noteworthy analyses of the emergence of task and relational leaders were contributed by Bales (1958), Bales and Slater (1955), Borgatta and Bales (1956), Carter (1954), and Slater (1955).

It is important to note that not all of these studies consistently showed the emergence of the same pattern of two differentiated high status leadership roles and resulting follower roles for the remaining group members. For example, Bales and Slater (1955) found that member roles were differentiated along three dimensions. Two of the dimensions did correspond to the typical task and relational functions. But the third dimension simply reflected the member's activity level. Individual group members scoring highly on the three dimensions gained respect from other members and were thus accorded higher status in reciprocation for their special contributions to the group. An interesting finding from the Slater (1955) study was that the degree of group consensus in the identification of the status hierarchy was related to the pattern of emergent role differentiation. The strongest consensus was generally achieved among the status appraisals of the members when the two most active individuals emerged into distinct roles, one as task specialist and the other as a relationship specialist. The task specialist would then have the highest status and the relationship specialist would have the second highest status. Consensus was lowest when a third member, who did not score highly on either the task or relational dimensions, was at least as active as either or both of the members scoring highest on the task and relational dimensions. This pattern indicates that group members disagreed on the value of the relative contribution made to the group by member behaviors along the task, relationship, and activity dimensions. At least a significant portion of the individual members of a group apparently accord high status to an individual who contributes by participating a great deal despite making relatively little contribution to group maintenance or task achievement.

Studies of status emergence have generally attempted to purify the phenomenon of interest by minimizing the possibilities for anything other than interaction among members in the group context to affect individual perceptions of member status. Chief among such biasing factors ruled out by experimental control in a well-designed laboratory study of status emergence is any prior relationship among subjects as members of the same group, as their prior acquaintance could overcome any experimental manipulation of socialization cues. Yet we know that most self-directed work teams will actually be composed in ongoing organizations of members who have prior acquaintance with each other from past work experience. One might then question the usefulness of the findings from the long stream of psychological laboratory studies, not only regarding the emergence of influence leaders of higher status, but indeed regarding any of the interpersonal and group dynamics material to the function of work teams. Yet to treat this massive body of research as uninformative risks not only the reinvention of the wheel, but also the misinterpretation of contemporary research. With respect to the establishment of internal leadership in self-directed work teams when the members have worked together previously, we should examine how the prior experiences of work team members may pre-dispose (or even predetermine) the behavioral patterns of leading and following in their new groups.

While research that examines emergent leadership among strangers is abundant, research that incorporates the interpersonal knowledge of group members from prior interaction is rare. However, several studies of emergent group status have used the conceptual framework of expectation states, which can accommodate member expectations based on prior knowledge (Berger et al., 1980). Briefly, the expectation states model of emergent status explains individual assessments of member status in terms of expectations held for the various contributions to task accomplishment and group maintenance to be made by group members. This approach has withstood a challenge from advocates of a demeanor explanation for the emergence of dominant members in groups. Lee and Ofshe (1981) found that deference-demanding body language including a relatively loud, fast, and firm tone of voice with little hesitation, strong eye contact, and traditional business attire yielded high influence while deferential body language including soft, slow, and hesitating speech with disjunctive pauses, poor eye contact, and overly casual attire yielded low influence, while the identification of an individual as holding a high versus low status job title had no effect on the resulting influence.

However, a 1984 study by Tuzlak and Moore found effects on influence for both demeanor and status. Furthermore, the effect of demeanor was found to diminish over time, suggesting the possibility that the behavioral cues of demeanor might serve as a temporary surrogate for the more enduring cues of role expectations in establishing which members lead and which members follow. Ridgeway (1984) formulated a model that integrated the demeanor and expectation states approaches and found support for it in a subsequent study (Ridgeway, 1987). An important feature of Ridgeway's model for our purposes is its characterization of demeanor contests as dyadic phenomena while the emergence of a status hierarchy requires the establishment of an effective degree of consensus across the entire group membership. Members of newly formed teams will need to sort out their perceptions of which members can and will best facilitate the task and relational needs of the group. If they have prior knowledge of each others' group behavior patterns, we should simply expect this knowledge to be incorporated into their sent expectations for these other group members. Given what we know about Pygmalion effects (Eden & Shani, 1982), we should expect that emergent leadership should stabilize rather quickly when teams are formed from members with prior shared experience. We can also see again that conceptualizing how each member may have a role that is defined in relation to the group as a whole presents a useful tool for understanding how some members of a group may come to follow the lead of certain other members. While no empirical studies to date have addressed the issue, future research should certainly examine whether status in a group is a linear function of the relative standing of members on TMX. Team member exchange may prove to be a key mediating construct in the establishment of emergent team leadership.

Norms

While roles comprise those patterned behaviors characteristic of certain members in a group, norms involve patterned behaviors characteristic across members of the group. Thibaut and Kelly (1959) suggested that norms evolve as a functional response to sources of discord among group members. Thus, norms may be seen as implicitly negotiated agreements on rules of conduct to be observed by all group members. In this sense behavioral compliance with group norms constitutes a special portion of the roles negotiated by individual members. Roles include certain patterned behaviors that differentiate members from one another, but they also include patterned behavior that is simultaneously expected to be acceptable for all members, and which ritualistically signifies each member's social identity as a group member.

While much of the literature explaining group norms emerged before interest in teams became widespread, more recent contributions have continued to expand our knowledge of how norms may arise in work teams. Opp (1982) suggested three types of processes that could give rise to norms. The first type was called institutional. An institutional norm would be one that arises because the members of a group consistently comply with the mandates of external leaders or other authority figures. Here members shift from doing something "because the boss said so" to doing something "because that's the way we do it here." The second type was labeled voluntary. Voluntary norms correspond to those identified by Thibaut and Kelly (1959), which arise from negotiation among members in the resolution of a conflict. The third category suggested by Opp (1982) was called evolutionary. An evolutionary norm would be one that arises as members model the behaviors that a single member exhibits, simply because they find this behavior to be as easy and comfortable as does the originating member. Another suggestion regarding the origin of norms comes from Bettenhausen and Murnighan (1985). They suggest that individuals have cognitive scripts that they bring to groups as members. They act out behavior according to which script fits the situation. When members classify situations similarly and share scripts, norms develop around the common behaviors.

Norms are useful to members, as well as groups, in several ways. Norms reinforce group identity by reminding both the individual members of what they have in common and what may differentiate them from other groups. Norms also provide an exchange opportunity for members to reaffirm their psychological contract with the group, as this contract cannot be a static arrangement between the parties. The individual members of a group, and the group as a social entity, must both continue to evolve through normal patterns of growth and development. As events proceed, behavioral compliance with norms provides the group and its members with the comfort of consistency. Related to this, norms govern member perceptions of fairness and equity. Even as role differentiation yields relatively great status and influence to some members, norms provide a signal that, at least in some sense, all members remain equal. As norms are standards for behavior, they offer economies to group functioning. Common behavioral standards save efforts by making certain group operations relatively automatic, analogous to the way that an individual person's habits can save effort by automating behavior. Functions of a group that might otherwise require taking the time to meet and make a decision can be taken care of via convention. For example, a norm might require individual team members to publicize in a particular fashion those actions taken on one's job that might affect other team members. So long as a note does not get posted on a bulletin board, members need not pay any more attention than usual to what coworkers are doing, nor do they need to hold a team meeting to hear the announcement that "there's no news today."

Norms constitute a major medium of social exchange between groups and their members. That group members collectively want conformity to their norms is evidenced by the sanctions for deviations applied to non-conforming members (Blau & Scott, 1962). That social norms are of particular relevance to group productivity is illustrated in Whyte's (1955) analysis of rate restrictions, as well as in detailed analysis of the Hawthorne effect (Kahn, 1975). While we already have at least some evidence that the average level of TMX predicts performance at the group level of analysis, future research should further examine this linkage. It seems quite likely that we should also find that teams with the highest aggregate level of TMX would have the strongest norms concerning the task performance of members. Teams characterized by strong exchange relationships between the group and its members should be least dependent on external team leadership.

Group Working Relationships and Coordinated Efforts

We should also expect working relationships within a workgroup to affect both formal and voluntary means of coordination. Constructive working relationships require and encourage skilled interaction among members who have a very clear understanding of what they can expect from other members, as well as what others expect from them and how they can meet those expectations. If members work together with such skilled interaction, they should be able to focus their efforts toward establishing and maintaining a high degree of collaboration. A workgroup with constructive working relationships is, therefore, more likely to make effective use of administrative systems, liaison officers, formal meetings, and other formal mechanisms to achieve coordination than a group with poor working relationships.

While group working relationships can thus affect the formal means of coordination, working relationships should likely have a greater influence on the voluntary means of coordination. In a workgroup with effective working relationships, members will have a high level of mutual understanding and trust. They can expect help and assistance from their coworkers and can be confident that they can rely on others. In this way, groups whose members maintain effective working relationships should have the greatest capacity for voluntary coordination.

We should also see the effects of the quality of working relationships within individual group members. An individual member's working relationship with coworkers should influence the member's decisions about the direction of efforts. As shown by previous research (Katerberg & Blau, 1983; Naylor et al., 1980; Terborg & Miller, 1978), some of an individual member's efforts are directed toward productive work activities and some are not. In a workgroup, the efforts of an individual member allocated to productive work activities can be directed toward the achievement of the group goals and/or individual goals. In a study combining group and individual goal-setting, Crown and Rosse (1995) found that individuals could develop a high degree of commitment to both individual and group goals, thus simultaneously optimizing both individual and group performance.

Our present analysis suggests that an individual's working relationship with coworkers will influence a team member's commitment to group performance. High levels of commitment to both individual and group goals should be evident when a member has effective peer working relationships, as that person should be generally exhibiting behaviors that contribute to the group in return for optimal social rewards.

We propose that when members of a group act in ways that influence others to better coordinate their efforts, they are providing leadership. Thus, individuals high on TMX can serve as internal team leaders, not only because they achieve influential status, but also because they adopt patterns of behavior that effectively complement the behavioral patterns of other team members. Our analysis suggests that the ability of members to coordinate their efforts depends on their perception and recognition of the interdependent network of roles and relationships through which they are linked to other team members and that the motivation of members to coordinate their efforts depends on their perception and recognition of the instrumentality of reciprocal exchange among team members. Thus, teamwork should be produced when team members clearly understand their roles and how those roles are interdependent, and when mutually beneficial reciprocal exchanges characterize the working relationships among those members.

The Question of Role Chemistry

Evidence that teams can differ systematically on their average level of TMX (Seers et al., 1995) implies that we should not simply expect a normal distribution of TMX scores within groups such that most group members score in a middle range with the emergent leader anchoring the high end of the distribution and a laggard (or deviant) anchoring the low end. The average level of TMX may roughly index the proportion of members with the ability and willingness to serve, in some capacity, as emergent leaders. As reviewed previously, studies of emergent leadership showed that, left to their own devices, groups usually produced two emergent leaders, but could produce more or less than two. Thus, Benne and Sheats' (1948) identification of multiple role types within the two major categories of group roles might be viewed as providing prototypes for differing types of task leaders and differing types of relational leaders. Just as the task and relational leadership types have been found to constitute mutually compatible leadership roles, some of the specialized roles within those task and relational categories may prove to provide compatible forms of leadership.

Perhaps the first place to look for compatible roles from which shared leadership could be exercised would be the finer distinctions generated in studies of the dimensionality of leader behavior. In fact, we get a very consistent set of distinctions by retracing the evolution of traditional leader behavior models. While the most commonly remembered characterization of the leader behavior studies emanating from the University of Michigan studies identifies the two dimensions of job-centered and employee-centered behaviors, Bowers and Seashore (1966) separated the job-centered behaviors into work facilitation and goal emphasis, and also separated the employee-centered behaviors into leader support and interaction facilitation. House and Dessler's (1974) formulation of path-goal theory identified two similar types of leader task behavior and two similar types of leader relational behavior. The directive and goal-oriented behaviors identified in path-goal theory correspond to the work facilitation and goal emphasis behaviors from Bowers and Seashore (1966), just as the supportive and participative behaviors from path-goal theory correspond to leader support and interaction facilitation.

Table 1 lists the task and relational roles identified by Benne and Sheats (1948) in approximate correspondence to the four categories of leader behavior

Table 1.   Group Roles and Leadership Dimensions

University of Michigan	Path Goal Theory	Benne and Sheats
Work Facilitation	Directive	Information Seeker
		Initiator
		Contributor
		Information Giver
		Opinion Giver
		Elaborator
		Coordinator
		Procedural Technician
		Recorder
Goal Emphasis	Goal Oriented	Evaluator/Critic
		Orientor
		Energizer
Leader Support	Supportive	Encourager
		Standard Setter
		Follower
Interactioin Facilitation	Participative	Harmonizer
		Compromiser
		Gatekeeper
		Observer/Commentator

common to path-goal theory and the Michigan studies. Almost one-half of Benne and Sheats' group role types correspond to the directive/work facilitation category. This may reflect an implicit theory that emphasizes the structuring aspects of leadership, but all of the remaining three leader behavior categories still can be associated with at least three of the group role types from Benne and Sheats (1948). An initial working hypothesis might be that groups with members whose behavioral tendencies reflect all four categories proportionately might have better shared leadership chemistry than groups composed of members whose behavioral tendencies tend to concentrate within certain categories. The latter type of groups might experience more conflict and power struggles among the members.

Our analysis, of course, only sketches a crude outline from which a model of shared internal leadership relevant for self-directed work teams could be developed. Much conceptual elaboration remains to be done. Still, the previously suggested rough outline may serve as a useful starting point for developing preliminary empirical investigations to begin exploring the potential for a model of shared internal leadership in which multiple group members can serve influential leadership roles for various important functions common to work teams, while these members in turn accept the leadership influence of each other at different times for different functions. A major practical benefit of increased knowledge about the team member exchange relationships underlying the notion of shared leadership may be that training programs designed to enhance team member exchange could significantly improve the coordination of effort, and thus effective teamwork, among members of self-directed work teams. There is existing evidence (Graen, Novak, & Sommerkamp, 1982) that analogous training for external leaders can improve their abilities to form more effective working relationships with members of traditional workgroups.

SUMMARY

Members of self-directed work teams have a unique opportunity to share the leadership function, as external supervision is minimized. Our analysis suggests that the role-making process can serve to facilitate team members' ability to identify the compatibilities among their behavioral tendencies and to negotiate relationships that capitalize on those compatibilities to the mutual benefit of team members. The emergent pattern of group working relationships may have the potential to explain the distribution of influence among team members in a manner such that they can effectively divide the labor of team leadership and achieve unity of direction by the integration of the efforts of team members within their differentiated roles. This process should produce a high degree of coordinated teamwork. While additional refinement is clearly needed for the constructs and relationships suggested by our analysis, research addressing these ideas appears to offer the potential for major advances in our understanding of how people work together.

REFERENCES

Allport, F.H. (1924). *Social psychology*. Cambridge, MA: Riverside Press.

Allport, F.H. (1962). A structuronomic concept of behavior: Individual and collective. *Journal of Abnormal and Social Psychology, 64*, 3-30.

Argote, L. (1982). Input uncertainty and organizational coordination in hospital emergency units. *Administrative Science Quarterly, 26*, 349-377.

Bales, R.F. (1958). Task roles and social roles in problem-solving groups. In E.E. Maccoby, T.M. Newcomb, & E.L. Hartley (Eds.), *Readings in social psychology* (pp. 437-447). New York: Henry Holt.

Bales, R.F., & Slater, P.E. (1955). Role differentiation in small decision-making groups. In T. Parsons & R.F. Bales (Eds.), *Family, socialization, and interaction processes* (pp. 259-306). New York: Free Press.

Barnard, C.I. (1938). *The functions of the executive*. Cambridge, MA: Harvard University Press.

Beer, M. (1976). The technology of organizational development. In M.D. Dunnette (Ed.), *Handbook of industrial and organizational psychology* (pp. 937-973). Chicago: Rand McNally.

Bem, D.J. (1967). Self-perception: The dependent variable of human performance. *Organizational Behavior and Human Performance, 2*, 105-121.

Benne, K.D., & Sheats, P. (1948). Functional roles of group members. *Journal of Social Issues,* *4,* 41-49.

Berger, J., Rosenholt, S.J., & Zelditch, M. (1980). Status organizing processes. *Annual Review of Sociology, 6,* 479-508.

Bettenhausen, J., & Murnighan, J.K. (1985). The emergence of norms incompetitive decision-making groups. *Administrative Science Quarterly, 30,* 350-372.

Blau, P.M., & Scott, W.R. (1962). *Formal organizations: A comparative approach.* San Francisco: Chandler Publishing Co.

Borgatta, E.F., & Bales, R.F. (1956). Sociometric status patterns and characteristics of interaction. *Journal of Social Psychology, 43,* 289-297.

Bowers, D.G., & Seashore, S.E. (1966). Predicting organizational effectiveness with a four factor theory of leadership. *Administrative Science Quarterly, 11,* 238-263.

Buller, P.F., & Bell, C.H. (1986). Effects of team building and goal setting on productivity: A field experiment. *Academy of Management Journal, 29,* 305-328.

Campion, M.A., Medsker, G.J., & Higgs, A.C. (1993). Relations between workgroup characteristics and effectiveness: Implications for designing effective workgroups. *Personnel Psychology, 46,* 823-850.

Carter, L.F. (1954). Recording and evaluating the performance of individuals as members of small groups. *Personnel Psychology, 7,* 477-484.

Cheng, J.L.C. (1983). Interdependence and coordination in organizations: A role-system analysis. *Academy of Management Journal, 26,* 156-162.

Cheng, J.L.C. (1984). Organizational coordination, uncertainty, and performance: An integrative study. *Human Relations, 37,* 829-851.

Crown, D.F., & Rosse, J.G. (1995). Yours, mine and ours: Facilitating group productivity through the integration of individual and group goals. *Organizational Behavior and Human Decision Processes, 64,* 138-150.

Cummings, T.G. (1977). *Management of work: A socio-technical systems approach.* Kent, OH: Kent State University Press.

Deaux, K. (1993). Reconstructing social identity. *Personality and Social Psychology Bulletin, 19,* 4-12.

Durkheim, E. (1898). *The rules of sociological method.* New York: Free Press.

Dyer, W.E. (1987). *Team building: Issues and alternatives.* Reading, MA: Addison Wesley.

Eden, D., & Shani, A.B. (1982). Pygmalion goes to boot camp: Expectancy, leadership, and trainee performance. *Journal of Applied Psychology, 67,* 194-199.

Ethier, K.A., & Deaux, K. (1994). Negotiating social identity when contexts change: Maintaining identification and responding to threat. *Journal of Personality and Social Psychology, 67,* 243-251.

Festinger, L. (1950). Informal social communication. *Psychological Review, 57,* 271-282.

Fiedler, F.E. (1967). *A theory of leadership effectiveness.* New York: McGraw-Hill.

Gabarro, J.J. (1987). The development of working relationships. In J.W. Lorsch (Ed.), *Handbook of organizational behavior* (pp. 171-189). Englewood Cliffs, NJ: Prentice Hall.

Gladstein, D.L. (1984). Groups in context: A model of task group effectiveness. *Administrative Science Quarterly, 29,* 499-517.

Goffman, E. (1959). *The presentation of the self in everyday life.* New York: Free Press.

Goodman, P.S., Ravlin, E., & Schminke, M. (1987). Understanding groups in organizations. *Research in Organizational Behavior, 9,* 121-173.

Graen, G. (1976). Role making processes within complex organizations. In M.D. Dunnette (Ed.), *Handbook of industrial and organizational psychology* (pp. 1201-1245). Chicago: Rand McNally.

Graen, G., & Cashman, J.F. (1975). A role-making model of leadership in formal organizations: A developmental approach. In J.G. Hunt & L.L. Larson (Eds.), *Leadership frontiers* (pp. 143-165). Kent, OH: Comparative Administration Research Institute, Kent State University.

Graen, G., Novak, M.A., & Sommerkamp, P. (1982). The effects of leader-member exchange and job design on productivity and satisfaction: Testing a dual attachment model. *Organizational Behavior and Human Performance, 30,* 109-131.

Hackman, J.R. (1987). The design of work teams. In J.W. Lorsch (Ed.), *Handbook of organizational behavior* (pp. 315-342). Englewood Cliffs, NJ: Prentice-Hall.

Hackman, J.R., & Morris, C.G. (1975). Group tasks, group interaction process, and group performance effectiveness: A review and proposed integration. *Advances in Experimental Social Psychology, 8,* 45-99.

Hage, J. (1980). *Theories of organizations.* New York: John Wiley & Sons.

Hare, A.P. (1976). *Handbook of small group research.* New York: Free Press.

Harrison, R. (1973). Role negotiation: A tough minded approach to team development. In W.G. Bannis, D.E. Berlew, E.H. Schein, & F.I. Steele (Eds.), *Interpersonal dynamics: Essays and readings on human interaction,* 3rd ed., (pp. 467-479). Homewood, IL: Dorsey Press.

Homans, G.C. (1950). *The human group.* New York: Harcourt, Brace and World.

Homans, G.C. (1961). *Social behavior: Its elementary forms.* New York: Harcourt Brace and World.

House, R.J., & Dessler, G. (1974). The path-goal theory of leadership: Some post-hoc and a priori tests. In J.G. Hunt & L.L. Larson (Eds.), *Contingency approaches to leadership* (pp. 29-55). Carbondale, IL: Southern Illinois Press.

Jacobs, T.O. (1970). *Leadership and exchange in formal organizations.* Alexandria, VA: Human Resources Research Organization.

Janz, T., & Tjosvold, D. (1985). Costing effective versus ineffective work relationships: A method and a first look. *Canadian Journal of Administrative Science, 2,* 43-51.

Kahn, R.L. (1975). In search of the Hawthorne effect. In E.L. Cass & F.G. Zimmer (Eds.), *Man and work in society* (pp. 49-62). New York: Van Nostrand Reinhold.

Kahn, R.L. (1956). The production of productivity. *Journal of Social Issues, 12,* 41-49.

Katerberg, R., & Blau, G.J. (1983). An examination of level and direction of effort and job performance. *Academy of Management Journal, 26,* 249-257.

Katz, D., & Kahn, R.L. (1966). *The Social Psychology of Organizations.* New York: Wiley.

Katz, D., & Kahn, R.L. (1978). *The Social Psychology of Organizations,* 2nd ed. New York: Wiley.

Kolodny, H.F., & Kiggundu, M.N. (1980). Toward the development of a sociotechnical systems model in woodlands mechanical harvesting. *Human Relations, 33,* 623-645.

Kozlowski, S.W.J., Gully, S.M., Salas, E., & Cannon-Bowers, J.A. (1996). Team leadership and development: Theory, principles, and guidelines for training leaders and teams. In M. Beyerlein, D. Johnson, & S. Beyerlein (Eds.) *Interdisciplinary advances in the study of work teams,* Vol. 3. Greenwich, CT: JAI Press.

Lee, J.W. (1989). Technological interdependence, working relationships, and group-task effectiveness. Unpublished doctoral dissertation, University of Alabama.

Lee, M.T., & Ofshe, R. (1981). The impact of behavioral style and status characteristics on social influence: A test of two competing theories. *Social Psychology Quarterly, 44,* 73-82.

Levine, J.M., & Moreland, R.L. (1990). Progress in small group research. *Annual Review of Psychology, 41,* 585-634.

Liebowitz, S.J., & DeMeuse, K.P. (1982). The application of team building. *Human Relations, 35,* 1-18.

Litterer, J.A. (1973). *The analysis of organizations,* 2nd ed. New York: John Wiley & Sons.

Manz, C.C. (1986). Self-leadership: Toward an expanded theory of self-influence processes in organizations. *Academy of Management Review, 11,* 585-600.

Manz, C.C., & Sims, H.P., Jr. (1987). The external leadership of self-directed work teams. *Administrative Science Quarterly, 32*, 106-128.

Moreland, R.L., & Levine, J.M. (1982). Socialization in small groups: Temporal changes in individual-group relations. *Advances in Experimental Social Psychology, 15*, 137-192.

Moreland, R.L., & Levine, J.M. (1984). Role transitions in small groups. In V.L. Allen & E. van de Vliert (Eds.), *Role transitions: Explorations and explanation* (pp. 181-195). New York: Plenum.

Naylor, J., Pritchard, R., & Likert, D. (1980). *A theory of behavior in organizations.* New York: Academic Press.

Opp, K.D. (1982). The volutionary emergence of norms. *British Journal of Social Psychology, 21*, 139-149.

Ridgeway, C.L. (1984). Dominance, performance, and status in groups. In E.J. Lawler (Ed.), *Advances in group processes* (pp. 59-93). Greenwich, CT: JAI Press.

Ridgeway, C.L. (1987). Nonverbal behavior, dominance, and the basis of status in task groups. *American Sociological Review, 52*, 683-694.

Roger, D.B., & Reid, R.L. (1982). Role differentiation and seating arrangements: A further study. *British Journal of Social Psychology, 21*, 23-29.

Sarbin, T.R., & Allen, V.L. (1968). Role theory. In G. Lindzey & E. Aronson (Eds.), *Handbook of social psychology*, Vol. 1 (pp. 488-567). Reading, MA: Addison-Wesley.

Seers, A. (1989). Team-member exchange quality: A new construct for role making research. *Organizational Behavior and Human Decision Processes, 43*, 118-135.

Seers, A., Petty, M. M., & Cashman J.F. (1995). Team-member exchange under team and traditional management: A naturally occurring quasi-experiment. *Group and Organization Management, 20*, 18-38.

Slater, P.E. (1955). Role differentiation in small groups. *American Sociology Journal, 20*, 300-310.

Shea, G.P., & Guzzo, R.A. (1987). Groups as human resources. *Research in Personnel and Human Resources Management, 5*, 323-356.

Stogdill, R.M., & Coons, A.E. (Eds.) (1957). *Lender behavior: Its description and measure.* Columbus, OH: Ohio State University.

Terborg, J., & Miller, H. (1978). Motivation, behavior and performance: A close examination of goal-setting and monetary incentives. *Journal of Applied Psychology, 63*, 29-39.

Thibaut, J.W., & Kelly, H.H. (1959). *The social psychology of groups.* New York: Wiley.

Trist, E.L., & Bamforth, K.W. (1951). Some social and psychological consequences of the long-wall method of coal getting. *Human Relations, 4*, 3-38.

Tuzlak, A., & Moore, J.C. (1984). Status, demeanor, and influence: An empirical reassessment. *Social Psychological Quarterly, 47*, 178-183.

Van de Ven, A.H., Delbecq, A.L., & Koenig, R., Jr. (1976). Determinants of coordination modes within organizations. *American Sociological Review, 41*, 322-338.

Weick, K.E. (1979). *The social psychology of organizing*, 2nd ed. Reading, MA: Addison Wesley.

Whyte, W.F. (1955). *Money and motivation.* New York: Harper & Row.

Woodman, R.W., & Sherwood, J.J. (1980). The role of team development in organizational effectiveness: A critical review. *Psychological Bulletin, 88*, 166-186.

Zurcher, L.A. (1983). *Social roles: Conformity, conflict and creativity.* Beverly Hills: Sage.

BUILDING HIGHLY DEVELOPED TEAMS:
FOCUSING ON SHARED LEADERSHIP PROCESSES, EFFICACY, TRUST, AND PERFORMANCE

Bruce J. Avolio, Dong I. Jung, William Murry, and Nagaraj Sivasubramaniam

ABSTRACT

In this paper, we provide an alternative framework for examining team leadership development, focusing specifically on the type of shared leadership observed at different levels of group/team development. Results are provided from two longitudinal studies that offer preliminary support for the conceptual model of team development presented in this paper.

INTRODUCTION

A team: To join forces or efforts.;
teamwork: subordinating prominence to the efficiency of the whole.
—*Webster's Unabridged Dictionary*, 1986

Advances in Interdisciplinary Studies
of Work Teams, Volume 3, pages 173-209.
Copyright © 1996 by JAI Press Inc.
All rights of reproduction in any form reserved.
ISBN: 0-7623-0006-X

In many popular outlets today, we hear a growing call for restructuring organizations around teams, usually ones that are multifunctional, fluid, and more boundaryless. Concurrently, there is a fundamental shift occurring in many organizations toward increasing employee involvement in leadership and decision-making roles (Lawler, 1986, 1992). The strategic makeover in numerous organizations seems to be borne out of necessity, rather than simply being the current trend. As organizations decrease levels of management, while increasing spans of control, the creation of *natural work teams* is fast becoming the core unit in the redesign of organizational systems. Coupled with these organizational transformations is the need to compete with other countries who are far more advanced in their use of teams than is the United States.

Shifting to Team Systems

Today, nearly 66 percent of the largest North American organizations have set up some form of self-managed teams, up from 28 percent in 1987. Some recent surveys project that up to 40 percent of U.S. employees will participate in self-managed teams by the year 2000 (Manz & Sims, 1993). It appears that teams rather than individuals will characterize the organizational structures of the next millennium.

The numerous ongoing organizational restructuring efforts, coupled with employees having far greater access and need for all forms of information, points to an obvious conclusion that more teamwork is needed (Cohen, 1990). Team systems appear to be emerging as the fundamental building block in what many writers describe as the post-bureaucratic age of organizations (Kanter, 1983; Ogilvy, 1990; Parker, 1992).

The shift toward team-based organizational structures has not always come about easily, particularly when the development of teams has occurred from the inside out, versus by way of setting up greenfield operations. Some of the difficulty stems from the fact that many organizations have to shift from a control-oriented culture based on external rules and procedures, to a culture that has internal controls based on consensual values and beliefs. As Barker (1993) indicates, "In a sense, concertive control reflects the adoption of a new substantive rationality, a new set of consensual values, by the organization and its members" (p. 412). In this new environment, it is the workers who determine the social rules that guide and, if necessary, sanction the conduct of members in an organization and/or team. They create the framework that provides the basis for a system of their own controls, which is at the core of self-directed teams. The net result is the transformation of a traditional, hierarchically-based organization to one that is directed and controlled by a collaborative framework that operates within and between self-managing teams (Barker, 1993).

If team systems are to become highly developed, the external controls that have traditionally determined how work gets accomplished, must give way to self-control, which is value-based (Jermier, Slocum, Fry, & Gaines, 1991). Such value-based controls will become the source of influence for controlling the actions and directions of teams in the organizational contexts of the future.

Teams, as they develop value-based norms, will go from having a loosely coupled set of norms known to the group, to a more controlled system of guideposts (Barker, 1993). In this team systems environment, the locus of control will shift significantly from one based on transactional agreements, between an external leader and the group, to a new set of consensual values that have emerged and will guide (sometimes constrain) the team's behavior (Tompkins & Cheney, 1985). This shift requires that teams learn how to coordinate themselves and work collaboratively on projects that have been previously directed by supervisors external to the team (Bass, 1985).

We argue in this paper that the new, emerging organizational system requires more sharing of leadership responsibilities between and within organizational levels (Manz & Sims, 1987). According to several writers, the primary reason often identified for the failures associated with shifting to a more team-based environment, is the problems associated with building effective team leadership (Cummings, 1978; Klein, 1984; Stewart & Manz, 1994). Sinclair (1992) is even more specific on this issue, indicating that the most critical ingredient of team success is its leadership, where the abdication of leadership in any group, just like any other organizational setting, is a recipe for failure.

It is quite clear that a shift in control can effectively occur where one goes from an external supervisor to internal members of a team taking responsibility for supervision. Yet, an alternative set of rules and procedures may simply shift the bureaucracy in which a group was embedded into the team itself, where rewards and punishments are used to gain compliance at the expense of commitment. Moreover, the shift in responsibility for directing the team should by no means be perceived as an end point, but rather a developmental transition toward creating idealized relationships among team members, based on trust, commitment, and a common sense of purpose. What we must avoid is creating a new iron cage in the form of team systems (Barker, 1993).

Providing groups with more control over their own activities and in setting direction requires that they are able and willing to assume leadership responsibilities for themselves, and for their engagements with other groups in their organization, and/or with other organizations. Getting employees and employers to abandon hierarchical structures, and the command and control thinking that goes along with such structures, has been a formidable challenge with some, but not many widespread successes. It appears that many team initiatives have failed because of a lack of attention to leadership development (Lawler, 1986; Yukl, 1994). Yukl summarizes the work of Hackman (1987) and Lawler (1986), noting that, self-managed teams are very difficult to implement, and they can be a dismal failure when used in inappropriate structures or without sufficient leadership and support (Yukl, 1994, p. 182). Teams, like any other entity, must be capable of handling increased responsibilities, otherwise what may be perceived by some as empowerment simply becomes entrapment!

As organizations move toward team-based structures, there are several compelling questions that have not yet been fully addressed in the literature. Specifically, what are the implications for leadership processes and leadership development in the new team-based organizational structure? Clearly, the leadership role is an integral part of the structure of self-directed teams, yet to date, it has not been fully explored (Stewart & Manz, 1994). Complicating matters, as leadership becomes shared within a collection of roles, it must be developed and learned to fill the void where the lines of authority and decision making in team-based organizations are blurred. Indeed, the need for leadership will not go away, and will be even more challenging for groups developing their own authority structures (see Schneier & Goktepe, 1983).

One Significant Example of a Shift Toward Teams

A dramatic example of the shift toward teams is unfolding in New York State, and is driven by the New Compact for Learning, recently approved by the New York State commissioner of education. The compact required that all public schools have in place a strategic plan for implementing shared decision-making teams by February 1995. Administrative leaders in the public school system were required by law to involve others in their decision-making processes. The directive from the commissioner to establish shared leadership and decision-making processes in many school systems which were used to working under a more authoritarian, control-oriented structure, represented a radical shift from past practices. Following the commissioner's directive, numerous questions remain unanswered, such as:

1. How much formal leadership should be shared with others?
2. What obligation does the school system's leaders have to develop members of shared decision-making teams to handle their increased responsibility?
3. What should a school officer do when others in the school do not want to be involved in the decision-making process? Each of these questions have significant implications for the leadership processes, as well as the organizational culture that will eventually emerge in our public school systems. In our opinion, these questions also have implications for all other organizations moving toward team-based structures.

The dramatic change occurring in today's organizational structures raises some serious questions as to how well prepared we are in the United States to move toward effectively implementing team-based organizations. In this regard, we need to consider several additional questions beyond those just mentioned. First, to what extent have organizations created selection systems which choose individuals who are able and willing to share leadership roles and responsibilities? Simply put, do we have the right people in place to lead the next generation of team-based organizational systems?

Second, Hofstede's (1980) cross-cultural work on *individualism* versus *collectivism* indicated that North Americans were by a large margin the most individualistic culture out of the 40 countries participating in his study. The *I* has traditionally been the common denominator in U.S. organizations versus the *we* or the *us*. To achieve the higher developmental level associated with teams, individuals must evolve from focusing on self-interest, and developing their own competence, to supporting the collective interest of the team and the full development of its members (Kozlowski et al., 1994).

Third, most reward and performance evaluation systems are still individually-based, with relatively little emphasis on recognizing group accomplishments. Similarly, most organizations do not use peer evaluations to determine merit increases, or promotions, which is a critical element in developing high performance teams. Many systems that are still in place in U.S. organizations may inhibit rather than contribute to the changeover toward implementing team-based organizational structures. Indeed, given the individualistic base in U.S. society, and the accrued experiences of individuals, we cannot simply assume that all individuals will prefer to work in teams. Since rewards in many organizations are individually-based, the belief that a group and/or team will help individual employees achieve their personal goals is a critical issue that must be addressed (Vancouver & Ilgen, 1989). Similarly, we must also examine whether some individuals simply prefer to work alone rather than in groups (Loher, Vancouver, & Czajka, 1994). Such preferences are likely to be affected by previous, as well as current, experiences in working with groups or teams (Lawler, 1981; Pritchard et al., 1988).

Summary

On the one hand, there has been a surge of interest in developing teams and many organizations are now captivated by the wisdom of such structures. However, the systems presently in place in many organizations make it difficult, if not impossible, to fully implement a team-based organization. Above and beyond these critical issues, another essential ingredient for introducing teams in organizations lies in the team members' collective perspective regarding their responsibility to each other and their mission. A collective perspective can develop as the team learns to guide and govern its own direction. It is where the team realizes that it is fully responsible for controlling its own behavior, and has the interpersonal skills and perspectives to do so (Lawler, 1992; Manz & Sims, 1987). In our opinion, how this perspective-taking capacity develops, represents the holy grail in both building highly developed teams and in the quality of leadership observed in those teams. It also represents a formidable challenge for an individualistic culture like that of the United States where we must shift our support from external control-oriented managers to internal controls exercised by members of the team in the form of shared leadership. Only when a team has developed the skills and perspective to govern itself, is it ready to lead itself (Manz, 1992). To be successful, this will require that we create in U.S. organizations a balance between the benefits derived from an individualistic culture, such as innovation and creativity, with those of a collectivistic culture, including high integration and collaboration.

An overall dilemma for evolving leadership processes in the team development process was succinctly articulated by Stewart and Manz (1994), when they asked, "How does one lead others who are supposed to lead themselves?" (p. 3). This is by no means an easy question to resolve, and presents the challenge for leadership development in these new, emerging organizational structures.

CONSIDERING AN ALTERNATIVE FRAMEWORK FOR EXAMINING TEAMS

Why Most Teams Are Really Groups

While all teams are groups, not all groups can be considered teams (Tannenbaum et al., 1992, p. 118). Minimally, for a group to be a team they *must* share a common goal. Collective goals, perspective, and interest must be aligned with individual interests and agendas which are often in conflict (Sinclair, 1992). The shift between a *group* and a *team* can therefore be stressful, and even dissatisfying, to the extent that such conflicts exist, and the guidelines and rules for optimal team development and performance are unclear. Yet, the team can continue to develop over time and to work toward sharing responsibilities to the extent that the team provides for itself a sense of meaning and collective purpose with which its members can personally identify over time (Shamir, 1990).

In Figure 1, we have presented a simple framework to help examine how a collection of individuals evolve into a structured group, team, and, ultimately a highly developed team which has established common goals and/or shared purposes. Later we expand this framework by highlighting some of the variables one can track to mark different phases of group and team development. Underlying this simple framework, are several facets of group

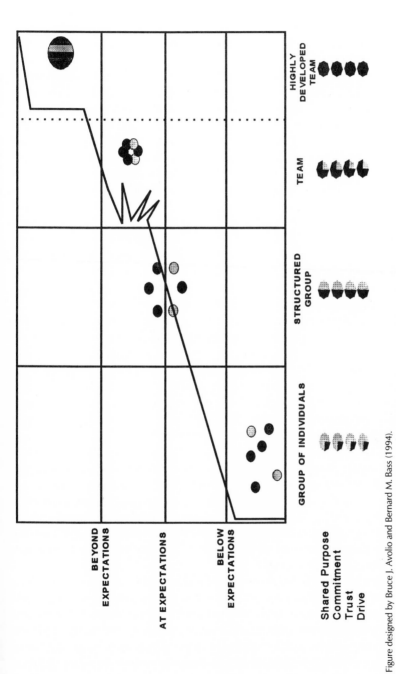

Figure designed by Bruce J. Avolio and Bernard M. Bass (1994).

Source: *Creating the High Performance Team*, by Steve Buchholz and Thomas Roth, edited by Karen Hess for Wilson Learning Corporation.

Figure 1. Overview of Team Development

development which are pertinent to understanding how groups become teams, and ultimately how leadership processes impact on the process of team development. We have intentionally used the term highly developed versus high performing to focus on the process and perspective associated with the highest levels of team development.

We begin our examination of the relationship of individuals to each other, using a level of analysis framework (see Dansereau et al., 1984 for a detailed discussion of levels of analysis issues). Specifically, at the lower left-end of Figure 1, we have a label indicating a collection of individuals, which are depicted as being heterogenous by different shaded circles. At this level, the appropriate unit of analysis would be the individual. Specifically, individual differences are the norm rather than the exception with respect to group member's levels of trust, commitment, drive, and shared leadership. The degree to which these perceptions are present for a group is noted by the amount of the circle colored in gray, for example, the lower the amount the less it is present. At this level, there is attention to learning how to do my task, or how to master my own work. The roles and relationships within the group are ill-defined and are not generally on the radar screen of individual members.

At the next phase of group development depicted in Figure 1 the group has now become more structured based on the establishment of specific agreements and role specifications. Certain expectations are set by individuals for each other where compliance to those expectations is sought. The learning process involved may focus on learning the roles required to function as a team, but at this level members are not thinking of team roles, rather they view their individual roles within the context of a group in which they are a member. Tannenbaum, Beard, and Salas (1992) describe a team as being based on a range of overlapping roles from which the teams' collective behavior can be best understood in terms of the individual member's perceptions of their roles.

Most team-building efforts are, in fact, geared toward clarifying individual versus collective roles, while at the same time reducing role ambiguity and conflict. As shown in Figure 1, there is less heterogeneity within the group in terms of certain characteristics, such as level of drive, shared purpose, commitment, and trust. This phase of the group's development can be characterized by higher within versus between group homogeneity, on the indicators shown at the bottom of Figure 1. The relevant unit of analysis is now emerging at the group level.

One expects at this level of development that individual members are learning to assume partial responsibility for other group members' roles. The assumption of these new responsibilities occurs as the group takes on new challenges and opportunities in its external environment. Kozlowski and coworkers (1994) refer to this evolutionary process as going from the individual to the dyad, to multiple dyads to flexible networks within developing groups.

Moving further to the right, if we were to compare the more developed target group depicted in Figure 1 to other groups back at earlier phases of their development, we would see that the variance within these earlier groups in levels of trust and shared purposes, would be much lower and would differ significantly from groups at earlier cycles in their own development. Another way of stating this is that there is a shared perspective among group or even team members, concerning key team indicators, for example, sense of purpose, core values, and so forth. This shared perspective would reflect a team's higher stage of development. In terms of shared perspective, the team now views itself as a relevant entity of social networks/roles. Development of members is now more closely tied to the changing roles and expectations for the team. If questioned, members would be able to articulate their view of what comprises the team and its developmental process (Rentsch et al., 1994).

Tracking these people, who began as a collection of very different individuals, toward being a highly developed team, can be accomplished by examining how they collectively view the meaning of their work goals, the agreements they have on future direction, how they treat one another, what they are ultimately striving to accomplish, and their willingness to sacrifice their own gain for the gain of others. Specifically, at a lower level of group development, a collection of individuals may not perceive the need to comply with the group in that there is no shared purpose, commitment, nor any good reason to work together that has been clearly articulated for its members (Ilgen et al., 1993). Beyond simply being reasonable and cooperative, levels of trust and/or a shared sense of purpose will likely have little impact on compliance among group members. Goals are not perceived to be at a collective level. Consequently, we expect that levels of collective efficacy or personal identification with the group's purpose/goals would not be very high at this point in the group's development (Bandura, 1986; Shamir et al., 1993).

If there is no compelling reason for a collection of individuals to work together, except perhaps an external threat, then there is likely to be some confusion about the group's purpose, its expectations, roles, responsibilities, and so forth. Such confusion can often lead to process losses in groups. The presence of social loafers or free riders in this collection of individuals is likely to be high, to the extent there are varying levels of motivation and commitment to contribute to a specific end goal or outcome. Clearly, members do not identify with the goal or collective purpose, and therefore their tasks are not considered meaningful (Price, 1987; Steiner, 1972). To provide some focus to the group and direction requires leadership, shared or otherwise. The group begins to develop and design its focus based on continuous transactions with each other, and those transactions require effective leadership.

If a reason for being still exists, then often groups will attempt to structure their activities, roles, and expectations to comply with the challenges or goals confronting the group. At this level of development, one expects levels of trust and a common sense of purpose to be relatively low. However, as the group works to structure itself, there should be some gains in member compliance. Generally at this level of development, the group establishes transactional agreements or contracts which specify what each member is expected to contribute to the overall group. Of course, the specificity in these contracts generally varies quite extensively, as a function of the type of leadership emerging in the group. Specifically, the clarity of the contract depends on whether the group's mission and goals are clearly set, and the extent to which members of the group understand those goals and how each member needs to contribute. These are all critical transactions that provide the foundation for structuring effective groups. And, these transactions parallel what Bass and Avolio (1994) have labeled transactional leadership. However, the unit of analysis is now at the group rather than the individual level.

As we move further up on the development curve, compliance with obligations can turn into consent over time, if each group member's perspective changes regarding their overall contribution and purpose. Also contributing to a change in perspective is whether the group provides greater external and internal rewards/recognition for accomplishing the group's objectives. In Figure 1, we have labeled this phase of development as being a fully structured group, which could be at the lower-end based on compliance, or at the higher-end based on consent, and the prior transactional agreements established within the group.

Some Preliminary Anecdotal Evidence

Over the past several years, we have conducted open-ended interviews with project leaders, technical specialists, and middle-to-upper-level managers, offering the framework in Figure 1 to judge their group's rate of development. When these groups were asked where they were in terms of development, most concluded they were not a team, but were typically at the level of a structured group. Yet, prior to examining their team, most interviewees had labelled it a team. The importance of this realization was that they had not yet built a common sense of purpose or goal, a collective vision, adequate levels of trust, or commitments to each other. Interestingly enough, they were often relieved to discover that what they and others had called a team (which they often implicitly knew was incorrect), was in fact another entity—a structured group.

Going From the I To the We: A Core Transformational Process

There is an African expression that goes as follows: "I am because you are, you are because we are." This represents one facet of Afrocentric thinking and philosophy called Ubuntu—literally translated by some authors as teamship (Christie et al., 1993). We introduce this philosophy and perspective to help address the inherent problems that result when we ask individuals to subordinate their own interests for the good of the group or collective.

In Figure 1, we represented the developmental transition from the *I* to the *we* with a squiggly line, because it is a more fundamental and systemic change in the way the group derives meaning from internal and external events, including ones tied to the group, its tasks, its commitments, interdependence, and so forth. The group transformation depicted in Figure 1 is analogous to what Burns (1978), Bass (1985), Kuhnert and Lewis (1987), Avolio and Gibbons (1988), and Torbert (1991) have labeled individual transformational leadership development. It is also similar to Bennis and Nanus's (1985), as well as Tichy and Devanna's (1986) representations of organizational transformations. Specifically, a transformation in the perspective of the team is represented by a shift from an *I* to a *we* perspective. Now, the common reference point for individual members is not so much the individual where in the structured group the expectation of members was focused on each other's goals, but rather it is based on commitments to something the group desires to accomplish. At this level of development there has now emerged a shared sense of purpose and goals.

At these higher levels of development, reality for a team is created and interpreted with respect to the impact that both internal and external events have on the team rather than on each individual, although the individual is by no means left behind, as groups develop into teams. Having established a collective goal and/or sense of purpose, the group would also be expected to exhibit higher levels of cohesion and collective efficacy (Bandura, 1982), potency (Guzzo, Yost, Campbell, & Shea, 1993), outcome interdependence (Shea & Guzzo, 1987), and active transactional and transformational leadership (Bass, 1985; Bass & Avolio, 1994; Burns, 1978).

At these higher stages, the locus of control has now shifted significantly from one based on transactional agreements, oftentimes between an external leader and the group, to a new set of consensual values that have emerged and will guide (sometimes constrain) the team's behavior (Tompkins & Cheny, 1985). The shift in development requires that the team learn how to coordinate itself, and work collaboratively on projects that had been previously directed by external supervisors (Bass, 1985). These developmental changes are associated with team members who are more willing to sacrifice their own gain for the good of the group. Supporting this claim, Evans and Dion (1991) found a moderately strong +0.42 correlation between level of cohesion and group performance. Thus, we expect teams at this level of development to also be higher performing teams. Teams that have compatible needs, alignment around purpose and cohesion, are likely to be the ones exhibiting the highest performance.

Figure 1 depicts the transformational phase in groups evolving into teams as being represented by a tightening of the group around its central core purposes. To achieve this level of cohesiveness, the group must go through what, in many cases, is a radical breakpoint, transformation, and/or conflict in perspectives among its members. We believe this is analogous to what Gersick (1988) referred to as the punctuated equilibrium phase of group development. Such transformations in groups are often driven by an external challenge to the group, or it may be a self-induced challenge generated by its members. In either case, active, constructive leadership is required to move the group from a lower to a higher level of development.

Davis-Sacks, Denison, and Eisenstat (1990) reported that teams of professional experts often sought out crises if they had to wait too long for their development to be caused by natural events. When interactions raise conflicts there are opportunities to resolve them, to build faith and trust, to learn of other members' strong versus weak positions, and to learn about oneself, while clarifying, modifying, and revising group norms. The literature on transformational leadership also indicates that such leaders often create or take advantage of crises to move groups and individuals to higher levels of commitment and performance (Avolio & Bass, 1988; Klein & House, 1995).

Whether caused by internal or external forces, if development has occurred, the group's perspective will be transformed in Kegan's sense of perspective-taking capacity, to operate at a higher level of moral expertise and/or development (see also Gaas & Ponemon, 1995). In the highly developed team, the core values will have become internalized through the transformations described previously, which in turn leads to greater levels of predictability and trust among members. Team members are more willing to go against received wisdom, confronting and even abandoning beliefs central to the group's focus. The abandonment occurs not only at the behavioral level, but also in terms of the team's assumptions and beliefs. To be highly developed, the team has to be able to restructure its beliefs and assumptions over time, when they no longer apply to new challenges and opportunities. To go from the *as is*, to the *desired*, requires leadership at any level of analysis, including the team.

The transformation in perspective and perspective-taking capacity described previously parallels discussions of group development using a more psychodynamic framework. For instance, a highly developed team would be expected to view confrontation and conflict as a mechanism for liberating the group to develop itself—to recognize conflict as an index of vitality. Smith (1982) has argued that belonging to a group (or team) creates a sense of frustration between the need to conform versus the need to remain as an individual. The central dilemma is for members of the group to maintain their individuality, while achieving the satisfaction and synergy that comes with being a member of a highly developed team. The inference we can draw here is that members of highly developed teams have resolved this dilemma through their personal identification with the group's common mission and/or sense of purpose. Yet, conflict over perspectives will still exist, and should be encouraged to maintain the vitality and continuous development of the team. Conflict, development, and performance must go hand-in-hand for highly developed teams.

An awareness of the team's transformation and the desire (more than a willingness) to sacrifice for their beliefs and to work for a common cause are two of the qualities that we would expect to find in a highly developed team. A collective desire for attaining the group's goals is seen as being much stronger than any one individual's goal attainment (Cartwright & Zander, 1968).

The most highly developed teams have the ability to establish their own judgments, exhibiting what Sims and Manz (1993) have called self-directed leadership. They operate based on a core set of values and principles versus simple transactions and contracts, which moves them collectively to a higher stage of internalization and development. The highly developed team is one that is able to perform beyond expectations and has a clear sense of its own identity. However, it is also willing to abandon courses of action which no longer make sense even when faced by external or internal pressures to remain the same. These characteristics parallel exactly what Burns (1978) and Bass (1985) have described in terms of transformational leadership.

Summary

In sum, at the highest level of development, we expect that a team will exhibit a higher sense of collective efficacy, a shared sense of purpose and vision, higher trust, and commitment as well as a greater willingness to share in its leadership responsibilities, represented by active transactional and transformational leadership. We expect that such highly developed teams will continue to develop themselves, never quite reaching a plateau since they will continuously confront new challenges and paradoxes that must be overcome (Berg & Smith, 1987). Paralleling the stages of moral development discussed by Kegan (1982), the highly developed team is more able to judge between right versus wrong, and in doing so continues to adapt to new, challenging situations.

REINTRODUCING AFROCENTRIC VIEWS OF GROUPS AND VITAL FORCES

Returning to an Afrocentric philosophy of groups, we now use the team as our reference point without neglecting the very critical contributions made by each individual. In fact, one advantage of an Afrocentric, humanistic view is that it considers the vital forces of individuals to be a function of each individual's connection to the group, or communal to which they belong. Thus, one's personal forces are enhanced by an affiliation with others, while the group's vital forces are enhanced by its affiliation with each individual. Thus, the *we* becomes a relevant entity, but only with respect to the *I*, and vice versa.

As Burns (1978) noted in describing the distinction between transactional and transformational leadership, the individual sacrifices personal gain for the gain of others. To some extent, the rights of individuals are devolved to enhance the individual's ties to the group, as is often observed in teams, and especially highly developed teams.

Based on our prior discussion, there are two critical questions that must be answered with respect to the U.S. culture. First, to what degree will North Americans be willing to tolerate de-emphasizing the individual in terms of decision making, evaluation, and rewards? Equally important, how will such groups of individuals be led? There is very little research available which has examined leadership processes at the team level versus examining a team leader and his or her influence on members of the team (Ilgen et al., 1993). We believe the answer to these questions lies in both the leadership and moral development literature cited earlier. Moreover, an Afrocentric view and philosophy provides a range of insights into the linkages between the need to be individualistic, coupled with the desire to belong to a group. Indeed, we may be able to have both, in that it appears to represent the best of what a highly developed team should achieve.

Building Unity Based on Diversity

We have stated that the most highly developed team is one that has achieved unity through its diversity. Such teams have typically evolved through a series of transitions and/or transformations, shifting from a more integrated to a more differentiated level of development, followed by a higher level of integration. At each integrated level of development, there are standard ways of operating and functioning which are fully accepted by group members. As the group moves to a more differentiated level, there is greater fragmentation and less agreement among members over how they should relate to each other. At the higher levels of integration and/or development, the teams derive meaning from events using their group as a primary point of reference, as opposed to the individual. They exhibit a strong psychological identification with the team and an internalization of the team's norms (Shamir, 1990).

The alignment in highly developed teams, creates a collective lens through which events are interpreted. It provides a road map to help guide the team toward higher cohesion and a common set of goals (Mitchell, 1986). Yet, as was shown in Figure 1, although the team is now itself an entity, each individual still remains an important element in their team. Specifically, highly developed teams recognize that their diversity, in terms of perspectives, can lead to conflict, which often results in a better way of operating and achieving the team's collective objectives. Conflict is not avoided. Indeed, the use of conflict in this manner represents a significant transformation in the team's leadership behavior.

One of the 10 positive factors identified by Eisentat and Cohen (1990) as being relevant to successful team development was addressing difficult internal and external issues for the team. The willingness to confront these issues was shown by Eisentat and Cohen to be correlated with greater learning capacity over time, as well as levels of trust among team members. We believe that conflict over perspective, which leads to more profound insights, represents a very high level of developmental potential.

Summary of Team Development

In sum, in our overview of group/team development, we have been able to capture several significant facets relevant to shared leadership behavior and its development. These included the different levels of collective perspective-taking or meaning-making that characterize the group or team over time, the relationship of these different perspectives to the drive and motivation of the group or team, and parallels to the type of influence processes expected at each phase of the group's and ultimately the team's development. We expand on this latter point in the following section on shared leadership.

It suffices to say that one of the most important changes that occurs as individuals develop into teams is that they go from a focus on self-interest to interest in others, and finally demonstrate an interest in the principles and values shared by all team members. This shift in perspective provides the foundation for building a highly developed team.

Figure 2 summarizes some of the parallel dimensions that were discussed previously, which are associated with the development of teams. These dimensions include: how the group or team observes events, its learning capacity, levels of functioning and commitment, as well as styles of leadership.

In the first column of Figure 2, at the earliest phases of a group's development, there is little focus on what the group is supposed to be doing, and their direction is therefore unspecified. As the group develops, it builds a concrete view of what it should do in the short term, which over time helps the group to transcend current problems and conflicts, to envision possibilities and potential avenues for future direction. At the highest level, teams can examine abstract patterns and trends to determine a course of action or vision for the team to pursue. Hence, the team goes from having no specific direction to one that is abstract and extends into the future.

Paralleling the ability to go from a more concrete to an abstract level of observation, at the early stages of a group's development the members do not know what they do not know. Thus, learning is unsystematic, unprogrammed, and lacking in focus and strategic emphasis. As a group develops, it builds a core knowledge base that it relies upon to address problems either internal or external to the group. To develop, however, the group must learn to go beyond its basic knowledge structure to include new ideas, perspectives, and

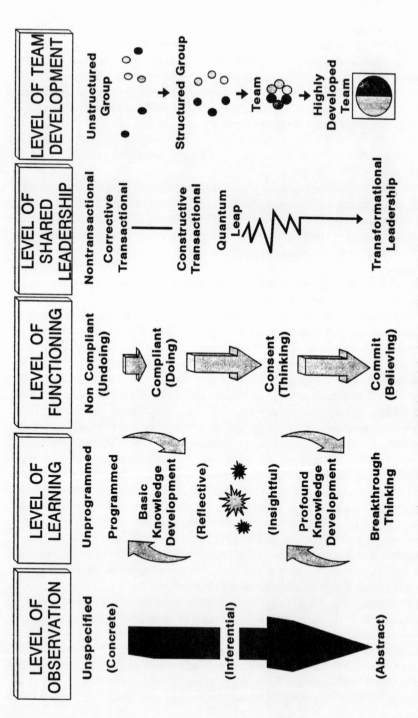

Figure 2. Expanded Model of Team Development

insights about unique problems which the group has not previously confronted. Many groups become constrained by their own core knowledge base, forcing them to routinely address problems, even when their old approaches and basic knowledge no longer apply to either new problems and/or opportunities. Breakthrough thinking occurs as the team develops an ability to question its own basic assumptions and knowledge. The team must be willing and able to attack its installed base of knowledge to continuously develop to its full potential.

In terms of functioning, at the very onset of a group's development there are no rules or guideposts. There are no specific objectives and rules the group must comply with in its work together. Once the group establishes these guideposts or rules, there are now standards it can comply with, and if helpful to the group's development, rules and procedures its members can likely consent to over time. Eventually, the group will commit to what they stand for as principles evolve from the group's interactions. Rules become ways of operating, that is, norms, standards, and values which form the basis of what the group member's truly believe in and work toward. Transactions based on rules lead to transformations based on values and beliefs.

The fourth column in Figure 2 depicts the type of shared leadership (or lack thereof) observed at each level of a group or team's development. At the lower end, where a group has very little shared purpose, we can observe a non-transactional leadership style. This parallels the lack of direction exhibited by the group. As the group develops rules and procedures it must learn to comply with them by establishing agreements on what members are supposed to do, as well as the implications for lack of compliance. Both corrective and constructive transactional leadership styles are observed at this level of a group's development. Only when the group sees itself as a team having a collective purpose, will we see a significant shift toward more transformational leadership behaviors being exhibited by team members. Now, members are inspired by the vision for the team, are willing to challenge each other's viewpoint, care deeply about each others' development, and exhibit a collective sense of purpose.

The last column in Figure 2 integrates the components of Figure 1, showing the parallels between levels of shared leadership and team development. Indeed, what we have now provided is a detailed analysis of what underlies a team's development with a specific focus on its shared leadership development.

In the next section, we briefly expand on the concept of shared leadership, before presenting some of our preliminary results, where we have examined leadership processes in teams, and how they relate to some of the indicators presented in Figure 1.

SHARED LEADERSHIP IN TEAMS

One thing has become clear in our overview of team development, and will become a focal point for the measurements of team development described below, is that shared leadership should not imply that there is no designated leadership. According to Bowers and Seashore (1966) "There are both common sense and theoretical reasons for believing that a formally acknowledged leader through his supervisory leadership behavior sets the pattern of the mutual leadership which subordinates supply each other" (p. 249). Bradford and Cohen (1984) use the concept of balance in their discussion of shared leadership. Balance can be seen in a management team of varying competencies where one member balances the other by complementing his or her skills or expertise. It can also be seen in the visions developed by many organizations, which often come from a shared leadership process (Nanus, 1992). One point is clear, we have barely begun to examine one of the more important ingredients of group development—its leadership processes, shared or otherwise.

SUMMARY

We have presented in Figures 1 and 2, a general conceptual framework for examining the team development processes. This framework links together several areas including the work on transformational and transactional leadership, perspective-taking, shared leadership, and organizational change and transformation. Our intent was to highlight the importance of focusing on the transformational process, through which a collection of individuals eventually become a team. We have also emphasized that the escalation of both transformational and transactional leadership to a group level of analysis is needed to examine the type of leadership that can be observed in teams. The method and results described below are based on two preliminary studies, which are each described in more detail in the following section.

METHOD

Participants in the studies reported below came from two separate samples. The first sample was comprised of undergraduate students who participated in two sections of an introductory course in organizational behavior. In the first sample, there were 188 male and female undergraduates participating in groups of five to seven members. In the second sample, there were 60 undergraduate students pooled from all departments on campus. These students participated in a two-year project funded by the Dwight D. Eisenhower program, Department of Education. The goals of this project were to develop student groups into teams (7-9 members each), who where then responsible for completing a socially responsible project in the community. Each sample contained participants who were generally not familiar with each other prior to either beginning the organizational behavior course or the Eisenhower training program.

Procedure

Each of the groups in the two samples were formed at either the outset of the training program or organizational behavior course.

Sample 1

In the two organizational behavior classes, ratings of team leadership, effectiveness and satisfaction using the *Team Multifactor Leadership Questionnaire* (Form 5X) developed by Bass and Avolio (1995) were collected one month into the semester (Time 1), as well as ratings of group collective efficacy and potency. The group process survey measures were repeated toward the end of the semester, at Time 2.

Sample 2

In the training sample, measures of team leadership, efficacy, trust, and cohesiveness were collected pre- versus post-training intervention. A measure of perspective-taking capacity paralleling Rest's (1986) Defining Issues Test (DIT), called the *Test of Business Issues* (TBI) developed by Escoffer and Kroeck (1990), was used to assess the moral development level of members in each group. The TBI has been developed and construct validated against other measures of moral development including the DIT (see Escoffer & Kroeck, 1990). The TBI was administered during the training intervention.

Sample Items of Survey Measures

Instructions for Bass and Avolio's (1995)
Team Multifactor Leadership Questionnaire (TMLQ Form 5X)

Please evaluate each statement in terms of your evaluation of your team's collective leadership behavior. The constructs comprising the TMLQ (Form 5X) refer to aggregate level constructs or phenomenon. A five-point rating scale was used ranging from frequently if not always to not at all. Sample items from each scale are presented in Table 1.

In addition to the leadership scales, participants also rated themselves in terms of three outcome measures, including level of effectiveness, satisfaction, and extra effort, and on three group process scales: collective efficacy, potency, and collective trust.

Table 1. Factor Analysis Results for the TMLQ(5X) and Group Process

Sample Items by Scale	Loadings	Total # of Items
Idealized Influence/Inspirational Motivation		10
Set high standards	0.60(0.53)*	
Talk about how trusting each other can help overcome their difficulties	0.47(0.49)*	
Intellectual Stimulation		5
Question the traditional ways of doing things	0.78(0.81)*	
Encourage each other to rethink ideas which had never been questioned before.	0.62(0.62)*	
Individualized Consideration		5
Treat each other as individuals with different needs, abilities, and aspirations	0.71(0.68)*	
Provide useful advice for each other's development	0.50(0.73)*	
Contingent Reward		5
Work out agreements about what's expected from each other	0.56(0.73)*	
Clearly communicate what each other needs to do to complete assignments.	0.53(0.62)*	
Management-by-Exception (Active)		5
Focus attention on irregularities, mistakes, exceptions and deviations from standards.	0.52(0.45)*	
Track each other's mistakes.	0.48(0.81)*	
Management-by-Exception (Passive)/Laissez-faire		5
Delay taking actions until problems become serious.	0.79(0.74)*	
Avoid addressing problems.	0.51(0.76)*	
Collective Efficacy		11
When unexpected problems arose, I'm sure we can handle them.	0.76(0.77)*	
If something looked too difficult, I expect we'll give up before trying. (Reverse)	0.78(0.91)*	
Group Potency		8
Our group feels it can solve any problem it encounters.	0.88(0.86)*	
Our group believes it can become unusually good at producing high-quality work.	0.78(0.89)*	

Note: * The values in parentheses are factor loadings from time 2. The factor loadings indicated a rather stable factor structure emerged across time for Sample 1 data.

Outcomes:[1]

- Effectiveness—The overall effectiveness of your group can be classified as _____. (The five-point scale used for rating effectiveness ranged from "Not Effective" through "Extremely Effective.")

- Satisfaction—In all, how satisfied are you with the leadership abilities of the team you are rating? (The five-point scale anchors used for rating satisfaction ranged from "very satisfied" through "very dissatisfied.")
- Extra Effort—Encourage each other to do more than they expected they could do. (The rating scale used here was the same as the scale previously described for the leadership dimensions.)

Group Process Measures

- Collective Efficacy—When we set goals, I'm sure we will achieve them. (These items were rated on a five-point scale with anchors ranging from "strongly disagree" through "strongly agree.")
- Potency—Our group expects to be known as a high-performance team. (These items were rated on a five-point scale with anchors ranging from "to no extent" through "to a great extent.")
- Cohesion—Members of our team have established a close working relationship. (These items were rated on a five-point scale, with anchors ranging from "a great deal" through to "not at all.")
- Trust—I mistrust members of my team. (These items were rated on a five-point scale, with anchors ranging from "a great deal" through to "not at all.")

Data collected from Sample 1 at Times 1 and 2, were subjected to a factor analysis to establish the dimensionality of the scales. The TMLQ was factor analyzed separately from the other two measures, collective efficacy and group potency, in that each of these latter instruments were validated in prior research. The results of these analyses are discussed briefly in the following paragraphs for each respective survey measure. All results presented in Tables 1-3 were based on Sample 1 data.

TMLQ (Form 5X)

The 40 items comprising the TMLQ (Form 5X) were written to represent the eight transformational, transactional, and non-leadership factors discussed earlier. The four transformational leadership factors were expected to be highly correlated, as they are component dimensions of the higher order factor of transformational leadership. More extensive details on the factor analyses that were employed with the TMLQ (5X) are reported in Avolio, Jung, Sivasubramaniam, and Murry (1995).

Results of the factor analyses produced six interpretable factors, which held up across the two data collection periods. These factors represented three transformational leadership dimensions—idealized influence/inspirational motivation, intellectual stimulation, and individualized consideration; two transactional dimensions—contingent reward and management-by-exception-active; and one passive transaction and/or non-transactional leadership factor—passive management-by-exception and laissez-faire leadership. Sample items and their factor loadings are presented in Table 1.

Collective Efficacy

Moving to the group process measures, a single factor representing collective efficacy was expected, as it was the conceptual basis of developing the 11 items. However, results across both time periods yielded more than one factor. A closer examination of these results indicated that the items did not consistently relate to the primary factor of collective efficacy. We decided to remove those two items from further analyses to retain uniformity across the two time periods. It should be pointed out that all other items had very high loadings on the collective efficacy factor.

Group Potency

The group potency scale was developed based on the work of Guzzo, Yost, Campbell, and Shea (1993). The eight items representing this construct were included in a factor analysis, which yielded a single factor solution for both Times 1 and 2. These results clearly confirm those of Guzzo and coworkers (1993), regarding the unidimensionality of this construct. Representative items from this scale are provided in Table 1 along with their factor loadings.

Testing for Group Level Effects

Next, we conducted a series of analyses to test whether the TMLQ scales could be assessed at the group level, that is, was there more variation within groups participating in the study, or between the groups in terms of ratings of leadership. Greater between as compared to within group differences in ratings, suggests that it is appropriate to aggregate to the group level (Dansereau et al., 1984). A detailed explanation of these analyses and results appear in the Appendix and Table A1.

With Sample 1, for Time period 1, there were no group effects found. This pattern of results indicates that the amount of variation in ratings within any particular group was greater than between any particular group. At Time 2, some group effects were observed with the following scales: Individualized Consideration, Intellectual Stimulation, Contingent Reward, Active and Passive Management-by-Exception, and Laissez-faire Leadership. These group effects however, did not consistently hold up using Within and Between Analyses (WABA), which is also described in more detail in the Appendix.

Group level results of the WABA analyses are presented in the Appendix. Of the leadership variables measured at Time 1 versus Time 2, some showed significant between group effects. When examining results of WABA II, Individualized Consideration, Contingent Reward, Management-by-Exception-Active, and Laissez-faire leadership did appear to operate at the group level going from Time 1 to Time 2. In general terms, each group became more consistent, that is, yielded a group effect in their ratings of their group's leadership style. This pattern of results provides preliminary support for the model in Figure 1, in that it shows a greater level of consistency over time within groups, in their ratings of leadership.

Since the group effects only began to emerge at Time 2, we will present Time 1 versus Time 2 comparisons at the individual level of analysis. The choice of whether to aggregate or not is a difficult one, in that we may be witnessing a developmental progression over time, where a collection of individuals are evolving to a group level. Yet, the key question is when should we interpret it as a group effect? By not aggregating, we run the risk of interpreting a phenomenon at the wrong level of analysis. However, if we went to the group level, we could also be mixing levels of analysis prematurely, and perhaps erroneously.

Reliabilities and Predictive Results

Generally, the reliability estimates for the leadership and group process measures achieved acceptable levels. However, several within time period scale reliabilities did fall below the conventional cutoff of 0.70. In most instances, however, the average reliability per scale across both time periods, either exceeded or approximated the prescribed cutoff of 0.70.

Results presented in Table 2 indicated that active transformational and transactional team leadership styles were generally positively correlated with the rated outcome measures of Extra Effort, Effectiveness, and Satisfaction. Similarly, these active styles of leadership were also positively correlated with ratings of team Collective Efficacy and Group Potency.

Contrasting the results presented for active transformational and transactional leadership, correlations between passive Management-by-Exception and Laissez-faire leadership with each of the outcome and group process measures were consistently negative. The pattern of results for both active and passive leadership styles was consistent with results reported by Bass and Avolio (1994) for individual leadership ratings using the *M*ultifactor *L*eadership *Q*uestionnaire (MLQ).

Correlations across the two time periods represent the predictions of both outcome and group process measures using the various team leadership styles as predictors. These correlations were significantly lower than correlations generated within a particular time period. However, the pattern of correlations

Table 2. Descriptive Statistics and Reliabilities for the TMLQ(5X), Group Outcomes and Process Measures for Time 1 versus Time 2

Team Leadership	Time 1			Time 2		
	Mean	SD	α	Mean	SD	α
Transformational						
Idealized Influence/						
Inspirational Motivation	2.37	0.73	0.88	2.39	0.64	0.84
Intellectual Motivation	2.29	0.69	0.79	2.11	0.57	0.65
Individual Consideration	2.49	0.69	0.77	2.56	0.74	0.79
Transactional						
Contingent Reward	2.90	0.72	0.83	2.75	0.75	0.84
Management-by-Exception						
(Active)	1.67	0.64	0.60	1.58	0.70	0.68
Passive/Nontransactional						
Management-by-Exception						
(Passive)/Laissez-faire	1.03	0.53	0.71	1.02	0.73	0.87
Outcomes						
Extra Effort	1.33	0.92	0.85	2.39	0.96	0.87
Effectiveness	2.70	0.65	0.85	2.71	0.85	0.91
Satisfaction	2.89	1.00	0.87	2.82	1.06	0.87
Group Process Measures						
Collective Efficacy	23.08	0.52	0.88	2.81	0.58	0.82
Group Potency	2.79	0.69	0.92	2.83	0.75	0.92

Note: Items underlined indicate that one of the original items was deleted from these scales.

was generally in the same direction, as the results reported for Time 1. Generally speaking, these results supported those reported by Lindsley and coworkers (1994), which showed that Team Efficacy and Group Potency were highly correlated with performance data collected over time.

There are a number of potential reasons for the drop-off in relationships noted in Table 3, across the two time periods. First, there may have been an inflation in the correlations reported for Time 1, due to single source bias effects. Second, a variety of changes in these groups over time may have resulted in a non-linear relationship between leadership, group process, and outcome measures perhaps reducing the magnitude of the relationships reported at one point in time. Third, as the groups developed over time there may have been other factors which could have impacted the observed relationships that were not captured in our survey assessments at either Time 1 or at Time 2. Although not collected, one could examine the type of interactions within the group, as well as communication patterns to determine how much the group matured over time. Finally, as group effects emerged over time (refer to WABA results in Appendix A), they may have also impacted the observed relationships reported in Table 3.

Table 3. Preliminary Correlations Between Team Leadership
Measured at Time 1 and Outcomes Measured at Time 2

	Outcomes (Time 2)					
Team Leadership (Time 1)	Extra Effort		Effectiveness		Satisfaction	
Transformational						
Idealized Influence/						
Inspirational Motivation	0.55**	(0.81**)	0.38**	(0.59**)	0.30**	(0.46**)
Intellectual Stimulation	0.11	(0.66**)	0.03	(0.42**)	0.01	(0.34**)
Individualized Consideration	0.08	(0.72**)	0.10	(0.60**)	0.01	(0.49**)
Transactional						
Contingent Reward	0.12	(0.71**)	0.17**	(0.66**)	0.08	(0.51**)
Management-by-Exception						
(Active)	0.09	(0.41**)	0.14	(0.07)	0.12	(0.11)
Passive/Nontransactional						
Management-by-Exception						
(Passive)	-0.18*	(-0.25**)	-0.32**	(-0.43**)	-0.27**	(-0.32**)

	Group Process Measures (Time 2)			
	Collective Efficacy		Potency	
Transformational				
Idealized Influence/Inspirational				
Stimulation	0.33**	(0.63**)	0.49**	(0.66**)
Intellectual Stimulation	0.10	(0.39**)	0.09	(0.47**)
Individualized Consideration	0.12	(0.56**)	0.15	(0.58**)
Transactional				
Contingent Reward	0.11	(0.63**)	0.18**	(0.63**)
Management-by-Exception (Active)	0.18*	(0.10)	0.10	(0.15)
Passive/Nontransactional				
Management-by-Exception (Passive)/				
Laissez-faire	-0.33**	(-0.45**)	-0.33**	(-0.41**)

Notes: [1] Values in parentheses are correlations within time period 1. All analyses are based on Sample 1 data
$(n = 171)$.
* $p < 0.05$.
** $p < 0.01$.

It suffices to say that the pattern of correlations were generally in the expected direction. Moreover, several of the transformational and active transactional scales were more positively correlated with levels of Extra Effort, Effectiveness, Satisfaction, Collective Efficacy, and Group Potency than either passive transactional or nontransactional leadership. Conversely, the inactive or corrective styles of leadership appeared to negatively predict each of the outcome and group process measures discussed previously. Again, this pattern of results was similar to those reported at an individual level of analysis using the *M*ultifactor *L*eadership *Q*uestionnaire in non-team settings.

Next, we examined the extent to which transactional and transformational team leadership collected at Time 1, predicted levels of Collective Efficacy and Group Potency at Time 2. The results of a series of regression analyses indicated that both transactional Contingent Reward and the components of transformational leadership combined to significantly predict levels of Collective Efficacy and Group Potency perceived by team members over time.

Findings with Sample 2 Data

Moving to our second sample, preliminary results regarding Sample 2, which went through a year-long team development program, are presented in Table 4. Factor analysis of this data revealed that the two scales measuring trust and cohesiveness each loaded on the same factor. Thus, these scales were combined in a single scale using those items that loaded on one overall factor.

Comparing relationships across time with the leadership and group process measure of Group or Collective Efficacy, indicated that these relationships were more positive for transformational, transactional contingent reward at Time 2 versus Time 1. Since the training program focused on developing transformational, transactional Contingent Reward and Collective Efficacy, these results are not all that surprising. A similar pattern of results were obtained with relationships between the team leadership measures and the combined measure of Trust/Cohesion. The relationship between *less* active Management-by-Exception, Laissez-faire, and Collective Efficacy was significantly more negative at Time 2 versus Time 1.

The pattern of results presented in Table 4, indicated that groups who perceived themselves as exhibiting more transformational leadership also saw themselves as being characterized as having higher levels of Collective Efficacy, and as noted previously, greater levels of Trust/Cohesiveness among team members. Groups that were at a more transactional level in terms of Management-by-Exception and nontransactional Laissez-faire Leadership rated themselves as exhibiting lower levels of Collective Efficacy and Cohesiveness/Trust. All of those relationships were in the expected direction and in line with the model presented in Figure 1.

Finally, we examined the relationship between the collective moral development level of each group with each of the leadership scales, but found no significant relationships. The sample sizes for these respective analyses was relatively low (approximately 10), perhaps contributing to the lack of any significant effects.

A General Summary of Preliminary Results

Evidence for group level effects varied across two separate time periods in Sample 1. Stronger group-level effects were shown moving from Time 1 to

Table 4. Correlations Between Leadership and Group Process Measures at Time 1 versus Time 2, Following Training for Sample 2

	Collective Efficacy		Trust/Cohesiveness	
Team Leadership	Time 1	Time 2	Time 1	Time 2
Transformational				
Transformational Influence/Inspirational Motivation	0.10	0.52**	0.06	0.38**
Intellectual Stimulation	0.00	0.45**	0.09	0.23*
Individual Consideration	0.11	0.28*	0.08	0.25*
Transactional				
Contingent Reward	-0.04	0.47*	0.02	0.36*
Management-by-Exception (Active)	-0.26*	-0.06	0.17	0.05
Passive/Nontransactional				
Management-by-Exception (Passive)/ Laissez-faire	-0.19	-0.15	-0.01	-0.07

Notes: The reliability for the collective efficacy scale used with this sample was 0.82 ($N = 57$).
  * $p < 0.05$.
  ** $p < 0.01$.

Time 2 for Individualized Consideration, Intellectual Stimulation, Transactional Contingent Reward, Active Management-by-Exception, and Passive Management-by-Exception/Laissez-faire leadership. Transformational and transactional contingent reward team leadership ratings were positively correlated within and, less so, between time periods with group process/outcome measures. Whereas, transactional management-by-exception (active/passive) and nontransactional laissez-faire leadership were either not correlated or negatively correlated within and between time periods with group process and outcome measures. The perspective-taking capacity of groups as measured by the T.B.I. did not significantly correlate with team leadership ratings over time. Preliminary trends in the data indicated the following nonsignificant pattern: higher levels of perspective-taking were positively associated with team transformational leadership ratings; conversely, higher levels were negatively associated with team leadership ratings of corrective and nontransactional laissez-faire leadership.

In Sample 2, there were stronger positive correlations found between Transformational, Transactional Contingent Reward leadership, and group process measures following team leadership training. This pattern of results was expected in that the training program's goal was to enhance the relationships among leadership factor scales that were predicted to be more positively related to each other, and/or negative in the case of transformational leadership with Management-by-Exception and Laissez-faire leadership.

GENERAL DISCUSSION

The purpose of this paper was to present an alternative framework for examining the development of teams by placing greater emphasis on the full range of leadership processes associated with different phases of team development. Specifically, we examined the relevance of Bass and Avolio's (1994) full range model of leadership to the development of team leadership behavior and styles, and how those styles related to group process measures such as collective efficacy, potency, trust/cohesion. Underlying the focus of this paper is the idea that leadership styles, such as transformational and transactional, can and should be examined at multiple levels of analysis, including teams (Avolio & Bass, 1995).

We were also interested in exploring in greater detail what other authors have referred to in rather general terms as shared leadership. Using the full range model as a basis for operationalizing different styles of shared leadership we examined how groups can collectively exhibit nontransactional, transactional, and transformational styles of leadership.

It is essential that the concept of shared leadership be more clearly defined relevant to the stage of a group and/or team's development. Indeed, in this paper we made a clear distinction between groups, teams, and highly developed teams by importing models of leadership such as Burns' (1978), as well as models of moral development such as Kegan's (1982), to examine differences in the process dynamics between groups versus teams.

We view a team, particularly one that is highly developed, as paralleling the higher stages associated with personal leadership development, in that members go beyond their self-interest for the good of the team and/or larger collective; establish a common sense of purpose and/or vision that all members can identify with; view conflict as a healthy challenge to each others' perspectives and as a basis of development; and view leadership as an investment in the development of relationships. Finally, rather than examine team leadership with respect to one individual who has emerged over time to guide his or her group, we examined leadership constructs as they would manifest themselves at the group or team level. By escalating our unit of analysis to the group level, we intended to refine the discussion of shared leadership at the level it is expected to emerge.

A review of the most recent literature on team development clearly shows that leadership is a critical ingredient in the formation and development of teams. Leadership in teams will likely have both a direct and indirect impact on all aspects of group and/or team development including how the team handles its growth, conflicts, rewards, strategic focus, and so forth. Yet, given the central role that leadership plays in a team's development, for the most part it has been largely ignored and/or oversimplified in prior research on teams, as well as in training programs (Ilgen, Major, Hollenbeck, & Sego, 1993).

As organizations move toward greater use of multifunctional/multi-level teams, the need to lead coordinated activities versus simply manage them becomes increasingly more relevant. Developing a collection of individuals to go beyond their self-interests for the collective good of the team is at the heart of what Burns (1978), Bass (1985), and Bass and Avolio (1994) have called transformational leadership. Uhl-Bien and Graen (1992) similarly highlight the importance of transformational leadership by suggesting that the leadership in teams gets members to go beyond a narrow view of their roles, to a commitment and belief in the team's common purposes. In doing so, they also cite the connection to Burns' (1978) views on the higher end of leadership development, showing that it transforms selfish, individual interests into team interests. Self-management/leadership must now be viewed at both the collective and individual level (Uhl-Bien & Graen, 1992).

Some General Conclusions and Implications

In this section, we provide an overview of the general pattern of results and implications for team development. It is important to note that we have been successful in escalating an individual leadership model and its range of styles to a group level of analysis.

1. The hierarchy of relationships between team leadership ratings, group process and outcome measures were similar to earlier patterns reported for the *M*ultifactor *L*eadership *Q*uestionnaire (see Bass & Avolio, 1994).
2. Although requiring some refinements, there is some preliminary evidence to support measuring leadership behaviors using the group as the unit of analysis, after the group has had time to develop itself.
3. As expected, team transformational leadership ratings positively correlated with measures of Group Efficacy, Group Potency, Trust/Cohesion, Extra Effort, Effectiveness, and Satisfaction, both within a particular time period, and over a three-month time span.

A next logical step is to examine the reciprocal relationship between measures of team leadership, cohesion/trust, efficacy, potency, and performance. We expect, as has been shown at the individual level with relationships between self-efficacy and performance (Bandura, 1982; Gist & Mitchell, 1992; Wood & Bandura, 1989), that there is likely to be a reciprocal, causal relationship found over time that will parallel a team's development. This notion of reciprocal causation is also consistent with Hackman's (1987) view of team development. Hackman (1987) indicates that teams evaluate their performance as they work, and that these evaluations can affect team processes, which in turn can affect team performance. Hackman's cyclical framework probably comes close to representing the dynamic nature of continuous team development.

Some Next Steps

Based on our preliminary research, we can now point to several avenues for improving our measurement scales and instruments. Also, we can examine the process of team development, which is associated with transformational change and then link the developmental focus on teams to literature on self-directed, high performance teams.

First, the current findings indicate that we need to refine the team leadership survey, and measures of efficacy, cohesion, and so forth. Yet, the general pattern of results supported the construct validity of these instruments.

Second, we need to focus on group development over time, examining shifts common and uncommon to different groups of individuals. Preliminary evidence indicates that there may be some nonlinear effects associated with changes in leadership, group processes, and outcomes associated with different phases of group and/or team development. Specifically, there may be critical periods where the group dynamics change in terms of their influence and impact on achieving higher levels of team development (Gersick, 1988, 1989; Tuckman & Jensen, 1977). Some of these changes will parallel the transformational changes discussed by Bass and Avolio (1994).

Third, we must begin to differentiate the higher versus lower performing groups and examine any unique patterns with respect to group leadership and process development over time. Comparing successful versus unsuccessful groups should provide further insights into the team leadership development process.

Finally, there is a clear need to resolve the issue of group versus individual level effects with respect to measurement and developmental differences/ patterns. The fact that a measure does not exhibit a group level effect early on in a group's development, that is, the variance in individual perspectives is high, suggests at least two possibilities. First, the survey measure may not be appropriately constructed to measure group level effects. Second, in the early phases of a group's development, one would likely find wide variation in individual perceptions of the group that could legitimately eliminate any group-level effect. By resolving this issue, we will have a much clearer idea on how and when to measure a group's progress in terms of its development.

In sum, this paper provided a general conceptual framework and measures to help study the team development process, as well as to promote development via training interventions. Shifting the focus from performing to highly developed teams will hopefully provide a clearer path for helping teams and their members maximize their full range of leadership potential.

APPENDIX

Levels of Analysis Results

First we conducted a series of one-way analyses of variance. As noted in the text, the results of these analyses produced significant between group effects. The scales exhibiting these significant group effects were individualized consideration, intellectual stimulation, contingent reward, passive management-by-exception, and laissez-faire.

Within and Between Analysis (WABA)

In order to further test whether the leadership and group process measures operated at the group level of analysis, for example, should the TMLQ scales be aggregated to the group level, we used an analytical technique for simultaneously comparing between- and within-group sources of variance called WABA. This procedure, termed Within and Between Analysis (WABA), is based on foundation work done by Robinson (1950), and subsequently expanded by Dansereau, Alutto, and Yammarino (1984). WABA has been widely used to assess the appropriate level of analysis on which constructs should be interpreted (e.g., Markham, 1988; Markham & McKee, 1991; Yammarino & Markham, 1992; Yammarino & Dubinsky, 1992; Yammarino, 1995).

One of the advantages of using Within and Between Analysis (WABA) is that it is possible to determine at what level phenomena can reliably be observed and, ultimately, to what level they have evolved (Dansereau et al., 1984). For instance, since we collected data over time on our survey measures, we can determine whether variables such as individualized consideration emerged from an individual level at Time 1, to a group level at Time 2. This would suggest that the group is beginning to see itself displaying (or not displaying) individualized consideration consistently over time, relative to other leadership behaviors. Whereas, in the first time period, we would expect that the lack of experience with the group would result in individual differences in opinion within a group, regarding perceptions of leadership. Essentially, we used WABA here to determine whether a group level effect emerges as groups of individuals interact over time. With respect to the model in Figure 1, we expected there would be a group effect as groups structure themselves and their relationships over the course of time.

In the first step in WABA (WABA I) we aligned the groups in our study into cells, similar to a one-way ANOVA, to test for significant between versus within group differences on all variables. WABA I produces tests of group differences, which are not based on degrees of freedom, such as ANOVA. Thus, effect sizes can be computed independent of the number of degrees of freedom, thus eliminating the problem of interpreting small but significant effects.

Table A1. Summary WABA Equations—Group LEVEL—Time 2

Variable 1: Individualized Consideration: WITH

Variable 2	TOTAL Corr.	=	BETWEEN WABA 1 Variable 1	WABA 1 Variable 2	WABA 2	+	WITHIN WABA 1 Variable 1	WABA 1 Variable 2	WABA 2	Z	Final Inference
Contingent Reward	0.73***	=	0.72*	0.73*	0.82*	+	0.70	0.68	0.63	2.18*	Between Group
Management-by-Exception—Active	-0.18**	=	0.72*	0.74*	-0.61*	+	0.70	0.67	0.30	2.18*	Between Group
Laissez-faire Leadership	-0.52***	=	0.72*	0.81*	-0.79*	+	0.70	0.59	-0.16	4.83**	Between Group

Variable 1: Contingent Reward: WITH

Variable 2	TOTAL Corr.	=	BETWEEN WABA 1 Variable 1	WABA 1 Variable 2	WABA 2	+	WITHIN WABA 1 Variable 1	WABA 1 Variable 2	WABA 2	Z	Final Inference
Management-by-Exception—Active	-0.12ns	=	0.73*	0.74*	-0.43ns	+	0.68	0.67	0.25	1.12ns	Weak Between Group
Laissez-faire Leadership	-0.48***	=	0.73*	0.81*	-0.69**	+	0.68	0.59	-0.18	3.59**	Between Group

Variable 1: Management-by-Exception—Active: WITH

Variable 2	TOTAL Corr.	=	BETWEEN WABA 1 Variable 1	WABA 1 Variable 2	WABA 2	+	WITHIN WABA 1 Variable 1	WABA 1 Variable 2	WABA 2	Z	Final Inference
Laissez-faire Leadership	0.62***	=	0.74*	0.81*	0.78*	+	0.68	0.59	0.38	3.54**	Between Group

The second and simultaneous step in WABA (WABA II) imports correlations based on cell averages generated from WABA I, contrasting the between cell correlations with the within, which can be interpreted as a residual term in the covariance equation used in WABA. In the ideal whole-group case, a group that exhibits a high rating on one scale represented by the group's average score, would also have a high rating on another scale expected to be highly correlated with that first scale. Hence, WABA provides us with a statistical tool to accurately assess the emergence of group effects with respect to a single measure, and also the relationships among measures comprising our survey instruments.

Results of WABA I and WABA II analyses are summarized in Table A1.

ACKNOWLEDGMENT

The authors wish to thank Bernard M. Bass for comments and contributions to an earlier draft of this paper.

NOTE

1.   These outcome scales have been used extensively in prior research, and thus were not included in our preliminary factor analyses (see Bass & Avolio, 1990).

REFERENCES

Avolio, B.J., & Bass, B.M. (1988). Transformational leadership, charisma and beyond. In J.G. Hunt, B.R. Baliga, H.P. Dachler, & C. Schriesheim, (Eds.), *Emerging leadership vistas* (pp. 29-50). Elsmford, NY: Pergamon Press.

Avolio, B.J., & Bass, B.M. (1995). Individualized consideration viewed at multiple levels of analysis: A multi-level framework for examining the diffusion of transformational leadership. *Leadership Quarterly, 6,* 199-218.

Avolio, B.J., & Gibbons, T. (1988). Developing transformational leaders: A lifespan approach. In J. Conger & R. Kanungo (Eds.), *Charismatic leadership: The elusive factor in organizational efectiveness* (pp. 276-308). New York: Jossey-Bass.

Avolio, B.J., Jung, D., Sivasubramaniam, N., & Murry, W. (1995). Construct validation of the TMLQ (Form 5X). Unpublished manuscript, Binghamton University.

Bandura, A. (1977). *Social learning theory.* Englewood Cliffs, NJ: Prentice Hall.

Bandura, A. (1982). Self-efficacy mechanism in human agency. *American Psychologist, 37,* 122-147.

Bandura, A. (1986). *Social foundations of thought and action: A social cognitive theory.* Englewood Cliffs, NJ: Prenctice Hall.

Barker, J. (1993). Tightening the iron cage: Concertive control in self-managing teams. *Administrative Science Quarterly, 38,* 408-437.

Bass, B.M. (1985). *Leadership performance beyond expectations.* New York: Free Press.

Bass, B.M., & Avolio, B.J. (1990). *Manual for the multifactor leadership questionnaire.* Palo Alto, CA: Consulting Psychologists Press.

Bass, B.M., & Avolio, B. (1995). Manual for the Team Multifactor Leadership Questionnaire. Unpublished manuscript, Binghamton University.

Bass, B.M., & Avolio, B. (1994). *Improving organizational effectiveness through transformational leadership*. Thousand Oaks, CA: Sage.

Bennis, W.G., & Nanus, B. (1985). *Leaders: The strategies for taking charge*. New York: Harper & Row.

Berg, D.N., & Smith, K. (1987). *Paradoxes of group life*. San Francisco: Jossey-Bass.

Bion, W.R. (1961). *Experience in groups*. London: Tavistock.

Bowers, D.G., & Seashore, S.E. (1966). Predicting organizational effectiveness with a four-factor theory of leadership. *Administrative Science Quarterly, 11*, 238-263.

Bradford, D.L., & Cohen, J. (1984). *Managing for excellence: The guide to developing high performance organizations*. New York: John-Wiley.

Burns, J.M. (1978). *Leadership*. New York: Free Press.

Cartwright, D., & Zander, A.W. (Eds.) (1968). *Group dynamics research and theory*, 3rd ed. New York: Harper & Row.

Christie, P., Lessem, R., & Mbigi, L. (1993). *African management: Philosophies, concepts and applications*. Randsburg, South Africa: Knowledge Resources.

Cohen, S.G. (1990). Corporate restructuring team. In J.R. Hackman (Ed.), *Groups that work and those that don't: Creating conditions for effective teamwork* (pp. 36-55). San Francisco: Jossey-Bass.

Cummings, T.G. (1978). Self-regulating work groups: A sociotechnical synthesis. *Academy of Management Review, 3*, 625-634.

Dansereau, F., Alutto, J.A., & Yammarino, F.J. (1984). *Theory testing in organizational behavior: The varient approach*. Englewood Cliffs, NJ: Prentice-Hall.

Davis-Sacks, M.L., Denison, D.R., & Eisenstat, R.A. (1990). Summary: Professional support teams. In J.R. Hackman (Ed.), *Groups that work and those that don't: Creating conditions for effective teamwork* (pp. 195-202). San Francisco: Jossey-Bass.

Eisenstat, R.A., & Cohen, S.G. (1990). Summary: Top management groups. In J.R. Hackman (Ed.), *Groups that work and those that don't: Creating conditions for effective teamwork* (pp. 36-55). San Francisco: Jossey-Bass.

Escoffer, M., & Kroeck, K.G. (1990). Manual for the test of business issues. Unpublished manuscript.

Evans, C.R., & Dion, K.L. (1991). Group cohesion and performance: A meta-analysis. *Small Group Research, 22*, 175-186.

Gaas, J.C., & Ponemon, L.A. (1995). Toward a theory of moral expertise: A verbal protocol study of public accounting professionals. Unpublished manuscript, Binghamton University.

Gersick, C.J.G. (1989). Marking time: Predictable transitions in work-groups. *Academy of Management Journal, 32*, 274-309.

Gersick, C.J.G. (1988). Time and transitions in work teams: Toward a new model of group development. *Academy of Management Journal, 31*, 9-41.

Gist, M.E., & Mitchell, T.R. (1992). Self-efficacy: A theoretical analysis of its determinants and malleabilitiy. *Academy of Management Review, 17*, 183-211.

Guzzo, R.A., Yost, P.R., Campbell, R.J., & Shea, G.P. (1993). Potency in groups: Articulating a construct. *British Journal of Social Psychology, 3*, 87-106.

Hackman, J.R. (1987). The design of work teams. In J.W. Lorsch (Ed.), *Handbook of organizational behavior* (pp. 315-342). Englewood Cliffs, NJ: Prentice Hall.

Hofstede, G. (1980). *Culture's consequence: International differences in work related values*. Beverly Hills, CA: Sage Publications.

Ilgen, D., Major, D., Hollenbeck J., & Sego, D. (1993). Team research in the 1990s. In M. Chemers, & R. Ayman (Eds.), *Leadership theory and research: Perspectives and directions* (pp. 245-270). New York: Academic Press.

Jermier, J.M., Slocum, J.W., Jr., Fry, L.W., & Gaines, J. (1991). Resistance behind the myth and facade of an official culture. *Organization Science, 2*, 170-194.

Kanter, R.M. (1983). *The change masters.* New York: Simon & Schuster.

Kanter, R.M., & Hofstede, G. (1980, summer). Motivation leadership and organizations: Do American theories apply abroad? *Organizational Dynamics*, 42-63.

Kegan, J. (1982). *The evolving self: Problem and process in human development.* Cambridge, MA: Harvard University Press.

Klein, J.A. (1984). Why supervisors resist employee involvement. *Harvard Business Review, 62*, 87-95.

Klein, K.J., Dansereau, F., & Hall, R.J. (1994). Level issues in theory development, data collection and analysis. *Academy of Management Review, 19*, 434-474.

Klein, K.J., & House, R.J. (1995). On fire: Charismatic leadership and levels of analysis. *Leadership Quarterly, 6*, 183-198.

Kozlowski, S., Gully, S., Nason, E., Ford, K., Smith, E., Smith, M., & Futch, C. (1994). A composition theory of team development: Level, content, process, & learning outcomes. Paper presented at the Ninth Annual Conference of the Society for Industrial and Organizational Psychologists. Nashville, TN.

Kuhnert, K.W., & Lewis, P. (1987). Transactional and transformational leadership: A constructive developmental analysis. *Academy of Management Review, 12*, 648-657.

Lawler, E.E. (1992). *The ultimate advantage: Creating the high involvement organization.* San Francisco: Jossey-Bass.

Lawler, E.E. (1986). *High involvement management.* San Francisco: Jossey-Bass.

Lawler, E.E. (1981). *Pay and organization development.* Reading, MA: Addison Wesley.

Lindsley, E., Matthieu, J., Heffner, T., & Brass, D. (1994). Team efficacy, potency and performance: A longitudinal examination of reciprocal processes. Paper presented at the Ninth Annual Conference of the Society for Industrial and Organizational Psychologists, Nashville, TN.

Loher, B., Vancouver, J., & Czajka, J. (1994). Preferences and reactions to teams. Paper presented at the Ninth Annual Conference of the Society for Industrial and Organizational Psychologists, Nashville, TN.

Manz, C.C. (1992). Self-leading work teams: Moving beyond self-management myths. *Human Relations, 45*, 1119-1139.

Manz, C.C., & Sims, H.P., Jr. (1987). Leading workers to lead themselves: The external leadership of self-managing work teams. *Administrative Science Quarterly, 32*, 106-128.

Manz, C.C., & Sims, H.P., Jr. (1993). *Business without bosses: How self-managing teams are building high performance companies.* New York: Wiley.

Markham, S.E. (1988). Pay-for-performance dilemma revisited: Empirical example of the importance of group effects. *Journal of Applied Psychology, 73*, 172-180.

Markham, S.E., & McKee, G.H. (1991). Declining organizational size and increasing unemployment rates: Predicting employee absenteeism from within- and between-plant perspectives. *Academy of Management Journal, 34*, 952-965.

Mitchell, R. (1986). Team building by disclosure of internal frames of reference. *Journal of Applied Behavioral Science, 22*, 15-28.

Nanus, B. (1992). *Visionary leadership: Creating a compelling sense of direction for your organization.* San Francisco: Jossey-Bass.

New York State Education Department. (1992). *A new compact for learning: Improving public elementary, middle and secondary education results in the 1990's.* New York: University of the State of New York, Education Department.

Ogilvy, J. (1990, February). This postmodern business. *Marketing and Research Today*, 4-20.

Parker, M. (1992). Post-modern organizations or post-modern organizational theory? *Organizational Studies, 13*, 1-17.

Price, K.H. (1987). Decision responsibility, task responsibility, identifiability, and social loafing. *Organizational Behavior and Human Decision Process 40*, 330-345.

Pritchard, R.D., Jones, S., Roth, P., Stuebing, K., & Ekeberg, S. (1988). Effects of group feedback, goal-setting, and incentives on organizational productivity. *Journal of Applied Psychology, 73*, 337-358.

Rentsch, J., Heffner, T., & Duffy, L. (1994). Teamwork schema representations: The role of team experience. Paper presented at the Ninth Annual Conference of the Society for Industrial and Organizational Psychologists, Nashville, TN.

Rest, J. (1986). *Moral development: Advances in research and theory*. New York: Praeger.

Robinson, W.S. (1950). Ecological correlations and the behavior of individuals. *American Sociological Review, 15*, 351-357.

Salas, E., Montero, R.C., Glickman, A.S., & Morgan, B.B. (1988). Group development, teamwork skills and training. Paper presented at the American Psychological Association Meetings, Atlanta, GA.

Schneier, C.E., & Goktepe, J.R. (1983). Issues of emergent leadership: The contingency model of leadership, leader sex, and leader behavior. In H.H. Blumberg, A.P. Hare, V. Kent, & M.F. Davies (Eds.), *Small groups and social interaction*, Vol. 1, pp. 413-412. Chichester, UK: Wiley.

Shamir, B. (1990). Calculations, values, and identities: The sources of collectivistic work motivation. *Human Relations, 43*, 313-332.

Shamir, B., House, R.J., & Arthur, M.B. (1993). The motivational effects of charismatic leadership: A self-concept based theory. *Organizational Science, 4*, 577-594.

Shea, G.P., & Guzzo, R.A. (1987). Group effectiveness: What really matters? *Sloan Management Review, 28*, 25-31.

Sims, H., & Manz, C. (1993). *Businesses without bosses: How self-managing teams are building high performing companies*. New York: Wiley.

Sinclair, A. (1992). The tyranny of a team ideology. *Organization Studies, 13*, 611-626.

Smith, K.K. (1982). *Groups in Conflict*. Dubuque, IA: Kendall-Hunt.

Steiner, I.D. (1972). *Group process and productivity*. Orlando: Academic Press.

Stewart, G., & Manz, C. (1994). Leadership for self-managing work teams: A theoretical integration. Paper presented at the Annual Conference of the Society for Industrial and Organizational Psychologists, Nashville, TN.

Tannenbaum, S.I., Beard, R.L., & Salas, E. (1992). Team building and its influence on team effectiveness: An examination of conceptual and empirical developments. In K. Kelley (Ed.), *Issues, theory and research in industrial/organizational psychology* (pp. 117-153). Amsterdam: Elsevier.

Tichy, N., & Devanna, M. (1986). *Transformational leadership*. New York: Wiley.

Tompkins, P.K., & Cheney, G.M. (1985). Communication and unobtrusive control in contemporary organizations. In R.D. McPhee & P.K. Tompkins (Eds.), *Organizational communication: Traditional themes and new directions* (pp. 179-210). Newbury Park, CA: Sage.

Torbert, W.R. (1991). *The power of balance: Transforming self, society and scientific inquiry*. Beverly Hills, CA: SAGE Publications.

Tuckman, B.W., & Jensen, M.C. (1977). Stages of small-groups development revisited. *Group and Organizational Studies, 2*, 419-427.

Uhl-bein, M., & Graen, J.B. (1992). Self management and team-making in cross-functional work teams: Discussing the keys to becoming a team. *The Journal of High Technology Management Research, 3*, 225-241.

Vancouver, J.B., & Ilgen, D.R. (1989). The effects of individual difference and the sex-type of the task on choosing to work alone or in a group. *Journal of Applied Psychology, 74*, 927-934.

Wood, R., & Bandura, A. (1989). Social cognitive theory of organizational management. *Academy of Management Review, 14*, 361-384.

Yammarino, F.J. (1995). Group leadership: A levels of analysis perspective. In M.A. West (Ed.), *Handbook of work group psychology.* Chichester, UK: John Wiley & Sons.

Yammarino, F.J., & Dubinsky, A.J. (1992). Superior-subordinate relationships: A multiple levels of analysis approach. *Human Relations, 45*, 575-600.

Yammarino, F.J., & Markham, S.E. (1992). On the application of within and between analysis: Are absence and affect really group-based phenomena? *Journal of Applied Psychology, 77*, 168-176.

Yukl, G. (1994). *Leadership in organizations.* Englewood Cliffs, NJ: Prentice Hall.

LEADERSHIP, TEAMS, AND CULTURE CHANGE:
CHANGING PROCESSING STRUCTURES AND DYNAMICS

Robert G. Lord and Elaine M. Engle

ABSTRACT

This paper addresses the role of leaders in producing dramatic change. Several perspectives are assimilated to develop the theory underlying leadership and change. First, Lord and Maher's (1993) work on leadership and culture change is reviewed. It is argued that leaders can produce changes in culture via two main strategies—by changing organizational members underlying knowledge structures (schema) or by changing the way organizational members process information. Second, building on recent thinking by Mischel and Shoda (1995), it is argued that personality involves affective-cognitive systems which must be considered in understanding the link between information processing and behavior. Culture and personality are viewed as being reciprocally interdependent, each providing a potential mechanism for leader initiated change. Using this perspective, we then discuss the options leaders have for producing

Advances in Interdisciplinary Studies
of Work Teams, Volume 3, pages 211-237.
Copyright © 1996 by JAI Press Inc.
All rights of reproduction in any form reserved.
ISBN: 0-7623-0006-X

dramatic change, likely obstacles, expected costs, and potential outcomes. Finally, this approach is applied to three alternative views of leadership and work teams: traditional hierarchical views of leadership, leadership in self-managing work teams, and self-leadership work teams.

It is widely recognized that leadership is an important component of group dynamics, yet the mechanisms by which leaders impact on group or team processes are often not clearly specified, particularly when our concern is with top management teams (Hambrick, 1994). Much of the work on leadership and teams has focused on observable processes such as leadership behavior, influence (Hollander & Offerman, 1990), and motivational processes. In this paper we go beyond these perspectives to emphasize the role of information processing structures and processing dynamics of group members in generating behaviors. Processing structures and dynamics represent the confluence of individual personalities, group processes, and organizational culture. We maintain that for leaders to produce dramatic changes in behaviors or team functioning, they must understand and be capable of changing these underlying processing structures and dynamics.

These ideas have many parallels to Lord and Maher's (1993) thinking on leadership and cultural change. Cultural change, in their perspective, is highly dependent upon follower schema and type of information processing. In this paper, we extend the Lord and Maher perspective to include the cognitively-oriented treatment of personality recently developed by Mischel and Shoda (1995). We develop an integrated treatment of cognitive factors underlying behavior that spans topics such as personality, group culture, team mental models, organizational culture, learning, and transfer of training. We then use this framework to address the potential for leader-guided change. We posit that to be effective, leaders must be able to change the underlying cognitive-affective units used by team members to generate behavior. That is, leaders must be able to overcome team members' prior learning and socialization processes that often develop very early in individual or team learning (Jackson et al., 1993).

In order to develop this perspective, we begin by reviewing prior thinking on leadership and organizational culture (Lord & Maher, 1993). We then extend this work by explaining the notion of processing structure, focusing on the relation of knowledge to performance. Additionally, we build on recent thinking by Mischel and Shoda (1995) by conceptualizing personality as micro-level schema that act as a basis for proceduralized knowledge. The implications for leaders guiding group members through cultural change are also discussed. We illustrate these processes with an example contrasting traditional hierarchical leadership, self-managing work teams, and self-leadership work teams (Manz, 1990). Of particular concern are the requirements and problems associated with changing from one type of team leadership structure to another.

CULTURE AND INFORMATION PROCESSING

Group or team processes often depend on a common learning history that produces similar interpretations of organizational situations and similar expected actions. We argue that this common understanding reflects cognitive processes that are shared by group members. In other words, as group members gain familiarity with each other and with work tasks, they develop a common culture and shared meanings which can be viewed as a subsystem of a larger organizational culture (Rentsch, 1990). Consequently, much of the literature on organizational culture has direct relevance for understanding team or group processes, particularly those processes related to leadership.

In initiating and managing cultural change efforts, many researchers have highlighted the importance of both leader and follower cognitive schema (Hollander, 1992; Lord & Maher, 1993). Hollander (1992) addressed the importance of followers' leadership schema by proposing that such schema serve as situational constraints for the leader's behavior. Followers' perceptual structures may also interact with leader behavior in determining the way a leader is perceived and the influence that he or she can exert (Hall & Lord, forthcoming). In addition, the cognitive schema of followers have other important effects on their task performance and social skills. Thus, dramatic changes in teams or organizations require supporting changes in a variety of knowledge structures.

Knowledge structures can exist at multiple levels (Walsh, forthcoming). At the *individual level* knowledge structures typically serve to produce efficient processing and understanding. At the *group level* they provide a basis for group structure and climate to the extent that they are shared by group members. At the *organizational level* shared knowledge structures provide a basis for organizational culture, which also exists at multiple levels. Changing knowledge structures for team members must simultaneously address all three of these levels of analysis to be effective.

Multiple Levels of Culture

Two complementary models of organizational culture, which we believe are particularly relevant for understanding group or team processes, are those offered by Schein (1985) and by Lord and Maher (1993). Schein's conceptualization of culture involves three different levels that vary in the extent to which organizational members are aware of them: (a) artifacts, (b) values and beliefs, and (c) assumptions and schema.

Artifacts constitute the first level and reflect tangible aspects of culture, such as the physical layout of the organization, typical language, ceremonies, organizational stories, and behavioral patterns. According to Lord and Maher (1993), artifacts result from organizational members' information processing applied to context-specific knowledge structures. Thus, insight into an organization's culture can be obtained more fruitfully by examining the scripts and categories that create patterns of behavior than by examining artifacts of culture.

Values and beliefs comprise the second component of Schein's model, and they are also a component of Lord and Maher's (1993) model. In both models, values and beliefs represent organizational members' perceptions of the way things are and the way things should be. Values and beliefs are more conscious aspects of culture that provide justifications for behavior. It is important to note, however, that values and beliefs may not actually drive behavior, they may simply provide a post hoc interpretation for it. Thus, attempts by leaders to change values and beliefs may not change actual behavior, though they may change the way past behavior is justified.

Assumptions and schema: The third level in Schein's (1985) model corresponds to the second aspect of culture in Lord and Maher's (1993) model. What Schein terms "assumptions," Lord and Maher call "schema," while still other researchers describe this aspect as "organizational frames of reference" (Wilkins & Dyer, 1988). *Assumptions and schema* are knowledge structures stored in long-term memory that guide the interpretation of organizational information. Assumptions and schema are what actually drive behavior. Essentially, schema and assumptions reflect the organization's culture and are therefore of great importance in understanding organizational behavior and cultural change attempts. Whereas values and beliefs reflect a more controlled process, schema and assumptions serve as cognitive filters that allow for the automatic processing of cultural information.

Schemas provide a natural point for leaders to intervene to change culture or group climate. Generally, people have multiple schema that could be used to guide processing in a specific situation, but usually one of these competing schema is chronically available and is automatically accessed to guide processing. In many cases, change may only require that leaders prime an already existing schema so that it is more available to automatically guide processing. Changing the accessibility of competing schema can be achieved explicitly by altering the organization or group reward structure. Under the revised reward structure, actions associated with alternative schema are rewarded instead of those actions associated with previous operating schema.

While not a simple task, changing the accessibility of competing schema is still easier than creating an entirely new schema or modifying existing schema. Labeling is an important "tool" in this regard, because labels access associated schema. Thus, one important leadership tactic to bring about change may be relabeling familiar events so that they correspond to existing but unused schema. For example, leaders involved in cultural shifts that emphasize product quality as opposed to product quantity may relabel previously used quality control procedures as a "zero-defect" policy. The relabeling of the familiar event so that it corresponds to the existing but unused schema makes the previously unused schema more salient, and therefore more accessible. Importantly, this view of change describes a dyadic level interaction or fit between leaders and organizational members (Hall & Lord, forthcoming). Labeling, as a type of leadership, may not be effective with subordinates who lack appropriate schema.

Cultural Information

The manner in which cultural information is processed reflects the third aspect of organizational culture in Lord and Maher's (1993) model for which there is no analog in Schein's (1985) model. They identify four qualitatively different types of information processing—limited capacity, expert, rational, and cybernetic information processing. These four information processing models are described in a subsequent section. They are important because, according to Lord and Maher (1993), the translation of assumptions or schema (the second level of culture) into behavior depends on the type of information processing used by organizational members. In addition, various types of information processing provide an avenue for leader-directed change. Leaders may promote change, at least temporarily, by altering the type of information processing used by team or organizational members from a more automatic to a more rational or cybernetic mode of processing.

In sum, as shown in Table 1, Schein (1985) and Lord and Maher (1993) each use three levels to define organizational culture. From our perspective, Lord and Maher's second and third levels are most critical because they specify the knowledge content that gives meaning to group or organizational features

Table 1. A Comparison of Schein (1985) and
Lord and Maher's (1993) View of Culture

Schein (1985)	*Lord and Maher (1993)*
Artifacts: Physical layout, organizational stories, language, ceremonies, behavioral patterns.	**Artifacts:** Cognitive processes are the source of artifacts.
Values and Beliefs: Generate behavior through conscious, controlled processes.	**Values and Beliefs:** May also provide post hoc justifications of behaviors.
Basic Assumptions: Pr3econscious perspectives that are taken for granted.	**Cognitive Schema:** Knowledge structures that permit automatic processing.
	Type of Information Processing: Limited Capacity, Expert, Cybernetic and Rational processing modes.

and the information processes that produce observable behavior. Because of their importance to understanding leadership and change, we examine the effects of these latter two levels, knowledge and information processing, in the following two sections.

Knowledge Structures

Lord and Maher (1993) maintain that context-specific knowledge structures are critical to understanding the impact of culture on behavior. Knowledge structures are cognitive schema, otherwise known as scripts, plans, categories, prototypes, implicit theories, or heuristics. They are organized sets of knowledge, stored in long-term memory which can be activated by combinations of environmental cues, current goals, recent thoughts, and feelings.

Frequently, knowledge structures are represented by sets of productions, which are condition-action statements. These productions can be organized into systems, which with experience become proceduralized and are able to operate with minimal load on working-memory (Anderson, 1987). Hence, proceduralized knowledge structures permit relatively automatic processing that can affect interpretations of situations, the development of intentions and plans, or the actual behaviors that occur.

The fact that proceduralized knowledge structures can operate relatively automatically, creates considerable problems in changing group or organizational cultures. Because behavior is salient to perceivers, behavioral definitions of culture, and behaviorally-oriented change attempts seem reasonable. However, as already noted, behavior may merely be an artifact of culture and when behavior is generated automatically thoughts and associated values may be more of a rationalization for behavior, rather than a cause (Lord & Maher, 1993). In such situations, attempts to change values, even when successful, may not change behaviors. For this reason, we focus on underlying knowledge structures and their role in producing thoughts and behaviors in our attempts to understand culture and culture change. Emphasizing knowledge structures in understanding culture and culture change has another important advantage—it helps us understand effective performance and why change may disrupt performance.

Knowledge structures learned over time permit efficient task performance and efficient social processes. It is well known that experts differ from novices mainly in the accumulation of rich, highly organized stores of domain-specific knowledge.

Also, knowledge is organized at a different level for experts than novices. Novices tend to emphasize surface features tied to directly observable phenomena such as cultural artifacts, whereas experts rely more on underlying principles or meaning (Glaser & Chi, 1988; Day & Lord, 1992). Importantly, for experts, many different surface features may be associated with similar underlying meanings, allowing their knowledge to be more generally applied. Novices, in contrast, may encode and retrieve information based more on surface features, thereby restricting the application of their knowledge to superficially similar situations. The knowledge base of experts also supports qualitatively different types of processing for experts as compared to novices (Glaser & Chi, 1988; Lord & Maher, 1990). Frequently, experts can move directly from stimulus information defining problems to solutions stored in long-term memory (Logan, 1988). Novices, on the other hand, must construct solutions on-the-fly, consuming time and attentional resources in the process. Experts also have many domain-specific procedures, learned through experience, which can be applied efficiently and with minimal demands on working memory when solutions must be constructed on-the-fly (Anderson, 1987).

In short, experts can substitute knowledge for resource intensive processing (Newell, 1990) when performing tasks in their domain of expertise. This potential tradeoff between knowledge and processing is shown in Figure 1, which is patterned after Newell (1990). In this figure, each curved line represents equivalent task or work performance produced by different combinations of knowledge and processing. Performance increases as one moves from one line to another, along the 45 degree diagonal leading away from the origin. Experts or expert systems are typically in the top portion of this figure, while systems relying on pure processing capacity are far to the right.

This knowledge/processing capacity tradeoff is particularly important in understanding group or team processes, for as teams or tasks become familiar, team members become experts in this limited domain. In other words, performance increases as they move toward the top of the figure and to lines further from the origin. With such changes, both performance of well learned tasks and social processes can then function in an automatic, taken-for-granted manner. Efficient and stable processing will not occur, however, for novel or changing tasks. Therefore, automatic processing leads to efficient and stable performance of well learned tasks, but it may also limit individual growth, learning, and the capacity to adjust to environmental changes. For example, in the leadership domain, widely shared leadership prototypes allow us to recognize and evaluate leadership qualities in others with little cognitive effort (Lord & Maher, 1993). However, leadership skills not consistent with traditional patterns (for example, characteristics typically associated with females) require more effortful processing in order to be recognized as leadership. In the absence of controlled processing, the potential contribution of some members may not be adequately used.

These schema-driven processes create "cognitive inertia" which creates a passive obstacle to change. There are also more active processes that resist change. Because changing team processes often makes old learning obsolete,

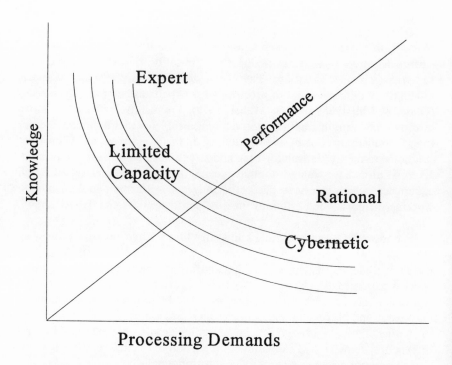

Figure 1. Knowledge/Processing Tradeoff in Influencing Performance

such changes can destroy social competencies in much the same way that technological change can destroy technical competencies (Keck & Tushman, 1993; Tushman & Anderson, 1986). Dramatic change often triggers a complex sequence of events involving changing social structures, uncertainties associated with learning new ways of thinking and behaving, and temporary declines in task and social functioning. Consequently, leaders can expect considerable resistance when they attempt to initiate substantial changes in group functioning, particularly when such change is viewed as being initiated by external rather than internal factors (Arrow & McGrath, 1995). An additional problem with dramatic change is that it often has a negative short-run effect on performance, reinforcing the notion that old ways were in fact better and undercutting the motivation for learning new ways of thinking and behaving. Such changes are naturally resisted by individuals whose performance is reduced, even though they are exerting more cognitive effort.

Leaders may be able to minimize the negative effects associated with competence-destroying change by developing a learning culture within the group. Such a culture should emphasize the importance of the potentially significant increases in performance in the long run as opposed to temporary decreases in performance in the short run. This type of culture would require organizational policies that recognize the importance of errors in learning new skills. In practice, zero-defect or error free policies may operate in direct opposition to such learning processes.

In short, leaders attempting to produce dramatic change must deal with a number of cognitive and social issues related to resistance and reduced performance. One way to help understand such effects is to recognize that movement away from familiar schema is in fact a shift in terms of the isoperformance curves shown in Figure 1. As the knowledge base supporting performance becomes less relevant, the only way to maintain prior levels of performance is with increased allocation of computational resources. Another way to understand such changes is to conceptualize them as shifts in the *type* of information processing used, a topic addressed in the following section.

Alternative Information Processing Models

Figure 1 provides a useful framework for understanding the effects of knowledge on organizational behavior, but we also need to specify the type of information processing being used. Lord and Maher (1990) identify four types of information processing which are described in this section.

Two of the four models described by Lord and Maher (1990) are schema based and therefore of particular relevance in processing cultural information. *Limited capacity models* reflect the limitations of working memory, while emphasizing reliance on generic schema or heuristics in the processing of information. Limited capacity models are not very effective because they do not incorporate domain-specific knowledge (Anderson, 1987). *Expert models* also emphasize reliance on schema but differ in the type and structure of the schema that are used. The expert model assumes that people have highly detailed, well organized schema with regard to a given content domain. This knowledge is proceduralized and therefore, can be used with little load on working memory (Anderson, 1987). Consequently, expert schema are both efficient and effective in terms of performance in routine situations.

Lord and Maher (1993) suggested that cultural information, which is often encountered under cognitively busy conditions, is often processed according to these schema-driven models. Reliance on schema for the processing of cultural information can have inhibiting implications for change efforts. Once formed, schema tend to be highly resistant to change. As previously discussed, it may be more efficient for change agents to prime alternative schema or, as will be discussed in the following section, it may be easier for change agents to switch to a more effortful type of information processing than to focus on changing existing schema.

The two other information processing models offered by Lord and Maher (1990) require more conscious processing of cultural information and may not accurately describe the type of information processing that *typically* occurs in organizational settings. In particular, *rational models* emphasize the deliberate and thoughtful processing of information. These models assume that people have extensive information stored in long-term memory that is optimally combined in making decisions (Lord & Maher, 1990). Though effective, rational models are slow and effortful, and hence are not typically used in fast-paced group or organizational settings. *Cybernetic models* adjust behavior based on a comparison of feedback to internal standards. Through negative feedback a need for alternative behaviors or schema may be recognized. In addition, new productions (condition → action rules) are formed by addressing problems identified by feedback processes. With further experience, these productions can be compiled, forming new schema. Thus, cybernetic processing links change to careful monitoring of environmental information and openness to the new interpretations such feedback may suggest.

In short, whereas people processing cultural information in a limited capacity or expert manner·are likely to resist cultural change, those who process this information in a cybernetic or rational manner are more likely to recognize the need for change and build alternative schema. Rational and cybernetic processing are more cognitively demanding, however, and will be used mainly in contexts where organizational members lack the schema needed to support limited capacity or expert processing.

These four modes of information processing are shown in Table 2. In this table the left to right dimension involves the automatic/controlled processing distinction, or the capacity to rely on schema-driven processing. While this distinction has traditionally been viewed as a dichotomy, Bargh (1994) has recently noted that mental processes often do not rely on exclusively automatic or controlled processes. Rather, mental processes frequently rely on a combination of these two processes. For instance, a well-learned task may be performed automatically, but the intention to perform that task reflects more of a conscious process.

The top to bottom dimension in Table 2 reflects the extent to which information processes make use of domain-specific knowledge and therefore enhance performance. Thus, these two dimensions reflect amount of processing resources used and amount of domain-relevant knowledge, respectively, which are the same dimensions of the isoperformance curves shown in Figure 1. Consequently, these four types of information processing can be located on Figure 1.

This organization·emphasizes the performance differences that could be expected with different forms of information processing. Differences in flexibility can also be expected, with schema-based processing being more efficient, but rational and cybernetic processing being more flexible in their

Table 2. Four Modes of Information Processing
by Type of Processing and Amount of Knowledge

Knowledge	Automatic Processing	Controlled Processing
Low	Limited Capacity	Cybernetic
High	Expert	Rational

Note: The distinction between automatic and controlled processes is presented here as two ends of a continuum, and not as a true dichotomy.

capacity to deal with new situations. Understanding these distinctions is helpful in understanding the consequence of change attempts and the inherent tradeoffs associated with change.

Importance of Context

As well as creating cognitive inertia, schema-based processing may produce cognitions and behaviors which are highly dependent on contextual factors because they trigger context-specific productions and meanings for specific individuals. Thus, the effects of context depend on the match between features of a particular context and the currently activated schema of people in that organizational context.

This interaction between situational features and the schema of organizational members has some interesting implications for understanding the generation of effects associated with group or organizational culture. First, the effects of culture depend on situation-specific interpretations and reactions. Thus, we should *not* expect broad, cross-situational tendencies associated with a culture, for example, a customer-based culture. Instead, culture will be manifest in reactions to specific situations—treatment of a particular type of customer with a particular type of need or problem. For this reason, broad attempts to change culture may occur at a level that is too general to change actual behavior.

The limiting aspects of context may be less severe for experts than novices because experts organize knowledge at a deeper, more principled level. Novices may depend on concrete factors to trigger previously learned productions—tasks with identical physical features, teams comprised of the same members, or a particular organizational setting. The productions of experts, on the other hand, depend more on underlying principles which transcend physical features, specific individuals, or specific organizational contexts. Thus, the skills of experts should be more generalizable. However, they are still domain specific in the sense that they do not generalize to domains where different principles are operating.

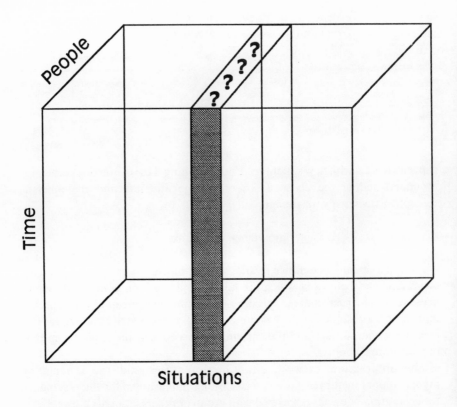

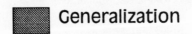 **Generalization**

Figure 2.   Generalization of Behavior Based on Similar Pressing Structures
and Dynamics Across Individuals, Time, and Situations

While cultural effects may not generalize across situations, they may be
consistent across time, if the same individual interprets and reacts to the same
situation consistently. Cultural effects may also be consistent across people to
the extent that a specific situation elicits similar productions and meanings.
In either case, we would expect greater consistency for experts than novices,
because novices are responding to surface features, whereas experts base
responses on underlying meaning. However, this consistency is domain specific.

These points are shown in Figure 2, which shows generalization/consistency
in behavior in terms of a shaded band. People show consistency over time,

perhaps across people, and infrequently across situations. For example, a team member may behave consistently in a particular work group but may behave quite differently when different members are added to a group or when the same group is in a different situation. In each case, the key factor is whether the same productions and meaning structures exist and are elicited by situational features. As already noted, consistency/generalization may be greater when expert processing is involved.

PERSONALITY AS PROCESSING STRUCTURES AND DYNAMICS

The knowledge-based view of culture, cognitions, and behavior that has been developed thus far is consistent with recent views on personality developed by Mischel and Shoda (1995). According to their model, personality reflects patterns of cognitive-affective unit relations that may vary across time, contexts, or people. *Processing structures* are comprised of these cognitive-affective units, which are analogous to the knowledge structures discussed previously. *Processing dynamics* pertain to the sequences of activation of these processing structures. We describe each of these two components more fully in the following sections.

Processing Structures

The processing structures of personality dispositions involve characteristic sets of cognitions, affect, and behavioral strategies, which are similar to our use of the term knowledge structures. The components of processing structures—particular cognitions, affect, or behavioral strategies—are interrelated in a manner that constrains their mutual activation. That is, particular components can activate or inhibit other components in a manner consistent with connectionist architectures (see Lord & Maher, 1991). The key idea is that these components operate as a *network* rather than in isolation.

Mischel and Shoda (1995) identify five types of cognitive-affective units (see Table 3) that define processing structures. These units are critical in mediating between environmental features and behavior. It is important to note that Mischel and Shoda's first three types of units correspond to factors critical in formulating intentions or setting goals. They represent micro-level factors involved in interpreting environmental features and creating meaning. *Encodings* are critical in automatically translating environmental features into internal meanings for organizational members. *Expectancies and beliefs* are critical in setting and revising goals. *Affect* is inseparable from the processing of social information according to Mischel and Shoda.

Table 3.   Types of Cognitive-Affective Units in the Personality Mediating System

1. **Encodings:**   Categories for self, people, events, and situations.

2. **Expectancies and Beliefs:**   About social world, situation-specific behavior outcomes, and self-efficacy.

3. **Affects:**   Feelings, emotions, and affective responses.

4. **Goals and Values:**   Desirable/aversive outcome of affective states, goals, values, and life projects.

5. **Competencies and Self-regulatory Plans:**   Potential behaviors and scripts, plans, and strategies for organizing actions and for affecting outcomes, behavior, and internal states.

Note: Adapted from Mischel and Shoda (1995).

Others (Edwards, 1990; Izard, 1991) also provide evidence that affect exerts its influence very quickly and automatically (Murphy & Zajonc, 1993; Srull & Wyer, 1989). Affect can also be associated with any of the other four units shown in Table 3. Affect can be a powerful retrieval cue for long-term memory that influences encodings or expectancies (Eich, 1995), it can be a goal in itself (Hyland, 1988), or it can influence self-regulatory competencies (Kuhl, 1992).

The units under goals and values in Table 3 pertain more to pursued outcomes, while category 5 reflects the self-regulatory processes that actually produce these outcomes. *Goals and outcomes* are particularly interesting because they can exist at different levels of abstraction. For example, outcomes are organized in hierarchies ranging from values to self-identities to personal projects to task goals (Cropanzano, James, & Citera, 1993). Cropanzano and coworkers note that these hierarchies *are* personality, a view somewhat more narrow than Mischel and Shoda's (1995) treatment of personality. Importantly, leaders (and leadership theories) can focus on different levels in this hierarchy— transformational leadership may deal with values and identities, whereas transactional leadership may focus on task goals (Cropanzano et al., 1993).

Competencies and self-regulatory plans include both the store of scripts and tacit knowledge individuals bring to team or organizational situations, and cognitive hardware differences in the ability to implement these plans.

Each of these five cognitive-affective units may be a critical aspect of knowledge that affects group or organizational functioning. Each is also a potential target of interventions aimed at changing processing. When explaining individual behavior, these units may become activated in predictable sequences such as encodings and affect-activating expectancies, which in turn activate goals, which then activate implemental competencies and self-regulation processes.

In groups, however, interpersonal processes also are critical in activating each of these units. Thus, leadership practices influencing these units may have relatively unseen effects which operate implicitly in individuals, but are much more explicit when teams or larger social units are involved. For example, in self-managed work teams, leaders may change the team's goals, which will in turn affect group member interpersonal interactions, task-related interactions, and group level regulatory activities. The resulting changes in group activities will be readily apparent to team members. In contrast, change attempts at the individual level may not alter the individual's task-related or interpersonal interactions. Therefore, the effects of these attempts are likely to be less noticeable.

Processing Dynamics

In Mischel and Shoda's (1995) theory, *processing dynamics* of dispositions refer to the pattern and sequences of activation among units that mediate between situational features and individual reactions. For example, a set of stimulus features may activate a sequence of internal thoughts or external actions characterized as a script. Such sequences involve many important aspects which impact on the final observable behavior. Rather than being mindless (Langer, Blank, & Chanowitz, 1978), scripts involve several interesting types of cognitive operations:

1. Situations may elicit memories, specific knowledge, and relevant affect;
2. These components may lead to the formulation of specific goals and plans for their implementation (Tubbs & Ekeberg, 1991);
3. Goals and plans, in turn may implement action-related scripts increasing the accessibility of script-related knowledge while making competing knowledge less accessible (Diefendorff et al., 1995; Goschke & Kuhl, 1993); and
4. Finally, during implementation, script tracts or general strategies may be reconsidered and altered based on outcome feedback (Wofford & Goodwin, 1990).

The connection among each of these intermediate steps, though unseen to outsiders, may reflect important assimilations of past learning and potential points at which change agents can intervene to change processing dynamics. In connectionist architecture terminology (Lord & Maher, 1991), they represent multilayered networks and the operation of "hidden units." While connections may be very difficult to change, one way to change processing dynamics is to change from one information processing mode to another. Different modes of information processing engage different networks for interpreting environmental information, and may even involve different brain systems (Reber et al., 1991). Thus, as shown in Figure 1, changes in information processing also involve changes in knowledge used and required processing resources, which must also be considered in developing change strategies.

Each of these intermediate steps may represent a point where processes and behaviors diverge for different individuals or for the same individual across different situations. However, where processing structures and processing dynamics are similar, individuals may be said to have similar *processing dispositions*. In other words, processing networks operate similarly for individuals with similar processing dispositions.

Mischel and Shoda (1995) use their framework to explain why personality often produces stabilities *over time* in reactions to specific situations, but does not provide the general cross-situation consistencies in behavior often expected of personality. These are precisely the type of effects that we have suggested apply to culture, consistencies over time in reacting to specific situations, but a lack of general cross-situational effects of culture.

Drawing on our discussion of expert/novice differences in the use of knowledge structures offers some insights into Mischel and Shoda's (1995) theory of personality. Specifically, we would predict that where "expert" processing is involved, there will be greater consistency and greater generalization across situations. This is because responses will be based on a deeper structure rather than surface features. Generalization of behavior should occur when different surface features map into the same "deep" structure.

One area where people operate as experts with respect to their own personality is in domains that they view as self-descriptive—domains for which they are schematic in Markus' terms. *Self-schema* are chronically available schema that are used to encode information about the self. For example, athleticism or intelligence may be important as an encoding category for some individuals, but not others. When operating in a schematic domain, one would expect much greater consistency as noted by several researchers (Bem & Allen, 1974; Markus, 1977; Markus et al., 1985).

This line of reasoning provides some important insights for leaders attempting to produce consistency or stability. All possible self-schema are not activated in any situation. As Markus and Wurf (1987) note, there are many potential self-views, and only a few are currently active at any one time. These active self-schema comprise the *working self*. Leaders can influence the working self and thereby affect the nature of the expert personality schema that are used to understand and generate behavior in a particular situation. For example, by emphasizing professional identifications, leaders can elicit a working self associated with competence, initiative, and professional training. These factors, in turn, may influence the type of attitudes and work behavior that occurs. Where individuals share similar self-schema, which are similarly activated by situational features, common histories or leadership activities, we would expect considerable generality in behavior across people. Generalization across time or situations may also depend on the relevance of self-schema and the extent to which the same working self is activated.

We suggest that personality, group structure, and cultural patterns reflect the same underlying processes involved in generalizability. Where processing structures and dynamics are similar, generalizability will exist, whether across time, people, or situations. The differences among organizational culture, group culture, and personality are mainly in the origin of consistency in processing structures and dynamics, but the underlying cognitive mechanisms are very similar. The critical issues in determining whether individual, group, or organizational levels are more appropriate levels of analysis are the extent to which knowledge structures and type of processing are consistent across individuals, as well as the theoretical focus of research (Klein et al., 1994).

Interestingly, over time, culture, group cognitions, and personality may become quite similar in terms of their source and effect. Attraction-selection-attrition factors (Schneider, 1987) may produce homogeneity in the types of people found in an organization or group. That is, organizational culture acts as a filter, eliminating or retaining members based on the member's stable processing disposition. In the long run, however, organizations can also change personality. Frese and Zapf (1994) suggest that work can change personality itself as a consequence of the tremendous amount of task-based learning or socialization that occurs in work situations.

Processing Dispositions and Leadership

The prior discussion of knowledge, culture, and personality in terms of information processing factors provides a basis for understanding the potential role of leaders in mediating between stability and change. Stability involves transfer of learning in the sense that the same processing structure and processing dynamics is used in two situations. Transfer can occur within a person across time or across situations; it can also be a between-person phenomena if team or organizational members have similar processing structures and dynamics.

Leaders can foster stability by actions that promote these forms of transfer of learning. Anderson (1987) has argued that goals are of particular relevance in the acquisition and transfer of new task and social skills. Goals indicate which aspects of problem solving belong together and can therefore be compiled into new productions. Compilation marks the transition from declarative to proceduralized knowledge and thus a reduction in working memory load. Once the productions become strengthened, they can be fired quickly, effortlessly, and accurately, but only when context-specific cues are present. Knowledge of other people's goals also helps us understand their actions (Albrecht et al., 1995; Goschke & Kuhl, 1993; Lord & Kernan, 1987). Thus, by emphasizing specific goals leaders can affect both the knowledge structures that generate behavior and the way behavior is interpreted by others.

In order for new learning to transfer to another setting, goal structures that were present during skill acquisition must also be present in the transfer setting (Anderson, 1987), and the goals in the new setting must cause the same interaction among the components of the personality system as they did in the learning environment. This argument is consistent with Mischel and Shoda's (1995) conceptualization of personality. Situations that share similar psychological features should elicit common patterns of activation of cognitive-affective units for individuals with similar processing dispositions.

The actions of leaders that produce stability will also make change more difficult to achieve. Basically, change involves exposure to different organizational features, different translations of these features into processing structures, or different processing dynamics. Leaders can be a force for change by affecting any or all of these factors. Attempts to change any one of these three components without consideration of the other two are likely to result in unanticipated change outcomes. Further, we suggest that dramatic, frame-breaking change would require changes in all three components: the organizational situation in which employees operate, the affective-cognitive structures that give meaning and coherence to these situations, and the processing dynamics that produce eventual responses. Similar arguments can be made at the level of work teams, a topic which we now address.

GROUPS AND TEAMS

To better understand the relevance of the approach that has been developed thus far, we now apply this approach to workgroups and teams. Workgroups have been defined as everything from quality circles to completely autonomous teams (Manz, 1990; Manz & Sims, 1986). In this section, we contrast traditional hierarchical structures of leadership to those leadership structures that are present in self-managed and self-leadership work teams. We begin by first addressing the role of knowledge structures in group processes and then by discussing group-level processing dynamics. Together, these processes reflect a group's processing disposition. At the group level, processing disposition provides the framework for understanding the potential role of leaders to bring about cultural change, as well as understanding factors that will interfere with leaders' change efforts.

Group-level Knowledge Structures

Based on their shared organizational experiences, employees within the same workgroup are likely to hold common leadership and culture knowledge structures. This does not imply, however, that categories are identical across members of a workgroup. It simply means that leadership and culture categories are probably more similar within work units than they are across work units. Support for this contention comes from Walsh (forthcoming) who asserts that individuals in a group share similar cognitive categories. These categories are somewhat "fuzzy" and set the stage for gap filling among members. That is, some common ground for interpreting leader behaviors and cultural information is found in an overall group-level schema. Those who are unable to find any common ground on which to gap fill will have different perceptions of the leader and the culture than those who engage in gap filling.

Several researchers have provided evidence of differences in cognitive categorization among members of different workgroups. Rentsch (1990) found that members of an accounting firm who interacted with one another had similar interpretations of organizational events, but that members of qualitatively different interactive groups interpreted organizational events differently. Rentsch further argued that organizational subcultures may be operationalized as those individuals who interpret organizational events similarly. Thus, if there are differences across work teams in the interpretation of organizational events, each work team operationally represents a subculture. Change efforts could not then just focus on a broad conceptualization of culture; rather, to be successful, these efforts must take place at the group level.

Rentsch's (1990) line of reasoning is consistent with work done by Weick and Roberts (1993). Weick and Roberts proposed that a collective mind exists within work teams that are highly interdependent. According to these researchers, a collective mind determines consistent patterns in a social system. In order for the collective mind to develop, cooperation among group members is essential. Newcomers to the group internalize and perpetuate the social interrelationships and therefore the collective mind. Weick and Roberts argued that as the cooperative interrelations increase, that the number of organizational errors decrease. Thus, as the working and social relationships among team members becomes proceduralized, they are able to work more efficiently and minimize task and social errors. Referring back to Figure 1, proceduralization results in the movement by group members from the purely process-driven area on the graph to the more knowledge-driven area (i.e., they begin to engage in expert processing). The well developed nature and automaticity of task and social relationships within work teams then allows for effective task and social performance. Consequently, team members are unlikely to willingly participate in change efforts which destroy their task or social competence, and thus impair their performance.

Group-level Processing Dynamics

Group-level processing dynamics refer to similarities in patterns of activation of the cognitive-affective units held by group or team members. As was the case for individual-level processing dynamics, group-level processing dynamics mediate the relationship between situational features and group member's reactions to those features. Similarities in patterns of activation among group members eventually lead to consistencies in member responses to context specific task and social situations.

There are differences, however, between group-level and individual-level processing dynamics. One primary difference is that dynamics tend to be more explicit at the group level than they are when applied at the individual level. Whereas individual-level scripted behavior occurs relatively automatically, groups engage in the same sort of processes in a more controlled manner, and they communicate explicitly though not always verbally. A single group member's reaction to situational characteristics likely elicits feedback from other group members. (Cybernetic information processing involves the comparison of feedback to internal standards.) Continual social feedback may lead to behavior change among group members who engage in a cybernetic mode of information processing. This mode of information processing is in contrast to the limited capacity or expert processing that non-group members rely heavily upon.

Group-level processing dynamics also differ from individual processing dynamics in that the interpersonal aspects of group interaction exert a substantial influence on the patterns of activation of the cognitive-affective units. The interpersonal nature of group interactions probably impacts on each of the units in Mischel and Shoda's (1995) model and on the interaction of these units (see Table 3). That is, the interpersonal aspect of a group's interaction may impact on the group's affect, which in turn influences expectations, and subsequent goals and actions. It is important to take this factor into account, because individuals in non-group settings may process cultural information based on one pattern of processing dynamics, but use other, more group consistent patterns in group or team settings.

Group-level Processing Dispositions

Similarity among group members in terms of knowledge structures and processing dynamics results in a consistent group processing disposition. Processing dispositions are similar to Weick and Roberts' (1993) use of the term "collective mind." The guiding forces behind the group's processing disposition are likely shared leader and cultural implicit theories, similar organizational experiences, and common group goals. Leaders have the potential to impact on these factors, but they are also constrained by the implicit leadership and culture theories held by group members (Hollander, 1992; Lord & Maher, 1993). We argue that the salience of goals and the content of implicit leadership and culture theories differ depending on whether the leader is dealing with traditional, hierarchically organized employees, self-managed work teams, or self-leadership work teams. The differing leadership requirements associated with each of these situations are addressed next.

Alternative Types of Group Leadership

Hierarchical Leadership

Hierarchical leadership operates as a link with other aspects of organizations, as a source of structure and motivation, and as a center of group processes. Thus, hierarchical leadership provides one basis for leader initiated change. Traditionally, leadership theories have explained change in terms of control over organizational reward structures (Kerr & Slocum, 1987). In addition, the potential of hierarchical leaders to initiate changes is dependent on leadership status which is extended to an individual because of formal positions, but also because an individual is perceived as a leader by other group members.

Leadership perceptions, particularly when recognition based, serve as a constraint on leadership, but also as a basis for exercising hierarchical influence. Recognition-based processing is dependent upon the fit between stimuli and culturally-based perceptual schema (leadership prototypes) which specify appropriate leader behavior (Lord & Maher, 1993). Those individuals who conform to leadership prototypes are likely to be perceived as leaders and consequently increase their latitude of discretion. This line of reasoning is consistent with Hambrick and Finkelstein's (1987) argument that top level managers who act within the "zone of acceptability" of powerful stakeholders, increase their latitude of discretion.

An important point of this paper is that leaders have many cognitive-affectively based means to change behavior that compliment their use of organizational rewards and social influence processes. According to the view developed in this paper, leaders can initiate change efforts by priming alternative schema, collective minds, working selves, and goal structures which are congruent with their change-related objectives. The greater the leader's latitude of discretion, the more likely this is to happen.

There are several ways that leaders can prime alternative schema, including developing these schema within themselves or appointing powerful others who deviate from existing cultural norms. Leaders may also look to existing subcultures as a source for alternative schema. In order to activate alternative schema, it may be necessary to also shift the type of information processing used by team members. This change often involves a switch from schema-based processing to more cybernetic modes for processing information.

In short, leaders operating in traditional hierarchical organizations have a variety of ways to initiate change—they can change rewards, exercise social influence, prime alternative schema, emphasize different goals, or change the mode of information processing used by team members. Priming new schema or goals may be difficult in both hierarchical and group settings. In hierarchical settings, leadership and cultural schema may not be as widely shared by organizational members and therefore not as easily recognized by leaders.

Importantly though, a lack of widespread shared cultural schema can actually facilitate change efforts (Lord & Maher, 1993) by reducing widespread resistance to change.

Additionally, leaders must take into account the limiting aspects of personality in trying to initiate change. An important point of Mischel and Shoda (1995) was that cognitive-affective units operated as mutually activating networks. Thus, for substantial change to occur, the operation of many types of units must be changed simultaneously. The implication is that for both individuals and teams, many of the factors discussed previously must be systematically altered for substantial, frame-breaking change to occur.

Self-managed Work Teams

Self-managed work teams represent a qualitatively different context than more traditional hierarchical organizations of employees. Consequently, the role of both leaders and group members, as well as the interaction among these individuals, differ in the self-management setting. Manz (1990) argued that members of self-managed work teams have a high degree of control over their immediate behaviors, but not over the larger regulatory system that governs the group. Thus, self-managed group members likely have a high degree of task influence, but a much smaller impact on the culture which provides the task standards regulating behavior. It is important to note that Manz (1990) indicated that members of self-managed work teams generally do not evaluate the appropriateness of the standards imposed on the group. Thus, these individuals are not likely to independently identify and switch to alternative schema.

The role of leaders in providing appropriate standards depends on whether stability or dramatic change is required. During periods of cultural stability, the role of leaders in mature self-managed work teams is characterized by monitoring and evaluation behaviors. Therefore, the responsibility of leader's is to recognize discrepancies from existing standards and also to evaluate the appropriateness of such standards. If dramatic change is required in self-managed work teams it is likely that leaders must build new cultural schema for the members and teach the team members how to operate according to the new schema. These new schema involve new knowledge structures, new standards, and new procedures for monitoring discrepancies from standards.

The building of new schema may be a difficult task to accomplish, since it involves a switch from well learned structures to an unfamiliar orientation. Members of self-managed work teams likely possess expert-like schema for their specific task and social domain. As mentioned earlier, once these schema become obsolete, task and social performance will likely decline. This competence-destroying change is likely to be most pronounced in self-managed work teams because most self-managed work teams are organized around specific tasks. Indeed, the team identity and team structure may be dependent on task activities and accomplishments. Consequently, task-related changes are most vehemently resisted in self-managed work teams, because they involve very fundamental change. In contrast, group identity in hierarchical leadership situations may be more dependent on identification with the particular hierarchical leader, and changing task operations does not require changes in social structures.

Self-leadership

Not all group members are as deficient in self-influence as those members of self-managed work teams. For instance, Manz (1986) described *self-leadership* as encompassing self-management strategies in addition to strategies for managing the motivational value of the task and the patterns of group member's thinking. Thus, the focus is on both behavior and cognition. Whereas members of self-managed work teams tend not to judge the appropriateness of the standards imposed on their group, members of self-leadership teams do. In fact, the amount of self-control possessed by members of self-leadership teams allows them to both reduce discrepancies associated with task performance and also to increase deviations from the larger system.

Essentially, the self-leadership perspective provides that members of these groups can and do actively change group standards. Members of these groups are not likely to be as constrained by organizational culture as are members of self-managed work teams and traditional, hierarchically-structured organizations. Members of self-leadership teams are more apt to recognize the need for change and to be willing to develop and implement new schema. Ironically, though comfortable with team-initiated change, these members may be more resistant to *external* change efforts. Thus, the role of leaders in these situations may be to build consensus for the acceptance of existing, alternative cultural schema or to guide group members in the setting of context appropriate goals.

The collective mind described by Weick and Roberts (1993) reflects the patterns of effective working relationships among group members. The collective mind, as well as the subcultures described by Rentsch (1990), is likely to be more pronounced in self-leadership teams than in self-managed work teams or traditional hierarchical organizations. Since members of self-leadership teams exert a degree of self-control that allows them to question an organization's culture, it is likely that they actively reinterpret organizational events, while other, non-group members do not. These reinterpretations become the basis for a collective mind or the subculture of the group. Unless an influential member of the group leads the group to change its interpretation, a large-scale change is unlikely to occur.

Table 4.   Leader Approaches to Managing Change
at the Individual and Group Levels

Individual Level	Processing Structure 1. Mapping features into meaning by influencing endocing categories through priming and label ing or providing new schema. 2. Changing expectancies, increasing self-efficacy. 3. Changing affect. 4. Prime relevant aspects of goal hierarchies. 5. Change self-regulatory plans and scripts. Processing Dynamics 1. Encourage rational or cybernetic processing. Managing Transfer 1. Create consistency in learning and transfer setting. 2. Provide practice in implementation situations. 3. Tolerate temporarily lower performance. 4. Accept errors as bassis for learning. 5. Address sources of resistance associated with competence destruction. 6. Encourage encoding at deep rather than surface levels. 7. Engage the same working self in learning and transfer situations.
Group Level	Processing Structure Changes Involving: 1. Group encodings and meaning. 2. Group affect. 3. Planning and implementation processes. Processing Dynamics Changes Involving: 1. Group feedback processes such as social feedback creating a reluctance to change. 2. Nature of information processing. Managing Transfer 1. Maintain some social structure. 2. Preserve social competencies across situations.

Changing Type of Leadership

Changing from hierarchical to self-managed or self-leadership work teams is a good example of dramatic change that is likely to be resisted because of both cognitive and social factors. It illustrates the value of the perspective developed in this paper. As groups become familiar with leadership, group processes become proceduralized and provide a basis for expert processing. Norms, differentiated roles, and social status differences coalesce to buttress leadership structures and group practices. Movement to alternative ways of operating are competence destroying in a social sense and require an initial shift to information processes that are temporarily less effective. They require changes in each component of processing structures (see Table 4) and are coupled with increased uncertainty, stress and negative affect, lower self-efficacy, and increased task and social mistakes. Such changes are likely to be actively resisted by *both* former leaders who experience changed status and competence and by group members who must assume different amounts of responsibility.

CONCLUSIONS

The framework developed in this paper provides guidance in managing dramatic change. We summarize this material in Table 4 where approaches to managing change are cumulative as one moves down the table. That is, group level change includes both approaches mentioned at the individual level as well as those mentioned at the group level. Leadership changes also include individual and group level approaches.

Three points are critical. First, dramatic change at any level will require that most of the factors listed in Table 4 be addressed. Second, managing change is certainly more complicated than just recognizing and reinforcing appropriate behaviors. Thus, a cognitive information processing approach like the one developed in this paper suggests ways of managing change not considered by more traditional behavior modification approaches. Third, at times organizations need stability, not change. Stability can also be managed by leaders by emphasizing the factors associated with transfer in Table 4.

ACKNOWLEDGMENTS

We would like to thank Annette Girondi and Skip Blechle for helpful comments on prior drafts of this manuscript.

REFERENCES

Albrecht, J.E., O'Brien, E.J., Mason, R.A., & Myers, J.L. (1995). The role of perspective in the accessibility of goals during reading. *Journal of Experimental Psychology: Learning, Memory, and Cognition, 21,* 364-372.

Anderson, J.R. (1987). Skill acquisition: Compilation of weak-method problem solutions. *Psychological Review, 94,* 192-210.

Arrow, H., & McGrath, J.E. (1995). Membership dynamics in groups at work: A theoretical framework. In L.L. Cummings & B.M. Staw (Eds.), *Research in Organizational Behavior,* (pp. 373-411). Greenwich, CT: JAI Press.

Bargh, J.A. (1994). The four horsemen of automaticity: Awareness, intention, efficiency, and control in social cognition. In R.S. Wyer & T.K. Srull (Eds.), *Handbook of Social Cognition,* (pp. 1-40). Hillsdale, NJ: Lawrence Erlbaum Associates.

Bem, D.J., & Allen, A. (1974). On predicting some of the people some of the time: The search for cross-situational consistencies in behavior. *Psychological Review, 81,* 506-520.

Cropanzano, R., James, K., & Citera, M. (1993). A goal hierarchy model of personality, motivation, and leadership. In L.L. Cummings & B.M. Staw (Eds.), *Research in organizational behavior* (pp. 267-322). Greenwich, CT: JAI Press.

Day, D.V., & Lord, R.G. (1992). Expertise and problem categorization: The role of expert processing in organizational sense-making. *Journal of Management Studies, 29,* 35-47.

Diefendorff, J.M., Lord, R.G., Quickle, J., Sanders, R.E., & Hepburn, E.T. (1995). Goal-related inhibition: Application of a negative priming paradigm. Manuscript presented at the 10th Annual Society Industrial and Organizaitonal Psychologists' convention, Orlando, FL.

Edwards, K. (1990). The interplay of affect and cognition in attitude formation and change. *Journal of Personality and Social Psychology, 59,* 202-216.

Eich, E. (1995). Searching for mood dependent memory. *Psychological Science, 6,* 67-75.

Frese, M., & Zapf, D. (1994). Action as the core of work psychology: A German approach. In H.C. Triandis, M.D. Dunnette, & L.M. Hough (Eds.), *Handbook of Industrial and Organizational Psychology* (pp. 271-341). Palo Alto, CA: Consulting Psychologists Press.

Glaser, R., & Chi, M. (1988). Overview. In M. Chi, R. Glaser, & M. Farr (Eds.), *The nature of expertise.* Hillsdale, NJ: Erlbaum.

Goschke, T., & Kuhl, J. (1993). Representation of intentions: Persisting activation in memory. *Journal of Experimental Psychology: Learning, Memory and Cognition, 19,* 1211-1226.

Hall, R.J., & Lord, R.G. (1995). Multi-level information Processing explanations of followers' leadership perceptions. *Leadership Quarterly, 6,* 265-287.

Hambrick, D.C. (1994). Top management groups: A conceptual integration and reconsideration of the "Team" label. In B.M. Staw & L.L. Cummings (Eds.), *Research in Organizational Behavior* (pp. 171-213). Greenwich, CT: JAI Press.

Hambrick, D.C., & Finkelstein, S. (1987). Managerial discretion: A bridge between polar views of organizational outcomes. In B.M. Staw & L.L. Cummings (Eds.), *Research in Organizational Behavior.* Greenwich, CT: JAI Press.

Hollander, E.P. (1992). Leadership, followership, self, and others. *Leadership Quarterly, 3,* 43-54.

Hollander, E.P., & Offerman, L.R. (1990). Power and leadership in organizations: Relationships in transition. *American Psychologist, 45,* 179-189.

Hyland, M.E. (1988). Motivational control theory: An integrative framework. *Journal of Personality and Social Psychology, 55,* 642-651.

Izard, C.E. (1991). *The psychology of emotion.* New York: Plenum Press.

Jackson, S.E., Stone, V.K., & Alvarez, E.B. (1993). Socialization amidst diversity: The impact of demographics on work team oldtimers and newcomers. In L.L. Cummings & B.M. Staw (Eds.), *Research in Organizational Behavior,* (pp. 45-109). Greenwich, CT: JAI Press.

Keck, S.L., & Tushman, M.L. (1993). Environmental and organizational context and executive team structure. *Academy of Management Journal, 36,* 1314-1344.

Kerr, J., & Slocum, J.W. (1987). Managing corporate culture through reward systems. *Academy of Management Executive, 1,* 99-108.

Klein, K.J., Dansereau, F., & Hall, R.J. (1994). Levels issues in theory development, data collection, and analysis. *Academy of Management Review, 19,* 195-229.

Kuhl, J. (1992). A theory of self regulation: Action versus state orientation, self-discrimination, and some applications. *Applied Psychology: An International Review, 41,* 97-129.

Langer, E., Blank, A., & Chanowitz, B. (1978). The mindlessness of ostensibly thoughtful action: The role of "placebic" information in interpersonal interaction. *Journal of Personality and Social Psychology, 36,* 635-642.

Logan, G.D. (1988). Toward an instance theory of automatization. *Psychological Review, 95,* 492-527.

Lord, R.G., & Kernan, M.C. (1987). Scripts as determinants of purposeful behavior in organizations. *Academy of Management Review, 12,* 265-277.

Lord, R.G., & Maher, K.J. (1990). Alternative information processing models and their implications for theory, research, and practice. *Academy of Management Review, 15*, 9-28.

Lord, R.G., & Maher, K.J. (1991). Cognitive theory in industrial and organizational psychology. In M.D. Dunnette & L.M. Hough (Eds.), *Handbook of industrial and organizational psychology* (pp. 1-62). Palo Alto, CA: Consulting Psychologist Press, Inc.

Lord, R.G., & Maher, K.J. (1993). *Leadership and information processing: Linking perceptions and performance.* London: Routledge, Chapman & Hall.

Markus, H. (1977). Self-schemata and processing information about the self. *Journal of Personality and Social Psychology, 35*, 63-78.

Markus, H. (1983). Self-knowledge: An expanded view. *Journal of Personality, 51*, 543-565.

Markus, H., & Wurf, E. (1987). The dynamic self-concept: A social psychological perspective. *Annual Review of Psychology, 38*, 299-337.

Markus, H., Smith, J., & Moreland, R.L. (1985). Role of the self-concept in the perception of others. *Journal of Personality and Social Psychology, 49*, 1494-1512.

Manz, C.C. (1986). Self-leadership: Toward an expanded theory of self influence processes in organizations. *Academy of Management Review, 11*, 585-600.

Manz, C.C. (1990). Beyond self-managing work teams: Toward self-leading teams in the workplace. In L.L. Cummings & B.M. Staw (Eds.), *Research in organizational behavior*, Vol. 4 (pp. 273-299). Greenwich, CT: JAI Press.

Manz, C.C., & Sims, H.P. (1986). Leading self-managing groups: A conceptual analysis of a paradox. *Economic and Industrial Democracy, 7*, 141-165.

Mischel, W., & Shoda, Y. (1995). A cognitive-affective system theory of personality: Reconceptualizing situations, dispositions, dynamics, and invariance in personality structure. *Psychological Review, 102*, 246-268.

Murphy, S.T., & Zajonc, R.B. (1993). Affect, cognition, and awareness: Affective priming with optimal and suboptimal stimulus exposures. *Journal of Personality and Social Psychology, 64*, 723-739.

Newell, A. (1990). *Unified theories of cognition.* Cambridge, MA: Harvard University Press.

Reber, A.S., Walkenfeld, F.F., & Hernstadt, Jr. (1991). Implicit and explicit learning: Individual differences and IQ. *Journal of Experimental Psychology: Learning Memory and Cognition, 17*, 888-896.

Rentsch, J.R. (1990). Climate and culture: Interaction and qualitative differences in organizational meanings. *Journal of Applied Psychology, 75*, 668-681.

Schein, E.H. (1985). *Organizational culture and leadership.* San Francisco: Jossey-Bass.

Schneider, B. (1987). The people make the place. *Personnel Psychology, 40*, 437-453.

Srull, T.K., & Wyer, R.S., Jr. (1989). Person memory and judgment. *Psychological Review, 96*, 58-84.

Tubbs, M.E., & Ekeberg, S.E. (1991). The role of intentions in work motivation: Implications for goal-setting theory and research. *Academy of Management Review, 16*, 180-199.

Tushman, M.L., & Anderson, P. (1986). Technological discontinuities and organizational environments. *Administrative Science Quarterly, 31*, 439-465.

Walsh, J.P. (Forthcoming). Managerial and organizational cognition: Notes from a long trip down memory lane. *Organizational Science.*

Weick, K.E., & Roberts, K.H. (1993). Collective mind in organizations: Heedful interrelating on flight decks. *Administrative Science Quarterly, 38*, 357-381.

Wilkins, A.L., & Dyer, W.G., Jr. (1988). Toward culturally sensitive theories of culture change. *Academy of Management Review, 13*, 522-533.

Wofford, J.C., & Goodwin, V.L. (1990). Effects of feedback on cognitive processing and choice of decision style. *Journal of Applied Psychology, 75*, 603-612.

THE ROLES OF A FACILITATOR
IN TOP MANAGEMENT TEAM
DECISION MAKING:
PROMOTING STRATEGIC GROUP
CONSENSUS AND INFORMATION USE

William P. Anthony and Don D. Daake

ABSTRACT

Group strategic decision making has several advantages, as well as liabilities. The use of an independent facilitator can capitalize on these strengths and ameliorate many of these liabilities. For example, facilitators can help overcome certain dysfunctional political maneuvers such as hidden agendas and "back-stabbing." Facilitators can serve to equal the playing field between higher level organization members and others who may not be as politically strong, but whose opinions are critical to reaching informed consensus. Finally, the facilitator can make sure that important information gets considered and that the group stays on task. This paper discusses six roles a facilitator can play in the strategic planning process.

Advances in Interdisciplinary Studies
of Work Teams, Volume 3, pages 239-251.

STRATEGY FORMULATION AS
A GROUP DECISION-MAKING PROCESS

Much has been written about group decision making, although most of the research has focused on fairly narrow decisions such as acquisition of a new Management Information System or investment choices. Strategic decision making is more complex (Mintzberg et al., 1976) dealing with major allocations of resources which have long-term implications. Managers have a primary responsibility to interpret the environment (Daft & Weick, 1984), but there is usually no clear direction of where a firm should go three to five years into the future. There is great uncertainty and almost an infinite number of choices (March, 1994). Because of these characteristics, group decision making is often used in strategic decisions. Isabella (1990) has argued that the views of managers as a collective are important, because managers are at the heart of cognitive shifts that occur during change.

Group decision making has its strengths and limitations. Its strengths are as follow:

1.   Broader information base than individuals working alone;
2.   Ability to float trail balloons and react to suggestions;
3.   The creation of a climate of involvement that increases the ability to implement decisions;
4.   Can diffuse opposition;
5.   Can provide a means to represent stakeholders' interest; and
6.   Can generate a workable consensus.

Some of the limitations include the following:

1.   Very time and resource intensive;
2.   Over-commitment to cooperation can lead to "groupthink" (Janis, 1972) and the associated disasters that may result;
3.   Subject to political maneuvering;
4.   Lack of equality among status of participants may inhibit open and free discussion; and
5.   Differences in abilities of participants may lead to a sub-optimal decision.

Even so, group decision making with all of its limitations is widely used in organizations (Harrison, 1987). The sheer volume of information to be considered and the need to build consensus argues strongly for group decision making. Miller and Cardinal (1994) suggest that organizations use strategic planning to promote adaptive thinking that will maintain alignment with the

Table 1.   Information Based on Broad Scope
of 41 Top Management Teams

- Teams from 3-36 in size.
- Sessions conducted over the last 17 years.
- Planning conducted in retreats/workshops:
    50% One-time session
    35% Two to five sessions
    15% More than five sessions
- Types of organizations:
    Two manufacturers
    Four not-for-profit voluntary organizations
    Six financial institutions
    Five educational institutions
    Three hospitals
    Four medical practices
    Three legal practices
    Six credit industry companies
    Two real estate/resort operations
    Three construction companies
    Three retail companies

environment. However, many top management teams do not have the necessary skills to manage the group decision process in a way that capitalizes on the strengths and overcomes the limitations (Ginsberg, 1990). Korsgaard, Schweiger, and Sapienza (1995) argue that the process by which strategic decisions are made can have significant impact on the team members and the ability to implement those decisions.

A facilitator can help the CEO, top management team (TMT), and the board of directors make better strategic decisions and engender more positive attitudes (Korsgaard et al., 1995). Hambrick and Mason (1984) have argued that TMTs play a major role in determining the direction of their organizations. In most organizations what the TMT says goes. There are major costs of failure and large potential gains, thus, they have a strong stewardship role. TMTs usually include the CEO and his or her immediate subordinates. The definition can include a board of directors, as well. In most cases the team will be comprised of three to 15 members who have strong-willed personalities. This paper is based on the growing body of literature on managerial and organizational cognition and decision making (e.g., Corner et al., 1994; Meindl et al., 1994; Nonaka, 1994; Thomas et al., 1993) and the authors' experience working with 41 top management teams over 17 years. Table 1 summarizes the characteristics of these organizations.

CONDUCTING FORMAL STRATEGIC PLANNING

There are many ways to conduct strategy ranging from informal methods (Quinn, 1978) to formal planning departments to workshops and retreats of management teams (Anthony, 1985). Relying exclusively on a planning department tends to remove top management's commitment. Many strategic planning failures of the past are the result of delegating away this key responsibility of executives (Thompson & Strickland, 1996). Few small and middle-size organizations are likely to have a formal department anyway.

Our experience and research has demonstrated that a workshop or retreat format is the best way to get managers away from their daily pressures and commitments long enough to concentrate on strategic issues. Nonaka (1994) has suggested that new knowledge can be created in an organization by developing a dynamic dialogue among organization members. The retreat format provides a forum for that to happen and tends to put participants on a more equal footing which can insure greater diversity of thought.

USING A FACILITATOR TO MANAGE THE PROCESS

Rational decision making models predict that equal access and open discussion of issues based on consistent information should lead to an improved level of agreement. Models, such as Allison's (1971) Organization or Political Models, suggest that the information will be used in such a way as to further the interests of various power blocks. This can result in coalition building and improved consensus, or lead to further conflict and lack of consensus. Once an organization has decided to engage in strategic planning the next decision is whether an inside or outside facilitator should be used and which one can better cope with the decision making realities in that organization. Tables 2 and 3 outline the relative strengths and weaknesses of each approach. Most organizations do not have a qualified person on staff who can meet the demands of managing the process for top executives and powerful stakeholders. As Donaldson and Preston (1995) argue, stakeholder management requires the simultaneous attention to the rightful claims of all appropriate stakeholders. A company might have a skilled group facilitator from the training department, but that person is unlikely to have the political clout to stand up to or challenge the CEO, other top managers, or key stakeholders. Or take the example of a long-time, loyal, and successful employee who attempts to facilitate the process. He or she may even be viewed positively by virtually all of the planning team members. Even though she or he may be highly committed to the organization, he or she may be too myopic and likely to let the organization reinforce its current ways of doing things rather than challenging key assumptions (Starbuck & Hedberg, 1977).

Table 2. Strengths and Limitations of Using an Inside Facilitator

Strengths

- Knows company history, culture, and past strategic efforts
- Understands the political realities
- Has a direct stake in the outcome
- Understands the industry and markets involved
- Can provide follow-through over time
- Less expensive
- Guards confidentially

Limitations

- May lack professional expertise in group facilitation
- May reinforce current ways of doing things
- Subject to top management pressure for certain outcomes
- Too limited of a perspective knows only one company/industry
- May be ineffective in highly charged conflict situations

Table 3. Strengths and Limitations of Using an Outside Consultant/Facilitator

Strengths

- Experienced in group facilitation
- Immune to existing political struggles and conflicts in the organization
- May do dozens of workshops a year, experienced, and understands the process
- More likely to be respected by all participants as a neutral party able to arbitrate disputes
- Usually has experience across industries to bring new perspectives
- Does not have vested interest in maintaining status quo or in a particular outcome

Limitations

- May lack relvant background that is necessary to understand current situation and future needs of the organization
- No long-term interest in outcome may lead to reduced motivation for finding best strategy
- Can be more expensive
- May not provide adequate follow-through; lack of continuity between planning sessions

On the other hand, the CEO or another TMT member may be tempted to conduct the planning themselves. This rarely works effectively, because it conveys the hierarchical structure to the participants and dampens the atmosphere of free exchange of ideas. CEOs tend to surround themselves with a "dominant" coalition of powerful managers (Thompson, 1967). Under these circumstances diversity of thought may be discouraged, especially when like-mindedness and unity is a de facto objective of the discussions. Disastrous consequences from this type of "groupthink" (Janis, 1972) may result. Even

Table 4. Attributes Desired in a Strategic Group Facilitator

- Experienced in strategic planning and group facilitation, proper credentials, and certifications
- Respected by most or all of the participants
- Absolutely trustworthy with confidential information
- Broad experience across industries and some experience in industry in question
- Ability to take control and yet empower participants
- Ability to question, summarize, and communicate results
- Ability to manage group conflict
- Ability to encourage discussion and bring out reluctant participants
- A sense of humor

the best intended CEO usually will not have the skills to manage the strategic planning effort without professional help. Although Korsgaard and coworkers (1995) have argued that managers should display openness to input from subordinates, in many cases CEOs who are used to being in charge have difficulty in letting go of enough control to enable the process of discussion and debate to work.

Bringing in an outside facilitator, on the other hand, has numerous advantages and some risks (Bryson, 1988). Use of an outside facilitator can be very beneficial if the right steps are taken and care exercised. Table 4 outlines the ideal attributes of a strategic group facilitator. The primary advantage of the outsider is the independence they bring along with a fresh perspective and the ability to engage the group in "framebreaking" discussions that are difficult for insiders to conceive and manage. Furthermore, they generally have expertise to facilitate group decision making that takes advantage of its strengths while avoiding its traps. In addition a facilitator can provide a model or framework (Anthony, 1985), help resolve conflict, move the process along, and get laggards involved. The facilitator should never be viewed as a strategist but as an aid, or more properly, a catalyst, in helping the group write the plan. In some situations the facilitator becomes a convenient scapegoat on which to transfer anger and hostility.

There are clearly some situations where the use of an outsider is not desirable. If an ongoing strategic plan is already in place and the organization has a strong track record in effectively implementing the decisions, use of an inside facilitator for quarterly updates may make more sense. The outside consultant can be brought in when major revisions are made. Use of an insider will be most appropriate where there is little conflict and the industry is in a relatively predictable pattern. When an industry is experiencing rapid change, the insider may be too closely associated with the current ways of doing things and will not be able to stimulate discussion about change.

Strategic decision making is qualitatively different than operational decision making (Ansoff, 1984). A potential facilitator needs to have experience with this special decision making process. Not only is a theoretical and pragmatic understanding of the group planning process necessary, but the facilitator must have at their disposal *proven tools* such as SWOT (strengths, weaknesses, opportunities, threats), Porter's (1980) Five Forces Model, stakeholder analysis, and environmental scanning techniques (Anthony, 1985), to name a few. These help the group to focus on strategic issues without getting bogged down in short-term operational problems. That is not to say that these issues are not important, but they are not the focus of a strategic planning session. Also the facilitator must understand the strengths and limitations of group decision making that were discussed earlier.

The facilitator must have the respect of a majority, if not all, of the participants. Conflict and disagreement frequently arise and the facilitator must be able to negotiate through competing interests. The findings of Eisenhardt and Bourgeosis (1988) suggests that political behavior can result in an attempt to restrict information, but if power is more evenly distributed, there is less politics. The facilitator cannot be seen as an instrument of any one person or group. The role of the facilitator is not to impose his or her own views on the group, but to help the planning team negotiate a consensus that takes advantage of group diversity of experience, information, and opinion.

While confidentiality from consultants is generally assumed, when it comes to strategic discussions the issue is all the more critical because of the impact on an organization's competitive position should there be a leak that gets back to competitors. The facilitator's reputation must be impeccable. As mentioned previously, using an experienced outside facilitator can bring in new, fresh perspectives. There is of course a trade-off here. Bringing in someone who is narrowly focused on one industry provides depth of understanding. On the other hand, someone who has at least a limited understanding of the industry, but also understands several industries, can broaden the discussion and cross-pollinate the deliberations.

While the facilitator, in a sense, is a catalyst, he or she must be able to walk a fine line between taking charge, following an agenda, and empowering the group to participate and "customizing" the session to the organization's current needs. Research has demonstrated that there are many ways to construct a plan (Mintzberg, 1990; Quinn, 1980). An effective facilitator should be steeped in both the theoretical and pragmatic aspects of planning, so she or he can artfully manage the process with both rigor and flexibility. Finally, an effective facilitator needs to utilize his or her abilities to question, probe, and then summarize the results.

ROLES THAT A FACILITATOR CAN PLAY

Based on the large body of planning literature, decision-making literature, and the growing body of managerial cognition literature, along with our experience

Table 5.   Six Roles a Facilitator Can Play

1. An Educator
   - Planning and decision processes
   - Research
2. A Process Controller and Group Leader
3. An Information Provider and Prodder
   - Formal Information
   - Tacit Knowledge
4. A Cross Pollinator
5. A Mediator
6. A Clarifier

in facilitating group strategic planning sessions for more than 40 groups in all types of industries, we suggest six specific roles for facilitators. Table 5 summarizes these key roles.

Facilitator as Educator

In situations where diverse stakeholders are included, such as not-for-profit voluntary associations, chances are that many of the participants will never have utilized strategic planning (Bryson, 1988). In many of the groups we have worked with the participants are highly educated and skilled professionals, and yet they may not be used to thinking in strategic terms. In a group we worked with recently one of the participants said, "My strategic plan is to get up and go to work tomorrow." Even though this may have been said half in jest, the message is that most participants, unless they have previous planning experience, will not be familiar with the necessary planning concepts. For example, frequently participants will confuse mission, vision, goals, objectives, strategies, and tactics as used in the strategic context. Mintzberg (1990) points out that even among strategy researchers their is plethora of definitions and views on what strategy is. Therefore, a facilitator must be prepared to "educate" participants often on an ad hoc basis.

It is common for members of the planning team to get bogged down in day-to-day operational issues. The facilitator must skillfully manage these discussions to keep the group moving while at the same time not prematurely shutting off relevant debate and discussion. Fiol (1994) points out that to maximize organization learning and thus achieve organizational objectives, managers must "encourage the development of different and conflicting views of what is thought to be true, while striving for a shared framing of the issues that is broad enough to encompass those differences" (p. 418).

Facilitator as Process Controller and Leader

There is a large body of literature on group processes and their relative strengths and weaknesses during decision making (e.g., Allison, 1971; Harrison, 1987; Hogarth, 1987; Ungson & Braunstein, 1982) which we alluded to previously. A facilitator needs to be familiar with these. Three of the most important concerns they must pay attention to are outlined below:

1. Given the all-encompassing nature of strategic planning, the facilitator must keep the group focused. It is an art to balance the need for "getting on with it," with the need to have thorough discussion on the relevant topics. If participants are fully informed ahead of time and an agenda is used, this will aid in keeping everyone focused.
2. Intervention is often required, but *not* intervening at times is equally important as implied by Fiol (1994). For example, we have worked with groups where heated discussion has erupted. There is the temptation to intervene, but often underlying motivations and agendas can only be revealed when this is allowed to "play-itself-out." When to intervene is a judgment call.
3. Special attention must be paid to the level of participation of the team members. All who want to speak must be included without violating a person's right not to speak. The facilitator must remind participants that, at least during the retreat, all members are equal. The facilitator needs to get commitment from the CEO, before the session begins, that will assure this. Usually the CEO is willing make a statement to that effect at the beginning of the workshop.

Facilitator as Information Provider and Prodder

Strategic planning relies on having an effective information base (Thomas et al., 1993; Daft & Lengel, 1986; Nonaka, 1994). It is important that the facilitator remind the participants to consider information that has been gathered to support the planning process. Usually the facilitator, working with the organization's staff, serves to help coordinate and provide this information. It is important, though, not to over emphasize the latest reports, just because they exist.

Research has shown that individuals and groups can fall prey to the dual problem of "recency" and "availability" (Hogarth, 1987). Recency refers to the information that is among the most current or newest and, therefore, may have undue influence and overwhelm good quality information that is not as new. The availability problem states that information that is the most readily and easily available will get an extraordinary amount of attention. These two fallacies together can result in significant distortions in strategic decisions. For example, a prominent news item regarding a new proposed federal regulation that appears in the *Wall Street Journal* the day of the retreat, could result in a decision being made that over-reacts to the situation and is counter-productive in the long run. The facilitator, while not dictating which information should be used, must help to solicit a broad perspective of quality information from a variety of sources. In this sense, they are an information prodder.

Formal sources of information, for example, reports, journal articles, and media reports are not the only sources of information for making decisions, and indeed sometimes play only a minor role. Well educated professionals who participate will likely rely on their personal experience and knowledge gathered across the years (Wagner, 1987). This "tacit" knowledge is a valuable source (Nonaka, 1994), but the facilitator may have to draw-out and explore this elusive information base so that other group members can understand it and benefit from it. A skilled facilitator must balance the use of personal tacit knowledge with "hard data" sources, without introducing the bias through information recency, or availability discussed previously. They can do that by "eliciting" both types of information through sense making cues such as asking questions, asking for clarification, asking "why," providing information, examples, and insights, and providing summaries.

Facilitator as Cross-pollinator

It is very common for an organization to believe that its industry and particular situation is unique. A facilitator cannot just brush off those assertions. He or she must understand the unique aspects of the history, culture, and personnel and be sensitive to them. Certain industries manifest a structure and rules that do not apply to others (Porter, 1980). For example, safety is the most important issue in the airline industry, whereas 24 hour availability is crucial in the utility and communications industries.

However, it is important to recognize that an experienced facilitator can "cross-pollinate" with experiences, not only from other organizations in the same industry but across industries and from the literature, of which, in many cases, participants will not be aware.

Facilitator as Mediator

Conflicts usually arise during strategic planning. Feldman and March (1981) suggest that strategic information is often gathered and communicated amidst conflicting interests. Conflict is sometimes content related but may become personal as well (Sambamurthy & Poole, 1992). The facilitator's role is not to stop conflict but to use it and mold it in such a way as to make the planning productive. Stopping conflict too soon may mask the underlying issues that need to be resolved if there is to be an effective implementation of the plan.

Conflict can also emerge out of different professional perspectives (Ginsberg, 1990) and the meanings of words. For example, in one of our planning retreats we were working with a medical center. The strategic planning committee was made up of top level managers, the board of directors, and representatives from the medical staff. During the discussion one of the managers referred to his vision of the Center becoming a "Vertically Integrated" entity, by which he meant a broad-based organization that encompassed a wide range of services from basic medical care to home health care to psychiatric care and so forth. The doctors, however, interpreted the term vertically integrated as a very threatening concept assuming that vertically integrated meant the purchasing of private physician practices and making doctors employees. As it turned out, this misunderstanding had been brewing for months and had been one of the causes for a lack of trust.

It was of critical importance that this conflict over terminology be allowed to surface and then be redefined to enable shared meaning (Ginsberg, 1990). In a case like this, the facilitator needs to artfully guide this process but be prepared to intervene when no further useful progress is being made. Many times the "saving grace" of a facilitator will be his or her sense of humor. Knowing when and how to use humor can be an indispensable skill in using conflict positively, rather than letting it become destructive.

Facilitator as Clarifier

By carefully listening and then providing feedback to individuals and the group, the facilitator can glean and summarize for the planning team the most important conclusions. Frequently the facilitator must play the "naive" position in order to clarify for other group members what has been said. Certain members may not be as articulate but have some of the best ideas. Some participants assume that everyone knows what they mean by a term or concept. Side conversations (which should not necessarily be discouraged) may cause members to miss key points. The use of the journalist's tool kit of questions can serve to move the process along and help members process the vast amount of information that is produced during a workshop. These follow-up questions can help clarify, summarize, expand thoughts, define issues, and so forth:

1. What do you mean by that?
2. Who are you talking about?
3. How would you propose that be done?
4. Did everyone get that?
5. When should this be done?
6. Could you expand on that a bit?
7. Did everyone hear that?
8. Do you all agree with that?

SUMMARY

In this paper, we have advanced the idea that a skilled facilitator is needed to effectively carry out strategic planning. Group decision making has its strengths and weaknesses, and a facilitator can capitalize on the strengths and overcome many of the weaknesses inherent in group activity. Based on our experiences, it is highly advisable to utilize an outsider to conduct the process. An adept facilitator, whether an insider or an outsider, needs to play a number of roles as outlined in this paper.

Many strategic planning efforts that were disappointing in the decades of the 1960s, 1970s, and 1980s were failures because they delegated planning efforts to a bureaucratic structure and failed to engage the interest and commitment of the management team and key stakeholders. While an organization may find it desirable to keep or create staff planning positions, a planning process must have top priority interest and commitment from those selected to participate, particularly the top management team. An outside facilitator can greatly enhance the actual process but in the end he or she is no more than a catalyst. Ultimately the success or failure in writing and implementing a living/changing plan will fall upon the shoulders of the committed planning team led by the CEO.

More research is needed in the area of facilitation of tacit knowledge use. Nonaka (1994) has suggested that organizations can create new knowledge by tapping into this resource. This new knowledge aids in the process of effective strategic planning. Wagner (1987) argues that tacit knowledge is practical know-how that is generally not expressed openly. But our experience has shown that a skilled facilitator may be able to encourage the expression of this knowledge through a variety of means including story telling, metaphors, analogies, and envisioning. More theory needs to be developed and tested in this area.

REFERENCES

Allison, G.T. (1971). *Essence of decision: Explaining the Cuban missile crisis.* Boston: Little, Brown.
Ansoff, H.I. (1988). *The new corporate strategy.* New York: John Wiley & Sons.
Anthony, W.P. (1985). *Practical strategic planning.* Westport, CT: Quorum Books.
Bryson, J.M. (1988). *Strategic planning for public and nonprofit organizations.* San Francisco: Jossey-Bass.
Corner, P.D., Kinicki, A.J., & Keats, B.W. (1994). Integrating organizational and individual information processing perspectives on choice. *Organization Science, 5*(3), 294-308.
Daft, R.L., & Lengel, R.H. (1986). Organizational information requirements, media richness, and structure design. *Management Science, 32*(5), 555-571.
Daft, R.L., & Weick, K.E. (1984). Toward a model of organizations as interpretive systems. *Academy of Management Review, 9*, 284-295.
Donaldson, T., & Preston, L.E. (1995). The stakeholder theory of the corporation: Concepts, evidence, and implications. *Academy of Management Review, 20*(1), 65-91.

Eisenhardt, K.M., & Bourgeosis, L.J., III. (1988). Politics of strategic decision making in high-velocity environments: Toward a midrange theory. *Academy of Management Review, 33*(4), 737-770.

Feldman, M.S., & March, J.G. (1981). Information in organizations as signal and symbol. *Administrative Science Quarterly, 26*(2), 171-186.

Fiol, C.M. (1994). Consensus, diversity, and learning in organizations. *Organization Science, 5*(30), 403-420.

Ginsberg, A. (1990). Connecting diversification to performance: A sociocognitve approach. *Academy of Management Review, 15*(3), 514-535.

Hambrick, D., & Mason, P. (1984). Upper echelons: The organization as a reflection of its top managers. *Academy of Management Review, 9*, 193-206.

Harrison, E.F. (1987). *The managerial decision-making process*, 3rd ed. Boston: Houghton-Mifflin.

Hogarth, R. (1987). *Judgement & choice*. New York: John Wiley & Sons.

Isabella, L.A. (1990). Evolving interpretations as a change unfolds: How managers construe key organizational events. *Academy of Management Journal, 33*(1), 7-41.

Janis, I. (1972). *Victims of groupthink: A psychological study of foreign-policy decisions and fiascos*. New York: Houghton-Mifflin.

Korsgaard, M.A., Schweiger, D.M., & Sapienza, H.J. (1995). Building commitment, attachment, and trust in strategic decision-making teams: The role of procedural justice. *Academy of Management Journal, 38,*(1), 60-84.

March, J.G. (1994). *A primer on decision making*. New York: The Free Press.

Meindl, J.R., Stubbart, C., & Porac J.F. (1994). Cognition within and between organizations: Five key questions. *Organization Science, 5*(3), 289-293.

Miller, C.C., & Cardinal, L.B. (1994). Strategic planning and firm performance: A synthesis of more than two decades of research. *Academy of Management Journal, 37*(6), 1649-1665.

Mintzberg, H. (1990). Strategy formation: Schools of thought. In J.W. Fredrickson (Ed.), *Perspectives on strategic management*. New York: Harper Business.

Mintzberg, H., Raisinghani, D., & Theoret, A. (1976). On formulating strategic problems. *Administrative Science Quarterly, 21*, 246-275.

Nonaka, I. (1994). A dynamic theory of organizational knowledge creation. *Organization Science, 5*(1), 14-37.

Porter, M.E. (1980). *Competive strategy-techniques for analyzing industries and competitors*. New York: Free Press.

Quinn, J.B. (1978, fall). Strategic change: Logical incrementalism. *Sloan Management Review*, 7-19.

Sambamurthy, V., & Poole, S. (1992). Management of cognitive conflict in groups. *Information Systems Research, 3*(3), 225-251.

Starbuck, W.H., & Hedberg, B.L. (1977). Saving an organization from a stagnating environment. In H.B. Thorelli (Ed.), *Strategy + structure = performance: The strategic planning imperative*. New York: de Gruyter.

Thomas, J.B., Clark, S.M., & Gioia, D.A. (1993). Strategic sensemaking and organizational performance: Linkages among scanning, interpretation, action and outcomes. *Academy of Management Journal, 36*(2), 239-270.

Thompson, J.D. (1967). *Organizations in action*. New York: McGraw-Hill.

Thompson, A.A., & Strickland, A.J., III. (1996). *Strategic management: Concepts and cases*. Chicago: Irwin.

Ungson, G.R., & Braunstein, D.N. (Eds.). (1982). *Decision making: An interdisciplinary inquiry*. Boston: Kent Publishing Company.

Wagner, R.K. (1987). Tacit knowledge in everyday intelligent behavior. *Journal of Personality and Social Psychology, 2*(6), 1236-1247.

TEAM LEADERSHIP AND DEVELOPMENT:
THEORY, PRINCIPLES, AND GUIDELINES
FOR TRAINING LEADERS AND TEAMS

Steve W.J. Kozlowski, Stanley M. Gully,
Eduardo Salas, and Janis A. Cannon-Bowers

ABSTRACT

The increasing focus on work teams in organizations places emphasis on the role of the team leader to guide and structure team experiences that facilitate the development of teamwork skills, skills that underlie the coordinative and adaptive capabilities of effective teams. We present a theoretical framework that emphasizes two dynamic aspects of team leadership. One aspect specifies shifts in the leader's role as teams make developmental progress. A second aspect details how leaders can use natural variations in the team's task to create learning experiences. By integrating the task and learning cycles, leaders can enhance team coherence and adaptive capabilities. The theory provides the foundation for deriving principles and guidelines that specify leader behavioral capabilities. The guidelines are designed to be sufficiently specific to guide applications that aid leaders in the enactment of their roles, and to serve as training objectives and criteria.

Advances in Interdisciplinary Studies
of Work Teams, Volume 3, pages 253-291.
Copyright © 1996 by JAI Press Inc.
All rights of reproduction in any form reserved.
ISBN: 0-7623-0006-X

One of the key issues to emerge from the press toward quality, innovation, and accountability is the increased emphasis on work teams as the basic building blocks of organizations. Critical systems are being redesigned and restructured to enhance discretion, flexibility, and self-management. Organizations are continuing to downsize their administrative and middle-management layers, pushing problem solving and decision making downward—closer to the point in the system where problems arise (Kozlowski et al., 1993a). As this restructuring proceeds, upper-level managers are increasingly regarded as facilitators, and work teams take on the roles of innovators and implementors. This rise in the importance of work teams necessitates high levels of individual technical skills *and* the ability of individuals to effectively coordinate and adapt their actions to meet shifting problem contingencies.

It is increasingly clear that a gap exists between the capabilities desired of teams and our knowledge of the means by which those capabilities are developed. Training for teams typically focuses on the task-relevant skills needed for a particular role. Technical training for *taskwork* skills is generally targeted at the level of individual specialists or experts, who are usually trained collectively with like specialists. Often there is no formal training aimed at developing the skills needed to coordinate different types of expertise for cross-functional teams. Thus, the *teamwork* skills that enable individuals to meld their technical skills and operate effectively as a team are often overlooked in formal training. There seems to be a kind of faith that teamwork skills— communication, cooperation, and adaptive coordination—will simply develop within the team through experience (Salas, Dickinson, Converse, & Tannenbaum, 1992). Yet, there is little evidence that experience by itself is an effective teacher. Unguided experience does not focus attention on the mastery of key learning objectives, and their appropriate sequencing, that are necessary for the development of complex team skills. Even when an explicit effort is made to provide training on teamwork skills, it is often limited to social and interpersonal skills trained in isolation of the team's primary task context (Kozlowski & Salas, forthcoming). For the most part, training for critical teamwork skills that enable effectiveness is either neglected or not well integrated into the training system for teams.

Given these realities for team training in organizations, it is frequently the case that teamwork skills must be developed in the actual performance environment. Thus, the primary responsibility for the development of integrated task and teamwork skills necessarily falls to the team leader (Kozlowski et al., 1996). The leader encounters the new team in its work context. Newly formed teams are not holistic. Rather, they are a diverse set of individuals with heterogeneous knowledge and skills, who must be melded so they can operate as a well integrated and synchronous unit. This can only be accomplished in the team's work context as a developmental process, with the leader serving a central role as mentor, guide, and instructor.

What can the team leader do to fulfill these roles? What capabilities should the leader possess? What actions or techniques can be used to enhance the developmental process? When we turn to the literature on team development and leadership to answer these questions, we get surprisingly little information to guide applications. Although there are substantial literatures in both of these areas (e.g., Levine & Moreland, 1990; Yukl & Van Fleet, 1992), existing models are limited in their ability to provide prescriptions to guide team leadership and to enhance team development. In our view, this is due to a neglect of the work context and characteristics of the team, an insensitivity to variations and cycles inherent in team tasks, and a lack of appreciation for developmental processes.

For example, there are many existing models of group and team development that describe the stages groups pass through as they evolve (e.g., Bennis & Nanus, 1985; Bennis & Shepard, 1956; Bion, 1961; Francis & Young, 1979; Schultz, 1958; Tuckman, 1965). These models provide a rich description of developmental stages. Yet, virtually all of these models are limited by their focus on unstructured group situations that emphasize the development of norms to guide social interaction and to reduce interpersonal conflict. Although these issues are of some relevance to work teams, the models neglect the contextual and task characteristics that are of greater significance.

Leadership theories suffer from related limitations. First, most leadership theories used for training assume that the team is a collective, homogeneous, "average." The models are not sensitive to variations in individual roles, skill levels, and other individual factors that affect the leader's role. Second, most leadership theories assume that the team task has static characteristics. Although some models acknowledge that team tasks vary in complexity *across* teams, few existing models allow for variations in task complexity *within* teams. Yet, we know that most real world teams experience considerable variation in task complexity and work load. And, third, most models of leadership assume a team with no developmental history, yet we know that teams are often not very effective at initial formation. Indeed, we typically expect that "developing" the team is a key role for the leader. Although some leadership theories are sensitive to this leader developmental role, they are not very specific about leader behavioral capabilities, and how those capabilities can be used to build teamwork skills.

A theory of team leadership and development that can guide application requires a different approach than we see in most existing theories. It needs to focus on the melding of individuals into a team, and on the integration of taskwork and teamwork skills. To accomplish this, we need to construct a model that is sensitive to the teamwork context, task cycles, and developmental processes. Moreover, because these issues have generally not received much attention in the leadership and group development literatures, our theory will draw upon other research to provide empirical findings that illuminate different aspects of this overall process.

Our purpose is to present a theoretical framework that details the roles enacted by the team leader in the development of effective work groups and teams. The theory provides the foundation for deriving principles and guidelines that specify leader behavioral capabilities that enhance the development and integration of task and teamwork skills. The guidelines are designed to be sufficiently specific to aid leaders in the enactment of their roles, and to serve as training objectives and criteria.

We begin by first considering the nature of teams, their work context, and task requirements. This establishes basic assumptions necessary to ground our theory. We then describe our theoretical framework, and derive research-based principles and guidelines for enhancing the effectiveness of team leadership. The paper concludes with a discussion of issues relevant to the application of our theory, principles, and guidelines for leadership and team training.

TEAMS, LEADERSHIP, AND DEVELOPMENT

Leadership is one of the oldest and most studied phenomena in organizational behavior. Despite the considerable attention it has received in theory and research, the nature of effective leadership remains elusive. Several reviewers have noted the considerable variety, or what is sometimes labeled as confusion, evidenced by the multitude of leadership models (e.g., Phillips, 1995). One explanation for this variety in theory is that the concept itself is quite diverse, and will differ depending on the context, task situation, and temporal factors (e.g., Schein, 1980). Thus, in order to have an appropriately grounded theory, it is first necessary to establish the work context for teams and the nature of team tasks, and to consider some of the temporal dynamics associated with team developmental processes. We can then consider the key issues that need to be addressed by an applications oriented approach to team leadership.

The Team, Context, and Task

The labels "groups" and "teams" are often equated in the literature. Some researchers, however, distinguish the labels as the ends of a complexity continuum that represents differences in contexts, tasks, and interdependence requirements (e.g., Salas et al., 1992). From our perspective, the issue is not the labels themselves, but the nature of the underlying factors that distinguish the ends of the complexity continuum (Steiner, 1972; Sundstrom, De Meuse, & Futrell, 1990). In our use of "groups" and "teams" we mean: (a) multiple individuals, (b) formed to perform task-relevant functions, (c) who mutually interact, (d) exhibit task interdependence, (e) possess one or more shared goals, and (f) are embedded in a broader organizational setting (Argote & McGrath, 1993; Dyer, 1984; Salas et al., 1992).

The less complex end of the group/team continuum is characterized by clinical, therapeutic (Tuckman, 1965), and other consensus-oriented small groups (e.g., committees, councils, juries). The context in these situations is highly ambiguous. The task is essentially static, with any contingencies generally arising within the group. There is a common goal, although individual roles are unspecified and are essentially equivalent. There are no explicit task interaction or coordination demands. Members may or may not have task specialties, although there is often very little prior experience with the group task. Groups of this type are typically formed to make a single or limited number of decisions, as in a jury, committee, or task force. There is often a finite lifespan, although the time frame may simply be determined by the group's progress toward task accomplishment. Tasks of this type make few demands for specific interactions among team members in the achievement of their goal. Effectiveness is generally an additive, compensatory combination of individual contributions.

The context at the other end of the continuum is far more complex. Examples include surgical staffs, aircraft crews, and control system teams (e.g., nuclear power, air traffic control, military command and control). The task is driven by contingencies that are external to the team. It is highly structured, but in dynamic and cyclical flux. Team goals are shared, but individual responsibilities are highly specialized. And, although individual roles are distinguished, task interdependencies require particular patterns of interaction and coordination among team members. In this context, team effectiveness is based on the ability of team members to combine their efforts to satisfy task-relevant interaction demands, and to adapt their coordinated interaction to meet shifting external contingencies (Kozlowski et al., 1996; Salas et al., 1992). Team performance is a non-compensatory aggregate; a complex combination of linkages among individual tasks, roles, and goals that contribute to team performance. In this situation, the failure of a single team member to successfully integrate his or her performance with the team may hinder team effectiveness.

The current interest in work teams places a high premium on "leaderless" teams with self-leading or self-managing capabilities. We acknowledge the importance of these team attributes. However, we also recognize that many, if not most, work teams are hierarchically structured and have a formally designated leader. This is particularly the case as one examines team contexts at the more complex end of the continuum, where the consequences of team error become more serious. The premium here is on the ability of teams to coordinate, perform, and adapt, often without explicit directives or control. In our view, the leader plays a critical role in developing these adaptive team capabilities, and in guiding their effective application. Thus, we regard the leader as a central factor in the team context.

Teamwork Processes

Most models of team effectiveness acknowledge the importance of teamwork processes as critical factors for team effectiveness. From a theoretical perspective, teamwork processes mediate or intervene in the link between the team context and task characteristics, and the effectiveness potential of the team (Hackman, 1987). In this intervening position, teamwork processes either enable the team to cope effectively with its context and task, or prevent it from doing so. At a general level, teamwork processes include those factors relevant to social interaction (e.g., group norms, conflict, cohesion), as well as those factors relevant to task interactions (e.g., resource sharing, load balancing, coordination). For teams at the less complex end of the continuum, emphasis on social interaction processes predominate. As the team context and task shifts toward the complex end of the continuum, there is more emphasis on task-relevant interaction, in addition to the social process factors.

Many, if not most, work teams fall toward the complex end of the team task continuum (Sundstrom et al., 1990). Top management strategy teams, task forces, project/product teams, production teams, maintenance teams, and other exemplars possess several characteristic features: they are linked to external contingencies; have common, task-relevant goals; possess cross-functional roles, distributed expertise, and unique information across members; and must accomplish their objectives, while coping with coordination demands and time pressure. Research on the effectiveness of complex teams places heavy emphasis on the ability of the team to coordinate its diverse cross-functional roles, expertise, and information in response to externally driven task demands, and its ability to adapt coordination patterns to shifts in task contingencies and tempo. Often, team coordination and adaptation are accomplished implicitly, without explicit directives or commands (Adelman, Zirk, Lehner, Moffett, & Hall, 1986; Kleinman & Serfaty, 1989).

What are the bases of these essential teamwork capabilities? We maintain that the foundation is formed by affective, cognitive, and behavioral indicators that are *shared* among team members (Kozlowski et al., 1994). Shared affect in the form of interaction norms, mutual attraction, and group cohesion bond individuals emotionally to their team (Moreland & Levine, 1988). A cognitive foundation, represented by individual level cognitive structure and shared team mental models, provides a means for members to interpret the situation, anticipate, and respond collectively (Cannon-Bowers, Salas, & Converse, 1993). Behavioral factors such as mutual performance monitoring, mutual error detection, resource sharing, and load balancing are indicative of

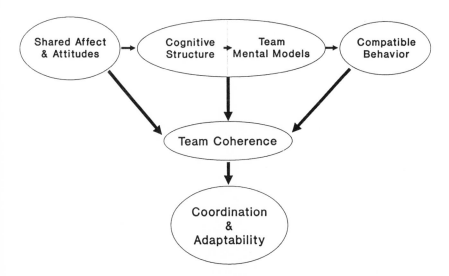

Figure 1.   The Sequence of Shared Affect, Mental Models,
and Compatible Behavior Underlying Team Coherence

compatible individual efforts to develop and maintain the team collective (McIntyre & Salas, 1995; Nieva, Fleishman, & Rieck, 1978).

By sharing similar emotional, conceptual, and behavioral tendencies, the team is able to anticipate, adapt, and coordinate as one. We refer to this shared affect, cognition, and behavior across the team as *team coherence* (Kozlowski et al., 1996). Consistent with models of team development, the components of coherence are presumed to be constructed sequentially. Coherence, then, represents a molar construct to capture the implications of shared affect, complementary cognition, and compatible behavior. It provides a conceptual basis for integrating taskwork and teamwork and, hence, team coordination and adaptability. This conceptual framework for team coherence is illustrated in Figure 1. Although there is a good research foundation for both the affective (Bettenhausen, 1991; Levine & Moreland, 1990) and behavioral factors (Fleishman & Zaccaro, 1992; Nieva et al., 1978), there has been relatively less attention devoted to the critical cognitive factors until recently. We now consider shared cognition in greater detail, as it is central to our model of team leadership.

The organizational literature has long stressed the importance of consensual perceptions and expectations that allow individuals to enact shared interpretations of their environment and its meaning (James & Jones, 1974; Kozlowski & Hattrup, 1992). Indeed, consensual perceptions have been used to predict important individual and organizational outcomes, including

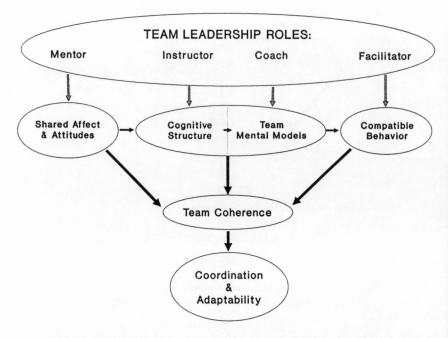

Figure 2.   Leader Roles and the Components of Team Coherence

performance (Kozlowski & Hults, 1987; Schneider & Bowen, 1985). Team researchers have created a similar, but more task focused and dynamic concept to account for team coordination and adaptability. Several researchers have proposed that complex teams develop *shared mental models* that enable individual team members to synchronize their actions (Cannon-Bowers et al., 1993; Cream, Eggemeier, & Klein, 1978; Kleinman & Serfaty, 1989; Orasanu & Salas, 1993; Rentsch & Hall, 1994; Rouse, Cannon-Bowers, & Salas, 1992). Shared mental models are conceptualized as a cognitive structure—a knowledge representation—that is shared across team members. These shared cognitive structures provide a basis for team members to comprehend the task situation, anticipate necessary individual and collective actions, and smoothly adapt the team's coordination. When the team is guided by a shared comprehension of its task situation and its corresponding goals, strategies, and role linkages, it is able to adapt to task variations and to maintain synchronicity without explicit directives (Kozlowski et al., 1996).

How do teams acquire the shared affect, mental models, and behavior indicative of coherence? In effect, this degree of sharing represents an integration of taskwork and teamwork capabilities. While we have the means with extant training methodologies to train taskwork skills, teamwork capabilities are presumed to develop through experience in the work setting. Team members must learn how to coordinate their individual performance with the ongoing moment-to-moment requirements of the team's task system. Thus, although the literature is not entirely clear, there is good consensus that coherence is an outcome of team developmental processes; processes which unfold in performance settings. Moreover, we know from the climate literature that leaders play a central role in promoting perceptual consensus (Kozlowski & Doherty, 1989). This focuses attention on the role of the team leader in the development of the shared knowledge underlying team coherence. Because the underlying shared knowledge is quite distinct at different points in the team's development, the particular focus of the leader's role is expected to be different as well. This is illustrated in Figure 2. We now consider a more detailed elaboration of these leader roles.

A MODEL OF TEAM LEADERSHIP AND DEVELOPMENT

Model Overview

Because team development occurs in the performance setting, as opposed to formal training environments, it focuses attention on the role of team leaders in the development of the knowledge and skills that underlie effective teams. How should leaders structure experiences to help integrate task and team skills? What learning objectives should they focus attention on and when should they shift the team's attention? In other words, what should we be training leaders to do to develop effective teams?

In our view, the factors for determining the role of leaders and for guiding their behavior can be derived by examining key implications of teams and their work contexts. A key implication in our discussion of teams is that their work contexts and tasks are dynamic, necessitating adaptive capabilities. This suggests a leverage point for going beyond current models of leadership training, which tend to be generic or static. Our previous analysis of the team context suggests two dynamic dimensions that have the potential to structure leader activities and behavior, and to provide the foundation for a theory of team leadership and development (Kozlowski et al., 1996). One dimension is *developmental*, represented by a temporal sequence that unfolds across the life cycle of the team. The other dimension is *task contingent*, represented by regular and/or aperiodic cycles that vary the complexity and workload of the team's task. Although these two dimensions are not independent in application, we treat them as conceptually distinct. These dimensions are the primary organizing features of the theoretical model illustrated in Figure 3.

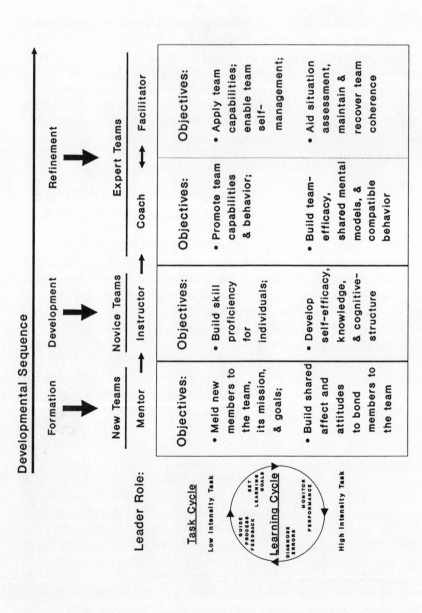

Developmental Sequence

	Formation	Development	Refinement	
	New Teams	Novice Teams	Expert Teams	
Leader Role:	Mentor	Instructor	Coach	Facilitator

Objectives:
- Meld new members to the team, its mission, & goals;
- Build shared affect and attitudes to bond members to the team

Objectives:
- Build skill proficiency for individuals;
- Develop self-efficacy, knowledge, & cognitive-structure

Objectives:
- Promote team capabilities & behavior;
- Build team-efficacy, shared mental models, & compatible behavior

Objectives:
- Apply team capabilities; enable team self-management;
- Aid situation assessment, maintain & recover team coherence

Task Cycle

Low Intensity Task

SET LEARNING GOALS

GUIDE PROCESS FEEDBACK

Learning Cycle

MONITOR PERFORMANCE

DIAGNOSE ERRORS

High Intensity Task

Figure 3. A Conceptual Model of Leadership and Team Development

262

The Developmental Dimension and Leader Roles

The developmental dimension represents the long-term evolution of the leader and team, their roles, and relationship. It is illustrated by the sequence of formation for new teams, development for novice teams, and refinement for expert teams that represents a natural progression of team evolution. Linked to this sequence, is a corresponding set of leader roles that are intended to develop the shared affect, cognitive structure, and behavior necessary for coherence. At formation, new teams are collections of individuals; they are teams in name only. The leader must guide the team through a process that allows members to bond with their teammates, develop cohesion to task, and commitment to the team's goals. The leader helps build shared affect and attitudes. By serving the role of *mentor*, the leader prompts the development of social structure, sets an example by modeling appropriate behavior, and promotes an orientation to the team, its mission, and objectives.

With this social structure in place, members are able to concentrate more on their tasks. The team makes the transition to a developmental phase in which members focus on demonstrating their individual task performance and building self-efficacy. These novice teams begin to work on the foundation for teamwork skills, but tend to be more focused on their individual capabilities rather than the teamwork skills that enable a well integrated team. Here the leader serves the role of *instructor*, providing explicit technical schooling and practice experiences that help each team member acquire or refine the proficiency he or she needs. This process begins the construction of individual, task-focused mental models, which get linked together as team level models in later developmental stages. As team members develop self-efficacy on their individual tasks, they are capable of attending to the broader team task and their role in it.

As individual proficiency improves, the leader shifts to take on the role of *coach*. Team members are individually capable, but need to develop an appreciation for the way in which their position fits into the team's task. This necessitates that they learn the interdependencies among individual positions, task priorities among positions, and the tempo and pacing that enables coordination. As a coach, the leader creates learning experiences that emphasize team goals and feedback, with the individual subordinate to the team. This helps shift the attention of members to development of the shared knowledge, mental models, and cognitive structure that links individual tasks, roles, and goals to the team. At this stage of development, behavioral indicators of adaptability, such as mutual performance monitoring, error detection, and load balancing should be apparent. Coaching completes the foundation for the development of team coherence, integrating taskwork and teamwork skills.

Over extended time periods, the leader is able to provide continued learning episodes to enhance and refine coherence. As the team develops greater and greater expertise, the leader role shifts to *facilitator*. At this level of team expertise, members have developed the meta-cognitive and self-regulatory capabilities that enable them to learn and to refine their shared cognition as a team without explicit direction. The leader's role is to facilitate effective team performance by helping the team to make the best use of its shared affect, cognition, and behavior. The leader facilitates team performance by assessing the task situation, clarifying team objectives and priorities, and monitoring the team's performance. The team self-manages as it adapts to changing task and situational conditions, with the leader lending a hand to maintain coherence.

The Task-contingent Dimension and Learning Experiences

Task cycles represent the natural variations in task intensity, complexity, and work load that occur for most work teams. These variations provide the leader with naturally occurring opportunities to create learning experiences or episodes. Under low intensity conditions, the leader is able to provide explicit structure and information, and team members are able to fully attend to these learning exercises. Under higher task loads, team members are more fully focused on task performance. Although the team may not be able to attend to instructional directives under these conditions, the leader can monitor actual performance under high load to determine how well the team applies the learning concepts and to diagnose needs for continuing development.

Our model utilizes these natural variations in the task to allow the leader to create, structure, and guide learning episodes. This learning cycle is designed around a sequence of goal-setting, monitoring, diagnosis, and feedback (Kozlowski et al., 1996). By matching the learning cycle to the task load variations, the leader can target the development of particular skills. Under low load conditions, the leader can provide information, instruction, and specific goals. As the task shifts to higher loads, the leader monitors team performance on the goals. As the intensity lessens at the end of a cycle, the leader engages the team in diagnosis and feedback. This dialogue with the team focuses attention on the skills to be developed and prepares for the next learning opportunity; it allows the leader to successively guide the development of team capabilities. The leader helps the team to derive the lessons learned from their experience and to revise learning objectives in preparation for subsequent episodes.

TEAM LEADERSHIP PRINCIPLES AND GUIDELINES

The primary value of our theoretical framework is that it provides a foundation for the identification of research-based principles, which in turn allow the derivation of guidelines for applications. Figure 3 summarizes key theoretical dimensions, links team developmental stages to leader roles, and identifies the learning content and outcomes associated with each of the leader roles that are important for the promotion of team coherence. We next elaborate the model by tracing the developmental sequence for a team and the corresponding evolution of the leader's role. As we describe the process, we will draw on research findings to generate principles relevant to each leadership role, followed by the derivation of guidelines to aid applications.

We define a *principle* as a theory and research-based fact or basic truth about a human phenomenon of interest (Salas, Cannon-Bowers, & Blickensderfer, forthcoming). In this sense, principles are designed to extract fundamental knowledge from empirical research and to summarize that knowledge succinctly and clearly. *Guidelines* are derived from the essential knowledge captured by a principle (Kozlowski et al., 1993b). Guidelines apply the principle by suggesting actions and/or conditions that, if properly implemented, can be used to improve a developmental activity or achieve an instructional objective (Swezey & Salas, 1992). In the following sections, we use these concepts to structure assertions about leader behavior, team development, and team effectiveness. For each developmental phase, we first present principles relevant to the leader's role based on relevant literature. We then derive guidelines for the application of the principles to enhance team development and performance. The intent is to provide guidelines that are theory driven and applications oriented.

Team Formation, New Teams, and the Leader's Mentor Role

When a new team is assembled for the first time, it is a team in name only; a collection of individuals. New situations emphasize high uncertainty and ambiguity, and individual members will be oriented to create social structure (Feldman, 1981; Ostroff & Kozlowski, 1992, 1993; Tuckman, 1965). Early during team formation, individuals seek information on the purpose of the team as a whole, the role of individual members within the team, and accepted norms for team operation, function, and social interaction. Until ambiguity regarding the social context is reduced, team members cannot focus effectively on performing their tasks (Katz, 1978; Kozlowski & Hults, 1986) and learning the coordination skills that underlie effective teamwork (Morgan, Glickman, Woodard, Blaiwes, & Salas, 1986).

Research indicates that a mentor who helps to orient newcomers to the key features of the new situation (Ostroff & Kozlowski, 1993) and who models appropriate and desired behavior (Weiss, 1977) can significantly reduce newcomer uncertainty and promote rapid adjustment. Thus, the leader's role as a mentor and model sets the foundation for future team effectiveness by creating an orientation among team members toward the team as a whole. The focus is on the development of shared perceptions of the social environment and cohesion within the team. The ability of the leader to affect the development of shared perceptions and cohesion is strongest very early during team formation. New team members are uncertain, and are most willing to accept information and structure that helps define the team and reduces ambiguity. Everything seems salient and meaningful to them. Thus, the advice and support provided by the leader, and the communication behavior the leader models will have significant influence on the team. The actions the leader takes during this earliest period of team formation will have immediate impacts that are likely to continue influencing the team throughout its developmental sequence.

Recommended leader role behavior for team formation focuses on the following key issues. First, leader mentoring behaviors are most effective very early during team formation. The first few minutes of interaction are critical, as individuals will be actively seeking to "make sense" of the leader, the team, and the situation. A miscue here is likely to have lasting and detrimental consequences. Thus, it is important for the leader to explicitly model the climate and demeanor that will set the tone for interpersonal interactions. Second, the leader needs to foster the bonding of individuals to the team. These behaviors are focused on reducing individual barriers and building an orientation to the team as a whole. Breaking down the "walls" that separate individuals and melding people to the team and its mission is a primary goal of the leader at this stage.

Principle 1.1: *New team members seek information, structure, and guidance from the leader to reduce social ambiguity during early team formation (Feldman, 1981; Ostroff & Kozlowski, 1992, 1993; Tuckman, 1965).*

During team formation, team members need a solid foundation regarding social norms, acceptable team member behavior, application of rules and regulations, and so forth. This information must be provided to team members to reduce ambiguity about social interactions. This helps to ensure that team members share perceptions and enact an appropriate social context for interaction, cooperation, and communication.

Guidelines:

- Leaders should promote the inclusion and acceptance of new team members for effective integration and cooperation of these new members.
- Leaders should openly discuss appropriate behaviors, attitudes, values, rules, regulations, and behavioral norms specific to interactions within the team to reduce ambiguity about appropriate team member behavior.

Principle 1.2: *New team members need to learn about each other as individuals prior to engaging in the team's task (Katz, 1978; Kozlowski & Hults,*

1986). The leader should promote and model self-disclosure during early team formation (Gabarro, 1987; Weiss, 1977).

Team members need to share social knowledge about each other regarding the skills, abilities, attitudes, and goals of the individual members on the team. This provides for the development of cohesion and trust within the team. Thus, leaders must provide informal opportunities that promote social interaction, and they must model appropriate self-disclosure to other team members.

Guidelines:

- Leaders should create informal opportunities for open communication by setting up events that promote conversation and non-work interactions.
- Information on the appropriate amounts and types of self-disclosure should be provided.
- Leaders should promote shared perceptions of an open and communicative climate by modeling desired self-disclosure to other members.

Principle 1.3: *Team members must understand and accept the goals of the team (Crown, 1993; Mitchell & Silver, 1990; Sundstrom et al., 1990). The leader must define, clarify, and instill team goals and objectives early during team formation (Shea & Guzzo, 1987).*

Part of the affective bond to the team is provided by shared goals. Effective team performance is hindered if members pursue individual goals without regard to the goals and objectives of the team. This is true even in situations where individual goals align with the goals of the team (Crown, 1993; Mitchell & Silver, 1990). Leaders must ensure that team members have a high degree of task cohesion and commitment to the team's mission. They can develop this by clearly defining team goals and objectives and by modeling their own commitment to the team and its goals.

Guidelines:

- Leaders should model commitment to the team as a whole.
- Leaders should proactively discuss team goals and objectives.
- Leaders should define the role of the team in the larger organization and define accepted performance standards.
- Leaders should ensure that team members have consensus on team goals and accepted performance standards.

Principle 1.4:   *Individual team members must understand the nature of their contribution to the mission of the team (Mitchell & Silver, 1990; Shea & Guzzo, 1987), and the way in which they fit within the team work system. Leaders clarify individual roles during early team formation.*

Role ambiguity has been linked to a number of problems in organizations, including withdrawal behaviors and increased stress. The leader can actively work to ameliorate this problem by clarifying individual roles, and encouraging an understanding of the ways in which individual roles contribute to the effectiveness of the team as a whole.

Guidelines:

- Leaders should proactively provide functional task information, and clarify roles for individual team members.
- The appropriate mutual influence of team members on one another should be clarified to develop a shared sense of the team climate.
- Leaders should discuss the importance of shared responsibility for team performance by all team members.

Team Development, Novice Teams, and the Leader's Instructor Role

Once team members establish their social fit within the team, they can shift their focus to the performance of their individual tasks within the team context (Feldman, 1981; Ostroff & Kozlowski, 1992). Although each member may bring unique skills and expertise to the team, it is still important for members to establish mastery over their individual tasks as they are linked to others in the team, and they must be able to demonstrate their competence to themselves and other team members. This develops the knowledge and cognitive structure that is later the foundation for shared mental models. Team members must also develop the confidence, or self-efficacy, required to operate as part of a team. Research indicates that such basic task competencies are important to later team performance (Glickman et al., 1987; Morgan et al., 1986; Salas et al., 1992). Additionally, individual feedback must be provided first for individuals to achieve task mastery, before focusing their attention on team performance feedback (Klaus & Glaser, 1970). Thus, members of novice teams will tend to be self-focused as they endeavor to learn about their new tasks and demonstrate competence to themselves and to others.

At this point, training instructors, leaders, and other high status experts are highly influential in facilitating the process of developing mastery of individual tasks and self-efficacy. Prior to performance as an intact team, members may have learned their individual technical knowledge and skills.

However, only within the team context do members learn how to perform their tasks within the constraints set by interdependencies with teammates (Kozlowski et al., 1993c). Leaders can affect skill acquisition, development of task knowledge, and self-efficacy through the provision of task-related information, modeling task effective behavior, and by providing opportunities for members to experiment and practice their individual tasks (Bandura, 1977, 1986; Ford, Quinones, Sego, & Sorra, 1992). Thus, the leader's role as an instructor is crucial to the development of individual proficiency and task mastery which sets the foundation for future team effectiveness (Kozlowski et al., 1996).

The ability of the leader to affect the development of individual skills is strongest very soon after social and interpersonal issues are resolved. New team members have resolved basic interpersonal issues and are prepared for the task at hand, but pressures of the team context are still minimal, providing opportunities for individual development. At this point, the opportunities the leader provides for the development of task mastery and self-efficacy will have a long-term impact on the team.

Recommended leader role behavior for instruction focuses on the following key issues. First, the leader must use the learning sequence in combination with task cycles to create experiences that help team members acquire basic skills. Prior to a learning episode, when task load is low, the leader guides the team through goal-setting to focus its attention on key learning objectives. As the task shifts to higher intensity and fully engages the team's attention on performance, the leader monitors individual and team behavior to identify critical behaviors for feedback. As the task cycles back to a lower intensity, the leader guides the team through a diagnosis of their performance and provides process feedback to focus attention on incidents and behaviors related to the learning objectives. This feedback and diagnostic process then sets the stage for the integration of learning objectives in subsequent task/learning cycles. Second, leader instruction must be focused on ensuring that basic competencies are established (Salas et al., 1992). Third, the leader must provide non-threatening environments that minimize the cost of error and which allow for the development of new or previously untested skills (Kozlowski, Gully, Smith, Nason, & Brown, 1995; Sitkin, 1992). Finally, the leader must ensure that members have opportunities to build their self-efficacy and demonstrate task competency to other members.

Principle 2.1: *Team members must develop task mastery and an orientation toward the acquisition of needed skills, even if such an orientation leads to early failures (Bandura, 1986; Dweck, 1986; Elliott & Dweck, 1988; Farr, Hofmann, & Ringenbach, 1993; Sitkin, 1992).*

During early team development fear of failure will discourage team members from using new skills (Sitkin, 1992), because they are more likely to exhibit inadequacies in the use of these new skills. In order to counteract the effects of this natural tendency, leaders must set specific task mastery goals. For example, the leader may create a learning orientation to prompt team members to practice and explore specific functions which they have not done before, even if it could adversely affect team performance. Research suggests that mastery goals are a very effective method for guiding exploration, accomplishing learning objectives, and building cognitive coherence during skill acquisition (Kozlowski et al., 1995). The leader should structure these early experiences so that the initial acquisition of new skills is more likely to succeed and seems less threatening. The leader should also provide process, or "how-to" feedback, instead of outcome, or "how well" feedback. This will help to orient members toward improvement and exploration rather than avoidance of failure (Kozlowski et al., 1996).

Guidelines:
- Leaders should provide specific learning goals that encourage the use of previously underutilized or unused individual skills.
- Leaders should provide positive feedback to individuals who actively engage in the acquisition of new skills and capabilities.
- Leaders should diagnose and provide process (how-to) feedback on how future performance can be improved rather than providing feedback on how well the individual performed.

Principle 2.2: *Self-efficacy provides a foundation for motivation, self-regulation, and resilience in the face of adverse circumstances (Bandura, 1986; Gist, 1987). Team members must develop self-efficacy for the performance of their individual roles within the team context (Kozlowski et al., 1994, forthcoming).*

The development of self-efficacy for individual role performance is important, because team members cannot focus on team goals and strategies until they are sure they can perform their own roles effectively (Kozlowski et al., 1994). Furthermore, self-efficacy enhances personal feelings of control over task performance, and perceptions of control are linked to reductions in stress, particularly under adverse circumstances (Bandura, 1986; Gist, 1987). Self-efficacy also maintains or increases motivation, especially in the face of failure experiences (Bandura, 1986; Dweck, 1986; Elliott & Dweck, 1988; Farr et al., 1993). Moreover, as team members gain experience with a task, prior performance has a diminishing influence on subsequent performance, while self-regulatory factors implicated by self-efficacy exert an increasing influence on performance (Kozlowski et al., 1995).

Team members should have opportunities to develop self-efficacy for their individual tasks. Initial learning episodes should emphasize simpler skill demonstrations that are more likely to be successful. Failure should be minimized in initial assignments, as it may increase anxiety and reduce self-efficacy (Gist & Mitchell, 1992). Self-efficacy is developed through exposure to models and the successful experience of others, verbal persuasion, and task mastery experiences (Bandura, 1982; Gist & Mitchell, 1992). Self-efficacy will provide resilience to stress and errors—indeed, errors are an important source of diagnostic information. Thus, later learning episodes will emphasize mastering more difficult and challenging aspects of the task where errors are likely, but useful for learning complex skills (Kozlowski et al., 1995). Leaders must proactively work to structure and guide the learning cycle to develop the self-efficacy of team members.

Guidelines:

- Leaders should structure instructional experiences such that they allow members to experience early success through the performance of less complex tasks. Over time, the leader can increase the difficulty of the goals of the learning cycle so that tasks become more complex and progressively higher skills are developed.
- Leaders should provide opportunities for members to observe the success and proper task performance of other team members.
- Leaders should diagnose and provide encouraging and constructive process feedback regarding task performance, and negative feedback should be provided carefully with a "how-to" orientation.

Principle 2.3: *Team members require equivalent opportunities to practice and explore the tasks they must perform in order to master necessary competencies (Ford et al., 1992; Hall et al., 1993).*

In a dynamic and interdependent setting like a team environment, team members may receive differential opportunities to master individual tasks. It is crucial for team members to perform a variety of assignments to ensure that all members have the opportunity to establish basic competence in required skills. Ford and associates (1992) found that individuals often receive differential opportunities to perform trained tasks. For teams, performance opportunities must engage the skills of all team members (Hall et al., 1993). Thus, initial task experiences should provide an opportunity for *all* team members to explore task contingencies, make errors, and receive process feedback relevant to the learning objectives. Without explicit structuring by team leaders, team members may attend to superficial aspects of the task.

Additionally, without opportunities to perform a task and learn from mistakes, team members may focus on avoiding errors without actually learning the underlying skills needed for long-term effectiveness.

Guidelines:

- Leaders should provide opportunities for experimentation and practice of needed skills to all team members.
- Leaders should set specific learning goals for experimentation and exploration which ultimately lead to better skill acquisition.
- Leaders should focus the attention of members on the underlying objectives of a learning cycle rather than on surface characteristics of a task.

Team Refinement, Expert Teams, and the Leader's Coaching Role

As team members build task competence and self-efficacy for performing individual tasks in the team environment, they are increasingly able to attend to team goals, team processes, and team performance. During the instructor role, the leader sets the foundation for effective team performance by developing the individual skills, self-efficacy, and the cognitive structure required to fulfill individual roles in the team. As individual skills are acquired and refined, the leader can divert attention to team processes and team performance. The purpose now is to build shared cognitive structures or team shared mental models (Cannon-Bowers et al., 1993), and the behavioral indicators that are relevant to team coordination and adaptability (Kozlowski et al., 1996). At this point the leader engages in coaching to develop the teamwork skills that improve team functioning and performance.

The leader's coaching role involves skill development for the team as a unit. Coaching requires the leader to foster the development of an understanding of member roles and mutual role relationships. Research has indicated that knowledge regarding other team member roles and interdependencies is a crucial component of effective team performance (Cream et al., 1978; Roth, Hritz, & Lewis, 1984). Furthermore, team members must minimize ambiguity about the role each member plays in the team and how each member contributes to effective team performance (Volpe, Cannon-Bowers, Salas, & Spector, forthcoming). As team members increase their understanding of team dynamics, team members will also be more able to engage in mutual performance monitoring, feedback, error detection (Boguslaw & Porter, 1962; Denson, 1981; Morgan et al., 1986; Nieva et al., 1978; Swezey & Salas, 1992), implicit coordination (Kleinman & Serfaty, 1989; Orasanu, 1990), and correct sequencing of communication (Glickman et al., 1987). Thus, team members can be guided to understand the complex network of interactions that lead to successful team performance (Kozlowski et al., 1994). Also, the leader can take advantage of opportunities for the team to perform under conditions where the effects of failure are minimized, but where the team is under high task load.

Recommended leader role behavior during coaching focuses on the following key issues. First, leader coaching behaviors must vary by task load. During low task load the leader provides team goals for performance or skill acquisition. As the team moves into high task load, the leader monitors by gathering information on team processes and team functioning. When the task cycles back to low intensity, the leader engages in diagnosis and feedback. New learning goals are set that are designed to improve the acquisition of teamwork skills, and another coaching cycle ensues. Second, the leader must ensure that team members understand how their roles and task performances interrelate to affect team performance. This is essential to the development of shared mental models. Third, leaders must focus on building teamwork skills that underlie coordination, such as error detection and mutual performance monitoring, by providing opportunities to exercise and develop such skills in a non-threatening environment that minimizes the cost of making errors. Fourth, leaders as coaches must provide opportunities to develop team efficacy, or task confidence in the team.

Through coaching, the leader can set goals for the improvement of team skills, then monitor team performance paying specific attention to the teamwork skills requiring improvement. This type of continued instruction for the team is critical, because team performance is not the simple amalgamation of individual task skills (Tziner & Eden, 1985). Although individual members have gained task competence, it is at this point that teams must develop the smooth and coordinated interactions that are the hallmark of effective team performance.

Principle 3.1:   *Team members must establish competence in teamwork skills such as mutual performance monitoring, error detection, load balancing, and coordination (Boguslaw & Porter, 1962; Nieva et al., 1978; Kleinman & Serfaty, 1989; Swezey & Salas, 1992; Morgan et al., 1986).*

In contrast to the instructor role, the leader must now focus primarily on the team level when coaching expert teams. Members of expert teams should have acquired sufficient basic technical skills, cognitive structure, and confidence in their ability. It is important, however, for team members to fully develop their teamwork skills so that they can function effectively in a variety of situations. It is through this process that the leader helps team members to link-up their individual mental models and to develop shared mental models that enhance teamwork.

Since the leader is primarily focused on coaching the team, evaluation and assessment at the team level becomes increasingly important, although individual feedback and skill diagnosis cannot be ignored. Through coaching and repeated exposure to various team performance conditions, team members can develop a sense of role relationships and expected role behaviors (Rentsch & Hall, 1994). During the coaching cycle, teams can develop task routines that save critical time and energy (Gersick & Hackman, 1990; Novak, 1991) and reduce process losses (Steiner, 1972) for a normative range of tasks and situational contingencies. Furthermore, stabilization of team member's expectations reduces role conflict and ambiguity; team members learn what must be done by whom and when for normative tasks. An understanding of team interactions allows team members to learn role relationships and implicitly coordinate their efforts, thus improving team performance (Kleinman & Serfaty, 1989). Although leaders must increasingly focus the team on achieving performance outcomes, members of expert teams must also continue to develop teamwork skills that help them to cope and adapt to unusual, emergent, and non-routine situations. Thus, leaders should encourage teams to acquire new skills when facing new or novel situations, but this encouragement must be interspersed with assessment or evaluation of skills which the team and team members should have already acquired (Kozlowski et al., 1996).

Guidelines:

- Leaders must set clear learning goals for teamwork skills that underlie coordination, such as mutual performance monitoring, error detection, load balancing, and resource sharing.
- Leaders must provide opportunities for team members to develop teamwork skills in an environment that minimizes the costs of making errors.
- Leaders should emphasize awareness of more complicated interdependencies and role relationships among team members by emphasizing teamwork and team goals.
- During coaching for new, unusual, or difficult situations, the leader should provide specific learning goals that encourage the use of previously unused teamwork skills.

Principle 3.2: *In expert teams, leaders must guide the development of a collective, team-level efficacy, or the belief that the team can work together effectively to accomplish the task or goals set before it (Bandura, 1982; Campion, Medsker, & Higgs, 1993; Shea & Guzzo, 1987; Shamir, 1990; Spink, 1990).*

Leader coaching behavior must also encourage the development of confidence in the team, or team efficacy. Individual members may have established and developed confidence in their ability to function in their respective roles, but the team must still learn to work together under a variety of conditions. Coaching can ameliorate these problems by developing teamwork skills. As teams develop competence in teamwork skills, increases in team functioning and team performance will lead to the development of team efficacy. Team efficacy provides resilience in the face of adverse task demands, and is similar to the function of self-efficacy for individual skills (Bandura, 1982; Shamir, 1990). If team members do not believe that the team can work together as a unit, then they will be less likely to use teamwork skills like coordination, mutual performance monitoring, and error detection to achieve team outcomes (Travillian, Baker, & Cannon-Bowers, 1992). Also, they will be increasingly stressed because of the decreasing lack of control they will feel in response to external stimuli. Team efficacy will help to maintain or increase team motivation, especially in the presence of a difficult situation, and it provides the foundation for the development of team self-regulatory skills.

Guidelines:

- Leaders should provide goals to improve teamwork skills and constructive team feedback to enhance the team efficacy of the team members.
- Leaders should provide coaching experiences which are designed to enhance the likelihood of success for the team as a whole but which are challenging enough to provide opportunities to develop teamwork skills.
- Leaders must diagnose and proactively set goals for the team which are attainable and which lead to preparation for performance in difficult or stressful situations.
- Leaders must diagnose and provide process feedback on how well teamwork goals have been met and how future goals may be better attained.

Team Refinement, Expert Teams, and the Leader's Facilitator Role

Through coaching team members have developed a full understanding of their own roles and how their role performance affects other members, that is, they fully understand their role relationships and how their mutual interdependence affects team performance. Team members have fully shifted from an individual self-focus to a focus on the team as a unit; this enhances their ability to cooperate and work with other members (Kozlowski et al., 1994). They possess shared mental models of the team and task, and exhibit behavioral indicators of coordination and adaptability. This compatible understanding allows team members to understand and predict member role performances, and facilitates adaptation to shifting task environments (Cannon-Bowers et al., 1993; Kozlowski, Gully, & McHugh, 1993; Rentsch & Hall, 1994).

Expert teams must be able to adjust team member tasks, task boundaries, and task responsibilities as the situation requires (Novak, 1991). To facilitate adaptability, the team must initially have clear objectives and strong self-regulating skills. Team adjustment to tasks will require shifts in role linkages and negotiations between team members. These role negotiations are continuous and impact all linkages between team members. To adapt to changing situations, team members must learn to recognize situational cues which dictate changes in team goals, task strategies, and member role linkages (Kozlowski et al., 1994). Routinized task behavior must be adapted to fit the demands of situational contingencies. This allows the team to adjust to new situations in which one or more members of the team cannot fulfill their normative functions. This, in turn, gives the team enhanced control of the environment.

Until this point in team development leader roles have primarily been focused on creating team coherence by building shared affect, basic task competencies and self-efficacy, and shared cognitive structure and compatible behavior. Now, as a facilitator, the leader's role shifts from a focus on instruction and the creation of learning episodes, to one of facilitating and utilizing the team capabilities that have already been acquired. In this sense, the team is increasingly capable of self-leading and self-managing its performance. To help the team maintain its coherence and performance focus, the leader facilitates by buffering the effects of external environmental contingencies, and by monitoring the impacts of the contingencies on internal team functioning (Kozlowski et al., 1996). In this sense, the leader steps in to direct or negate team decisions only when the team has become caught in the press of the moment and has lost perspective on the external situation, or has lost the coherence needed to maintain internal team processes.

Teams increase their self-regulatory capabilities as members develop a shared perception of the team and its environment and as they acquire teamwork skills critical to team effectiveness through leader behaviors like mentoring, instruction, and coaching. Team self-regulation involves an understanding of how to coordinate member actions, engage in error detection, and monitor each other's performance, so the team can balance workloads and stay on track toward stated objectives. Moreover, the members have developed confidence in themselves and the team, so they can function effectively under adverse task conditions. Although teams may vary in the amount of self-regulation available to them (Sundstrom et al., 1990), self-regulation is likely to be an important component of team effectiveness (Hackman, 1987).

In teams that are self-regulating, success will depend on both the team and the leader (Manz & Sims, 1987; Rentsch & Hall, 1994). Once a team is functioning as an intact system, it will control its own destiny to a considerable extent. However, leaders can still affect and facilitate team performance by engaging in a variety of activities like encouraging reevaluation of the aspects of the team situation that impede performance, ensuring that members get the ongoing assistance they need to operate well as a team, helping the team to learn from its experiences, and assisting the team in environmental scanning and interpretation (Gersick & Hackman, 1990; Hackman, 1987; Kozlowski et al., 1996; Manz & Sims, 1987).

Since the team has developed the skills to be self-regulating, the leader's role shifts away from that of providing instruction or coaching to one in which the leader facilitates the application of the self-regulating capabilities of the team. Self-regulation, however, requires knowledge of one's environment. Because team members can rarely obtain complete or accurate views of the broad environmental contingencies, they must turn to other sources of information, like leaders, to learn "how things are" (Hackman, 1992). Leaders can facilitate team regulation by scanning the external environment and framing the anticipated situation, ensuring that sufficient resources are available for the task at hand, and providing periodic updates as the situation unfolds. In addition, to the extent external contingencies disrupt internal coherence and hinder performance effectiveness, the leader may intervene through redefinition of the task, the team, or its goal to aid the recovery of coherence (Boguslaw & Porter, 1962; Hackman, 1987; Kozlowski et al., 1996). The potential of the leader to facilitate the application of learned skills is strongest after the team has established competency in teamwork skills.

Recommended leader role behaviors for facilitation focus on the following key issues. First, the leader must ensure that sufficient resources exist within the team to accomplish stated objectives. This occurs through planning. Second, the leader must establish shared expectations among members regarding the tasks that need to be performed, what information is important, and the strategy to be used to attain objectives. This is accomplished by framing the upcoming situation and establishing objectives. Third, the leader must gather and interpret information and then revise or refine member expectations as external conditions change. This occurs through situation assessment. Fourth, the leader can facilitate performance by redefining the team, task, or objectives if coherence breaks down in an unusually complex or difficult situation. This is accomplished through task/team redefinition. A fifth facilitation behavior involves reconsideration and learning from recent task experiences. This occurs through reassessment.

Reassessment is also linked to the ability to know when to shift back to the role of mentor, instructor, or coach. Although the leader is working with an expert team with advanced teamwork skills, there may be occasions when interpersonal understanding must be reestablished, basic task competencies need to be developed or honed, and different teamwork skills need to be acquired. An effective facilitator will understand when such activities need to be pursued. An effective facilitator must also be sensitive to how task-contingent workloads interface with different forms of facilitation to affect team effectiveness.

Principle 4.1: *Teams require sufficient resources within the team to accomplish stated objectives (Goodman, Ravlin, & Argote, 1986; Hackman, 1987).*

Research suggests that teams are highly influenced by the amount of leader support and team resources that can be brought to bear on a given task (Hackman, 1987; Manz & Sims, 1987; Pearce & Ravlin, 1987). Teams that are highly competent in both individual and teamwork skills will still be unable to achieve objectives if there are too few resources available. Leaders can ensure sufficient resources exist by planning and organizing prior to task engagement (Yukl & Van Fleet, 1992).

Guidelines:

- Leaders must work with the team to determine long-term objectives and strategies and then allocate resources according to priorities.
- Leaders must work with the team to determine how to assign members and resources efficiently to accomplish a given task or project.
- Leaders must determine how the utilization of resources can be maximized through additional mentoring, instructing, or coaching.
- Leaders must proactively search the team, organization, and environment to find alternative methods of procuring needed resources.

Principle 4.2: *Teams must share an understanding of how team objectives and strategies relate to the team environment (Cannon-Bowers et al., 1993; Gersick & Hackman, 1990; Kozlowski et al., 1996; Orasanu & Salas, 1993; Rentsch & Hall, 1994).*

A team requires a relatively clear map of the performance situation in order to develop a task-appropriate performance strategy and to maintain effective self-regulation (Hackman, 1987). A leader can provide such a map by engaging in situation framing behaviors. Situation framing includes presentation of the primary objectives of the team, as well as the situational contingencies which may be enacted as the task environment changes. Situation framing prepares the team for action by "cuing up" previously learned goals and strategies (Kozlowski, Gully, & McHugh, 1993c). Thus, the role of leader facilitation is to prepare the team for dealing with upcoming situations by reviewing and identifying appropriate sets of previously learned responses for different contingencies. Team self-regulation is assisted in this manner because the team becomes aware of what is likely to occur and all members know how they should respond as the situation unfolds. The focus of situation framing will tend to be on the team as a unit, except when particular individuals or sub-teams need to make specific responses to a given situation.

In order for team members to coordinate their actions effectively, they must share the ultimate goal or objective of the team. By sharing this information, team members can self-regulate to determine if their individual actions are congruent with the team's objective. Also, knowledge of key team objectives will allow greater flexibility and adaptability to the situation as it unfolds, since there are often multiple paths to a given outcome. The leader must also stress the importance of team objectives to ensure that all team members are committed to the team's ultimate goal.

It is also important for leaders to discuss strategies or plans for a variety of situational contingencies which will lead to the fulfillment of the team's objectives. Since strategies or plans consist of a sequence of sub-goals which lead to some desired outcome (Kozlowski et al., 1996; Lord & Kernan, 1987), the leader can highlight the strategy being used by the team by specifying sub-goals. The sub-goals may change as the situation unfolds, so the leader must also work with the team to identify key situational contingencies which may lead to a switch in strategies (Cannon-Bowers, Tannenbaum, & Salas, 1995; Gersick & Hackman, 1990). Finally, the leader should also link the anticipated strategies to previous learning experiences so that team members will share an understanding of their specific roles in achieving the team's desired outcomes.

Guidelines:

- Leaders must discuss and help the team clarify its objectives, especially when task loads are at a minimum and members can attend to their objectives.
- Leaders must help ensure that all team members have consensus on the nature of the team's objectives and that they understand their importance.
- Leaders must work with the team to identify key sub-goals which will lead to desired outcomes, especially when task loads are at a minimum.
- Specific situational contingencies that can change sub-goals must be defined. Alternative strategies in response to such contingencies must be explored.
- Leaders should compare the different possible strategies to previous learning experiences, and the leader must ensure that the team has consensus on the strategy to be used for a given situational contingency.

Principle 4.3: *Teams require periodic updates on how the external environment relates to current team objectives and performance (Kozlowski et al., 1996; Salas, Cannon-Bowers, & Johnson, forthcoming).*

During facilitation under high task loads, the leader must provide situation assessment updates which provide team members with information on how the team must adapt to the changing environment and how it is progressing toward fulfillment of its objectives. Situation assessment and awareness has been defined as "continuous extraction of environmental information, integration of this information with previous knowledge to form a coherent mental picture, and the use of that picture in directing further perception and anticipating future events" (Dominguez, 1994, p. 11). Situation assessment updates enhance team regulation and maintain coordinated and effective team performance by providing team members with needed information which allows them to share perceptions regarding the team and its relation to the external environment. Also, situation assessment updates can encourage situation scanning and strategy planning on the part of team members. Hackman and colleagues (Gersick & Hackman, 1990; Hackman, 1987), have noted that it is often necessary to prompt or encourage members to engage in situation scanning and strategy planning activities; leaders can focus member attention on such activities by presenting relevant situational updates.

Information disseminated through situation assessment updates might include current status and positioning of the team in its environment, how the team might adjust to the current situation, and how the situation could change in the near future. Through previous instruction and coaching, the team will be able to adjust in a coordinated fashion in response to the updates provided. This provides for seamless interaction between team members in response to changing situational contingencies. Situation assessment updates must typically be kept simple when the team is in a high task load environment. They must also be frequent enough to allow the team to make whatever adjustments might be needed as a given situation unfolds.

Guidelines:

- Leaders must provide situation assessment updates to team members to maintain a shared perspective on how the team is currently performing and how it must adapt to a changing environment.
- Leaders should periodically provide information on how the team is doing, what it should be doing, and how it might adjust to the changing situation.
- Leaders should provide information on what events might be expected to occur in the near future.

Principle 4.4: *Teams require redefinition of the team, task, or objectives if the current situation is too complex, overwhelming, or difficult (Boguslaw & Porter, 1962; Kozlowski et al., 1996).*

Planning, situation framing, and situation assessment updates facilitate team performance and help to maintain self-regulatory processes within the team. There are some occasions, however, when situational demands can become so complex or difficult that the leader must intervene by engaging in task/ team redefinition. Task/team redefinition involves the establishment of intermediate goals, changing the priorities of the team as a unit, and simplification of the task and team member interactions. Task/team redefinition can also include reassignment of workloads among team members or redefinition of their respective roles to match their current capabilities. Once the team has achieved the intermediate goals and stabilized its performance, the leader can provide situation assessment updates until the task load lightens or the team reaches its objective.

Task/team redefinition·ensures that work loads are equally balanced among team members to meet their abilities to fulfill their respective role requirements. It also focuses attention onto tasks which must be accomplished immediately until such a time as the environment stabilizes and the team can refocus on the long-term objectives of the team.

Guidelines:

- When workloads exceed the capabilities of the team members to reallocate resources or load balance, the leader must redistribute work such that everyone is operating within their maximum capabilities.
- When events occur which require adjustment to an unexpected situation, the leader must quickly redefine the roles of the various team members and establish intermediate task objectives for the team.
- If situations become too complex or too difficult to handle, the leader must focus on intermediate objectives by letting some inputs wait, omitting some inputs from processing, allowing certain errors or approximations to take place, prioritizing or processing some inputs before others, increasing the number of people working on a particular task, or if necessary, by withdrawing from the task or situation.
- Once the team has reestablished its ability to deal with a given situation, the leader must continue to provide situation assessment updates which link with the overall team objective until the team reenters low task load conditions or the objective is attained.

Principle 4.5: *Teams require an opportunity to reflect, reexamine, and learn from recent task experiences (Gersick & Hackman, 1990; Hackman, 1987, 1992).*

Although an expert team can typically function together effectively, there are often opportunities to learn from recent task experiences that can improve future task performance. It is unlikely that any team will execute every required task and behavior perfectly under all conditions. Leaders can take advantage of the learning that can accrue as a result of naturally occurring task performance efforts and the errors that occur during such efforts. The leader can facilitate such learning through reassessment behaviors. Reassessment involves a systematic review of the proper and improper actions undertaken by the team, as well as a consideration of alternative strategies that could have been pursued. Reassessment is also linked to diagnosis of individual and team skills and competencies. Depending on the outcome of the reassessment process, the leader may have to shift from the role of facilitator to that of mentor, instructor, or coach. Reassessment is facilitated by providing occasions for explicit review and renegotiations between team members regarding their respective tasks.

Guidelines:

- Leaders should set aside times for reflection and learning when task loads are relatively low.
- Leaders should encourage reevaluation of previous team strategies and performance with a focus on future improvement.
- Leaders should assist the team in diagnosis of individual skill and teamwork competencies, and engage in mentoring, instruction, and coaching when necessary.
- Leaders should use information gathered during reassessment for future framing, situation assessment updates, and task/team redefinition.

Thus, we envision a continuing facilitator role for the leader as teams refine and enhance their expertise and adaptive capabilities across their life cycle. Although, in time, many of these leader activities may become internalized by the team, the natural renewal of team members, and finite team life cycle, are likely to provide continuing opportunities for leaders to aid in the development and maintenance of effective teams.

DISCUSSION

Theoretical and Research Implications

The purpose of this paper was to present a theoretically based model of team leadership and development. Our model takes the focus of team training and development out of the classroom and puts it in the workplace, where the workplace, in effect, becomes another element in a sequence of learning experiences across different training environments (Kozlowski et al., 1993b). From this perspective, team leaders become an integral aspect of team training systems, and the key focal point for the development of effective work teams.

Our model posits that the primary goal of team leaders is to build integrated taskwork and teamwork skills for the team. This goal is accomplished through the creation of team coherence, a term we use to describe the development of shared affect and attitudes, team mental models or individual and shared cognitive structure, and compatible behaviors that link individuals to the team and its goals. Ultimately, this shared affect, cognition, and behavior provides a foundation for team performance, regulation, and adaptability, that is, a basis for the creation of self-managing teams.

Our leadership model is dynamic along two dimensions: the team's developmental sequence and cycles of task contingencies. The developmental dimension specifies a sequence of leader roles that are linked to different phases across the evolution of the team. Each leader role is intended to contribute differentially to the components of team coherence. For new teams at initial team formation, the leader exercises a mentoring role that is intended to build the bonds of shared affect and attitudes. As the new team melds interpersonally, members are able to shift attention to their individual task proficiency in the team context. During this stage of team development, the leader exercises an instructional role that builds individual task knowledge and self-efficacy. As teams develop their basic competencies, they become more expert. At this stage the leader shifts to a coaching role, seeking to combine the individual knowledge developed in the prior stage in order to build shared mental models and team efficacy. Teams develop shared cognitive structure about the team and its task, and are able to begin exhibiting behavioral mechanisms that regulate coordination and adaptability. They exhibit the behavioral foundations for self-management. As teams improve and refine their expertise, the leader shifts to a facilitating role intended to aid team self-regulation. By interpreting the environment, managing expectations, and monitoring goals, the leader helps the team maintain its common foundation of shared affect, cognition, and behavior.

The task cycle dimension refers to variations in the workload and complexity of team tasks which create differential learning opportunities for the leader to use to build the components of team coherence. We propose a learning cycle that is compatible with these natural or created variations in workload that is based around a sequence of goal setting, monitoring, diagnosis, and feedback. The specific content, outcomes, and level of learning varies with the particular leader role under consideration. By iterating this learning cycle in combination with ongoing task variations, the leader is able to successively build the foundation for team coherence. Thus, the two dimensions provide a theoretical basis for integrating team leadership and development into the work environment and the natural flow of work in organizations.

Our presentation of the theoretical model follows the leader and team through the entire developmental sequence from team formation to refinement. As the team progresses across the sequence, the leader adapts his or her role to take advantage of task variations and learning cycles. Note, however, that application of the principles and guidelines derived from the model may occur at any point in the team developmental sequence. Thus, the principles and guidelines can be used to assist existing teams that have already progressed beyond the formation stage. Assuming that prior learning objectives have been accomplished, principles applicable to more advanced stages of development can be used to build and refine coherence. By assessing an existing team's current point of development, the appropriate portion of the model can be used to guide further progress and improvement.

Although our theoretical model is grounded by broad-based support in the literature, research is currently in progress in an effort to provide more direct supporting evidence, particularly for those principles that are of a more inferential nature. We are currently engaged in laboratory and field experimentation to test key aspects of the model. The results have been encouraging.

For example, laboratory research has examined the benefits of creating a mastery orientation when novices are trying to acquire the adaptive skills needed to perform complex tasks. Our theoretical framework indicates that a leader's instructional role should focus attention on individual skill mastery, frame errors as opportunities to learn, and guide trainees through a sequence of increasingly more challenging learning objectives. Most learning situations emphasize performance and attempt to minimize trainee errors. Although this approach may improve task performance during training conditions, it may prevent trainees from focusing attention on key learning objectives, learning from their errors, and acquiring adaptive skills. This inability to comprehend the task at a deeper level of understanding may later hinder their ability to transfer skills to more complex task conditions. Results indicated that a mastery orientation yielded a improved learning relative to a performance orientation during training. A mastery orientation improved learning of basic knowledge and the development of a coherent meta-cognitive structure, representing trainee comprehension of key task concepts, appropriate strategies, and linked behaviors needed to implement the strategies. It also substantially improved the development of task self-efficacy. In addition, these learning outcomes were significant predictors of skill adaptation. Indeed, the full model accounted for nearly 75 percent of the variance in adaptive performance (Kozlowski et al., 1995). Extensions of the laboratory research will shift to the next phase of the model, which focuses on the team level development.

In addition to the laboratory work, a recent field experiment has demonstrated support for a leader training intervention that is consistent with our model (Smith-Jentsch & Tannenbaum, 1995). Leaders were trained to use a debriefing approach which emphasized the link between teamwork processes and performance outcomes. Teams whose leaders had been trained to use this approach outperformed teams whose leaders had not received training on how to debrief in a series of simulation exercises. Thus, although both experiments represent preliminary efforts to evaluate the model, the results appear to be promising.

Application Implications

We believe that our model provides a theoretically grounded, research-based approach to team leadership that has important implications for applications. One way to get a sense of its application potential, is to compare it to existing models of leadership and leadership training. Organizational surveys indicate that leadership training is regarded as the most pressing training need (Human Technology, 1993), and is among the top three areas in which organizations sponsor training activity (Lee, 1991). Three theoretically based approaches have proved to have enduring popularity for leadership training in organizations (Tetrault, Schriesheim, & Neider, 1988), although there are also newer approaches that have assumed more recent prominence. Some approaches assume that the leader should possess basic behavioral capabilities, and that those behaviors are applicable to all people and situations (e.g., Blake & Mouton, 1978). Although these leader behaviors are undoubtedly useful, training that emphasizes generic leader skills assumes uniform followers and static tasks. Where is the focus on team skills? Other approaches are more sensitive to variations in situational contexts. There is a theoretical emphasis on fitting the leader to characteristics of the group situation or modifying the situation to better fit the leader's personality or skills (e.g., Fiedler, Chemers, & Maher, 1976; Hersey & Blanchard, 1977). While these approaches allow for variations in task complexity across teams, they neglect cycles in task load that occur within teams. Leaders are assumed to exhibit relatively stable role behaviors within their teams. Finally, those approaches that do acknowledge variations of the situation within teams, focus exclusively on leader and team decision making (e.g., Vroom & Yetton, 1973). Although this is an important consideration, it is a relatively restricted view of the range of leader role behavior needed to manage effective work teams.

We believe that the focus of our approach on the dynamic dimensions of developmental processes and task cycles, and the emphasis on creating team coherence, highlight three important practical implications. First, team training is best accomplished in the actual performance setting. It is only in the team context that cross-functional specialists can begin to fully appreciate the interdependencies that will link them together as a team (Cannon-Bowers et al., 1995; Kozlowski & Salas, forthcoming). The interpersonal skills training that often passes as team training may have some value, but it is not a substitute for learning experiences grounded in the team's work setting. Organizations that emphasize team-based work units must see team training and development as an integral aspect of the work environment.

Second, leaders must be sensitized to their central function as team trainers. This is a complex function, transcending multiple roles, that is often neglected, because pressing work demands are more salient. Leaders often assume a new team is fully capable and ready to perform. Although a new team may be composed of individually proficient experts, it is not yet an expert team. That is a function that should be guided by the leader. Leaders need to learn how to take advantage of natural learning and adaptation processes and to create experiences to enhance team development.

Third, leader role behaviors and intended outcomes should drive instructional objectives and training design for team leadership skills training and subsequently the instructional objectives for team training by leaders in work contexts. The model specifies a sequence of leader roles, each linked to stages of team development. In addition, key role behaviors, learning objectives, learning level, and outcomes relevant for each role are identified. Relative to existing models of team leadership, our framework provides considerable specification to aid training design and operationalization. The principles are research based. The guidelines are applications oriented. When combined with that research foundation, they provide a basis for specifying instructional objectives to train team leaders, and for leaders to train teams.

Teams are emerging as key factors in the drive to improve organizational effectiveness. When we turn to the small group and team literatures to aid us in the development of effective work teams, we find few hard answers. Most of the literature has focused on relatively simple groups that have little in common with work teams. However, the resurgent interest in teams has prompted theorists to remark on the renaissance that is occurring in small group and team research. Lest we fall into prior pitfalls, this time we need to make sure that our theory development translates into meaningful applications. To paraphrase the great psychologist, Kurt Lewin, "there is nothing so practical as a good theory" (see Stagner, 1988, p. 289). Our goal was to develop a theory of team leadership with the potential for practical impact; we hope that our approach stimulates application.

REFERENCES

Adelman, L., Zirk, D.A., Lehner, P.E., Moffett, R.J., & Hall, R. (1986). Distributed tactical decision-making: Conceptual framework and empirical results. *IEEE Transactions on Systems, Man, and Cybernetics, 16*, 794-805.

Argote, L., & McGrath, J.E. (1993). Group processes in organizations: Continuity and change. In C.L. Cooper & I.T. Robertson (Eds.), *International review of industrial and organizational psychology*, Vol. 8 (pp. 333-389). New York: John Wiley & Sons.

Bandura, A. (1977). Self-efficacy: Toward a unifying theory of behavioral change. *Psychological Review, 84,* 191-215.

Bandura, A. (1982). Self-efficacy mechanisms in human agency. *American Psychologist, 37,* 122-147.

Bandura, A. (1986). *Social foundations of thought and action: A social-cognitive theory.* Englewood Cliffs, NJ: Prentice-Hall.

Bennis, W.G., & Nanus, B. (1985). *Leaders.* New York: Harper & Row.

Bennis, W.G., & Shepard, H.A. (1956). A theory of group development. *Human Relations, 9,* 415-437.

Bettenhausen, K. (1991). Five years of groups research: What we have learned and what needs to be addressed. *Journal of Management, 17,* 345-381.

Bion, W.R. (1961). *Experiences in groups.* London: Tavistock.

Blake, R.R., & Mouton, J.S. (1978). *The new managerial grid.* Houston: Gulf Publishing.

Boguslaw, R., & Porter, E.H. (1962). Team functions and training. In R.M. Gagne (Ed.), *Psychological principles in system development* (pp. 387-416). New York: Holt, Rinehart, & Winston.

Campion, M.A., Medsker, G.J., & Higgs, A.C. (1993). Relations between work group characteristics and effectiveness: Implications for designing effective work groups. *Personnel Psychology, 46,* 823-850.

Cannon-Bowers, J.A., Salas, E., & Converse, S.A. (1993). Shared mental models in expert team decision making. In N.J. Castellan, Jr., (Ed.), *Current issues in individual and group decision making* (pp. 221-246). Hillsdale, NJ: LEA.

Cannon-Bowers, J.A., Tannenbaum, S.I., & Salas, E. (1995). Defining team competencies and establishing team training requirements. In R. Guzzo & E. Salas (Eds.), *Team effectiveness and decision making in organizations* (pp. 333-380). San Francisco: Jossey Bass.

Cream, B.W., Eggemeier, F.T., & Klein, G.A. (1978). A strategy for the development of training devices. *Human Factors, 20,* 145-158.

Crown, D.F. (1993, May). Maximizing group level performance for nonsummative interdependent tasks: Integrating individual and group goals. Paper presented at the Eighth Annual Conference of the Society for Industrial and Organizational Psychology, San Francisco.

Denson, R.W. (1981). *Team training: Literature review and annotated bibliography* (Tech. Report AFHRL-TR-80-40). Dayton, OH: Air Force Human Resources Laboratory, Logistics and Technical Training Division.

Dominguez, C. (1994, June). Can SA be defined? In M. Vidulich, C. Dominguez, E. Vogel, & G. Mcmillan (Eds.), *Situation awareness: Papers and annotated bibliography* (pp. 5-15). (Report No. AL/CF-TR-1994-0085).

Dweck, C.S. (1986). Motivational processes affecting learning. *American Psychologist, 41,* 1040-1048.

Dyer, J.C. (1984). Team research and team training: State-of-the-art review. In F.A. Muckler (Ed.), *Human Factors Review* (pp. 285-323). Santa Monica, CA: Human Factors Society.

Elliott, E.S., & Dweck, C.S. (1988). Goals: An approach to motivation and achievement. *Journal of Personality and Social Psychology, 54,* 5-12.

Farr, J.L., Hofmann, D.A., & Ringenbach, K.L. (1993). Goal orientation and action control theory: Implications for industrial and organizational psychology. In C.L. Cooper & I.T. Robertson (Eds.), *International review of industrial and organizational psychology,* Vol. 8 (pp. 193-232). New York: John Wiley & Sons.

Feldman, D.C. (1981). The multiple socialization of organization members. *Administrative Science Quarterly, 21,* 433-452.

Fiedler, F.E., Chemers, M.M., & Mahar, L. (1976). *Improving leadership effectiveness: The leader match concept.* New York: John Wiley.

Fleishman, E.A., & Zaccaro, S.J. (1992). Toward a taxonomy of team performance functions. In R.W. Swezey & E. Salas (Eds.), *Teams: Their training and performance* (pp. 31-56). Norwood, NJ: Ablex.

Ford, J.K., Quinones, M.A., Sego, D.J., & Sorra, J.S. (1992). Factors affecting the opportunity to perform trained tasks. *Personnel Psychology, 45*, 511-527.

Francis, D., & Young, D. (1979). *Improving work groups: A practical manual for team building.* San Diego, CA: University Associates.

Gabarro, J.J. (1987). The development of working relationships. In J. Lorsch (Ed.), *Handbook of organizational behavior* (pp. 172-189). Englewood Cliffs, NJ: Prentice Hall.

Gersick, C.J.G., & Hackman, J.R. (1990). Habitual routines in task-performing groups. *Organizational Behavior and Human Decision Processes, 47*, 65-97.

Gist, M.E. (1987). Self-efficacy: Implications for organizational behavior and human resource management. *Academy of Management Review, 12*, 472-485.

Gist, M.E., & Mitchell, T.R. (1992). Self-efficacy: A theoretical analysis of its determinants and malleability. *Academy of Management Review, 17*, 183-211.

Glickman, A.S., Zimmer, S., Montero, R.C., Guerette, P.J., Campbell, W.J., Morgan, B., & Salas, E. (1987). *The evolution of teamwork skills: An empirical assessment with implications for training* (Tech. Report No. 87-016). Orlando: Naval Training Systems Center.

Goodman, P.S., Ravlin, E.C., & Argote, L. (1986). Current thinking about groups: Setting the stage. In P.S. Goodman (Ed.), *Designing effective work groups* (pp. 1-33). San Francisco: Jossey-Bass.

Hackman, J.R. (1987). The design of work teams. In J.W. Lorsch (Ed.), *Handbook of organizational behavior* (pp. 315-342). Englewood Cliffs, NJ: Prentice-Hall.

Hackman, J.R. (1992). Group influences on individuals in organizations. In M.D. Dunnette & L.M. Hough (Eds.), *Handbook of industrial and organizational psychology*, Vol. 3 (pp. 199-267).

Hall, J.K., Dwyer, D.J., Cannon-Bowers, J.A., Salas, E., & Volpe, C.E. (1993). Toward assessing team tactical decision making under stress: The development of a methodology for structuring team training scenarios. *Proceedings of the Fifteenth Annual Interservice/Industry Training Systems and Education Conference* (pp. 87-98). Washington, DC: National Security Industrial Association.

Hersey, P., & Blanchard, K.H. (1977). *Management of organizational behavior.* Reading, MA: Addison-Wesley.

Human Technology. (1993). *Training and development framework and descriptions of best practices.* McLean, VA: Author.

James, L.R., & Jones, A.P. (1974). Organizational climate: A review of theory and research. *Psychological Bulletin, 81*, 1096-1112.

Katz, R. (1978). Job longevity as a situational factor in job satisfaction. *Administrative Science Quarterly, 23*, 204-223.

Klaus, D.J., & Glaser, R. (1970). Reinforcement determinants of team proficiency. *Organizational Behavior and Human Performance, 5*, 33-67.

Kleinman, D.L., & Serfaty, D. (1989). Team performance assessment in distributed decision making. *Proceedings of the Symposium on Interactive Networked Simulation for Training* (pp. 22-27), Orlando.

Kozlowski, S.W.J., & Doherty, M.L. (1989). Integration of climate and leadership: Examination of a neglected issue. *Journal of Applied Psychology, 74*, 546-553.

Kozlowski, S.W.J., & Hattrup, K. (1992). A disagreement about within-group agreement: Disentangling issues of consistency versus consensus. *Journal of Applied Psychology, 77*, 161-167.

Kozlowski, S.W.J., & Hults, B.M. (1986). Joint moderation of the relation between task complexity and job performance for engineers. *Journal of Applied Psychology, 71*, 196-202.

Kozlowski, S.W.J., & Hults, B.M. (1987). An exploration of climates for technical updating and performance. *Personnel Psychology, 40*, 539-563.

Kozlowski, S.W.J., & Salas, E. (Forthcoming). An integrated approach for the implementation and transfer of training interventions. In J.K. Ford, S. Kozlowski, K. Kraiger, E. Salas, & M. Teachot (Eds.), *Improving training effectiveness in work organizations.* Hillsdale, NJ: Lawrence Erlbaum Associates.

Kozlowski, S.W.J., Chao, G.T., Smith, E.M., & Hedlund, J.A. (1993a). Organizational downsizing: Strategies, interventions, and research implications. In C.L. Cooper & I.T. Robertson (Eds.), *International review of industrial and organizational psychology*, Vol. 8 (pp. 263-332). New York: Wiley.

Kozlowski, S.W.J., Ford, J.K., & Smith, E.M. (1993b). *Training concepts, principles, and guidelines for the acquisition, transfer, and enhancement of team tactical decision making skills I: A conceptual framework and literature review* (Contract No. N61339-91-C-0117). Orlando: Naval Training Systems Center.

Kozlowski, S.W.J., Gully, S.M., & McHugh, P.P. (1993c). *Leadership skills to enhance team tactical decision making effectiveness: Theory, principles, and guidelines* (Contract No. DAAL03-86-D-0001, D.O. No. 2666). Research Triangle Park, NC: U.S. Army Research Office.

Kozlowski, S.W.J., Gully, S.M., Nason, E.R., Ford, J.K., Smith, E.M., Smith, M.R., & Futch, C.J. (1994, April). A composition theory of team development: Levels, content, process, and learning outcomes. In J.E. Mathieu (Chair), *Developmental views of team processes and performance.* Symposium conducted at the Ninth Annual Conference of the Society for Industrial and Organizational Psychology, Nashville.

Kozlowski, S.W.J., Gully, S.M., Smith, E.A., Nason, E.R., & Brown, K.G. (1995, May). Sequenced mastery training and advance organizers: Effects on learning, self-efficacy, performance, and generalization. In R.J. Klimoski (Chair), *Thinking and feeling while doing: Understanding the learner in the learning process.* Symposium conducted at the Tenth Annual Conference of the Society for Industrial and Organizational Psychology, Orlando.

Kozlowski, S.W.J., Gully, S.M., McHugh, P.P., Salas, E., & Cannon-Bowers, J.A. (1996). A dynamic theory of leadership and team effectiveness: Developmental and task contingent leader roles. In G. Ferris (Ed.), *Research in personnel and human resources management*, Vol. 14 (pp. 253-305). Greenwich, CT: JAI Press.

Lee, C. (1991). Who gets trained in what? *Training, 28*, 447-456.

Levine, R.L., & Moreland, R.L. (1990). Progress in small group research. *Annual Review of Psychology, 41*, 585-634.

Lord, R.G., & Kernan, M.C. (1987). Scripts as determinants of purposeful behavior in organizations. *Academy of Management Review, 12*, 265-277.

Manz, C.C., & Sims, H.P. (1987). Leading workers to lead themselves: The external leadership of self-managing work teams. *Administrative Science Quarterly, 32*, 106-128.

McIntyre, R.M., & Salas, E. (1995). Team performance in complex environments: What we have learned so far. In R. Guzzo & E. Salas (Eds.), *Team effectiveness and decision making in organizations.* San Fransico: Jossey-Bass.

Mitchell, T.R., & Silver, W.S. (1990). Individual and group goals when workers are interdependent: Effects on task strategies and performance. *Journal of Applied Psychology, 75*, 185-193.

Morgan, B.B., Glickman, A.S., Woodard, E.A., Blaiwes, A.S., & Salas, E. (1986) *Measurement of team behaviors in a Navy environment* (Tech. Report No. 86-014). Orlando, FL: Naval Training Systems Center.

Moreland, R.L., & Levine, J.M. (1988). Group dynamics over time: Development and socialization in small groups. In J.E. McGrath (Ed.), *The social psychology of time: New perspectives* (pp. 151-181). Newbury Park, CA: Sage.

Nieva, V.F., Fleishman, E.A., & Rieck, A. (1978) *Team dimensions: Their identity, their measurement and their relationships* (Contract No. DAHC 19-78-C-0001). Washington, DC: Advanced Research Resources Organization.

Novak, M.A. (1991). Toward a model for leading self-managing individuals. *Journal of Management Systems, 3,* 1-13.

Orasanu, J. (1990, October). Shared mental models and crew performance. Paper presented at the 34th Annual meeting of the Human Factors Society, Orlando, FL.

Orasanu, J., & Salas, E. (1993). Team decision making in complex environments. In G. Klein, J. Orasanu, R. Calderwood, & C. Zsambok (Eds.), *Decision making in action: Models and methods* (pp. 327-345). Norwood, NJ: Ablex.

Ostroff, C., & Kozlowski, S.W.J. (1992). Organizational socialization as a learning process: The role of information acquisition. *Personnel Psychology, 45,* 849-874.

Ostroff, C., & Kozlowski, S.W.J. (1993). The role of mentoring in the information gathering processes of newcomers during early organizational socialization. *Journal of Vocational Behavior, 42,* 170-183.

Phillips, J.M. (1995). Leadership since 1975: Advancement or inertia? *The Journal of Leadership Studies, 2,* 58-80.

Pearce, J.A., & Ravlin, E.C. (1987). The design and activation of self-regulating work groups. *Human Relations, 40,* 751-782.

Rentsch, J.R., & Hall, R.J. (1994). Members of great teams think alike: A model of team effectiveness and schema similarity among team members. In M. Beyerlein (Ed.), *Advances in interdisciplinary studies of work teams,* Vol. 1 (pp. 223-261). Greenwich, CT: JAI Press.

Roth, J.T., Hritz, R.J., & Lewis, C.M. (1984). *Method for understanding, describing, assessing, and training teamwork* (Contract No. MDA903-81-C-0198). Alexandria, VA: U.S. Army Research Institute for the Behavioral and Social Sciences.

Rouse, W.B., Cannon-Bowers, J.A., & Salas, E. (1992). The role of mental models in team performance of complex systems. *IEEE Transactions on Systems, Man, and Cybernetics, 22,* 1296-1308.

Salas, E., Dickinson, T.L., Converse, S.A., & Tannenbaum, S.I. (1992). Toward an understanding of team performance and training. In R.W. Swezey & E. Salas (Eds.), *Teams: Their training and performance* (pp. 3-29). Norwood, NJ: Ablex.

Salas, E., Cannon-Bowers, J.A., & Blickensderfer, E.L. (Forthcoming). Enhancing reciprocity between training theory and practice: Principles, guidelines, and specifications. In J.K. Ford, S. Kozlowski, K. Kraiger, E. Salas, & M. Teachout (Eds.), *Improving training effectiveness in work organizations.* Hillsdale, NJ: LEA.

Salas, E., Cannon-Bowers, J.A., & Johnston, J. (Forthcoming). How can you turn a team of experts into an expert team?: Emerging training strategies. In C. Zsambok & G. Klein (Eds.), *Naturalistic decision making.* Hillsdale, NJ: LEA.

Schein, E.H. (1980). *Organizational psychology.* Englewood Cliffs, NJ: Prentice-Hall.

Schneider, B., & Bowen, D. E. (1985). Employee and customer perceptions of service in banks: Replication and extension. *Journal of Applied Psychology, 70,* 423-433.

Schultz, W. (1958). Interpersonal underworld. *Harvard Business Review, 36,* 123-135.

Shamir, B. (1990). Calculations, values, and identities: The sources of collectivistic work motivation. *Human Relations, 43,* 313-332.

Shea, G.P., & Guzzo, R.A. (1987). Groups as human resources. In K.M. Roland & G.M. Ferris (Eds.), *Research in personnel and human resources management,* Vol. 5 (pp. 323-356). Greenwich, CT: JAI Press.

Sitkin, S.B. (1992). Learning through failure: The strategy of small losses. In B.M. Staw & L.L. Cummings (Eds.), *Research in organizational behavior,* Vol. 14 (pp. 231-266). Greenwich, CT: JAI Press.

Smith-Jentsch, K.A., & Tannenbaum, S.I. (1995, May). Team leader training at the surface warfare officer's school (SWOS). Presentation at the Tenth Biannual Meeting of the Technical Advisory Board for the Tactical Decision Making Under Stress (TADMUS) Project, Moorestown, NJ.

Spink, K.S. (1990). Collective efficacy in the sport setting. *International Journal of Sport Psychology, 21*, 380-395.

Stagner, R. (1988). *A history of psychological theories.* New York: Macmillan.

Steiner, I.D. (1972). *Group processes and group productivity.* New York: Academic Press.

Sundstrom, E., De Meuse, K.P., & Futrell, D. (1990). Work teams: Applications and effectiveness. *American Psychologist, 45*, 120-133.

Swezey, R.W., & Salas, E. (1992). Guidelines for use in team-training development. In R.W. Swezey & E. Salas (Eds.), *Teams: Their training and performance* (pp. 219-245). Norwood, NJ: Ablex.

Tetrault, L.A., Schriesheim, C.A., & Neider, L.L. (1988). Leadership training interventions: A review. *Organizational Development Journal, 6*, 77-83.

Travillian, K., Baker, C.V., & Cannon-Bowers, J.A. (1992, March). Correlates of self and collective efficacy with team funcitioning. Paper presented at the Thirty-eighth Annual Meeting of the Southeastern Psychological Association, Knoxville, TN.

Tuckman, B. (1965). Developmental sequence in small groups. *Psychological Bulletin, 63*, 384-399.

Tziner, A., & Eden, D. (1985). Effects of crew composition on crew performance: Does the whole equal the sum of its parts? *Journal of Applied Psychology, 78*, 85-93.

Volpe, C.A., Cannon-Bowers, J.A., Salas, E., & Spector, P. (Forthcoming). The impact of cross-training on team functioning: An empirical investigation. *Human Factors.*

Vroom, V.H., & Yetton, P.W. (1973). *Leadership and decision making.* Pittsburgh: University of Pittsburgh Press.

Weiss, H.M. (1977). Subordinate imitation of supervisor behavior: The role of modeling in organizational socialization. *Organizational Behavior and Human Performance, 19*, 89-105.

Yukl, G.A., & Van Fleet, D.D. (1992). Theory and research on leadership in organizations. In M.D. Dunnette & L.M. Hough (Eds.), *Handbook of industrial and organizational psychology* Vol. 3 (pp. 147-197). Palo Alto, CA: Consulting Psychologists Press, Inc.

ABOUT THE EDITORS

Michael M. Beyerlein is director of the Center for the Study of Work Teams, and associate professor of Industrial/Organizational (I/O) psychology at the University of North Texas. Mike's work focuses on the implementation and development of SMWTs, especially knowledge teams. His research interests include all aspects of work teams, organizational change and development, cognitive styles, job stress, decision making, and measurement.

Douglas A. Johnson is director of the Industrial/Organizational psychology program, associate professor of psychology, and associate director of the Center for the Study of Work Teams, University of North Texas. Doug has published research in a variety of areas, ranging from leadership and job satisfaction to operant conditioning and interpersonal attraction. He cofounded and served as president of the Dallas-Fort Worth Organizational Psychology Group, and participated in the creation of the Dallas office of the I/O psychology consulting firm, Personnel Decisions International, with whom he works on a part-time basis.

Susan T. Beyerlein is a research scientist at the Center for Public Management, Department of Public Administration, University of North Texas. She has worked in project management and program development for the Center for the Study of Work Teams since 1992. Her areas of interest include professionals in teams in private and public sector organizations, research methods, and the new paradigm of business.

J A I   P R E S S

Advances in Interdisciplinary Studies of Work Teams

Edited by **Michael Beyerlein,** *Director, Interdisciplinary Center For The Study of Work Teams, University of North Texas*

Volume 2, Knowledge Work in Teams
1995, 301 pp. $73.25
ISBN 1-55938-926-5

Edited by **Michael M. Beyerlein** and **Douglas A. Johnson**, *Center for the Study of Work Teams, Department of Psychology, University of North Texas* and **Susan T. Beyerlein,** *Center for Public Management, University of North Texas*

Also Available:
Volume 1 (1994) $73.25

Research in Organizational Behavior
An Annual Series of Analytical Essays and Critical Reviews

Edited by **Barry M. Staw**, *Haas School of Business, University of California, Berkeley* and **L.L. Cummings**, *Carlson School of Management, University of Minnesota*

Volume 18, 1996, 373 pp. $78.50
ISBN 1-55938-938-9

CONTENTS: Preface, *Barry M. Staw and L. L. Cummings.* Affective Events Theory: A Theoretical Discussion of the Structure, Causes and Consequences of Affective Experiences at Work, *Howard Weiss and Russell Cropanzano.* Motivational Agendas in the Workplace: The Effects of Feelings on Focus of Attention and Work Motivation, *Jennifer M. George and Arthur P. Brief.* Why Do Workers Bite the Hand that Feeds Them? Employee Theft as a Social Exchange Process, *Jerald Greenberg and Kimberly S. Scott.* Culture as Social Control: Corporations, Cults, and Commitment, *Charles A. O'Reilly and Jennifer A. Chatman.* Consequences of Public Scrutiny for Leaders and Their Organizations, *Robert I. Sutton and D. Charles Galunic.* Entrainment: Pace, Cycle, and Rhythm in Organizational Behavior, *Deborah Ancona and Chee-Leong Chong.* Customer-Supplier Ties in Interorganizational Relations, *Mark Fichman and Paul Goodman.* Interfirm Relationships: A Grammar of Pairs, *Blair H. Sheppard and Marla Tuchinsky.*

Also Available:
Volumes 1-17 (1979-1995) $73.25 each

JAI PRESS INC.
55 Old Post Road No. 2 - P.O. Box 1678
Greenwich, Connecticut 06836-1678
Tel: (203) 661- 7602   Fax: (203) 661-0792

J A I   P R E S S

Research in Organizational Change and Development

Edited by **Richard W. Woodman,** *Texas A&M University* and **William A. Pasmore**, *Case Western Reserve University*

Volume 8, 1995, 302 pp. $73.25
ISBN 1-55938-871-4

CONTENTS: Preface, *William A. Pasmore and Richard D. Woodman.* Practitioner Attitudes about the Field of Organization Development, *Allan H. Church and W. Warner Burke.* Effects of Union Status on Employee Involvement: Diffusion and Effectiveness, *Gary C. McMahan and Edward E. Lawler III.* The Integration of Change in Organizations: Alternative Learning and Transformationn Mechanisms, *A.B. Shani and Txrbjorn Stjernberg.* The Moral Quandary of Transformational Leadership: Change for Whom?, *Carroll Underwood Stephens, Robert S. DIntino, and Bart Victor.* Transformational Change and Organizational Half-Lives, *Bruno Dyck.* The Consultants Dilemma: A Multiple Frame Analysis of a Public Housing Community, *David M. Boje, Judith White, and Terance Wolfe.* Justice in the Making: Toward Understanding the Theory and Practice of Justice in Organization Change and Development, *Anthony T. Cobb, Kevin C. Wooten, and Robert Folger.* Flawed Theories About Study Flaws, *John E. Hunter and Robert Rodgers.* About the Authors.

Also Available:
Volume 1-7 (1987-1993) $73.25 each

JAI PRESS INC.
55 Old Post Road No. 2 - P.O. Box 1678
Greenwich, Connecticut 06836-1678
Tel: (203) 661- 7602   Fax: (203) 661-0792

Research in Personnel and Human Resources Management

Research in Personnel and Human Resources Management, an annual series, includes monograph length conceptual papers designed to promote theory and research on important substantive and methodological topics in the field of human resources management. Although each volume contains papers on a variety of topics and is not designed to be theme-oriented, there exist a number of papers (across the several published volumes) that share common themes. The notion of reprinting such related papers into theme-oriented volumes was the stimulus for the development of this present series of books.

Volume 14, 1996, 419 pp. $73.25
ISBN 0-7623-0017-5

CONTENTS: Overview, *Gerald R. Ferris.* Interest and Indifference: The Role of Age and the Organizational Sciences, *Barbara S. Lawrence.* Establishing a Framework for Research in Strategic Human Resource Management: Merging Resource Theory and Organizational Learning, *Scott A. Snell, Mark A. Youndt, and Patrick M. Wright.* Mathematical/Computational Modeling of Organizational Withdrawl Processes: Benefits, Methods, and Results, *Kathy A. Hanisch, Charles L. Hulin, and Steven T. Seitz.* New Directions in Compensation Research: Synergies, Risk, and Survival, *Barry Gerhart, Charlie O. Trevor, and Mary E. Graham.* A Power Perspective of Empowerment and Work Groups: Implications for Human Resources Management Research, *Robert C. Liden and Sharon Arad.* A Dynamic Theory of Leadership and Team Effectiveness: Devlopmental and Task Contingent Leader Roles, *Steve W.J. Kozlowski, Stanley M. Gully, Patrick P. McHugh, Eduardo Salas, and Janis A. Cannon-Bowers.* Defining the Scope and Logic of Minority and Female Network Groups: Can Separation Enhance Integration?, *Raymond A. Friedman.* Organizational Socialization of Newcomers with Disabilities: A Framework for Future Research, *Adrienne Colella.*

Also Available:
Volumes 1-13 (1983-1995)
  + Supplements 1-3 (1989-1993) $73.25 each

JAI PRESS INC.
55 Old Post Road No. 2 - P.O. Box 1678
Greenwich, Connecticut 06836-1678
Tel: (203) 661- 7602   Fax: (203) 661-0792

J A I

P R E S S

Research in the Sociology of Work

Edited by **Ida Harper Simpson,** *Department of Sociology, Duke University* and **Richard L. Simpson**, *Department of Sociology, University of North Carolina, Chapel Hill*

REVIEW: " . . . .such breath has the potential to stimulate a broad range of research from sociologists who might otherwise have little common intellectual ground."

— *Contemporary Sociology*

Volume 5, The Meaning of Work
1994, 288 pp. $73.25
ISBN 0-89232-971-8

CONTENTS: Introduction, *Richard L. Simpson and Ida Harper Simpson.* The Concept of Work on the Rack: Critique and Suggestions, *Jan Ch. Karlsson.* The Meanings of Work, *Curt Tausky.* Some Effects of Gender on the Meaning of Work: An Empirical Examination, *Elizabeth A. Martin, Jennifer Hess, and Paul M. Siegel.* Work Orientation, Job Discrimination, and Ethnicity: A Focus Group Perspective, *Lawrence Bobo, Camille L. Zubrinsky, James H. Johnson, Jr., and Melvin L. Oliver.* Trends in Job Satisfaction in the United States by Race, Gender, and Type of Occupation, *Glenn Firebaugh and Brian Harley.* From the Instinct of Workmanship to Gift Exchange: Employment Contracts, Social Relations of Trust, and the Meaning of Work, *Margaret L. Krecker.* Cohesion or Conflict? Race, Solidarity, and Resistance in the Workplace, *Randy Hodson.* Job Satisfaction Theories and Job Satisfaction: A China and U.S. Comparison, *Shanhe Jiang, Richard H. Hall, Karyn L. Loscocco, and John Allen.* Researchers, Cultural Boundaries, and Organizational Change, *Tim Turpin and Stephen Hill.* Costs and Opportunities of Marketization: An Analysis of Russian Employment and Unemployment, *Susan Goodrich Lehmann.* Organizational Commitment and Job Performance in the U.S. Labor Force, *Arne L. Kalleberg and Peter V. Marsden.* Objective and Subjective Parental Working Conditions Effects on Child Outcomes: A Comparative Test, *Laura E. Geschwender and Toby L. Parcel.*

Also Available:
Volumes 1-4 (1981-1988) $73.25 each

Research in Corporate Social Performance and Policy

Edited by **James E. Post,** *School of Management, Boston University*

Supplement 1, Sustaining the Natural Environment: Empirical Studies on the Interface Between Nature and Organizations
1995, 388 pp. $78.50
ISBN 1-55938-945-1

Edited by **Denis Collins,** *University of Wisconsin, Madison* and **Mark Starik,** *George Washington University*

CONTENTS: A Breath of Fresh Air: Introduction to the Volume, *Denis Collins.* Research on Organizations and the Natural Environment: Some Paths We Have Traveled, The "Field Ahead", *Mark Starik.* An Empirical Investigation of Sustainability Strategy Implementation in Industrial Organizations, *W. Edward Stead and Jean Garner Stead.* The Determinants of Firms that Formulate Environmental Plans, *Irene Henriques and Perry Sadorsky.* Leading-Edge Environmental Management: Motivation, Opportunity, Resources, and Processes, *Anne T. Lawrence and David Morell.* Corporate Leadership and Policies for the Natural Environment, *Monika I. Winn.* Clash or Cooperation? Understanding Environmental Organizations and their Relationship to Business, *Judith A. Clair, John Milliman, and Ian I. Mitroff.* Conflict and Collaboration: The Interfaces between Environmental Organizations and Business Firms, *Marie-France Turcotte.* Changing and Converging Mindsets of Participants During Collaborative Environmental Rule Making: Two Negotiated Regulation Case Studies, *Ann E. Feyerherm.* Managing Complex Common Property Resources: Implications of Recent Institutional Reforms in New Zealand, *John W. Selsky and P.A. Memon.* Sustainable Development in Practice: The Management of Yellowstone Lake for Fishing and Ecosystem Protection, *Robert L. Swinth and Bruce C. Raymond.* The Performance of Environmental Mutual Funds in the United States and Germany: Is there Economic Hope for "Green Investors"?, *Mark A. White.* Conservation Strategies, Firm Performance, and Corporate Reputations in the U.S. Electric Utility Industry, *Daniel W. Greening.* The Complexity of Fresh Air: Summary of Findings and Recommendations, *Denis Collins.* About the Authors.

Also Available:
Volumes 1-14 (1978-1993) $78.50 each

J A I   P R E S S

New Approaches to Employee Management

Edited by **David M. Saunders**,
Faculty of Management, McGill University

**Volume 3, Employee Management in
Developing Countries**
1995, 255 pp. $73.25
ISBN 1-55938-930-3

Edited by **Rabindra N. Kanungo**,
Faculty of Management, McGill University

CONTENTS: Preface, *Rabindra N. Kanungo and David M. Saunders.* Going Beyond Traditional HRM Scholarship, *Nancy J. Adler and Nakiye Boyacigiller.* Transnational Corporations, Human Resource Development and Economic Growth: Directions for Future Research, *Susan Bartholomew.* Restructuring Public Enterprise in East Africa: The Human Resource Management Dimension, *Jan Jorgensen.* Social and Labor Issues of Privatization in South Asia: A Comparative Study, *C.S. Venkata Ratnam.* The Culture of Collectivism and Human Resource Management in Developing Countries, *Rabi S. Bhagat and Ben L. Kedia.* Performance Management Systems Designed for Total Quality: A Comparison Between Developed and Developing Countries, *David A. Waldman and Helena Addae.* State Policies and Career Structure and Strategies in an Asian Nie: The Singapore Case, *Ern-Ser Tan and Irene K.H. Chew.* Cultural Diversity in Managing The Employee Selection Event, *Peter B. Smith, Mark F. Peterson, and Zulfiqhuar Gilani.* Modal Orientations in Leadership Research and Their Implications for Developing Countries, *Rabindra N. Kanungo and Jay A. Conger.* Prospects of Participative Management in Developing Countries: The Role of Socio-Cultural Environment, *Miriam Erez.* Organization Development for National Development: A Review of Evidence, *Kalburgi M. Srinivas.* Impact of Management Practices on Employee Effectiveness in South Asia, *Zafar Iqbal Qureshi.* A Review of Human Resource Management Successes in Developing Countries, *Alfred M. Jaeger, Rabindra N. Kanungo, and Nidhi Srinivas.*

Also Available:
Volumes 1-2 (1992-1994) $73.25 each